MAMMALS
OF NORTH AMERICA
TEMPERATE AND ARCTIC REGIONS

MAMMALS
OF NORTH AMERICA
TEMPERATE AND ARCTIC REGIONS

ADRIAN FORSYTH

FIREFLY BOOKS

A FIREFLY BOOK

Published by Firefly Books Ltd. 1999

First Printing 1999

Library of Congress Cataloging-in-Publication Data

Forsyth, Adrian.
   Mammals of North America : temperate and arctic regions/Adrian Forsyth. – 1st ed.
[352] p. ;   col. ill. (maps) ;   cm.
Includes bibliographic references (p.) and index.
Summary : Reference guide includes scientific names, behavioral data, full anatomical descriptions, range maps and habitats.
ISBN 1-55209-409-X
1. Mammals – North America. I. Title.
599.097–dc21   1999   CIP

Published in the United States in 1999 by
Firefly Books (U.S.) Inc.
P.O. Box 1338, Ellicott Station
Buffalo, New York 14205

Produced by
Bookmakers Press Inc.
12 Pine Street
Kingston, Ontario K7K 1W1
(613) 549-4347
tcread@sympatico.ca

Design by
Janice McLean

Printed and bound in Canada by
Friesens
Altona, Manitoba

Printed on acid-free paper

Canadian Cataloguing-in-Publication Data

Forsyth, Adrian
   Mammals of North America : temperate and arctic regions

Includes bibliographical references and index.
ISBN 1-55209-409-X

1. Mammals – Canada. 2. Mammals – United States. I. Title.
II. Title: Mammals of the Canadian wild.

QL715.F66   1999   599'.0971   C99-930410-0

Published in Canada in 1999 by
Firefly Books Ltd.
3680 Victoria Park Avenue
Willowdale, Ontario M2H 3K1

Canada

The Publisher acknowledges the financial support of the Government of Canada through the Book Publishing Industry Development Program for its publishing activities.

ACKNOWLEDGMENTS

A special thanks to Fiona A. Reid of the Royal Ontario Museum and to John O. Whitaker, Jr., of Indiana State University for their thoughtful critical review of the text of *Mammals of North America*. (They bear no responsibility, however, for any errors that may appear here.) Brock Fenton graciously provided important insights into the material on bats.

My gratitude also to my friend and colleague Jody Morgan for acting as project editor and to Bookmakers Press for putting together the team that produced the book—art director Janice McLean, copy editor and indexer Mary Patton, editor Tracy Read, production coordinator Susan Dickinson, proofreader Catherine DeLury, typesetter Charlotte DuChene and cartographer Robbie Cooke.

Dedicated to Adam, Darwin and Sharon

CONTENTS

INTRODUCTION

Last summer, I was tide-pooling along a section of British Columbia's rocky coast with my 4-year-old son Darwin when we heard a piteous moaning and yelping issuing from some seaweed-coated rocks. The source was an infant harbor seal, pathetically miserable and seemingly stuck in a crevice. Against Darwin's fervent advice, I scrambled over to see whether I could free it or assist it in some other way.

Darwin was right. As I approached the seal, it suddenly turned on me, flashing a gaping pink mouth lined with formidable teeth and powered by bulging jaw muscles. I jumped back surprised and chastened, much to my son's amusement and satisfaction. Eventually, the rising tide floated the seal out into the bay. All was not well, however. The seal continued to bawl mournfully, perhaps missing its mother.

There was little we could do, but it seemed callous not to try. The impulse was hardly rational. Perhaps this seal's rightful destiny was to provide a snack for a hungry orca, a week's dining for an immature bald eagle or a repast for a hundred crabs. Moreover, harbor seals are thriving. Each year, thousands are born and die, just as always. Yet because the seal was a warm-blooded, milk-sucking infant with large eyes—an obviously sentient organism—it evoked emotions in my son and me more powerful than any large sea slug, jellyfish or other less-related organism could. It is only natural to be interested in a fellow mammal.

Mammalophilia, if we can call it that, can be a useful and rewarding trait. But it is one that requires nurturing. In an increasingly urban world, many North Americans find that their contact with mammals is limited primarily to pets such as dogs and cats, possibly rats, and the portions of cow or pig on their dinner plates. Yet it is not this thriving cadre of domesticates that deserves our concern. Instead, it is their wild brethren that demand our attention. Wild mammals are usually ecologically important, often magnificent and always interesting.

North Americans are lucky enough to live in a region that still supports wolves, grizzly bears, pronghorns, caribou, orcas—mammals that need large wild spaces. Where they thrive, ecosystems are normally healthy, generating the oxygen, clear water and other natural resources that sustain our own species. Unfortunately, even in this part of the world, wild mammals in general are diminishing, either slowly or rapidly, as natural habitats are converted to human use.

This book is a small attempt to interest readers in the wild mammals that live around them. It is generally true that the more one knows about something, the more one wants to know. And to conserve another organism, even to want to conserve another organism, knowledge seems necessary. This is my agenda.

A book can only skim the surface of any topic. And a book is always several steps removed from reality. As soon as you can, set this one aside and find a forest, a field or a mountain where you can pursue your own mammalogical discoveries. "Study Nature, not books," advised the great naturalist Louis Agassiz. But try not to get bitten.

Adrian Forsyth

The large, limpid eyes of pinnipeds such as this California sea lion are just one of the mammalian characteristics that inspire a natural bond between humans and wild creatures.

MARSUPIALS *Didelphimorphia*

All North American mammals except the opossum are placentals, which means that the female nourishes her undeveloped young through the placental membrane in the uterus. Marsupials such as the opossum have a different reproductive system and strategy. Most mother marsupials have a pouch, a fold of skin over the teats, where the immature marsupials feed and undergo much of their development.

Marsupials differ from placentals in many other aspects of their body plan. These differences arose early in mammalian history, as far back as the Cretaceous era between 75 and 100 million years ago. Marsupials are called "primitive" not only because of their ancient origin but also because their skeletal system is closer to that of the reptiles from which mammals evolved and because they appear to have been outcompeted and replaced by their placental competitors in many parts of the world.

Among the primitive features that marsupials exhibit are a narrow brain case, a small brain and more teeth. The common opossum, for example, has 50 teeth, whereas many placentals have only 44. The bones in a marsupial's inner ear are not the same as those in a placental's. But it is the evolutionary history of marsupials more than anything else that suggests they are less advanced than placental mammals.

At the time the earliest marsupials began evolving, the three southern continents—Australia, Africa and South America—were still joined in one large landmass known as Gondwanaland. When this landmass began breaking apart, Australia and South America became isolated from the other continents. In North America, Asia, Africa and Europe, the placental mammals began to diversify and increase. Marsupials declined until, by 15 to 25 million years ago, they were surviving only in Australia and South America. In Australia, where there was no competition from placental mammals, the marsupials diversified into a great variety of life-forms, such as the large grazing kangaroos, the digging rodentlike wombats, koala bears, marsupial lions and other carnivores such as the Tasmanian devil.

The reconnection of South America and North America suggests that competitive extinctions were important in the decline of many marsupial groups. For some 60 million years, South America was separated from North America. During that interval, the South American marsupials diversified into forms that resembled giant hyenas and saber-toothed tigers. But when the land bridge linking the Americas arose some two to five million years ago, large placental carnivores such as jaguars and pumas began invading South America, an event shown by the fossil record to correspond with the extinction of their marsupial counterparts.

Marsupials, however, are not simply "living fossils" that survived just because continental drift kept them isolated from competition by placental mammals. In spite of a long history of contact with placental mammals, marsupial opossums have survived and, indeed, have moved northward out of South America and well into Canada.

North America's only marsupial, the opossum evolved in South America at a time when that continent supported a wide variety of now extinct pouched mammals, including some that resembled giant hyenas and saber-toothed tigers.

NEW WORLD OPOSSUMS *Didelphidae*

The Didelphidae is primarily a South American family. Many mammalogists consider it to be the most primitive surviving marsupial family, the one from which all other marsupials have evolved. Opossums never get very large, no bigger than a small dog, and many are much smaller.

In South and Central America, some sort of opossum can be found in almost any habitat, from wet, marshy areas and dry savanna to the edge of the tree line high in the mountains. Opossums are omnivores—generalized feeders. Their adaptive radiation seems to be based more on adaptations to different ecological habitats than on food preferences. Nevertheless, groups within the family are relatively specialized in their habits in ways comparable to some North American placental mammals. Shrew opossums, for example, are indeed shrewlike in several respects, having reduced eyes, short tails adapted to a more terrestrial life, a small body size and an appetite for insects and small mammals. The water opossum is similarly specialized, having webbed hind feet and a pouch with a watertight seal.

As a group, opossums are somewhat arboreal; that is, they are adept at climbing and living in trees. This is reflected in the design of their feet, which are narrow and have an opposable big toe and an enlarged fourth toe that they use to grip branches. The naked, muscular prehensile tail is also used for hanging onto branches. Some of these animals, such as the woolly opossums, are almost completely arboreal, feeding on fruits and flowers in the canopy of tropical forests.

One of the most diverse groups of opossums is that of the mouse opossum, which fills many of the ecological niches occupied by mice in temperate and northern habitats. These animals seem to be generalized feeders, eating a wide variety of plant and animal matter. They differ in their use of habitats. Many species are highly arboreal and spend most of their time climbing trees. Other species spend more of their time on the ground, but in any case, virtually all mouse opossums have long, naked prehensile tails that act like a fifth limb. This not only makes climbing easier but enables them to dangle from branches to reach fruits and berries hanging from slender twigs. Thus at night, these creatures can harvest foods that are otherwise accessible only to day-flying birds and may be beyond the reach of heavier animals such as squirrels and monkeys.

In some species of opossum, such as the Patagonian opossum, the tail can act as a fat-storage organ, swelling and thickening when feeding is good. This may enable opossums to occupy seasonal habitats where the temperature or rainfall differs between winter and summer.

In spite of its success in Latin America, only a single species of this family has penetrated north of Texas. That species is the Virginia opossum, a highly generalized mammal that has extended its range into Canada.

Thought to be the most primitive surviving marsupial family, the Didelphidae includes 63 species that range from small mouse-sized shrew opossums to the omnivorous Virginia opossum, shown at right, which has extended its range as far north as Canada.

VIRGINIA OPOSSUM
Didelphis virginiana

Mammal: *Didelphis virginiana,*
Virginia opossum

Meaning of Name: *Didelphis* (double womb) refers to the pouch as a secondary womb in which the young develop after birth; *virginiana* (of Virginia)

Description: domestic-cat size; female has fur-lined abdominal pouch; naked prehensile tail; large, naked, paper-thin ears tipped with pink; male has gland on throat that stains the fur yellow; gray is most common color; white face

Total Length: 25.4 to 32.9 inches

Tail: 9.1 to 21.3 inches

Weight: 4.4 to 13 pounds

Gestation: 12 to 13 days

Offspring: 1 to 14; 1 or 2 litters per year

Age of Maturity: male, 8 months; female, 6 months

Longevity: 7 years

Diet: omnivore; unselective; will use most abundant foods; carrion forms a large part of diet, along with small mammals, insects, lizards, frogs, birds, eggs, fruits and vegetables

Habitat: open woodlands in association with streams; farming areas with sufficient cover

Predators: domestic dog, coyote, bobcat, fox, raccoon, raptors and large snakes

Dental Formula:
5/4, 1/1, 3/3, 4/4 = 50 teeth

VIRGINIA OPOSSUM
Didelphis virginiana

As one of the first white men to see a live opossum in its native haunts, Captain John Smith, who settled Virginia in the early 1600s, remarked: "An Opossum hath a head like a Swine, & a taile like a Rat, and is of the Bignes of a Cat. Under her belly, she hath a bagge, wherein she lodgeth, carrieth and sucketh her young."

It is often claimed that the Virginia opossum is a living fossil, a survivor in North America for the last 75 or 100 million years, but in truth, this species is one of our most recent arrivals from South America. Both genetic and geological evidence indicate that this species has evolved only since the last Pleistocene glaciations, and its arrival in North America is even more recent.

The Virginia opossum is a relatively recent immigrant to Canada. Prior to the European colonization of North America, the northern limit of this opossum was Virginia and Ohio. The opossum is one of the few animals that benefited from the changes wrought by the agricultural transformation of North America. The extermination of large predators, such as pumas, wolves and fishers, in the eastern United States and in southeastern Canada allowed the opossum to multiply and extend its range. Opossums will eat almost anything, and it is safe to say that the garbage generated by human settlements, a share of vegetable and fruit crops and a rise in various small-mammal populations associated with land clearing all increased the amount of food available to them.

In any case, the opossum has experienced a kind of ecological release, allowing it to increase its range both north and south. Its present northern limits seem to be set mainly by its ability to withstand the Canadian winter. The opossum has a naked tail, which is vulnerable to frostbite, and as an animal with recent origins in the tropics, it lacks adaptations such as food-storage techniques or hibernation to help cope with the lack of food and warmth in the northern winter.

The opossum does have the capability of putting on a huge quantity of body fat, which is one reason it can survive in southern Canada. Opossums can gain more than 30 percent of their body weight as fat and can lose as much as 45 percent of their body weight and still survive the overwintering period. Their ability to get very fat in autumn is, no doubt, why residents of some areas, such as the southern United States, once prized opossum as a food—in spite of its rank odor and pronounced taste for garbage and carrion. "Possum and taters" (sweet potatoes) is one of the traditional dishes of the southern United States.

As the only marsupial in North America, the opossum seems anatomically bizarre, and many misconceptions about its reproductive biology exist. Folklore often has it that male opossums copulate with the female's nose, a belief with a logical origin: Males do have a forked, two-pronged penis. But the notion is mistaken, since females have a forked vagina and two uteri. Less obvious but equally unusual is the fact that opossums produce paired sperm. Together, the sperm pairs swim in a straight line, but if they are separated, they swim in circles.

The opossum's courtship and mating procedure exhibits similar oddities. As with many kinds of mammals, male opossums will fight savagely for access to sexually receptive females, slashing at each other with their enlarged canine teeth and occasionally killing or maiming one another. Part of the threat display used in aggressive encounters is a clicking noise, probably produced with the canine teeth. When a male is courting a female, he shuffles after her, making a continuous clicking noise. If she is receptive, he will climb onto her back, grasp her neck in his mouth, grip her hind legs with his feet and proceed to mate, none of which is particularly unusual. What is unusual is that the pair of mating opossums almost invariably flops over so that the female is lying on her right side. Examinations of females from pairs that stayed upright or flopped to the left instead of the right revealed that they were not successfully inseminated.

The female's reproductive biology is as curious as the male's. The breeding season begins in January in the southern United States and in early spring in Canada. The female, reproductively mature at only 6 months, is in heat for less than two days, and her pregnancy is likewise quickly completed, the young being born after 13 days. At birth, opossums are very poorly developed compared with placental mammals. They are naked and only half an inch long; it would take 3,500 of them to weigh a pound. Their organs are still forming, the chambers of the heart have not been separated, the kidney does not work, there is no pigment in the eyes, and the hind limbs and tail are almost nonexistent. All the newborn opossum is equipped with are the tools needed to crawl up the furry belly of the mother and into her pouch: well-developed forearms and fingers with claws that are able to grab hair and pull the infant upward, hand over hand, to the fur-lined pouch that offers warmth and milk.

The mouth muscles that attach the newborn to the mother's nipple are also functional at birth. The nipple swells within the infant opossum's mouth, holding it firmly attached. As it swells, the nipple lengthens, until it is about an inch and a half long, a cordlike lifeline that enables the developing opossums to move about in the pouch and strengthen limb muscles and coordination. Once attached, the young feed on milk for roughly 60 days and complete the developmental changes that in other placental mammals, such as ourselves, take place inside the mother's uterus. At the end of 60 days, the young opossums have developed fur and will venture outside the pouch. The elongated nipples enable them to lie outside the pouch and continue suckling. After 30 to 40 more days, the young are

Born naked and poorly developed, up to two dozen half-inch-long young opossums must then crawl to the safety of their mother's pouch to suckle. Only the most vigorous survive.

ready to be weaned and eat solid food.

During their early life after weaning, the young opossums ride with their mother, clinging to the hair on her back, a period during which they are probably learning much about food and foraging. However, once they are able to forage independently, the young become unsociable. Normally within two to three months of weaning, all the offspring have dispersed. From then on, they remain as solitary animals, the only contact with other opossums being at mating and litter-raising time.

The opossum's ecological strategy is best described as opportunistic, or generalized. Originally, opossums were found primarily in deciduous woodlands, but they now occupy many habitats, including agricultural areas, marshland and even canyons in dry grassland areas. They depend on ready access to water, and because they do not excavate, they rely on burrowing mammals, rock cavities and hollow trees for their

dens. Although they depend on dens for reproduction and overwintering, opossums do not defend a specific foraging area or have a well-defined home range. Many seem to wander.

During the foraging season, most dens are used for only a single night. Opossums may cover several miles a night during foraging outings and move regularly to a new den site several hundred yards away. During any given night, an opossum makes many trips, usually a few hundred yards or less, between the denning site and some food source. Given the number of different den sites, its foraging range is roughly 50 to 500 acres. The home ranges of several resident opossums overlap, and opossum densities can range from one in 2 acres to one in 10.

The abundance of opossums and their wide distribution are made possible by their broad diet. They are nocturnal foragers that will eat carrion, mushrooms, grass and other green vegetation, fruits,

acorns, nuts, lizards, frogs, toads, many kinds of insect grubs, stinkbugs, hornets, worms and millipedes. Opossums can kill animals such as rabbits as well as small livestock such as chickens. They are one of the few predators that catch large numbers of shrews and moles.

Among the most interesting foods available to opossums are poisonous snakes in the family Crotalidae, which includes rattlesnakes, water moccasins and copperheads. Opossums, which evolved in the snake-rich regions of the south, are virtually immune to the venoms of these snakes. Researchers have injected opossums with as much as 60 times the lethal dose for other mammals. The opossums respond with only a mild increase in heartbeat and blood pressure and none of the massive bleeding or allergic and tissue-damaging reactions that mammals normally suffer. Treatment of human cases of snakebite still relies on the production of antivenins made from horse or sheep serum, which often produce violent allergic side effects. Somehow, opossums have evolved a biochemical alternative, and perhaps a study of their solution will lead medicine to a better form of snakebite therapy.

Many people have heard that opossums feign death when they are threatened, hence the phrase "to play possum." An opossum will, in fact, do this, a behavior that involves lying on its side with its mouth open, drooling saliva and often defecating and oozing a noxious stink from its anal glands, which must make the inert opossum uninteresting to all but the most avid predator. However, not all opossums play possum. Humans who harass them are surprised to discover that they will growl and attack aggressively with a formidable bite which can easily become seriously infected because of their carrion- and garbage-eating habits.

No predators appear to specialize on opossums. They are eaten by coyotes, bobcats, foxes, raccoons, snakes and some large birds such as eagles and the great horned owl.

INSECTIVORES *Insectivora*

One of the first things a mammalogist who sets out to livetrap animals must learn is that shrews and moles starve to death within hours if not supplied with large quantities of food. These animals are tiny. Some species would fit comfortably in an eggcup or even a thimble, but they have huge appetites, completely out of proportion to their size. The famous Canadian mammalogist Randolph Peterson once recorded what a single tiny pygmy shrew ate during 10 days of captivity: "the carcasses of 20 *cinereus* shrews, 1 white-footed mouse and 1 pygmy shrew, 20 houseflies, 22 grasshoppers, 2 craneflies, 1 beetle and the liver of a meadow mouse." In spite of this huge intake of food, the captive shrew did not get fat. A captive short-tailed shrew ate 20 crickets, 4 carabid beetles, a centipede and a beetle larva in a morning and was still hungry. Life for a shrew is one of seemingly perpetual hunger, although it can survive on a limited diet by going torpid.

Insectivores are a complicated blend of ancient primitive characteristics and highly evolved specialized traits. On one hand, insectivores are considered to be the most primitive placental mammals. Among the primitive features that many insectivores exhibit are the structure of the ears, the small brain, primitive teeth, testes that are usually inside the abdomen rather than in a scrotum, and the joining of the urinary and reproductive tracts and the intestine into a common channel called a cloaca. At the same time, the different families have developed highly specialized adaptations such as the mole's digging apparatus and the shrew's ultrasonic communication system, which are specific to particular groups and are of recent evolutionary origin.

Each family of insectivores has specialized abilities. Hedgehogs have evolved a unique prickly coat of quills along with the strange behavior of coating these spines with saliva and poison collected from toads. The solenodons, rat-sized predators of insects and other small animals on the isolated islands of Cuba and Hispaniola, have developed a potent venomous saliva that enables them to subdue lizards, frogs and birds. Moles have evolved into underground specialists. Each insectivore family has become substantially different from other families in the order as well as from their common ancestor.

North America has only two resident insectivore families: the shrews, Soricidae, and the moles, Talpidae. All species in this order tend to be small. They have reduced eyes and ears, and their feet have five clawed toes, distinguishing them from other small mammals such as mice, which have four clawed toes on their forefeet.

Shrews must spend most of their lives searching for food and will eat almost anything with a high calorie and protein content. One of the weapons in the northern short-tailed shrew's foraging arsenal is its neurotoxic saliva. Similar to a cobra's, it allows the shrew to kill lizards and prey larger than itself.

SHREWS *Soricidae*

The pygmy white-toothed shrew of Africa is the world's smallest terrestrial mammal. The next smallest mammal, the pygmy shrew, is a resident of North America and is scarcely larger than its African counterpart. Two hundred adult pygmy shrews would weigh a pound. The small size of shrews dominates their life history and behavior.

The small, hot bodies of shrews radiate a tremendous amount of heat energy. They have the highest surface area relative to body mass of all mammals, which means that the heat they generate metabolically to maintain their body temperature soon dissipates into the air. The calories they need to maintain their body temperature are acquired with the aid of a gargantuan appetite.

Shrews' high metabolic rate and large appetite mean they will attack almost any prey item they can subdue. They eat far more than just insects. They will prey on earthworms, seeds, fish, frogs and carrion, indeed almost any food with a high protein and calorie content that they can easily digest, including subterranean fungi.

One North American shrew has even evolved a poisonous venom so that it can immobilize a more diverse range of prey. The salivary glands of the short-tailed shrew contain a neurotoxin that quickly paralyzes and will kill other small mammals and even larger prey such as frogs. The venom is delivered along a special groove between the lower front incisor teeth. The poison is a water-soluble compound that is similar to cobra venom. A short-tailed shrew does not contain enough venom to kill a human, but a bite can cause swelling and a bad local reaction. Short-tailed shrew poison can kill mice within minutes and over time can be lethal to much larger animals such as cottontail rabbits.

Shrews possess many other adaptations related to their need for a continuous supply of food. The front incisor teeth of all shrews are enlarged to form a shearing and pinching apparatus for grasping and slicing up prey: The upper incisors, double-pronged and hooklike, cut against long horizontal lower incisors, which have a set of cusps. Shrews do not have time to shed a set of milk teeth—they might starve in the process—so they are born with a single set of permanent teeth. Mammalogists can calculate the age of a shrew from its tooth wear. Shrews rarely live longer than a year and a half, and even in that brief time, older ones have sometimes worn their teeth down completely.

The stomach and digestive tract of shrews are simple and short, designed to move, process and evacuate food at a high rate. If shrews kill more than they can eat immediately, they will cache the surplus. Shrews can immobilize grasshoppers, snails and earthworms with a specialized bite at a main nerve center that paralyzes but does not kill them, and a stash of fresh food can be built up for later consumption.

The northern water shrew, shown at right, is one of the largest of all shrews, but even so, it would take 30 of them to weigh a pound. It would take 200 of its diminutive relative, the pygmy shrew, to weigh the same amount.

Shrews usually work at night or underground along a series of runways and burrows (often those of other animals such as moles), so their eyes, of little use in prey capture, are reduced in size. To compensate, shrews have a well-developed sense of smell, and their pointed snouts always seem to be twitching and moving, reading the scents in the air. Some shrews use ultrasound to locate prey.

Small size opens foraging opportunities to shrews—they can profitably handle small prey items that are uneconomical for larger animals. For example, shrews will eat ants, fly and beetle larvae, centipedes and even mites and nematode worms that are scarcely more than a fraction of an inch long. Shrews can run through leaf litter and slip under logs and stones where insects and worms hide, places inaccessible to predators such as birds and larger mammals. Because of their ability to exploit such a huge resource base, shrews can be exceedingly abundant in spite of their high demand for food.

In winter, most shrew activity takes place beneath the insulating blanket of snow. Their fine fur is effective insulation. Unlike other northern mammals such as ground squirrels, shrews' high metabolic rate prevents them from hibernating. They would lose heat and burn body fat too quickly even if they reduced their body temperature like true hibernators. Instead, shrews respond to low temperatures in the environment by turning up their bodies' metabolism and generating even more heat. This is especially true of temperate-zone and northern shrews, known as "hot" shrews. Their metabolism is considerably faster than that of tropical and desert shrews, which are known as "cool" shrews.

Surviving winter is a challenge for shrews, and many starve to death. The successful ones, however, feed on the larvae and pupae of many dormant insects as well as other small mammals such as voles, which are available on the soil surface.

The success of their adaptations is made clear by the evolutionary history of shrews. Fossil shrews go back as far as 50 million years, and in overall body plan, they have changed little. They have spread from an apparently European origin through Africa, Asia and North America. In South America, they have penetrated only the north of the continent, and they never reached Australia because of its isolation. Shrews have radiated into a vast array of habitats from tropical rainforests to deserts, grasslands and high Arctic tundra.

In spite of their ubiquity, little is known about the social life of shrews. They are difficult to study under natural conditions, so what is known about their behavior is largely derived from captive animals. Studies of acoustic communication in shrews have recently revealed an unsuspected richness of signals. Shrews such as the short-tailed shrew and the least shrew have a vocal repertoire that includes chirps, clicks, twitters and buzzes. These sounds carry different meanings. Cheeping by the young, for instance, can trigger a search-and-rescue response by mother and father short-tailed shrews. Male short-tailed shrews in pursuit of estrous females produce a stream of dry, unmusical clicks similar to the sounds of a twig brushing against bicycle spokes.

Acoustic signals play an important role in fights between male shrews. Territorial male common shrews confront adversaries with screaming and staccato squeaking. These sounds are also used in echolocating objects and other shrews. Using a system similar to that of bats, shrews can read distortion and other features of the echo to assess the size and location of an object.

Shrews also communicate chemically. The male short-tailed shrew uses a large belly gland as well as sound to communicate with the female during courtship. In the words of one researcher, "The male appears to play a passive role—approaching the female, rubbing the substrate, tolerating bites from the female without biting her—while rubbing and exuding odor in new areas and gradu-ally increasing the receptivity of the female. The female repels the male with high-intensity chirps and buzzes; the male is easily repelled by the female's loud vocalizations. The male responds to bites and loud chirps by closing his eyes and ears and exposing his gland-covered neck. The male rubs his venter over the substrate and simultaneously over his body. His glandular odor, immediately detectable by the observer, is emitted after two or three minutes." Shrews also have conspicuous glands along their sides, but their function has yet to be established. They may act to deter predators. The males' glandular secretions also send a message to other males that the burrow is currently occupied. A single short-tailed shrew gives off enough scent to fill a room with a rank, repulsive smell.

Shrews have limited opportunity to communicate with each other. Females and males are normally hostile to each other and to members of their own sex during all but breeding season, when females may tolerate the presence of males. The only other well-developed communication is between the young and their mother.

There is, however, one North American shrew that has a greater propensity for social life—the least shrew. Adult least shrews often nest together, perhaps to increase heat retention, and both sexes reportedly care for their young. Short-tailed shrews also exhibit this behavioral pattern, but no detailed studies of their social behavior under natural conditions have been conducted.

Reproduction in shrews is as hurried as the rest of their lives. Copulation usually lasts only 10 seconds. The gestation period is three weeks or less. Litters of 2 to 10 young are born naked and helpless in a well-insulated nest of grass and other materials. They grow rapidly. Some species are ready to leave the nest within three weeks. This rapid development enables an adult female to breed several times during a season, which normally begins in early spring and continues through the summer months.

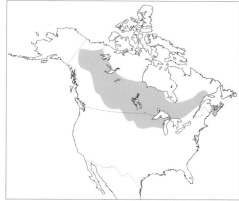

A denizen of the boreal coniferous forest, the arctic shrew, also known as the saddlebacked shrew, is one of the few species of shrew that has a color pattern in its fur.

ARCTIC SHREW *Sorex arcticus*

The tricolored pattern in adult and older juvenile arctic shrews—dark brown to black back, reddish sides and grayish belly—distinguishes the arctic shrew from most other shrews, which tend toward drab gray or black coloration. Despite its species name, *arcticus*, this shrew lives in boreal coniferous forests, especially in damp areas. In prairie regions, it is confined to moist shrub and forest edges. Where the arctic shrew occurs with the masked shrew, *Sorex cinereus*, it uses the drier parts of the habitat.

Arctic shrews also climb trees. Studies have found that the arctic shrew feeds heavily on sawflies found on larches and other coniferous trees. One shrew may require 123 sawflies a day, and at densities peaking at five individuals per acre, these shrews may have a major impact on the sawflies that sometimes invade northern forests. This shrew has also been seen climbing shrubs and jumping on grasshoppers. It will build runways and use those of other small mammals. Most of its foraging takes place in short bursts of a few minutes that alternate with rests. The pattern continues day and night, with somewhat more activity during the night.

Two generations may be produced in a season. Arctic shrews born in late summer begin to reproduce the following spring and die by fall. Spring-born arctic shrews may produce the late-summer and autumn generation, but this is not definitively known.

In captivity, the arctic shrew is docile and can be held in the hand.

Mammal: *Sorex arcticus*, arctic shrew, saddlebacked shrew, black-backed shrew
Meaning of Name: *Sorex* (shrew mouse); *arcticus* (land of the bear) refers to constellations of greater and lesser bear (i.e., the north)
Description: the most brilliantly colored shrew; tricolored, with dorsal region the darkest (brown to black); lighter brown flanks and paler, grayish brown underparts; younger juveniles are dull brown
Total Length: 3.8 to 5 inches
Tail: 1.2 to 1.9 inches
Weight: 0.18 to 0.5 ounce
Gestation: probably 21 to 25 days (possibly delayed implantation or ovulation)
Offspring: 5 to 9; 3 litters per year
Age of Maturity: female rarely breeds during first summer; varies with localities, depending on quantity and quality of available food
Longevity: 12 to 18 months
Diet: almost exclusively insects: caterpillars, centipedes, beetles and their larvae, sawfly cocoons
Habitat: swamps, bogs, grass/sedge marshes, edges of willow-alder zone, meadows or grassy clearings within forests
Predators: hawks, owls and lesser carnivores
Dental Formula:
3/1, 1/1, 3/1, 3/3 = 32 teeth

MASKED SHREW
Sorex cinereus

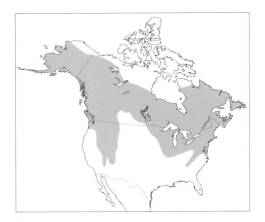

A keen hunter, the masked shrew has been observed stalking butterflies it has detected from a distance of 25 feet. Although insects are its dietary mainstay, it also eats small mammals.

Mammal: *Sorex cinereus*, masked shrew, common shrew

Meaning of Name: *Sorex* (shrew mouse); *cinereus* (ash-colored)

Description: slender body; long, slender snout that is always moving; brownish back and silvery or grayish white underneath; bicolored tail, brown above, paler below, with a black tip

Total Length: 2.8 to 4.9 inches

Tail: 0.98 to 2 inches

Weight: 0.09 to 0.28 ounce

Gestation: 17 to 28 days

Offspring: 2 to 10; 1 or sometimes 2 litters per year

Age of Maturity: female, some at 4 to 5 months, but most breed for the first time in the spring following birth; male, some individuals can breed at 2 months

Longevity: 12 to 18 months

Diet: mostly insects but also many small mammals; some seeds, moth and beetle larvae, slugs, mollusks, spiders, young mice and salamanders

Habitat: along margins of moist fields, bogs, marshes, moist or dry woods, willow-alder thickets and brushland

Predators: various small predators; larger shrews, hawks, owls, snakes, shrike, heron, merganser, fox, weasel and fish

Dental Formula:
3/1, 1/1, 3/1, 3/3 = 32 teeth

MASKED SHREW *Sorex cinereus*

The masked shrew is more widely distributed than any other shrew. It lives in forests and open meadows and marshes. In off years, populations may number only one per acre, but in peak years, masked shrew populations can climb as high as 13 per acre. For all its ubiquity, however, it is a relatively unknown mammal.

It is known that masked shrews are voracious hunters. One researcher observed a masked shrew stalking butterflies, which it could detect visually as far away as 25 feet. The masked shrew can also detect prey by smell. In an attempt to control sawfly pests in Newfoundland, the masked shrew was introduced to that province. The introduction was successful, and the shrew apparently does provide some biological control of those pests. It may also be able to kill young mice and salamanders. During winter, the masked shrew will also eat significant quantities of tree seeds, especially those of conifers.

Masked shrews do not build runways but will use those of other animals. They do, however, build grassy nests, which they defend from other shrews.

In the northern part of their range, masked shrews appear to breed only once a year, in spring. The young mature one year after birth. In the southern area of their range, masked shrews may breed several times in a season. The young show caravan behavior, following single file behind an adult. This may be of use if the female's nest is destroyed before the young shrews are fully mature.

The **prairie shrew**, *Sorex haydeni*, once thought to be a race of masked shrew, is now recognized as a distinct species. It is similar to the masked shrew, except that it specializes in prairie and parkland habitats. No study of the behavior or ecology of this shrew exists.

The **barren-ground shrew**, *Sorex ugyunak*, is another close relative of the masked shrew that is specialized to survive on the barren-ground habitat of the Northwest Territories. It is found in wet sedge-grass meadows and dwarf-willow and birch clumps.

SMOKY SHREW *Sorex fumeus*

The habitat of the smoky shrew is the mixed deciduous forest of the northeastern United States and eastern Canada. It builds nests of shredded leaves under stumps and logs and forages along the forest floor. Most of the time, the smoky shrew uses the runways of other small mammals, but it may make its own tunnels through loose leaf litter. It also modifies abandoned burrow systems of other small mammals. These burrows have openings scarcely larger than a dime and are easy to miss even when they are common. The smoky shrew's habit of rummaging through leaf litter may account for its preference for mature deciduous forests. Areas with rich loose soils such as stream and marsh edges are also suitable for this shrew. Like other shrews, the smoky feeds mainly on insects, but its use of mole runways may enable it to capture a large number of earthworms that other shrews, except for short-tailed shrews, either do not encounter or are too small to subdue.

When it is captured or harassed, a smoky shrew shrieks loudly. It is possible that the screaming may startle small predators such as short-tailed shrews and give the screaming animal an opportunity to escape.

The **wandering shrew**, *Sorex vagrans*, seems to be a western version of the smoky shrew, and like that species, it patrols the runways of other small mammals. It eats organisms associated with damp soil litter, including slugs, snails, insect larvae and even the underground fruiting bodies of a fungus in the genus *Endogone*.

Mammal: *Sorex fumeus*, smoky shrew
Meaning of Name: *Sorex* (shrew mouse); *fumeus* (smoky) refers to grayish brown color on back
Description: well-developed flank glands in both sexes; grizzled brown dorsally, slightly lighter underneath; tail is bicolored, yellow below and brown above; winter pelage is slate-gray to blackish
Total Length: 4.1 to 5 inches
Tail: 1.6 to 2.1 inches
Weight: 0.2 to 0.39 ounce
Gestation: less than 2 weeks
Offspring: 5 or 6; 2 or 3 litters per year
Age of Maturity: year after birth; does not breed in year of birth
Longevity: 14 to 17 months
Diet: insects, insect larvae, earthworms, moths, centipedes, snails, spiders, sow bugs, some mammals, salamanders and birds; also vegetable matter
Habitat: moist leaf mold, leaf litter, rotten logs in mature deciduous or mixed woods (uses tunnels in the leaf mold made by other small mammals)
Predators: owls and small predators such as short-tailed shrew
Dental Formula:
3/1, 1/1, 3/1, 3/3 = 32 teeth

The smoky shrew roots through the upper soil and leaf litter that covers the forest floor to capture prey such as earthworms, centipedes, snails and the occasional hatchling snake.

GASPÉ SHREW *Sorex gaspensis*

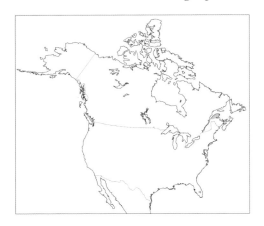

Mammal: *Sorex gaspensis*, Gaspé shrew; the least-known and rarest shrew
Meaning of Name: *Sorex* (shrew mouse); *gaspensis* (of Gaspé Peninsula)
Description: small with long tail; long whiskers; grayish; underparts are lighter than dorsum; bicolored tail
Total Length: 3.7 to 4.7 inches
Tail: 1.6 to 2.2 inches
Weight: 0.08 to 0.18 ounce
Gestation: not known (probably 13 to 28 days)
Offspring: possibly 5 or 6
Age of Maturity: not known (probably the spring following birth)
Longevity: 12 to 18 months
Diet: spiders, flies, beetles, insect larvae and plant matter
Habitat: coniferous and mixed forests; restricted to rocky-hilly terrain with a substrate of boulders; along small, swift-flowing streams
Predators: hawks, owls, snakes and carnivores
Dental Formula:
3/1, 1/1, 3/1, 3/3 = 32 teeth

GASPÉ SHREW *Sorex gaspensis*

Gaspé shrews are extremely rare and poorly understood. The species seems restricted to habitats along streams in the rocky and hilly areas of the Gaspé region of Quebec and New Brunswick. There is some dispute over whether this is a distinct species or merely a geographic race of the more southern and somewhat larger long-tailed shrew. It has a flattened skull, small body, long snout and long tail, all adaptations for moving through and hunting in rock crevices.

The **long-tailed shrew, *Sorex dispar***, is similar in appearance to the Gaspé shrew, although it is somewhat heavier and its fur is darker. The long-tailed shrew lives in mountainous regions in rocky talus slopes and areas with plenty of cracks and crevices among boulders, taking advantage of cover provided by moss and leaf mold and the roots of trees. The cool, moist habitat has resulted in a specialized diet: a high proportion of crevice-dwelling arthropods, especially the flat crack-dwelling centipedes, as well as spiders and insects.

Little is known of the long-tailed shrew. Experts assume that there is a substantial population near the Quebec/Maine border and throughout the Maritime Provinces, but study is nearly impossible given the species' subterranean life. Certainly, its predominant range is in the eastern mountains from Maine through to West Virginia and eastern Tennessee.

The primary predators of long-tailed shrews are the hawks, owls, snakes and carnivores with which it shares the talus mountain terrain. Long-tails are not considered territorial, as they are usually found in close proximity to red-backed voles and the masked shrew. It is likely that they avoid confrontation by concentrating on different sources of food.

Life expectancy is probably 12 to 18 months, and females average one litter of five young after maturity.

PYGMY SHREW *Sorex hoyi*

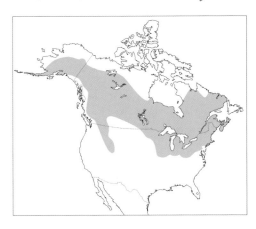

Mammal: *Sorex hoyi*, pygmy shrew
Meaning of Name: *Sorex* (shrew mouse); *hoyi* (named after Philip Hoy)
Description: sepia-brown above with paler grayish or brownish underparts; winter pelage is grayer and longer
Total Length: 2.8 to 4.1 inches
Tail: 0.9 to 1.4 inches
Weight: 0.07 to 0.22 ounce
Gestation: 13 to 24 days
Offspring: 3 to 8; 1 litter per year
Age of Maturity: not known (probably the spring following birth)
Longevity: 12 to 18 months
Diet: insect larvae, insects, beetles, spiders, invertebrates and carrion
Habitat: wooded areas (coniferous and deciduous); bogs, wet meadows
Predators: hawks, owls, snakes and carnivores
Dental Formula:
3/1, 1/1, 3/1, 3/3 = 32 teeth

Although its diet consists primarily of insects, the pygmy shrew will also eat carrion; it can digest animals much larger than itself within hours because of its high metabolic rate.

THE SPLITTING OF THE SHREWS

No one is certain how many kinds of shrews there are. This is surprising, because the taxonomy of most temperate mammals was worked out long ago. But new species of shrews continue to be recognized. In North America, more than 30 different shrew species have been described, many of them only in the past few years. One reason is that shrews are small and difficult to handle and study. The differences used to separate these newer species are subtle, requiring precise measurement and study of hundreds of specimens and sophisticated statistical analysis. The fact that many of our shrew species are so much alike suggests that these species are very recently formed and have not followed different evolutionary pathways for long.

The geographic range of closely related and newly formed species may give biologists insight into what causes speciation (the formation of new species). Normally, species are created by geographic isolation. A large population gets split into two or more populations isolated from each other by a geographic barrier such as a mountain range or large body of water. The split populations no longer mate and mix their genes. Because geographically separated populations live in different environments, they are subject to different forms of selection. Gradually, different genes and gene combinations develop in the populations until they become so distinct that they may be called separate species. This is especially true if the groups later come into contact but maintain their identity and do not interbreed.

There are good reasons why genetically different individuals ought not to interbreed. When a female and male mix their genes to produce offspring, each contributes a similar set of genes arranged in structures called chromosomes. During the fertilization of the egg and its division into cells, the male and female pairs of chromosomes must match reasonably well, or the resulting offspring will be genetically defective. Selection will favor individuals that choose not to mate with individuals who are too different from themselves because of the risk that their hybrid offspring will be defective. This reinforces the genetic separation of the two different populations, a process most biologists agree creates two or more new species out of one ancestral species.

It is more difficult to discover how populations become isolated, particularly for species that are millions of years old. But for some shrews, the isolation events may have been much more recent. It is quite possible that the waves of glaciation, which saw ice sheets march southward during cool times and then retreat northward during hot periods, played a major role in isolating populations and fostering the speciation process.

In the case of the Gaspé shrew and the related long-tailed shrew, a single ancestral species was probably distributed along the upper forest regions of the eastern mountain ranges running from the Gaspé through the southern Appalachian Mountains. During the peak of glaciation, the forested region moved to the south. There was a narrow strip of tundra in front of the glaciers. The northern forests spread out in a wide band, and populations of forest animals remained continuous for the most part. Some populations were isolated. Certain islands off the coasts remained unglaciated, and the animals were cut off from populations that had been pushed south.

When glaciers retreated, there were often pronounced hot and dry spells. During such spells, the northern forest home of the long-tailed and Gaspé shrew stock must have retreated higher and higher up mountainous areas until the two species were confined to strips and circles around mountaintops, separated from other similar forest pockets by grasslands and oak scrub. During one of these isolating episodes, the Gaspé shrew became separated and differentiated from the long-tailed shrew.

The same recent fragmentation appears to have happened to the common shrew. The prairie shrew, the barren-ground shrew, the Mount Lyell shrew and Preble's shrew have all recently been separated from the common shrew by taxonomists. The Mount Lyell shrew is found only in two counties in California, and it is probably a species formed from an isolated remnant population created when the common shrew was forced south by the ice sheets. It was left behind in an ecological island when the flora and fauna moved north with the retreat of the glaciers.

Many large mammals disappeared during the Pleistocene epoch for reasons that are not at all clear. But at the same time, the divisive influence of the ice sheets' waxing and waning across the continent had a creative effect and probably generated many of our most recent species of shrews and made the shrew family one of the most diverse groups of northern mammals.

DUSKY SHREW
Sorex monticolus

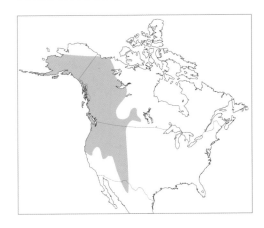

Mammal: *Sorex monticolus*, dusky shrew
Meaning of Name: *Sorex* (shrew mouse); *monticolus* (mountain-dweller)
Description: short rust-brown fur above in summer, with brownish to silver-gray underparts; tail indistinctly bicolored; winter pelage is darker above and below
Total Length: 3.7 to 5.5 inches
Tail: 1.2 to 2.4 inches
Weight: 0.16 to 0.36 ounce
Gestation: not known (probably 13 to 28 days)
Offspring: 4 to 7
Age of Maturity: not known (probably the spring following birth)
Longevity: 12 to 18 months
Diet: insects and their larvae, earthworms, spiders, snails and other invertebrates
Habitat: many different habitats subject to a wide range of climatic conditions; prefers wet meadows, grass/sedge marshes and coniferous forests near streams
Predators: hawks, owls, snakes and carnivores
Dental Formula:
3/1, 1/1, 3/1, 3/3 = 32 teeth

WATER SHREW
Sorex palustris

This large shrew has radiated into a niche unoccupied by other shrews and has therefore achieved a wide geographic range. It occurs along lakes, ponds, streams and rivers—any wet habitat where sheltering banks, tree roots or rocky debris offer protection. It is most abundant along fast-flowing streams with well-vegetated shorelines.

True to its name, the water shrew dives and swims well and is able to catch much of its diet underwater. It eats aquatic insects, fish and tadpoles. The water shrew makes very brief dives, usually lasting less than a minute.

Mammal: *Sorex palustris*, water shrew, northern water shrew

Meaning of Name: *Sorex* (shrew mouse); *palustris* (dwelling in marshes or bogs)

Description: large; big hind feet bear a row of stiff hairs along outer and inner margins of feet and toes; middle toes are partially webbed; soft, velvety fur is gray to black above and white or grayish underneath; distinctly bicolored tail

Total Length: 5.1 to 6.4 inches

Tail: 2.4 to 3.5 inches

Weight: 0.3 to 0.63 ounce

Gestation: not known (probably 13 to 28 days)

Offspring: 4 to 8 (average 6); 2 or 3 litters per year

Age of Maturity: male, winter of first year; female may breed when slightly more than 3 months old

Longevity: 12 to 18 months; dies after its second summer

Diet: primarily insects, insect larvae and nymphs of aquatic insects, planarians, small fish, spiders, slugs, snails, other invertebrates and larval amphibians

Habitat: streams, lakes and ponds if adequate cover is available along banks or on shores; can also adapt to habitats with little water

Predators: hawks, owls, snakes, weasel and mink

Dental Formula:
3/1, 1/1, 3/1, 3/3 = 32 teeth

The water shrew's adaptation to watery habitats has expanded its range of foods to items like tadpoles, frogs and fish.

Longer immersion risks soaking the coat, which would cause the shrew to lose large amounts of heat. Even half a minute underwater produces a drop in body temperature.

The water shrew is protected to some extent against heat loss by its coat, which traps air between the hairs. Underwater, the shrew looks silvery, an effect produced by air bubbles that are trapped in the coat. The trapped air makes the water shrew very buoyant. It paddles vigorously to submerge itself; when it stops swimming, it shoots up to the surface and floats well out of the water. It is buoyant and has actually been observed running across the surface of ponds with the help of the stiff hairs fringing its webbed hind feet.

Immediately after a dive, the shrew leaves the water and grooms and dries itself, allowing its body temperature to return to normal.

Trout and other fish eat the water shrew, another reason for it to minimize its time in the water.

The **Pacific water shrew, Sorex bendirii**, the largest of the northern long-tailed shrews, is highly aquatic. It also occupies wooded habitats, so it is not restricted to water. In wet weather, it may forage far from water.

TROWBRIDGE SHREW
Sorex trowbridgii

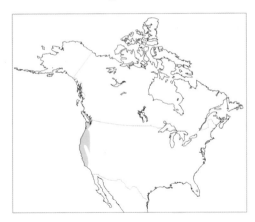

Mammal: *Sorex trowbridgii*, Trowbridge shrew
Meaning of Name: *Sorex* (shrew mouse); *trowbridgii* (named after W.P. Trowbridge)
Description: dark gray or blackish with brownish hue; lighter underparts; brownish in summer; strikingly bicolored tail (dark dorsally and white below)
Total Length: 4.1 to 4.9 inches
Tail: 1.9 to 2.3 inches
Weight: 0.43 to 0.53 ounce
Gestation: not known
(probably 13 to 28 days)
Offspring: 3 to 6; 1 or possibly 2 litters per year
Age of Maturity: not known
(probably the spring following birth)
Longevity: 12 to 18 months
Diet: insects, spiders, centipedes, isopods and some other invertebrates; in winter, conifer seeds and vegetable matter
Habitat: prefers moist ground litter of well-drained coniferous forests, where logs, stumps and decaying vegetation provide shelter; also found in brushlands and cutover areas
Predators: hawks, owls, snakes and carnivores
Dental Formula:
3/1, 1/1, 3/1, 3/3 = 32 teeth

A TEST OF THE MALE

Dogs, wolves and coyotes are well known for the "copulatory tie" in which two mating individuals seem stuck together for as long as an hour. In fact, the male is held in place and cannot easily separate from the female. This same situation is found in the northern short-tailed shrew. Most shrews copulate for only a few seconds, but in this species, the male and female remain stuck together for almost half an hour. When the male northern short-tailed shrew mates, his erect penis, when inserted into the female's vagina, bends in an S-shaped curve, following the vagina's shape. This lock-and-key mechanism holds the male in place. The tip of the penis also has a series of pointed hooking structures that further secure it. Even after he dismounts, the male remains attached to the female. She may drag him around backward for as long as 25 minutes.

The adaptive significance of this is unclear. It may prevent a male from being displaced by another male, and it may provide the female with some information about the status and competence of the male, as a subdominant male thus engaged would be extremely vulnerable to attack and unlikely to attempt copulation.

Another curious feature of the male northern short-tailed shrew's penis is that it can only be retracted into its storage sheath with the aid of the mouth. This seems a somewhat cumbersome arrangement, especially since a pair may mate as often as 20 times a day. Northern short-tailed shrews run down burrows much of the time, and like moles, they have grain-free fur and reduced external extremities, such as ears, that might be snagged by obstructions. An unretracted penis would seem to be a definite liability. Some form of female choice of male quality may be operating that results in a male reproductive morphology which inconveniences the male but gives the female information on his fitness.

TUNDRA SHREW
Sorex tundrensis

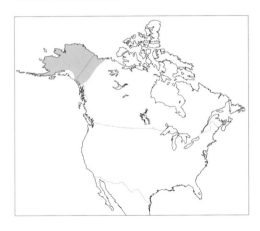

Mammal: *Sorex tundrensis*, tundra shrew
Meaning of Name: *Sorex* (shrew mouse); *tundrensis* (of the tundra)
Description: in summer, pelage is tricolored (brown back, pale grayish underparts and lighter sides); in winter, pelage is bicolored (grayish sides and underparts, brown back)
Total Length: 3.3 to 4.7 inches
Tail: 0.9 to 1.4 inches
Weight: 0.18 to 0.35 ounce
Gestation: not known
(probably 13 to 28 days)
Offspring: 8 to 12; several litters in quick succession
Age of Maturity: not known
(probably the spring following birth)
Longevity: 12 to 18 months
Diet: insects, earthworms, floral parts of small grasses
Habitat: well-drained habitats with dense vegetation; along northern border of boreal forest; dry tundra ridges
Predators: hawks, owls, snakes and carnivores
Dental Formula:
3/1, 1/1, 3/1, 3/3 = 32 teeth

WHY THERE ARE SO MANY SHREWS

One of the basic questions of ecology is: How do so many species coexist? If two species require the same resources to live, the species that is better at acquiring or controlling resources will outcompete and eventually displace the less efficient species.

How, then, do so many species of shrews coexist? Shrews seem similar. They are all small, hungry insectivores with a catholic diet. Shrews have to be voracious. Their high metabolism means they often must eat more than their own body weight each day, so one would expect shrews to compete intensely with each other for food. Yet one study found six species of shrews living in the same area.

Two kinds of competition confront an individual: competition from members of the same species (intraspecific competition) and competition from members of different species (interspecific competition). Normally, intraspecific competition will be most intense, because the more similarities there are among individuals in a population, the more likely they are to need exactly the same kinds of resources. Under the pressure of intraspecific competition, evolution will favor the individuals who use resources that are less used by other members of the species. If every northern short-tailed shrew is searching for sawflies, the individual who is able to eat earthworms may enjoy a great competitive advantage. The long-term evolutionary effect of intraspecific competition is a broadening of the resources a species will use. The resource base will grow until it is checked by inefficiency (a jack-of-all-trades is master of none) or opposed by interspecific competition.

Interspecific competition is hard to demonstrate experimentally under natural conditions, but there is evidence that it is important. Rarely have two different species ever been found to use exactly the same set of resources. One community of six shrews, each of a different

species, living on Sagamook Mountain in New Brunswick, showed important differences in diets and habitat choices. All six species shared the same kinds of foods, eating dozens of different invertebrates, but each species ate different proportions. The northern short-tailed shrew, a strong burrower, ate more earthworms and snails than the others; the water shrew ate more aquatic organisms; the Gaspé shrew, more spiders; the smoky shrew, earthworms and a mix of insects, including a high proportion of moths. The masked shrew favored insects, especially beetle larvae, while the pygmy shrew ate insect larvae and caterpillars.

Each shrew has access to a different microhabitat. The northern short-tailed shrew can reach earthworms by burrowing, but it cannot reach the items available to the Gaspé shrew, whose small body and flattened head enable it to reach into tight rock crevices. The tiny pygmy shrew might be a strong competitor of the Gaspé shrew, but it avoids rocky areas and prefers the understory of forested stream areas. When two shrew species share the same microhabitat, they will differ greatly in body size and will take different-sized prey. If two similar-sized shrews occur in an area, they will tend to prefer different microhabitats.

SMALL IS COSTLY

When an animal is warmer than its environment, it loses heat; when it is cooler than the environment, it gains heat. Any mammal generates heat because all the chemical reactions of the body create waste heat energy. The rate at which this heat is radiated and lost depends on the surface area of the mammal's body, how well it is insulated and other factors such as how windy and humid the weather is and the temperature difference between the animal and the environment. Mammals differ vastly in size, from tiny shrews to monstrous whales. Consequently, the rate

at which they lose heat energy varies tremendously.

Small mammals such as shrews, moles and mice must be capable of producing large amounts of heat. Their relatively large surface-to-volume ratio means that they lose heat at a high rate and thus must be able to generate heat at a high rate. Shrews have the smallest bodies and the fastest metabolism of any mammals. A shrew must eat several times its body weight each day to produce the calories needed to maintain its constant high body temperature. By contrast, a large mammal such as a moose or whale needs to eat only a small fraction of its body weight to maintain its body temperature.

The difference in metabolism between shrews and larger mammals is reflected in the rate at which they absorb and pump oxygen through their bodies to fuel their metabolic fire. A shrew's heart is capable of beating more than 1,000 times per minute when the shrew is active. A large mammal may have a heart rate of only 10 beats per minute. If the metabolic fire of the shrew goes out, it cools quickly. When a shrew dies, it is at the temperature of the environment within a few minutes. By contrast, a large whale that had been killed showed a drop in body temperature of only 2 Fahrenheit degrees in 28 hours.

An ounce of shrew or mouse biomass burns far more food and oxygen than an ounce of moose flesh, for example. One biologist has calculated that the plant food which would support a half-ton moose would support only about 90 pounds of mice and probably less than 40 pounds of shrews. This has some interesting behavioral and ecological consequences. It means that a larger animal will be able to survive longer than a smaller one on its energy stores, assuming both store the same proportion of their body weight. Some whales, for example, spend the better part of the winter migrating to tropical breeding sites and eat almost nothing. Large male seals and walruses may spend their two-month breeding season without eating,

NORTHERN
SHORT-TAILED SHREW
Blarina brevicauda

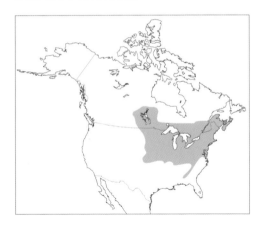

Mammal: *Blarina brevicauda*, northern short-tailed shrew

Meaning of Name: *Blarina* is a coined name for certain shrews—the actual meaning is unknown; *brevicauda* (short tail)

Description: large with a short tail and blunt nose; glandular hairless area on the midventral region; eyes are so small that they are barely apparent; slate-colored fur; paler underparts

Total Length: 3.5 to 5.7 inches

Tail: 0.7 to 1.4 inches

Weight: 0.53 to 1.2 ounces

Gestation: 21 to 22 days

Offspring: 3 to 10 (usually 5 to 7); 2 or 3 litters per year

Age of Maturity: male, 12 weeks; female, 6 weeks

Longevity: 1 to 2 years (a potentially greater longevity than long-tailed species)

Diet: insects, insect larvae, earthworms, snails, some vegetable matter and small vertebrates (young mice, meadow voles)

Habitat: hardwood forests with high humidity and loose humus; also coniferous forests, bogs, marshes, fields and grasslands if there is a lot of moisture

Predators: hawks, owls, shrike, weasel, skunk, fox, bobcat and coyote; domestic dog and cat may worry them to death

Dental Formula:
3/1, 1/1, 3/1, 3/3 = 32 teeth

but a shrew or mole starves to death after only a few hours without food. A large mammal can afford to eat low-energy foods such as twigs and shrubbery and to spend much of its life sleeping and digesting. Shrews must spend most of their lives foraging and can eat only high-quality, easily digested items.

Since oxygen consumption is proportional to metabolic rate, it is easy to see why there are no deep-diving small mammals. Only relatively large mammals such as seals and whales can be deep divers; a shrew or mole will burn up all its oxygen in a matter of minutes.

There are also some interesting life-history patterns associated with body-size variation. In general, small mammals are more fecund; that is, they breed more often and have more offspring than large mammals do, and their populations can grow faster than those of large mammals. Small mammals, however, mature earlier and die younger than large mammals do. Whales may live for a century, while many small mammals live at most a year or two, no matter how well they are fed and protected. Early death, a kind of planned obsolescence, seems designed into their bodies. The reason for this remains unexplained and is one of the most challenging questions of ecology and evolution.

NORTHERN
SHORT-TAILED SHREW
Blarina brevicauda

The northern short-tailed shrew can be one of the most abundant of mammals, at up to 80 animals per acre. It is tempting to attribute this to the range of food available. Its neurotoxic saliva enables it to kill animals such as garter snakes and young rabbits, prey much larger than itself and unavailable to other shrews and similar-sized rodents. This shrew also uses its venom to paralyze victims such as earthworms and then store them in caches, alive but immobile. Northern short-tailed shrews also cache large quantities of snails and sawfly pupae.

During some periods, half of this shrew's diet may consist of meadow voles. It is credited with controlling and depressing meadow vole population explosions, and in some years, huge increases in vole numbers are responsible for the extreme densities of northern short-tailed shrews. Short-tails and voles may cycle together in the same way that lynx and snowshoe hares do.

Despite the northern short-tailed shrew's venom, the voles and mice fight back. Although the venom slows and weakens the victim, reducing its respiration rate and reaction time, it can

take 10 to 30 minutes for the northern short-tailed shrew to deliver its *coup de grâce*: a bite to the base of the skull. Voles have evolved the ability to recognize and avoid the smell of the northern short-tailed shrew. Mammalogists trying to trap voles in devices that previously held northern short-tailed shrews have found that the voles avoid them.

Shrew venom is also reported to contain an enzyme, glycosidase chitinase, which may improve the digestive efficiency of this species. Insect skin and skeletons consist of chitin, a compound that most mammals cannot digest. The feces of other shrews often contain large quantities of undigested insect exoskeleton and chitin, recognizable as poorly digested legs and other body parts. The feces of the northern short-tailed shrew, however, are mushy and well digested.

There is also a suggestion that the side glands of this shrew produce such an unpalatable odor and taste that mammalian and bird predators avoid it, thereby allowing populations to reach great densities.

The northern short-tailed shrew is the most underground North American shrew and is a competent digger. Its short tail, slitlike ears and short, stout limbs all reflect its adaptation for life underground. The northern short-tailed shrew eats more earthworms than any other shrew, and moles could be its main competitors for food. It builds its own runways and constructs a nest that is well underground, often a foot below the surface.

This shrew is most common in rich deciduous forests but is found in a variety of other habitats, including coniferous forests and, to a lesser extent, in open and wet areas.

The northern short-tailed shrew has one of the most interesting and best-studied social behaviors of all shrews. Unlike most shrew species, the northern short-tailed shrew can be kept in captivity with other members of its species. They are antagonistic toward each other at times but will also sleep together and adjust to each other's presence.

These shrews are reproductively active for a large portion of the year, from early spring through to autumn. Females may breed two to three times in a season. They have the typically short shrew pregnancy of three weeks and a similar period passes before weaning.

LEAST SHREW
Cryptotis parva

Not much larger than a pygmy shrew, the least shrew looks like the bigger short-tailed shrew, but it is a surface dweller and does not burrow extensively. Least shrews are found in habitats ranging from open grasslands and salt marshes to forested areas.

Leasts may have the most interesting social lives of all shrews. Like the short-tailed shrew, the least shrew has a well-developed vocal repertoire, communicating with a variety of clicks and chirping sounds. Up to 31 individuals have been found in the same nest. In captivity, they do not fight. There is also an interesting observation of parental behavior: When a nest containing young was opened and the immature shrews were scattered, all the adults helped in retrieving the young. It is possible that these shrews live in large cooperative groups, which would make them completely unlike any other North American shrew species.

Normally a resident of deciduous forests, where it feeds mainly on earthworms, the short-tailed shrew also lives in open and wet areas, preying on frogs and other aquatic species.

LEAST SHREW *Cryptotis parva*

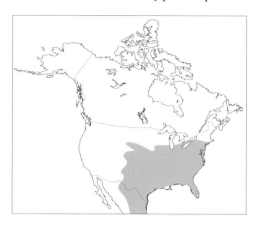

Mammal: *Cryptotis parva*, least shrew
Meaning of Name: *Cryptotis* refers to the fact that the ears are small and hidden under the fur; *parva* (small)
Description: small size and short tail distinguish it from other species; grayish brown above and silver-gray to white below; winter pelage is darker
Total Length: 2.7 to 4.1 inches
Tail: 0.5 to 0.9 inches
Weight: 0.16 to 0.2 ounce
Gestation: 21 to 23 days
Offspring: 1 to 9 (usually 3 to 6); 2 or 3 litters per summer
Age of Maturity: before the age of 40 days for both sexes
Longevity: 18 months in the wild; 20 months in captivity
Diet: insects, earthworms, centipedes, mollusks, amphibians, lizards and small mammals; also some fruit and plant material
Habitat: open grassy fields with scattered weedy or brushy vegetation
Predators: owls, hawks, snakes, weasel, domestic cat and short-tailed shrew
Dental Formula:
3/1, 1/1, 2/1, 3/3 = 30 teeth

MOLES *Talpidae*

Moles have been called the least understood major component of our mammalian fauna. The reason for this seems clear: Moles live mostly out of sight underground and in conditions hard to simulate in captivity. Most of what is known about moles is related to the sophisticated adaptations they have made to a subterranean life.

Like shrews and voles, which also spend much time in tunnels and under leaf litter, moles have a compact, elongate body. There are no awkward protruding limbs to snag on roots. Moles dig their own tunnel systems, and many features of their body reflect a design for digging. The evolutionary success of moles is tied to digging. The most primitive surviving mole, *Uropsilus*, looks much like a shrew and has no special adaptations for digging. The more modern moles have evolved a unique digging apparatus that enables them to occupy niches unexploited by primitive moles and other insectivores such as shrews.

A mole's forelegs and feet are its shovels. The limbs of other digging mammals such as squirrels, badgers and occasional excavators such as coyotes are under the body. These animals scrape and throw the soil under and behind them. Moles have developed a lateral-stroke digging technique, one that is unique among mammals. This special method has involved a radical redesign of their forelimbs. The shoulder and collarbone of the mole are joined in a different way than those of other mammals. Moles' shoulder blades are large, and their forepaws have grown into huge, flat paddles with stout claws. The fingers have flat ridges of skin along the sides, increasing their surface area. The breastbone is deeply ridged to allow the attachment of powerful chest muscles.

A mole digging in its tunnel braces its hind feet against the tunnel walls and then shoves its forepaws forward one at a time, scraping backward as if rowing. When placed on the soil surface, a mole can disappear in about five seconds. After two seconds, by pulling on the mole's tail, a person might be able to retrieve it, but when it has all four feet firmly planted, it is almost impossible to drag it back to the surface.

Eyes are all but useless in a dark tunnel, so the size of moles' eyes has been greatly reduced. Some moles are blind, the eyes completely grown over with skin, while others can distinguish light from dark and possibly perceive objects. Visual abilities are useful when moles are forced out of their burrows by flooding, fighting with territorial rivals, predators or lack of food, and there are some species that forage mainly above ground. It is not known how well moles smell; they may rely more on taste after touching objects, but they are apparently able to smell the slime of a worm several inches away. Some moles hear well. Evidence suggests that they may use ultrasonic echolocation as their shrew relatives do. They also produce sound audible to the human ear and can hear sounds useful in detecting both prey and predators. However, the mole perceives its environment largely through touch.

The snout of the mole is extremely sensitive and covered with a dense array of nervous receptors. The complexity of these nervous receptors, a tangle of various nerve cells including bare nerve endings and a rich supply of blood vessels, is unmatched in the animal kingdom. The nerves are

Moles, the Talpidae family, are well adapted for life underground. Sensitive nerve receptors on their noses—especially evident in the star-nosed mole shown here—lead them to worms and other food items.

organized into structures known as Eimer's organs, thought to be sensitive to touch, vibration, pressure changes, chemical sensation and possibly heat. The snout, paws, tail and back of the head also have sensitive bristles, like a cat's whiskers, that enable the mole to detect objects before a collision.

Streamlined body features assist moles in their movement through the soil. The most notable adaptation is in the fur. There was once a booming business in moleskins in both the United States and Europe, as they were used for various garments, gloves and purses. The demand for moleskin was so high that attempts were made to legally protect moles in countries such as Germany, because overtrapping threatened them with extinction. Moles are still trapped in England, but most moleskins now come from Russia. The appeal of moleskin is unexpected, since mole pelts are small and difficult to assemble into large items. Nevertheless, mole fur is of extremely high quality. It is shiny and dense and has no grain, which means it can be rubbed in any direction and still lie sleek and unruffled. This is because of the unique design of the hair itself. Moles have hinged hair. Each hair is made up of alternating sections: strong, cylindrical pigment sections joined by flat, flexible sections. The flat sections act as hinges, allowing the hair to bend easily in any direction. The adaptive significance of this design is that the mole can run both backward and forward in its tunnels unimpeded by fur friction against the walls.

Mole tunnels often form intricate networks. Different kinds of moles build different kinds of tunnels, but in general, two types of tunnel can be recognized for each species. The first are deep permanent tunnels that may go down 3 yards. These are used for sleeping, escaping from most predators and avoiding the cold of winter. They may have nesting and resting chambers attached to them. The second type of tunnel is a shallow network just below the soil surface. Familiar to those who have had moles in their yards, these tunnels can often be recognized as raised, meandering ridges in the ground surface. When a mole digs one of these shallow tunnels, it does not remove and pile the soil. Instead, it turns its body at a 45-degree angle and pushes the soil upward. These tunnels meander according to the texture of the soil and the ease of digging—hard and excessively wet soils are avoided. The energetic cost of digging is high, and accordingly, some mole tunnels are used for up to eight years.

It was once believed that moles spent most of their time digging in pursuit of prey such as worms and grubs buried in the soil. But it is now believed that moles spend little time searching for food in this way. No doubt, they will eat almost any food they encounter while excavating, but their burrows and tunnels are relatively permanent. Moles spend much of their time patrolling the system of runways and eating food that has crawled and fallen into the passageways. This is probably especially true in areas with hard-to-work soils such as clay, which have a high density of worms and soil animals. The burrow network acts as a giant pitfall trap. In loose soils and especially acidic, peaty ones that are poor in food, moles probably spend more time searching for food by digging shallow tunnels.

Usually, the only evidence of these tunnels is the piles of excavated dirt, molehills, that the animals bring to the surface. Otherwise, moles keep their burrows closed and inconspicuous as protection against predators.

Little is known about the social life of moles. Trapping evidence suggests that most species are solitary for much of the year. However, many species appear to share certain tunnel sections such as those for access routes to water. Some species, such as the star-nosed mole, may live as male-female pairs during winter, and shrew moles, which forage much of the time above ground, are sometimes seen in small groups. But other species appear to be socially intolerant. Male moles fight violently with, and even kill, intruders.

Mole courtship presumably involves some fighting between males for access to receptive females. Except for the star-nosed mole, the males of all mole species are considerably larger than females, usually a clear sign that male-male combat is well developed.

Some male moles employ another strategy to gain exclusive access to a female. After mating, a mixture of compounds from the prostate and Cowper's glands in the male reproductive tract are secreted into the female's vagina, where they solidify into a mating plug, a kind of chastity belt that prevents other males from mating with the female. This is exactly the kind of tactic to be expected in mammals in which the females are territorial and highly dispersed. A male can increase his reproductive success by mating with a female, then leaving to search for another mate while the mating plug guards his paternity. Without the plug, the male would risk being cuckolded, which would reduce his reproductive success. Males who use the plugging tactic also have reproductive systems in which testes and other glands swell to 14 percent of their body weight during mating season. Human testes weigh less than 1 percent of body weight, so for moles, the investment in mating is considerable.

Outside the reproductive period, females are unreceptive to the extent that a membrane grows over the vagina, sealing it off. They are receptive only once a year, usually in early spring. Southern populations may start reproduction several months ahead of northern populations. Pregnancy is thought to last four to six weeks and results in one to nine young, depending on the species. Females give birth in a nest that is usually lined with leaves and grass.

North American mole species vary in size, but all are small mammals, and like shrews and mice, they have a high metabolic rate. Moles are active day and night year-round and are incapable of hibernating. Consequently, they consume and burn large quantities of food.

The larger species may eat half to one-third of their body weight in a day, while smaller species can eat one or two times their body weight, making them comparable to shrews in food consumption. Earthworms form most of the mole's diet, and the rest is made up of soil insects. Some moles even attack the underground nests of hornets or invade ant mounds. On occasion, they will eat roots and bulbs and become pests in gardens and vegetable fields. The star-nosed mole is semiaquatic and eats many pond and stream dwellers, including fish. Like shrews, moles will cache an abundance of items such as earthworms, which they immobilize by biting off their digging end. The appetite of moles translates into a considerable ecological impact. A single mole may consume up to 80 pounds of food yearly, or roughly 8,000 earthworms, and its digging results in significant soil aeration and mixing.

SHREW MOLE
Neurotrichus gibbsii

As its name implies, the shrew mole's life history is similar to a shrew's in several respects. It is found on the Pacific slope of extreme southern Canada and the northwestern United States in areas where there is heavy forest along valley bottoms and hillsides. This habitat contains a rich and abundant leaf-litter layer, and the shrew mole is specialized in harvesting the small residents in the litter and on the surface. This mole is a habitat specialist associated with loose, productive soils in deciduous forest. It is rare in open habitats or areas with heavy and wet soils.

Shrew moles do less digging than other North American moles and, accordingly, are different structurally and behaviorally. The shrew mole's hind feet are relatively large, and so is its tail, which enables it to rear up, a difficult act for other moles. It is the only mole that can turn its front paws flat on the ground underneath it, and it can run on the backs of its claws. Unlike those of other moles, the front feet of a shrew mole are longer than they are wide, making it more efficient at locomotion than at shoveling and digging. It is even able to climb around low shrubbery. A powerful digger such as the eastern mole can move 35 times its own weight, but the shrew mole can move only 20 times its weight. Most shrew mole tunnels are shallow, running just below the leafy humus layer, and have many openings that are used as entrances and exits.

Although it forages extensively on the surface, the shrew mole has weak eyesight. To compensate, its snout is elongated and ends in a pink pad with the nostrils on the sides. This snout and its tip are thought to be highly sensitive, and they are used like a blind person's cane. As the shrew walks or runs, it taps its snout ahead and from side to side, reading tastes and textures as it goes. As a further aid to navigation, the shrew mole hears ultrasound and can echolocate.

The advantage to a mole of being more shrewlike is that it can exploit the rich fauna of the upper soil area, the surface and even low herb layers, a resource that is unavailable to conventional moles. Earthworms are a prominent element of its diet, as they are for other mole species, but the shrew mole also eats many litter arthropods, especially sow bugs, and an assortment of insects, mushrooms, seeds and other surface items. A disadvantage to its aboveground feeding is that it suffers heavy predation by owls, hawks, snakes and carnivorous mammals.

The behavior of this mole is little known. Several individuals have been trapped in a single set of runways, which suggests that the shrew mole may be more gregarious than other moles. It has an extended breeding season, from February to September, which may reflect the mild, damp climate where it occurs. This mole has a pronounced musky smell that is most noticeable in reproductively active males.

SHREW MOLE
Neurotrichus gibbsii

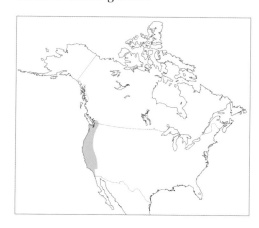

Mammal: *Neurotrichus gibbsii*, shrew mole; the smallest of American moles
Meaning of Name: *Neurotrichus* (new + tail + hairy); *gibbsii* (named after collector G. Gibbs)
Description: small and shrewlike; tail has sparse, coarse hairs projecting between annular scales and stiff brush of hairs at the tip; elongated flexible snout terminates in a naked pink nose pad; small eyes; feet are less modified for digging than other North American talpids; color is sooty blue to black with a metallic gloss
Total Length: 3.9 to 4.9 inches
Tail: 1.2 to 1.8 inches
Weight: 0.32 to 0.39 ounce
Gestation: not known (probably 4 to 6 weeks)
Offspring: 1 to 4
Age of Maturity: breeding season following birth
Longevity: not known
Diet: earthworms, isopods, sow bugs, insects and their larvae and pupae; some plant seeds and vegetable matter
Habitat: shady ravines; streambanks and riverbanks; forested hillsides and valley bottoms where there is moist, loose soil with high humus content, lots of leaf litter and no thick sod or turf
Predators: small predators such as snakes, hawks, owls and raccoon
Dental Formula:
3/3, 1/1, 2/2, 3/3 = 36 teeth

COAST MOLE
Scapanus orarius

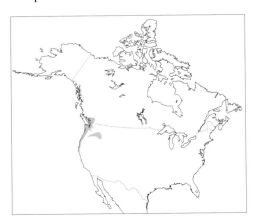

Mammal: *Scapanus orarius*, coast mole
Meaning of Name: *Scapanus* (spade or hoe) refers to its claws, which are specially adapted for digging; *orarius* (coastal)
Description: a small version of the larger Townsend's mole; pink snout, feet and tail are nearly naked; velvety fur is black above, paler below
Total Length: 5.8 to 6.9 inches
Tail: 1.0 to 1.6 inches
Weight: 2 ounces
Gestation: approximately 2 to 3 months
Offspring: 4; 1 litter per year
Age of Maturity: breeding season following birth
Longevity: not known
Diet: earthworms are main food; also eats fly larvae, insects, centipedes, snails, slugs and some vegetation
Habitat: moist deciduous and coniferous woods and thickets; tolerates drier, sandier loams than Townsend's mole
Predators: only a few natural predators, but may be taken by weasel, snakes or owls
Dental Formula:
3/3, 1/1, 4/4, 3/3 = 44 teeth

TOWNSEND'S MOLE
Scapanus townsendii

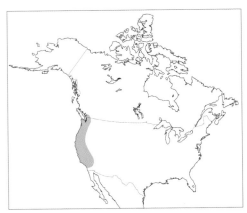

Mammal: *Scapanus townsendii*, Townsend's mole; largest North American mole
Meaning of Name: *Scapanus* (spade or hoe) refers to its claws, which are specially adapted for digging; *townsendii* (named after J.K. Townsend, 19th-century ornithologist)
Description: stocky and robust; slate-black fur with velvety sheen, darker in winter; pink snout is covered with sparse fine white hairs; tail is nearly hairless, as are front feet, which are whitish
Total Length: 7 to 9.3 inches
Tail: 1.3 to 2.2 inches
Weight: male, 5.2 ounces; female, 4.1 ounces
Gestation: 1 month
Offspring: 1 to 6; 1 litter per year
Age of Maturity: breeding season following birth
Longevity: not known
Diet: earthworms, insects and their larvae and pupae, centipedes, grubs and some vegetable matter, including bulbs of plants, wheat, corn and oats
Habitat: moist, loose soil of cultivated fields, meadows, open forests and valley bottoms
Predators: only a few natural predators, but may be taken by weasel, snakes or owls
Dental Formula:
3/3, 1/1, 4/4, 3/3 = 44 teeth

HAIRY-TAILED MOLE
Parascalops breweri

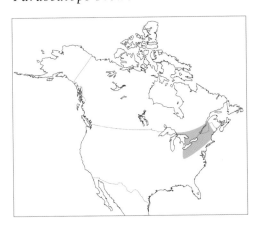

Mammal: *Parascalops breweri*, hairy-tailed mole; the smallest of eastern moles
Meaning of Name: *Parascalops* (resembles the digger, or mole); *breweri* (named after Dr. T.M. Brewer, zoologist and author)
Description: tail distinctly covered with long, stiff black hair; snout is conical and mobile; dense, velvety pelage; grayish black with metallic sheen; often a creamy, irregularly shaped spot on the breast or abdomen; light brownish secretions stain the fur of both sexes during breeding season
Total Length: 5.4 to 6.7 inches
Tail: 0.9 to 1.5 inches
Weight: 1.4 to 2.3 ounces
Gestation: 4 to 6 weeks
Offspring: 4 or 5; 1 litter per year
Age of Maturity: 10 months
Longevity: 4 to 5 years
Diet: earthworms, insects, soil invertebrates
Habitat: hardwood forests and fields near hardwood stands; prefers light, loose, moist but well-drained soils with well-mixed organic matter and minerals
Predators: fox, owls, snakes, bullfrog and opossum
Dental Formula:
3/3, 1/1, 4/4, 3/3 = 44 teeth

A prolific tunneler and one of the largest and strongest moles, the eastern mole can dig at a rate of nearly 13 feet per hour; one tunnel was found to extend 3,300 feet.

EASTERN MOLE
Scalopus aquaticus

A heavyset generalized mole, the eastern mole is found in a wide range of forested and open habitats. It is most common in rich, loose forest soils, avoiding stony soils but tolerating harder clay soils that some mole species stay away from. This may reflect the digging power of the eastern mole. It is one of the largest and strongest of moles and possibly the species most adapted for life underground. Its eyes are completely overgrown with skin. It is a prolific tunneler, able to construct its near-surface tunnels at a rate of almost 13 feet per hour. One of these tunnels was traced along a fenceline for 3,300 feet.

During dry and cold periods, eastern moles use their deep tunnel and nest system, which may run 18 inches or more underground. They are active all winter but may spend periods in a semidormant state. Each mole defends its own exclusive burrow system, which can occupy one-half to two acres.

The near-surface tunnels of the eastern mole are built and used during warm weather to gain access to the concentration of earthworms and insects in the rich upper organic layer of the soil. Most of the eastern mole's diet is earthworms, but it will eat a great variety of soil insects and a limited amount of plant material. Eastern moles also attack hornets, many of which nest underground. One mole was even observed extending one of its molehills up to reach an aerial nest of bald-faced hornets. Hornet nests are usually full of fat, helpless larvae.

During breeding season, males enter the burrow system of receptive females. They show the typical mole pattern of tremendous enlargement of the reproductive organs, 10 times their size at other times, and it is likely that these moles use mating plugs.

Females breed at age 1 and produce a litter of four in late spring. After four weeks, the helpless young are weaned.

Mammal: *Scalopus aquaticus*, eastern mole
Meaning of Name: *Scalopus* (a foot for digging); *aquaticus* (living in the water); this animal is not aquatic, however, even though it is a good swimmer and has webbed toes
Description: stocky; feet and snout are almost naked; webbed toes; small eyes are hidden in fur; wrists are lined with a row of short, stiff hairs; velvety, dense slate-colored fur
Total Length: 6.8 to 8.3 inches
Tail: 1.1 to 1.6 inches
Weight: 2.5 to 4.9 ounces
Gestation: approximately 4 weeks
Offspring: 2 to 5 (usually 4); 1 litter per year
Age of Maturity: 1 year (breeding season following birth)
Longevity: not known
Diet: primarily earthworms, insects and their larvae, as well as a small amount of vegetable matter
Habitat: moist, friable humus in open woodlands, fields, meadows and pastures
Predators: hawks, owls, snakes, shrews, skunk, coyote, fox and weasel
Dental Formula:
3/2(3), 1/0(1), 3/3, 3/3 = 36 or 38 teeth

ADAPTATION: NOBODY'S PERFECT

Hardly an evening goes by without some gravel-voiced television narrator explaining how perfectly adapted this or that animal is to its environment. In truth, no animal is perfectly adapted. Strictly speaking, adaptation can be defined as a characteristic that increases an individual's chances of leaving descendants. An adaptation increases the reproductive success of individuals possessing it over the success of individuals that lack the adaptation. More generally, non-biologists think of adaptations as structures or behaviors that match the environment and tasks that confront an animal. The digging apparatus of a mole is highly, even beautifully, adapted for tunneling in soil. However, it is misleading to say that the mole is perfectly adapted for its environment. It is more profitable to think of organisms and their evolutionary adaptations as compromises.

Everything an animal does and every part of its design by natural selection is the result of a series of cost-and-benefit trade-offs. For example, moles have degenerate eyes, which in some species are completely covered by skin. Yet moles do occasionally have to run across the ground's surface. At these times, moles could no doubt profit from having well-developed eyes. But the cost of having a conventional mammalian eye would be that during tunneling and fighting with worms and noxious insects, the mole eye would be continually assailed by dirt and organic debris and would probably be a vulnerable site for bacterial infections. Shrinking and covering of the eye has the benefit of reducing that risk, but it is a compromise. So, too, with the forelimb structure of moles. It is a su-

Designed for life underground, a star-nosed mole, like other members of its family, is at a disadvantage on open ground.

perb digging device, but for species such as the shrew mole, which obtains much of its food on the surface, the limb design is clumsy compared with that of true shrews.

Every adaptation has limits and virtues, and the discovery of these and the unraveling of the ecological and evolutionary forces that create them are a continual challenge for biologists. Perfection would be beautiful, but boring.

STAR-NOSED MOLE
Condylura cristata

Except for sea anemones, few animals have stranger appendages than the star-nosed mole, with its ring of tentaclelike Eimer's organs surrounding its snout. This unique appendage has a rich supply of nerves and blood vessels and remarkable mobility. The star-nosed mole is semiaquatic and adapted for a life in wet soils and shallow bodies of water. Its water-shedding fur is longer and coarser than that of other moles, its hind feet are flat and wide, and its tail is long, all adaptations that suit it for swimming. The star-nose can stay underwater for about 3 minutes and dive about 3 feet deep. It is often seen swimming beneath the ice of ponds in winter. In marshy areas, the star-nosed mole is normally the only mole present. The strange nose organs may be of most use when the mole forages in the bottom muck of streams and ponds. During tunnel digging, the tentacles lie folded together and are protected, but underwater, they are fully expanded and in constant motion. The star presumably provides a unique electric sense for detecting prey. Much of the mole's diet consists of aquatic insect larvae but also includes tadpoles, minnows, snails and leeches.

The star-nosed mole also builds the usual shallow and deep burrow systems, the former for foraging and the latter for reproduction and overwintering. The deep burrow system, by necessity, must be placed in solid ground above the waterline, a factor that may limit the abundance and distribution of these animals. The shallow system often has entrances right at the waterline and even underwater. During the winter, these moles also make a tunnel system through the snow. Several animals may use the same system of runways, and there is a possibility that the star-nose is more social than other mole species.

Because it forages in exposed conditions, the star-nosed mole is eaten by a number of raptors, carnivorous mammals and large fish.

STAR-NOSED MOLE
Condylura cristata

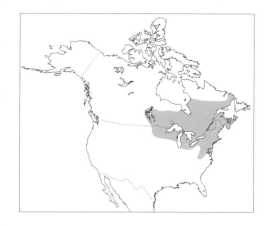

Mammal: *Condylura cristata*, star-nosed mole
Meaning of Name: *Condylura* (knuckle + the tail) refers to the knotty appearance of the tail in dried specimens; *cristata* (crested) refers to the star, or crest, of 22 pink fleshy fingers growing on the snout
Description: blackish brown; dense, long, soft pelage is waterproof; naked pink disk at tip of snout with 22 radially symmetrical tentacles; long fleshy tail thickens in winter with stored fat; large scaled feet are thinly furred on top and naked below
Total Length: 6.4 to 9.4 inches
Tail: 2.2 to 3.6 inches
Weight: 1.1 to 2.8 ounces
Gestation: 45 days
Offspring: 2 to 7 (usually 5); 1 litter per year
Age of Maturity: 10 months (the spring following birth)
Longevity: not known
Diet: aquatic insects, worms, crustaceans, mollusks and small fish; may be entirely dependent on benthic prey in winter
Habitat: prefers low wet habitats near lakes and streams; woods, marshes and meadows; soils ranging from clay loam to sand or muck
Predators: red-tailed hawk, great horned owl, skunk, weasel, chipmunk and perhaps large fish such as pike and bass
Dental Formula:
3/3, 1/1, 4/4, 3/3 = 44 teeth

BATS *Chiroptera*

Few mammals have been more successful than bats. There are close to 1,000 bat species, a richness exceeded only by rodents. The good fortune of bats has its origin in an event that took place millions of years before mammals existed, the moment when insects began to fly. The entry of insects into the air to escape predators, to mate and to disperse opened up a resource that remained unexploited until birds evolved into efficient fliers. Birds, however, remained primarily a day-active group. Accordingly, many insects evolved to become night fliers. The success of bats seems largely attributable to the night-flying insect resource. Most bats are night-active and eat insects that they catch on the fly.

Bats are thought to have originated in the same insectivore stock that gave rise to shrews and moles. The ancestors of bats were probably nocturnal and may have possessed the ability to echolocate, an ability that would preadapt them for night flight. How they went from being a small mammal that ran on the ground to one that flies is unknown. One idea is that the ancestral bat pursued prey by leaping and used its large webbed forefeet to catch its quarry. Using the webbed forefeet as a gliding device may then have led to an ever greater dependence on movement through the air. No one has found any fossils to disprove or support this notion. In fact, there is so little fossil record for bats that some scientists disagree about a common ancestry for all bats. Some believe that the fruit-eating bats evolved from mammals unrelated to those that gave rise to insectivorous bats.

Bats' mammalian body plan is substantially different from that of birds. Bats have strong jaws and teeth, making them nose-heavy. As a result, their necks had to become shorter to shift the weight back toward their wings. Consequently, they lack the abilities that come with the long, flexible neck of many birds. Birds have specialized their forelimbs for flight, but bats have pursued a mixed strategy. Their forelimbs not only act as wings but are used for crawling, capturing prey and grooming, while their hind limbs are used for perching, hanging and, in some species, capturing prey. The hind limbs also form part of the bat's wing, so they are less suited for terrestrial locomotion than birds' legs are.

Bats have not developed the large, powerful breast muscles and bones of birds. Bats roost in rock crevices, hollow trees, curled-up leaves and areas where a slender body is advantageous. The resulting wide, thin body of bats is not as aerodynamically efficient as the deep, rounded form of birds. The large ears and facial protuberance used in echolocation must also cause considerably more aerodynamic drag than the smooth head of a bird does. Mammalian fur lacks the lift-giving abilities of feathers. The membrane that gives lift to the bat wing is efficient at low flight speeds but offers more drag than a feathered wing at high speeds. Consequently, bats are less efficient at long-distance flight. However, they are superb at maneuvering and flying in total darkness.

Some other mammalian groups such as flying squirrels can glide, but bats are the only mammals that can actually fly by flapping their "wings" and

The northern long-eared bat displays the fiercely efficient jaws of all the Myotis *bats, one of the features that make members of the Chiroptera the most important predators of night-flying insects.*

lifting themselves by the power of their own muscles. Most of a bat wing is hand. The fingers of the hand have become tremendously elongated to support the wing membrane. The thumb has remained as a small and usually sharply clawed hook near the midwing. The wing membrane is a large flap of skin reinforced with muscles and cartilage that extends from the body along the forearm and hand back over the hind-leg bones. The resulting wing shape varies according to different species' particular styles of flight, which in turn reflect their preferred forage strategies and foods.

The wing is designed to both lift the bat and propel it forward. The large flap of skin running from the body to roughly midwing provides lift, while the movement of the wing-tip area generates propulsive power. Different shapes in the outer wing and varying use of the tail-membrane area (some species lack a tail membrane) affect maneuverability. Species that forage for insects such as moths and beetles by active pursuit are often small with relatively broad wings. Wide wings provide a large lift, enabling the bat to decelerate and turn at slow speeds without stalling, an adaptation useful for the pursuit of insects such as moths, which may take evasive dives and turns when they hear the sound of an approaching bat. Bats that are fast long-distance fliers have long, narrow wings that trade maneuverability and lift for greater propulsive power and efficiency. The Mexican free-tailed bat, which roosts in dense colonies in the southwestern United States, is an example of this design. These bats may fly 60 miles each night to foraging sites. One observer, using radar and a helicopter, recorded free-tailed bats flying 2 miles high and traveling at 65 miles per hour.

Bats have at least five patterns of wing design, each adapted to a different method of obtaining food. Specialized wings allow some bats to grab lone insects while flying. Other bats wait on perches and leap out after passing insects. One pattern of bat wing allows the bat to travel to and feed in fruit trees; another is designed specifically for flying long distances to feed on swarming insects. Bats are able to snag fish from the surfaces of ponds, rivers and other bodies of water. They can forage on the ground, pick frogs or roosting birds out of the vegetation or lap the blood of large mammals, activities that demand some modification in the wing. The bat wing, awkward though it may seem, has allowed bats to forage in ways that no bird can. Insectivorous bats are capable of continuous flight through a tree canopy in pursuit of flying insects, an unrivaled feat of slow, maneuverable flight. However, what truly separates bats from birds is the ability to echolocate and forage effectively at night. Bats that do not hunt by echolocation and birds that echolocate and forage primarily at night are minor exceptions.

In the northern temperate regions, all bats eat insects, but there seems to be a division based on whether hard insects such as beetles or soft insects such as moths are most important. The two different classes require different types of jaws and teeth. However, within each species, there is considerable variation among prey types according to the time of year. A certain amount of habitat specialization also occurs, some bats preferring to forage mainly above water, where there are large emergences of soft-bodied aquatic insects, while others forage above the land. Bats are also separated ecologically according to the type of roosts and hibernation sites they select. Big brown bats, for example, will tolerate drier hibernation sites than little brown bats. Some species will roost in rock crevices, others in trees and yet others in caves or house attics. The rate at which nest boxes and roosts created by human architecture are occupied suggests that roost type and availability play a major ecological role in bat populations. Some species frequently change roosts, while others stay at a particular site for years.

Bats are able to use senses other than echolocation. All bats can see. Their eyes are normally adapted for use under low-light conditions, which is why they appear disoriented and blind if disturbed during the day in bright light. Little is known about how important vision is to bats. Some species use visual cues to navigate over long distances. Bats also have functional noses capable of sophisticated discrimination. Mothers can sniff out their own infant from among thousands of others, and they rarely suckle the wrong one. Bats probably also use odor to identify their food, being drawn to fruits and flowers and avoiding distasteful insects. However, less is known about bat sight and smell than about echolocation.

Bats are small mammals, and one might expect them to have a high energy consumption. They do, in fact, burn energy at a rate comparable to that of shrews. During flight, a bat's heart may reach 1,300 beats per minute. Thus, like other insectivores, bats must

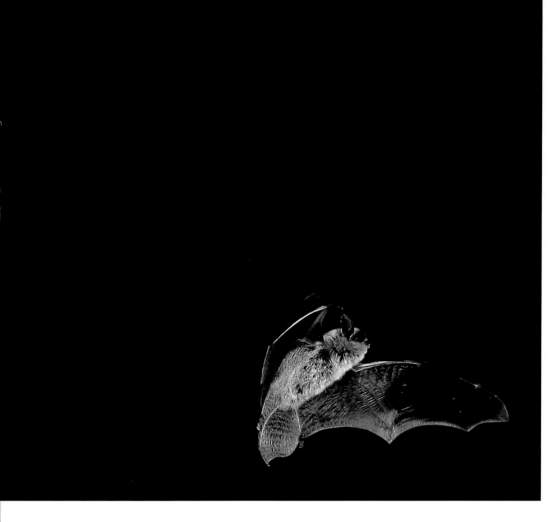

The western small-footed bat prefers to roost along the cliffs and steep banks of the badlands and the riverbanks of the prairies.

eat large amounts of food and process it quickly. Bats usually eat one-third to one-half their body weight each night. This is clearly less than shrews, which consume more than their body weight each day. Bats may be more efficient at energy conservation than shrews and moles because they are active during the night and torporous during the day. It was once thought that bats were poor thermoregulators, not always able to keep a constant body temperature, but daily torpor is clearly an energy-conservation device. By dropping its body temperature from near 100 degrees F to the temperature of its roost, say, 75 degrees, a bat saves huge amounts of energy. Bats may also lower their energy costs by choosing particular kinds of roosts. Warm roosts, like the tops of

buildings, may speed up digestion and reduce heating costs. On the other hand, during summer, bats that roost in attics may expend large amounts of energy staying cool. Hot bats will extend and slowly flap their wings to radiate body heat. In addition to sweating, they may urinate on their fur or lick it to increase evaporative cooling.

Shrews and moles have access to soil insects all winter, but bats' favored food, aerial insects, vanishes during winter in temperate areas. Thus many temperate species of bats have made use of body-temperature control and have developed true hibernation. They lower their body temperature to a few degrees above freezing, or even below freezing, and their heartbeat drops by a factor of 10 to 24—to 82 beats per minute. They stay in this dormant state for most of the winter, waking only occasionally to shift position or to fly about, perhaps to drink or merely for the exercise. Crucial

to the success of this strategy is finding suitable hibernation sites. For many species, the ideal place is an abandoned mine or cave. Underground cavities are usually humid, and water loss is a major stress on hibernating bats. Because these sites are limited in nature, many bats migrate considerable distances between their summer roosting and feeding areas and their winter hibernacula. Little brown bats, for example, may fly as far as 500 miles to reach an overwintering site. Banding studies show that individuals of many temperate bat species learn the location of caves and return to them year after year.

The reproductive biology of temperate-zone bats has also been modified according to the need for a long winter's dormancy followed by a summer of intense insect feeding and growth. Mating takes place in autumn, but surprisingly, the females do not ovulate until the spring. For as long as seven months, the sperm lie dormant, lined up along the uterine wall, where they may absorb nutrients and wait for spring and ovulation. Presumably, the female hormonal system provides a cue to awaken the sperm so that they can begin their competitive swim toward the eggs.

One advantage of this system is that it enables the female to time her pregnancy independently of male courtship. The northern spring comes at variable dates according to the weather. The already-bred female can wake from hibernation and become active and ovulate according to how she perceives conditions. If spring comes early, she does not have to wait for courtship and mating to proceed. She can, instead, ovulate and become pregnant, taking advantage of the early spring. Perhaps the best evidence that this is an important consideration is the convergence in the reproductive time of temperate bats. Virtually all species give birth at roughly the same time in late spring and early summer. Pregnancy is normally short, between two and three months depending on the species, and the young bats are weaned by midsummer.

Bats have a low reproductive rate, normally one or two offspring per female annually. The largest litter size is only four offspring. This small annual rate is compensated for by a long reproductive career, which may span two decades or more. The small litter size no doubt reflects the constraints imposed by flight. A female must still fly and feed while she is pregnant and lactating. Males provide no parental care. Temperate-zone bat females usually congregate at specific nursery sites (although some, such as the red and hoary bats, are solitary and do not cluster), where they give birth and rear their young. The infant bats cluster together while their mothers are out feeding.

Once the initial stage of juvenile mortality is past, a temperate-zone bat can expect a surprisingly long life. Some little brown bats have lived as long as 30 years. Few animals prey on bats, and no temperate-zone vertebrates are specialized as bat predators (in the tropics, some birds and some bats specialize in eating bats). Bats are host to a wide array of insect and microscopic parasites, but their impact is not enough to induce high adult mortality. The vulnerability of bat populations comes from their low reproductive rate, their dependency on traditional roost and hibernation sites, pesticides and public apprehension about bats as vectors of rabies. When hibernating bats are disturbed, many die as a result. Many more are gassed or poisoned by exterminators or killed by accumulated pesticides from the insects they eat. Several North American bats have declined to the point of being considered endangered species. These declines are undesirable, since bats are important insect predators. The risk of contracting rabies from them is minimal.

ECHOLOCATION

Echolocation is the term for the sonarlike method bats use to determine the size of objects and how far away they are. The process requires sending a sound that travels as a pressure wave through the air. When the sound wave hits an object, part of it is reflected back toward the sender.

Sound waves have various features that convey information to ears and brains designed to read them. Each wave has a given frequency that is measured in hertz, the number of vibrations per second. High-frequency sounds have shorter wavelengths and different transmission characteristics than low-frequency sounds.

Bats often use high-frequency sounds. While humans can hear from about 20 hertz to 20,000 hertz, bats can hear sounds from roughly 100 hertz to 200,000 hertz. The high-frequency sound is like a dog whistle. It can be blown with great energy right beside a human's ear, but our nerves will neither register nor transmit it. The tendency of most bats to use ultrasound is why bat navigation and echolocation remained a mystery for many hundreds of years.

The advantage of these high-frequency sounds is that they produce precise information about small objects. The best echo reflection occurs when the object being hit is roughly the same size as the wavelength. When the wavelength is larger than the target object, much of the sound wave will not be reflected as an echo.

However, high-frequency sound travels a shorter distance than low-frequency sound. For example, one is able to feel the low-frequency rumble of an earthquake or train many miles away, but the high-pitched squeak of a mouse travels only a few feet before its energy is dissipated. The cost of precision is a loss of range. Range is also affected by how many decibels of sound energy the bat produces. Some bats produce a sound comparable in intensity to a jet engine, although humans can never hear it. Bats can also focus the sound beam they send out by means of membranes and muscles in the nose and mouth.

The simplest sound a bat produces is a constant-frequency tone. The echoes returning from this enable the bat to estimate its velocity in relation to a target. Some bats can detect velocities as low as 1½ inches a second, about the speed of a caterpillar crawling. But a constant frequency cannot give much information about the target's texture—whether it is hairy or smooth, for example.

To compensate, many bats use a technique identical to that used in FM broadcasting by humans. They vary the sound by frequency modulation (FM). This also helps bats make use of the Doppler effect, which results in a sound familiar to anyone who has heard the wail of a train whistle. As a train approaches then passes a listener, the sound of its whistle seems to change in pitch. As the train rushes away, the number of waves reaching the listener in a second decreases, and the note is perceived as lower.

This is especially true in scenarios where the whistle is a tone of just one frequency. When a bat is stationary or moving at a constant speed in one direction, the Doppler effect from a constant-frequency signal can be used to calculate an object's speed, but it may also confuse the bat when it is flying complicated maneuvers. A bat can compensate for the Doppler effect by sweeping down a scale of frequency. Then it gets a variety of echo ranges and varying precision.

All of this happens extremely quickly over short distances, with the bat processing and reacting to sounds at a mind-boggling speed. A bat sending out a sound to strike an object 3 feet away is hit by the echo in 6 milliseconds. Bats may be able to detect objects as far away as 50 feet, but most echolocation takes place at closer range. Big brown bats are reported to detect a ¾-inch sphere 15 feet away from them. At shorter distances, bats are able to read fine details in the echo. They can detect an insect sitting on a leaf or a crevice in a cliff face. Some can detect a wire only 0.003 inch thick. These judgments are based on echoes that must be interpreted by the brain. To make sense of the echoes, especially FM echoes, there must be some space between the signals, which is why bats send their sounds out as pulses. It may also be energetically costly to produce these sounds, as exhausting as singing at full voice, so when bats are navigating, they may simply emit constant-frequency tones at a slow pulse rate, then increase the rate if a possible prey item is detected, adding FM to identify the item. As the bat zeroes in on the prey, the pulse rate may accelerate up to 200 times per second, 40 times higher than when navigating. More recent studies show that bats rely on vision to help them navigate over long distances.

In spite of the sophistication of their echolocation system, bats are not invincible predators of night insects. Various moths have ears capable of detecting the ultrasonic waves of an approaching bat from as far away as 100 feet, beyond the range at which the bat can detect the echo from the moth. This enables the moth to fly away from the bat, a reason for a bat to stay silent for brief intervals. If a bat does get close to a moth with ultrasonic hearing, the moth may dive, turn and plummet to the ground. Diving does not make a moth invulnerable, however. A little brown bat foraging for moths around a street-light, for example, is capable of sharp, diving turns. To compensate for that, some moths have evolved a series of grooves on their thorax that they can scrape together to produce ultrasound. As the bat dives in on the moths, they produce a burst of sound that jams the bat's navigation system with noise. In response, some bats have switched to frequencies higher than those the moths can produce, and so continues the co-evolutionary battle between the hunters and the hunted.

The huge ears of the Townsend's big-eared bat are indispensable for reading soft and low-frequency echoes and for detecting moths at a great distance.

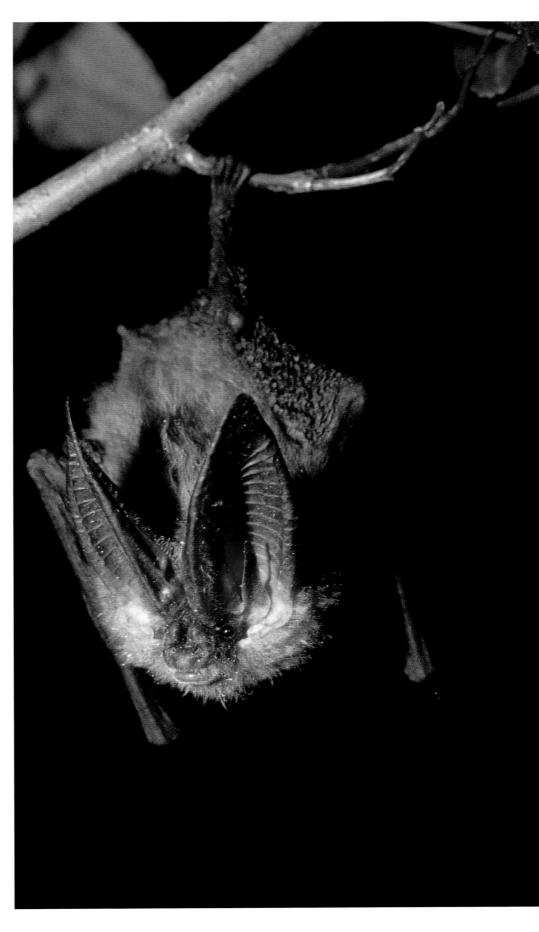

PLAIN-NOSED BATS *Vespertilionidae*

With 315 species distributed on every continent except Antarctica, the plain-nosed bats are the most widespread family of bats. Many plain-nosed species are tropical, but some range into the north, and the majority of temperate-zone bats are members of this family. Females are slightly larger than males, which is in keeping with what is known about their mating biology. Little male-male combat or highly demonstrative courtship occurs, and some species appear to be relatively promiscuous. True to their name, the plain-nosed bats lack the facial protuberances of many other bat groups. Except for a few tropical species that eat fish, plain-nosed bats are all insectivores and show the modification in their wings for highly maneuverable flight: The joint at the arm and shoulder blade is reinforced, the tail has a large membrane, the forelimbs are strong, and the wing is broad with a high lift at low speed—modifications that enable the bats to make sudden sharp turns in their pursuit of insects. All species have retained the ability to walk relatively well, and all have long legs.

HOME IS WHERE YOU HANG YOURSELF

Finding appropriate summer and winter roosting spots is a major concern for temperate and northern bats. In temperate climates, bats are vulnerable to cold. They also sleep and rest much of the time, which means they need a protected spot.

Half of a bat's life is spent dormant in a winter roost, and half of its more active summer life is spent in the summer roost.

The size and availability of roosts determine how far bats must migrate, how far they must commute to water and foraging grounds and how many potential mates they have to choose from. The shape of the roost and its accessibility have determined the ways in which different bats have evolved in body size, shape and posture as well as the degree to which they are exposed to predators and physical stresses.

There are several distinct kinds of roosts, and different syndromes of behavior, morphology and physiology are associated with each. Although there are as many roosts as there are cavities—from curled leaves to gigantic caverns—bat biologists, for convenience, classify roosts into three types: foliage, crevices and hollows. Each of these has a different set of costs and benefits.

Foliage roosts, in summer at least, are virtually unlimited, and foliage roosters, such as red bats, can hang themselves up almost anywhere. One disadvantage is that such a roost undergoes wild temperature and humidity fluctuations. Bats of this type can choose a sunny southern exposure when the weather is cold, but other than that, they are at the mercy of the weather. To compensate, foliage roosters typically have thick fur coats, which cause some drag during flight. The patagium (the skin membrane joining the forelimbs and hind limbs) is also furred, forming a "blanket" that the bat can stretch around itself.

With its large, powerful jaws and strong teeth, the big brown bat specializes in preying on hard-bodied beetles that other bats have a tendency to ignore. But it also eats other insects, including moths, mayflies and flies, and has been observed catching as many as 5 to 20 insects a minute.

These bats are also exposed to predators such as opossums and even blue jays, which will eat or otherwise molest them. Accordingly, many of the tree-roosting bats are cryptically colored. Tree-roosting hoary bats select roosts that are dark, have a minimum of reflected light from the ground and provide difficult access for arboreal predators. In the tropics, many foliage-roosting bats fold their wings around themselves for protection, using a special transparent part in the wing membrane to spot the arrival of predators.

Crevice roosters are more concealed, but they pay a morphological and anatomical price. Their body and head must be thin, which means that large chest muscles or, indeed, large body size are not possible. By contrast, bats that hang from either tree limbs or cave ceilings have large pectoral muscles and deep chests.

Rock crevices are cool and well protected but in limited supply, and they may be physically difficult to occupy. Many rock-crevice-dwelling bats have special pads on their feet and thumbs for gripping the substrate. Crevices under the bark of trees such as shagbark hickory are more common and offer some insulation and concealment to their residents, but these bats are still exposed to climbing snakes and mammalian predators.

Hollows are the most protected sites. While they offer moderated temperature and humidity, natural cavities such as

Female big brown bats often establish nursing colonies in the attics or eaves of buildings; the populations of these colonies can range from 40 into the hundreds.

caves are scarce, and they are not evenly distributed. This has the effect of crowding hundreds of thousands of bats into one area. Populations of fleas and other parasites increase. Competition for local food resources and travel time to foraging areas must increase. Some free-tailed bats, which congregate by the millions in the huge caverns of the southwest United States, fly hundreds of miles in search of food each night. The dung, or guano, they excrete into the cavern gives off large quantities of ammonia, which is toxic to some bat species.

CALIFORNIA BAT
Myotis californicus

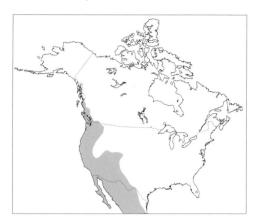

Mammal: *Myotis californicus,* California bat
Meaning of Name: *Myotis* (mouse + ear) alludes to large ears; *californicus* (of California)
Description: rich reddish brown dorsally and buffy brown ventrally; keeled calcar; dorsal base of interfemoral membrane is covered with fine hairs to approximately one-third of the way down the tibia
Total Length: 3.1 to 3.3 inches
Tail: 1.2 to 1.6 inches
Forearm: 1.2 to 1.4 inches
Weight: approximately 0.20 to 0.33 ounce
Gestation: not known (probably about 40 days)
Offspring: 1
Age of Maturity: 1 to 3 years
Longevity: not known
Diet: insects
Habitat: both forested areas and semiarid areas (in southwest); found mainly in crevices such as tunnels, hollow trees, buildings and bridges
Predators: lesser carnivores, snakes, hawks and owls
Dental Formula:
2/3, 1/1, 3/3, 3/3 = 38 teeth

WESTERN SMALL-FOOTED BAT
Myotis ciliolabrum

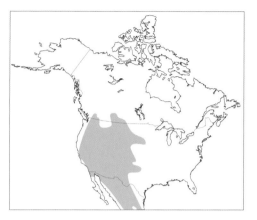

Mammal: *Myotis ciliolabrum,* western small-footed bat
Meaning of Name: *Myotis* (mouse + ear) alludes to large ears; *ciliolabrum* (eyelid + lip) refers to its whiskered lip
Description: small; long, dense fur varies from pale yellow-brown to flaxen dorsally and from buff to white ventrally; black flight membranes, ears and face
Total Length: 3.34 inches
Tail: 1.5 inches
Forearm: 1.27 inches
Weight: 0.17 ounce
Gestation: probably 40 days
Offspring: probably 1
Age of Maturity: 1 to 3 years
Longevity: not known
Diet: a variety of small insects
Habitat: arid habitats; cliffs, talus, clay buttes and steep riverbanks
Predators: owls, hawks, snakes, domestic cat and other carnivores
Dental Formula:
2/3, 1/1, 3/3, 3/3 = 38 teeth

LONG-EARED BAT
Myotis evotis

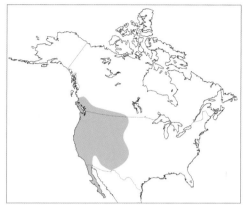

Mammal: *Myotis evotis,* long-eared bat
Meaning of Name: *Myotis* (mouse + ear) alludes to large ears; *evotis* (good, well + ear)
Description: pale brown; large, rounded black ears; long slender tragus
Total Length: 3.6 to 4.1 inches
Tail: 1.7 to 1.9 inches
Forearm: 1.4 to 1.6 inches
Weight: 0.35 ounce
Gestation: not known (probably about 40 days)
Offspring: 1
Age of Maturity: 1 to 3 years
Longevity: up to 22 years
Diet: small moths, flies, beetles and other insects
Habitat: forested areas; in crevices around buildings or trees; found in rocky habitats of the West Coast as well as on open plains
Predators: raptors, weasel, domestic cat, raccoon, skunk, rat and snakes
Dental Formula:
2/3, 1/1, 3/3, 3/3 = 38 teeth

KEEN'S BAT
Myotis keenii

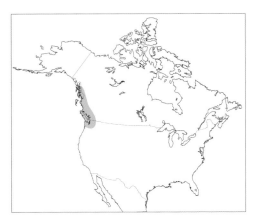

Mammal: *Myotis keenii*, Keen's bat
Meaning of Name: *Myotis* (mouse + ear) alludes to large ears; *keenii* (named after Reverend J.H. Keen, who collected the type specimen in 1894)
Description: similar to little brown bat but sheen is brassier; dark brown above, buffy gray below; dull brown shoulder spot; long, round ears; tragus is long
Total Length: 3.1 to 3.5 inches
Tail: 1.4 to 1.7 inches
Forearm: 1.4 to 1.6 inches
Weight: 0.25 to 0.32 ounce
Gestation: not known (probably about 40 days)
Offspring: 1
Age of Maturity: 1 to 3 years
Longevity: 18 years
Diet: caddisfly adults, small moths, mosquitoes
Habitat: forested areas near glades and rivers; also in mine tunnels, caves, buildings, storm sewers
Predators: owls are major predator
Dental Formula:
2/3, 1/1, 3/3, 3/3 = 38 teeth

EASTERN SMALL-FOOTED BAT
Myotis leibii

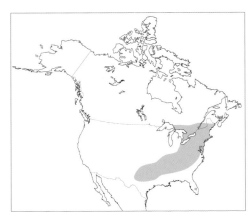

Mammal: *Myotis leibii*, eastern small-footed bat; also known as *Myotis subulatus*
Meaning of Name: *Myotis* (mouse + ear) alludes to large ears; *leibii* (named after Dr. G.C. Leib, collector of the type specimen)
Description: varies from yellowish to copper-brown to buffy gray dorsally; ears and wing membrane are dark brown to black; calcar has pronounced keel; external distinguishing mark is black facial mask
Total Length: 2.8 to 3.3 inches
Tail: 1.2 to 1.5 inches
Forearm: 1.2 to 1.4 inches
Weight: 0.21 to 0.32 ounce
Gestation: not known (probably about 40 days)
Offspring: 1
Age of Maturity: second year
Longevity: 9 years in the wild
Diet: soft-bodied insects; beetles are a predominant food source
Habitat: eastern range, hills covered with coniferous forests; western range, arid sites
Predators: hawks, owls, snakes, weasel, domestic cat, raccoon, skunk and rat
Dental Formula:
2/3, 1/1, 3/3, 3/3 = 38 teeth

LITTLE BROWN BAT
Myotis lucifugus

The little brown bat is the most common and best-known bat of the north temperate zone. Its natural habitat is forest areas with winter and summer roosts. Winter roost sites are often limited, and the bat may migrate several hundred miles between its winter and summer sites.

Overwintering takes place in caves and abandoned mines. Sometimes tremendous densities of up to 300,000 little brown bats cluster in a single cave. Large cavities that remain a few degrees above freezing and maintain a humidity close to 80 percent are preferred. Individuals show great fidelity to a wintering site and return to the same cave year after year.

In spring, groups of 50 to several hundred females move to daytime roosts or maternity colonies to give birth. Little brown bats often use human constructions such as cottage attics. In large structures such as barns, thousands may roost together. Males are usually solitary and spread out. The bats often find temporary nighttime roosts in various cavities near the foraging areas, which they occupy in the middle of the night between feedings.

Little brown bats are tolerant of high temperatures; they have been heated to 130 degrees F and survived, which makes summer roost sites such as hot attics more available to them than to other bats. Normally, roost locations are within a short flight of water.

Little brown bats pursue and eat a wide variety of soft-bodied insects as well as some hard beetles. They feed at a rate of some seven to eight insects per minute. They often feed on aquatic insects emerging from ponds and rivers and can skim insects from the water surface. If little brown bats crash into the water, they can swim. Like other small insectivores, the little brown bat has a large appetite and a high rate of digestion. It can fill its stomach in 15 minutes and empty its digestive system several times in an evening.

Mating takes place in late summer and early autumn and appears to be highly promiscuous. Males perch in caves and mine shafts and produce echolocation calls—apparently to court females. Females fly around and eventually land next to a male and copulate. Both males and females may mate with more than one partner. Gradually, torpor engulfs the bats, and they huddle together in the typical winter-hibernation group. Some males remain sexually active and crawl about attempting to inseminate dormant females.

Females ovulate in spring and give birth to a single offspring. The young bat is flying by itself after three weeks. Little brown bat mothers scent-mark trees outside nursery roosts with a glandular excretion. It is possible that scent-marked trees help young, inexperienced bats find their way back to the roost after their first excursions.

Females also communicate with their young through "isolation calls." A young bat that falls will call, and its mother will recognize and distinguish its call from that of other young but unrelated bats. Mothers also use a two-note signal that they direct toward their nursing infant.

Researchers report that little brown bats may live for as long as 33 years.

LITTLE BROWN BAT
Myotis lucifugus

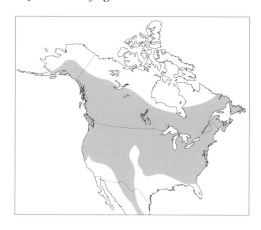

Mammal: *Myotis lucifugus*, little brown bat
Meaning of Name: *Myotis* (mouse + ear) alludes to large ears; *lucifugus* (shunning the light)
Description: brown pelage; hairs on back are long and have coppery, glossy tips; buffy gray underneath
Total Length: 3.1 to 3.7 inches
Tail: 1.2 to 1.6 inches
Forearm: 1.3 to 1.6 inches
Weight: 0.19 to 0.42 ounce
Gestation: 50 to 60 days
Offspring: 1 (sometimes 2)
Age of Maturity: male, 14 months; female, 1 year
Longevity: 24 to 30 years in the wild
Diet: primarily soft-bodied flying insects, especially flies and moths; some hard beetles
Habitat: caves, mine tunnels, hollow trees; has adapted to urban life during summer months and uses buildings as roosting sites
Predators: domestic cat, raccoon, weasel, snakes, hawks and bobcat
Dental Formula:
2/3, 1/1, 3/3, 3/3 = 38 teeth

The little brown bat, an extremely abundant species, communicates with ultrasonic squeals that are readily picked up by the large and precisely tuned ears of other bats.

NORTHERN LONG-EARED BAT
Myotis septentrionalis

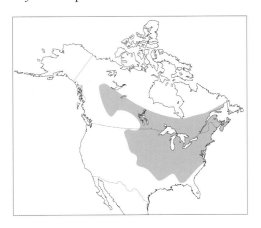

Mammal: *Myotis septentrionalis,* northern long-eared bat, northern bat

Meaning of Name: *Myotis* (mouse + ear) alludes to large ears; *septentrionalis* probably refers to northern distribution

Description: long, narrow tragus; light reddish brown above and buffy gray below

Total Length: 3 to 3.5 inches

Tail: 1.4 to 1.6 inches

Forearm: 1.3 to 1.5 inches

Weight: 0.10 to 0.20 ounce

Gestation: not known (probably about 40 days)

Offspring: 1 or 2

Age of Maturity: 1 to 3 years

Longevity: up to 18 years

Diet: flying insects

Habitat: dry forests, coniferous boreal forests

Predators: weasel, domestic cat, raccoon, skunk, rat, snakes, hawks and owls

Dental Formula:
2/3, 1/1, 3/3, 3/3 = 38 teeth

FRINGED BAT
Myotis thysanodes

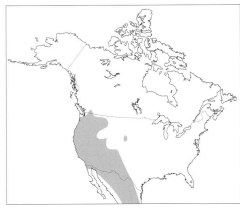

Mammal: *Myotis thysanodes,* fringed bat

Meaning of Name: *Myotis* (mouse + ear) alludes to large ears; *thysanodes* (fringelike) refers to short, stiff hairs along the posterior border of the tail membrane

Description: medium-sized, buffy brown; fringe of short, stiff brown hairs on free edge of interfemoral membrane

Total Length: 3.4 to 3.7 inches

Tail: 1.4 to 1.6 inches

Forearm: 1.6 to 1.8 inches

Weight: 0.19 to 0.30 ounce

Gestation: not known (probably about 40 days)

Offspring: 1

Age of Maturity: 1 to 3 years

Longevity: one lived at least 11 years

Diet: insects

Habitat: arid yellow-pine zone of Pacific Northwest in caves and attics of old buildings

Predators: weasel, domestic cat, raccoon, skunk, rat, snakes, hawks and owls

Dental Formula:
2/3, 1/1, 3/3, 3/3 = 38 teeth

The fringed bat has very precise echolocation and flight abilities. It hovers in front of leaves to search for insects then darts forward to capture them with great accuracy.

LONG-LEGGED BAT
Myotis volans

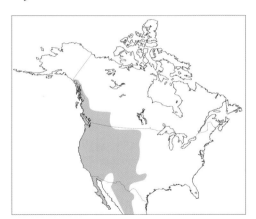

Mammal: *Myotis volans*, long-legged bat
Meaning of Name: *Myotis* (mouse + ear) alludes to large ears; *volans* (flying)
Description: large; dark brown above, smoky brown underneath; short, round ears; keeled calcar; sparse fur on wing membrane; fur on underside of interfemoral membrane goes as far out as the elbow and knee
Total Length: 3.5 to 3.9 inches
Tail: 1.5 to 2.1 inches
Forearm: 1.5 to 1.6 inches
Weight: male, 0.26 ounce; female, 0.30 to 0.38 ounce
Gestation: not known (probably about 40 days)
Offspring: 1
Age of Maturity: 1 to 3 years
Longevity: not known
Diet: insects (especially small moths)
Habitat: wooded areas and open scrub; found in buildings, small pockets and crevices in rock ledges
Predators: weasel, domestic cat, raccoon, skunk, rat, snakes, hawks and owls
Dental Formula:
2/3, 1/1, 3/3, 3/3 = 38 teeth

YUMA BAT
Myotis yumanensis

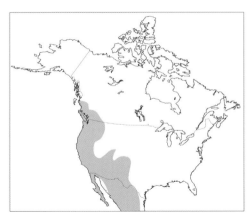

Mammal: *Myotis yumanensis*, Yuma bat
Meaning of Name: *Myotis* (mouse + ear) alludes to large ears; *yumanensis* (of Yuma) refers to the fact that the type specimen was described in Yuma, Arizona
Description: dull brown upper parts; buffy gray below; similar to little brown bat but smaller; interfemoral membrane is haired nearly to the knee
Total Length: 3 to 3.6 inches
Tail: 1.3 to 1.7 inches
Forearm: 1.3 to 1.5 inches
Weight: 0.21 to 0.25 ounce
Gestation: not known (probably about 40 days)
Offspring: 1
Age of Maturity: 1 to 3 years
Longevity: not known
Diet: flying insects; opportunistic and selective feeder
Habitat: open arid areas preferred over forests; found in caves, tunnels or buildings
Predators: weasel, domestic cat, raccoon, skunk, rat, snakes, hawks and owls
Dental Formula:
2/3, 1/1, 3/3, 3/3 = 38 teeth

WESTERN RED BAT
Lasiurus blossevillii

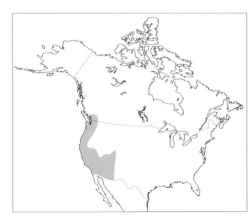

Mammal: *Lasiurus blossevillii*, western red bat
Meaning of Name: *Lasiurus* (hairy-tailed bat); *blossevillii* (+ shaggy hair)
Description: larger than eastern red bat with fewer frosted hairs and much less hair on margin of posterior tail membrane; hair is rusty red on back, and males are brighter red than females; white shoulder patch
Total Length: 3.4 to 4.8 inches
Tail: 1.4 to 2.4 inches
Forearm: 1.4 to 1.5 inches
Weight: 0.25 to 0.63 ounce
Gestation: not known (may be up to 90 days)
Offspring: 2 or 3 (only genus of bat that commonly has more than 2 young per birth)
Age of Maturity: 1 to 3 years (probably not during first summer)
Longevity: not known
Diet: variety of hard and soft flying insects, including moths, beetles, crickets, leafhoppers, ants, flies and cicadas
Habitat: trees, hedgerows and forest edges
Predators: hawks and owls
Dental Formula:
1/3, 1/1, 2/2, 3/3 = 32 teeth

EASTERN RED BAT
Lasiurus borealis

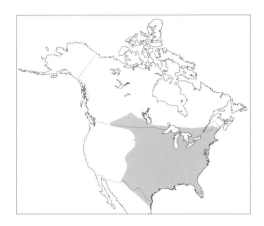

Mammal: *Lasiurus borealis*, eastern red bat
Meaning of Name: *Lasiurus* (hairy-tailed bat); *borealis* (of the north)
Description: male is bright brick-red above and paler below; frosting around neck area, pair of creamy shoulder flashes; dorsal surface of interfemoral membrane, hind legs and bases of the wing membrane are all heavily furred; orange fur covers face and back of ears; females are paler and have frosted appearance due to cream-colored tips of dorsal hairs
Total Length: 3.7 to 4.4 inches
Tail: 1.8 to 2.4 inches
Forearm: 1.4 to 1.8 inches
Weight: 0.25 to 0.53 ounce
Gestation: not known (may be up to 90 days)
Offspring: 1 to 4 (only genus of bat in which there are commonly more than 2 young per birth)
Age of Maturity: 1 to 3 years (probably not during first summer)
Longevity: not known
Diet: variety of hard and soft flying insects, including moths, beetles, crickets, flies and cicadas
Habitat: wooded areas; has also adapted to villages and towns
Predators: hawks, owls, opossum, blue jay and crow
Dental Formula:
1/3, 1/1, 2/2, 3/3 = 32 teeth

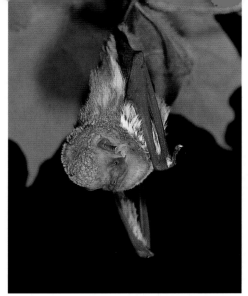

The female eastern red bat, above, is in one of its distinctive roosting places; the male, below, shows off its brighter red color.

EASTERN RED BAT
Lasiurus borealis

The red bat has long, narrow wings, and it may be one of the faster northern fliers, reaching speeds of up to 40 miles per hour. Their speed probably enables them to pursue prey that the broad-winged and flutter-style fliers cannot catch. Red bats are high fliers, capable of foraging at heights of 200 yards. After dark, they may lower their foraging height and work close to the ground and over water, but they continue to fly quickly. Their prey includes a mixture of hard-bodied beetles and soft-bodied insects such as moths.

Red bats also have distinctive roosting methods. In summer, they often hang up alone in a sheltered part of a tree, shrub or vine. This gives them freedom to range over a wide area but also exposes them to arboreal predators such as the opossum and some large aggressive birds such as blue jays and crows. Roost sites may be almost anywhere in the tree from top to bottom, but they are generally above an opening that allows the bat to drop freely.

The red bat has the highest fecundity of any northern temperate bat, giving birth to one to four young at a time.

Unlike other bats, the red bat has four nipples, not two. The young of a red bat are accordingly less precocial and developed at birth than those of other bats, and the mother must carry and feed them for a longer period of time. Pregnancy may last as long as 90 days, much longer than in *Myotis* bats, which produce only one infant after a pregnancy of roughly two months. Many *Myotis* can fly and forage effectively at the age of 3 weeks, but red bats take twice as long to reach the same level of competence. Care of the young takes place in the tree roost.

Red bats' high fecundity may be an adaptation to high mortality resulting from roosting in trees and being exposed to predators. The red bat has a tremendous geographic range, from northern Saskatchewan to as far south as Argentina and Chile. This may reflect an opportunistic character that trades off mobility and the chance to migrate to rich feeding areas against the higher risk that the offspring will fail to survive the autumn migration and first winter.

Red bats have an unusual courtship routine. Courtship in the air at dusk has been observed, with the pair descending to the ground to mate. There is a sexual dimorphism in color, males being brighter red than females.

The **western red bat**, *Lasiurus blossevillii*, was once considered to be the same species as the eastern red bat, but recent findings revealed that they are separate, the eastern red bat being a bit smaller and occurring farther east.

HOARY BAT
Lasiurus cinereus

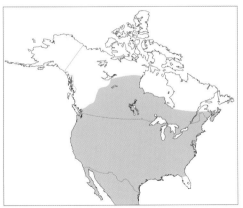

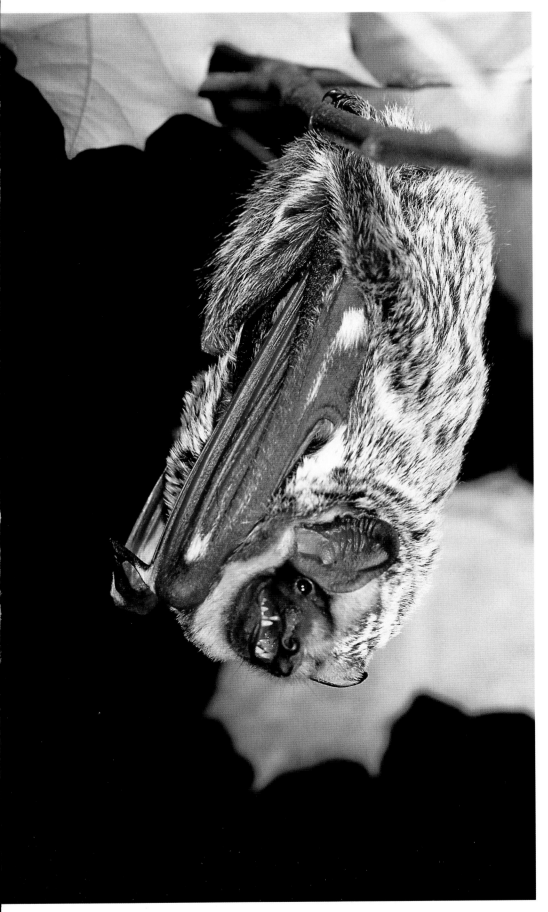

Mammal: *Lasiurus cinereus*, hoary bat

Meaning of Name: *Lasiurus* (hairy-tailed bat); *cinereus* (ash-colored); hoary can mean white or frosted grayish white

Description: dark brown with a silver frosting; ventral surface covered with tawny woolly hair; buffy patch at base of thumb and on throat; bases of wing membrane and dorsal surface of interfemoral membrane are covered with fur

Total Length: 5.1 to 5.7 inches

Tail: 2.2 to 2.6 inches

Forearm: 2+ inches

Weight: about 1 ounce

Gestation: not known (probably about 40 days)

Offspring: 1 to 4, usually 2 (only genus of bat in which there are commonly more than 2 young per birth)

Age of Maturity: 1 to 3 years

Longevity: not known

Diet: primarily a moth feeder; also dragonflies

Habitat: wooded areas, especially coniferous regions

Predators: weasel, domestic cat, raccoon, skunk, rat, snakes, hawks and owls

Dental Formula:
1/3, 1/1, 2/2, 3/3 = 32 teeth

The hoary bat prefers wooded habitats and roosts in trees in the open, wrapping its wings around itself to conserve body heat.

While most bats seek shelter in cool weather, the silver-haired bat continues to forage in below-freezing temperatures, though it migrates to warmer climes in winter.

SILVER-HAIRED BAT
Lasionycteris noctivagans

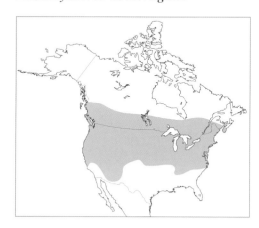

Mammal: *Lasionycteris noctivagans*, silver-haired bat; the slowest-flying bat
Meaning of Name: *Lasionycteris* probably translates as "playful at dusk"; *noctivagans* (wandering by night)
Description: blackish brown; silver-tipped hairs of back and belly give the appearance of a silver-frosted cape, since head and neck lack silver tips; short, rounded ears; blunt tragus; dark brown wing membrane; interfemoral membrane is covered with fine frosted hairs three-quarters of the way down
Total Length: 3.6 to 4.3 inches
Tail: 1.5 to 2 inches
Forearm: 1.5 to 1.7 inches
Weight: 0.21 to 0.49 ounce
Gestation: not known (probably about 40 days)
Offspring: 1 or 2
Age of Maturity: 1 to 3 years
Longevity: 12 years
Diet: insects; possibly prefers emerging aquatic insects
Habitat: flies along streams, rivers and lakes in forested areas, roosts under loose bark
Predators: weasel, domestic cat, raccoon, skunk, rat, snakes, hawks and owls
Dental Formula:
2/3, 1/1, 2/3, 3/3 = 36 teeth

EASTERN PIPISTRELLE
Pipistrellus subflavus

Mammal: *Pipistrellus subflavus*, eastern pipistrelle
Meaning of Name: *Pipistrellus* from Italian word meaning bat; *subflavus* (yellow beneath) refers to pale underparts
Description: yellowish brown woolly pelage; paler buffy brown underneath; short ears with tapered round tips; short, blunt tragus; calcar is prominent and unkeeled
Total Length: male, 2.9 to 3.5 inches; female, 3.5 inches
Tail: male, 1.4 to 1.8 inches; female, 1.6 inches
Forearm: about 1.2 inches
Weight: 0.12 to 0.21 ounce (depending on sex and season)
Gestation: not known (probably about 40 days)
Offspring: 2 (rarely 1 or 3)
Age of Maturity: over 1 year
Longevity: 7 to 10 years in the wild (maximum 15 years)
Diet: flying insects
Habitat: wooded areas along slow-moving streams or rivers; near water
Predators: weasel, domestic cat, raccoon, skunk, rat, snakes, hawks and owls
Dental Formula:
2/3, 1/1, 2/2, 3/3 = 34 teeth

BIG BROWN BAT
Eptesicus fuscus

The big brown bat, like its small cousin the little brown bat, is quite common and uses houses and other cavities created by humans. It is a strong flier and, unlike the small *Myotis*, includes many hard-bodied beetles in its diet. Its jaws and teeth are accordingly well developed and capable of a strong bite. Big brown bats can detect beetle-sized objects as far away as 15 feet. The low-frequency echo of a swarm of insects may be read from a remarkable range of 600 yards. Big brown bats can fly at 25 miles per hour.

The big brown bat has a remarkable tolerance for cold temperatures. Just before the start of severely cold and insect-free winter weather, it enters cold, drafty hibernation cavities that other bats avoid. Its broader tolerance means that it migrates comparatively short distances between its summer foraging and breeding grounds and its hibernation sites, but when it has to, the big brown bat can travel great distances—some banded big brown bats displaced by researchers traveled 450 miles back to their home territory, probably using celestial orientation.

Maternity colonies can number as high as 300 females but are usually half that size or smaller. Although eastern big brown bats frequently give birth to two young, the western big browns have only one offspring per year. Populations grow so large in some areas that the reproductive rate is depressed, which suggests that food availability is more important to the control of big brown bat populations than other factors such as the availability of roosting and hibernation sites, predation and winter mortality.

With a distribution that stretches over the entire mainland United States and across southern Canada, the big brown bat is one of the two best-known bat species.

BIG BROWN BAT
Eptesicus fuscus

Mammal: *Eptesicus fuscus*, big brown bat
Meaning of Name: *Eptesicus* (house flyer) refers to the fact that it is often seen flying near houses and roosting under eaves; *fuscus* (dark-colored)
Description: glossy, dark brown fur with reddish tips and grayish brown underparts; leathery black wing and tail membranes; calcar has pronounced keel; broad, blunt tragus; face is almost naked except for forehead; black skin and fleshy lips
Total Length: 4.5 to 5.2 inches
Tail: 1.7 to 2.1 inches
Forearm: 1.7 to 2 inches
Weight: 0.49 to 1.1 ounces (varies with season and hibernation)
Gestation: not known (probably about 40 days)
Offspring: western females, 1; eastern females, 2
Age of Maturity: usually first year; however, one-quarter of females do not mature early enough to bear young the first year
Longevity: 7 to 9 years in the wild
Diet: beetles are main food; also other flying insects
Habitat: urbanized areas and around farm buildings, pastures, meadows, creeks, ponds and wooded areas; suburban vegetation and city streets
Predators: grounded bats may fall prey to skunk, opossum and snakes
Dental Formula:
2/3, 1/1, 1/2, 3/3 = 32 teeth

A COMMUNAL COST

Many bats are gregarious, roosting together in large numbers. There are some benefits to communal roosting. Wintering bats stay warmer and maintain humidity better when clustered. If a predator finds the roost, a member of a large cluster is probably less likely to be eaten than one in a small cluster. Sometimes, females help other females guard and retrieve young that fall to the ground. Young, inexperienced bats may learn about foraging opportunities by tracking older, more experienced bats.

But communal roosting also carries costs. Because bats roost in tight packs and use the same small sites year after year, they are perfect hosts for a variety of parasites that flourish on social mammals. Bats rarely groom each other in the way that monkeys do. This makes communal bats vulnerable to an itchy version of a social disease: ectoparasitism. Bats are host to large numbers of external parasites such as fleas and bedbugs. Other mammals harbor fleas, chiggers, ticks and mites, but bats, in addition to hosting these pests, also have a unique range of parasites. Six entire insect families are found only on bats, and another, the bedbug family, has developed extensively on bats. Indeed, the bedbug that plagues humans probably first evolved on cave-roosting bats, gravitated to cave-dwelling humans and eventually moved with humans to their hovels.

Close to 700 species of insects live exclusively on the bodies of bats, and it is tempting to believe that this is because their gregarious roosting habits favor the lifestyles of parasites. Most families of bat insects spend part of their lives either living in the roost and feeding on bats that visit or living directly on a bat and using the roost mainly as a place to disperse offspring to new bat hosts.

Life on a bat that flies through the air at high speed and allows its body temperature to drop nearly to freezing during hibernation has led to some unique adaptations in certain bat insects. One group of flies, the streblids, or bat lice, hatch looking like most flies, with wings and legs. But in some species, as soon as the female finds an appropriate spot on a bat, her wings and legs fall off. She

Many bats are gregarious—densities of up to 300,000 little brown bats have been known to cluster in a single cave, a scenario that creates rich opportunities for parasitic insects.

embeds herself in the bat's skin, and her abdomen swells up like a balloon, completely enclosing her head and thorax. Mobility is traded for security.

The lack of mobility of bat lice means that they must be concerned with selecting bats that will be close enough to other bats for their offspring to find new hosts. This requires some sexual discrimination. The streblids that live on Townsend's big-eared bats, for instance, can distinguish male bats from females. They prefer females as hosts. This seems logical. Females form dense nursery roosts in summer, so the streblid and its progeny have a large food resource. Male big-ears are solitary, so a streblid on a summer male would have a dim future.

Streblids are also among the most devoted mothers in the insect world. Rather than simply laying eggs on the host or food source as most flies do, the female streblid hatches a single egg at a time inside her body and feeds it internally with special "milk" glands. When the fly emerges, it is almost adult size, and it pupates instantly, ready to become an adult. This would be comparable to a human pregnancy that lasts until the fetus is 18 years old. The reason that such a high degree of parental care in these flies is adaptive is clear: The adult female is much better at extracting resources from the host than a fly maggot could ever be, and the host's body is a better resource base than the detritus in the bat roost. A fly on a bat has an almost infinite supply of high-quality food, and since the bat roost is a predictable source of new hosts, there is no need to produce large numbers of young.

These parasites do not appear to harm bats seriously, but they are undoubtedly irritating, and the bats expend large amounts of energy grooming themselves.

Mammalogists, at least, are happy they exist. Most bat parasites are found on only one or a few closely related bat species, and by comparing the parasites of these bats, biologists gain insights into how various groups are related.

Although its high-pitched cry is audible to human ears, the spotted bat, photographed here from behind, is one of the rarest and least-known bats in North America.

SPOTTED BAT
Euderma maculatum

The most beautiful bat recorded in North America, the spotted bat is also one of the continent's rarest. This species is a resident of the arid west and ranges from open desert to ponderosa pine forest. It occasionally flies into Canada in the summer. Spotted bats roost in rock crevices in summer, but their winter habits are unknown.

They are moth specialists that fly a regular circuit through clearings and may defend their circuits from other spotted bats, avoiding echolocating foragers. Their echolocation call can be heard by humans as a high-pitched cry. The call's frequency means that the spotted bat has a long range, which may help it detect moths at a great distance. Humans can hear the sound from 250 yards, but moths probably find it hard to detect, since most of the moths that have ears hear only higher-frequency sounds.

Almost nothing is known about the reproduction of the spotted bat, nor have researchers explained why it is so beautifully marked.

SPOTTED BAT
Euderma maculatum

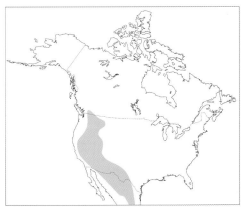

Mammal: *Euderma maculatum*, spotted bat, death's head bat
Meaning of Name: *Euderma* (nicely colored skin); *maculatum* refers to unique color pattern with white spots
Description: dark reddish brown to black; white spot on rump and on each shoulder; grayish ears and membranes
Total Length: 4.2 to 4.5 inches
Tail: 1.9 to 2 inches
Forearm: 1.9 to 2 inches
Weight: 0.54 to 0.60 ounce
Gestation: not known (probably about 40 days)
Offspring: 1
Age of Maturity: 1 to 3 years
Longevity: not known
Diet: moths and other insects caught in flight
Habitat: variety of habitats, but usually dry, arid, rough desert country
Predators: hawks, owls and snakes
Dental Formula:
2/3, 1/1, 2/2, 3/3 = 34 teeth

TOWNSEND'S BIG-EARED BAT
Plecotus townsendii

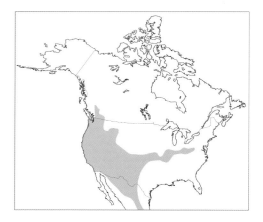

Mammal: *Plecotus townsendii*, Townsend's big-eared bat, western big-eared bat

Meaning of Name: *Plecotus* (twisted ear) may refer to its habit of coiling the ears back against the body during hibernation; *townsendii* (named after J.K. Townsend, an ornithologist and author)

Description: very long ears that are joined across the forehead; crescent-shaped nostrils are covered posteriorly by a pair of lumps consisting of sebaceous glandular tissue; dark and naked wing membrane; prominent calcar; grayish brown above, tan underneath

Total Length: male, 3.8 to 4.1 inches; female, 3.9 to 4.4 inches

Tail: male, 1.7 to 2 inches; female, 1.8 to 2.1 inches

Forearm: 1.6 to 1.8 inches

Weight: 0.32 to 0.39 ounce

Gestation: 60 days

Offspring: 1

Age of Maturity: female, in first autumn; male, probably not until the year after its birth

Longevity: average is about 5 years; 16.5 years is the record

Diet: moths

Habitat: cultivated valleys bordered by deciduous forests, brush, junipers or pine forest

Predators: weasel, domestic cat, raccoon, skunk, rat, snakes, hawks and owls

Dental Formula:
2/3, 1/1, 2/3, 3/3 = 36 teeth

RABIES

Rabies, a virus that feeds on mammals and subjects many of them, including humans, to a gruesome death, is both horrible and fascinating. Its manner of transmission is a marvel of evolutionary ingenuity. Rabies is transmitted in the saliva of its carrier. When the rabies virus contacts the victim's nerve tissue, it travels along the nerve until it reaches the brain and spinal stem, where it produces inflammation and usually death. However, before the affected animal dies, the virus manipulates the brain, changing the animal's behavior in a way that helps spread the virus.

There are two forms of rabies syndrome, the furious and the dumb. In the furious form of rabies, victims are likely to attack and bite other animals. Often, the throat is paralyzed so that swallowing is impossible and saliva accumulates in the mouth. The mad dog "foaming at the mouth" is the virus's way of transporting and perpetuating itself. The dumb form may spread itself by exposing the carrier to attack by predators. In either case, once the rabies virus enters the bloodstream, it usually results in the death of the carrier. All mammals are susceptible.

In North America, the vaccination of dogs has made rabies largely a disease of wildlife. In the eastern region, red foxes are among the most infected animals, while in the west, skunks and ground squirrels are most infected. The reservoir of rabies rarely affects humans directly, but it does represent a source of infection to animals such as dogs and livestock that have close contact with humans. In the tropics, vampire bats, which feed directly on the blood of livestock, are important agents of rabies transmission. However, in the temperate zone, most evidence suggests that bats are a minor source of rabies. In Canada, only one case of rabies transmitted by a bat bite has been recorded, while in the United States, bat bites cause fewer than one case every three years.

Since dogs, cats and livestock can be vaccinated, rabies is a highly avoidable disease. If the public would avoid handling obviously sick or strange-acting wildlife and vaccinate their pets, the risk of exposure to rabies would be minimal. Nevertheless, the fear of rabies has led to some excessive campaigns designed to stop its spread by means of wildlife eradication. In 1952, Alberta embarked on a famous poisoning campaign in which trappers were given cyanide and strychnine to set out for wildlife. In an 18-month period, the minimum estimate of wildlife destroyed by this unselective poisoning amounted to 50,000 foxes, 35,000 coyotes, 7,500 lynxes, 4,300 wolves, 1,850 bears, 500 skunks, 64 pumas, 4 badgers and 1 wolverine. Farmers were also given poison to use and may have killed comparable numbers of animals. Such programs did little except decimate wildlife populations. Fortunately, animals such as red foxes can now be vaccinated by broadcasting vaccine in meatballs dropped from airplanes.

The fear of rabies has allowed pest exterminators to sell bat-extermination services that needlessly destroy bats and actually increase the public's health risk. It is estimated that less than one half of one percent of North American bats carry rabies, a frequency no higher than that seen in many other animals. Bats that do become rabid rarely attack people. If sick bats are not handled, they present a minimal health risk. The best measure is simply for people to exclude bats from their dwellings—by screening and sealing attic vents, for example. Extermination programs that poison bats use toxins that are directly hazardous to other mammals, including humans, and the poisoned bats end up flapping around on lawns and in the street where they are more likely to be handled by children and pets. The best way to prevent bats from living inside a dwelling or building is to make it unattractive and inaccessible to them. Leave bright lights burning 24 hours a day to drive the bats out, and screen or otherwise seal all entrances wider than one-fifth of an inch.

PALLID BAT
Antrozous pallidus

The pallid bat is a large, big-eared bat of the southwestern United States that is sometimes caught in the north. Most information on its biology comes from populations in the arid southwestern United States.

Pallid bats inhabit dry areas with low shrubbery and rocky outcrops, but they also occur in dry forests, such as those of ponderosa pine, and along the riparian forest of desert streams. For day roosts, pallid bats use rock crevices and cavities and, at night, large cavities such as cave entrances. Unlike those of most other bat species, their summer colonies are home to adults of both sexes and the young, and they range in size from 30 to 100 individuals. The pallid bat hibernates in caves and mines near its summering areas.

Pallid bats' distinctive appearance is matched by a unique foraging technique. They fly low and slowly and are capable of hovering but are not highly maneuverable. Instead, they spend much of their time picking off larger prey species from foliage and the ground. They find prey items not by echolocation but by listening to the rustling sounds insects make as they crawl. Pallid bats crawl efficiently compared with other bats, and they will light on the ground and pursue their prey on foot. Small items are eaten on the spot, but larger items are taken to the night roost for consumption. Maternity colonies are formed in spring and may contain several hundred individuals of both sexes. Females give birth to one, two or even three young, born after a pregnancy of 7 to 10 weeks and weaned in a comparable time. Year-old females bear a single offspring.

Pallid bats are gregarious, and they communicate vocally. Four calls are recognized, three of which can be heard by humans: Directive calls communicate the location of individuals and roosting sites; squabble calls communicate positions and may keep the bats spaced within the roost; buzzing calls indicate aggressive intentions. The fourth call, an echolocation FM call in ultrasound, cannot be heard by humans but is used by pallid bats for orientation at night. The young bats call to their mothers, and the mothers can distinguish the individual calls and smells of their own offspring.

Pallid bats have a series of glands that exude a skunky odor when the animals are molested.

PALLID BAT
Antrozous pallidus

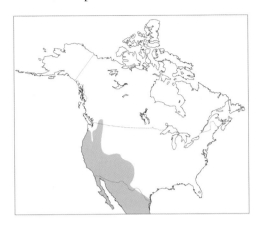

Mammal: *Antrozous pallidus*, pallid bat
Meaning of Name: *Antrozous* refers to the fact that it usually roosts in caves; *pallidus* (pale)
Description: creamy yellowish on upper parts; ventral surface is almost white; blunt bare pad at end of muzzle; scroll-shaped nostrils; two glandular swellings on each side of muzzle (behind nostrils) emit strong odor; large interfemoral membrane; weakly keeled calcar
Total Length: male, 4.4 to 4.9 inches; female, 4.2 to 5.1 inches
Tail: male, 1.4 to 1.7 inches; female, 1.5 to 1.9 inches
Forearm: 2 to 2.6 inches
Weight: male, 0.74 to 1 ounce; female, 0.84 to 1.2 ounces
Gestation: 53 to 71 days
Offspring: 1 to 3 (since there are only two teats, just 2 survive)
Age of Maturity: 1 to 3 years
Longevity: 9 years
Diet: moths, orthopterans (grasshoppers, crickets, etc.), beetles, neuropterans (fishflies, snakeflies), chilopods (centipedes), scorpions, mice and lizards
Habitat: rocky outcrops, open arid plains or cultivated areas; sometimes forested areas or open brushland; requires water surfaces nearby from which to drink
Predators: owls, hawks and snakes
Dental Formula:
1/2, 1/1, 1/2, 3/3 = 28 teeth

Less adept in the air than other bat species, pallid bats can land near prey and give chase by crawling on foot after large katydids, crickets, mice, horned toad lizards and even scorpions.

PIKAS, RABBITS & HARES *Lagomorpha*

Lagomorphs have suffered from a case of mistaken identity. Biologists once lumped them together with the rodents, but now they are recognized as a separate order.

The Lagomorpha is a small order of two families: One includes rabbits, while the other contains only pikas. Neither family is very diverse, but in many places, the animals are the dominant small herbivore. Like rodents, lagomorphs have chisel-shaped front incisors for chewing leafy vegetation and shrubbery. There are many morphological and behavioral differences between lagomorphs and rodents. For example, lagomorphs have two sets of upper incisors: a long front pair and a rear pair shaped like small pegs. Rodents, on the other hand, have just one set of upper incisors. Lagomorphs are strictly herbivores, whereas rodents have a highly diverse diet.

Lagomorphs evolved more than 50 million years ago in Asia, probably in large grassland and meadow areas. The greatest radiation of rabbits and hares has occurred in North America. More diverse at one time, lagomorphs were found even in Africa. In North America, pikas have never diversified, either taxonomically or ecologically, to the extent that rabbits and hares have.

Many of the lagomorphs' physical characteristics reflect their grazing habits, grassland origins and appeal to predators. Thus their wide-set eyes and erect heads give them a wide field of vision. Their long necks are easily swiveled, enabling them to look behind themselves; and their large ears help them to detect the stealthy sounds of predators. These features are most developed in hares that live in open areas and least developed in pikas, whose homes are in rockier regions that offer more shelter.

The digestive system of lagomorphs reflects their herbivorous specialization and is similar to that of other grazing ruminant mammals such as deer. Both lagomorphs and ruminants have a large, baglike digestive chamber. Chewed and semidigested food is collected in this chamber, where various microorganisms subject the contents to fermentation. Because the fermentation system of lagomorphs is not as extensive as that of large grazing ruminants, they must pass some of their nutrients through their system twice. They do this by eating some of their dung, a behavior called refection.

Lagomorphs excrete two kinds of dung pellets: One is a soft type that they eat, and the other is a hard, fully processed pellet that they do not eat. When the animals are inactive, they eat the soft pellets as they emerge from the anus. The pellets are then stored in the stomach, where they are mixed with a new load of vegetation and subjected to fermentation again. Refection increases digestive efficiency and enables the lagomorph to recapture nutrients, particularly vitamin B_{12}, which the gut bacteria produce. These go back to be stored in the stomach, where they will be mixed with new vegetation that the animal will harvest when it becomes active.

Little is known about the mountain, or Nuttall's, cottontail, which is smaller and paler than the eastern cottontail. Biologists speculate that its natural history is similar to that of Sylvilagus floridanus.

PIKAS *Ochotonidae*

The heyday of pikas has come and gone. Pikas arose in Eurasia and spread to Africa and North America, but they are now confined primarily to Asia, where 16 of the 18 surviving species live. Only two species remain in North America, where they inhabit the high mountains of the west.

Pikas have a peculiarly narrow range of temperature tolerance. They can survive long, frigid mountain winters but will die from heat stress at only a couple of degrees above their body temperature. This has limited them to the type of habitat in which they probably evolved: high-altitude rock slopes and grasslands.

Some Asian pikas burrow in grassland areas, but in North America, pikas occupy a single highly specific habitat: the rocky talus slopes next to mountain meadows. The rocks and boulders provide protected nest sites, while the meadows provide food. Unlike rabbits, pikas are diurnal, relatively sedentary creatures that scuttle into the rocks when threatened. Accordingly, they differ radically from rabbits and hares in body plan. Their legs are short, their eyes comparatively small and their bodies compact like those of rodents.

The habitat required by the North American pikas is extremely small in size. Talus with good forage nearby is limited, and as a result, they live in concentrated populations. Both males and females defend territories that cover several hundred square yards. Usually, a male's territory is adjacent to a female's, with the two sexes alternating along the rocky slope. During the mating season, a male's territory may overlap that of the adjacent female. Females repel other females during this time but are less aggressive toward males, and vice versa.

However, once the young are born, females vigorously exclude males from their territories.

There are two reasons for pika territoriality: a limited number of good nesting sites and the need to stock a winter food supply. Pikas live up to about six years and remain on the same territory for their lifetimes. The offspring of a pair will thus face limited prospects of finding their own territory, but if the parents aggressively exclude immigrants, the chances that their offspring may occupy adjacent vacancies will be increased. Females are aggressive toward males after the arrival of their young because of the limited food supply. Males provide no parental care, and they deplete the meadows closest to the talus slope.

Pikas remain active throughout the long mountain winter. To ensure enough food for this time, they store large piles of hay, which they cut in the meadow and dry on rocks within their territory. Vigilance and territoriality are probably required to keep others from stealing it.

Female territoriality forces the male pikas to be monogamous. Males cannot control access to a group of females, because the females are dispersed along the slope and are aggressive toward other females.

The **American pika**, *Ochotona princeps*, is the most common and widely distributed of the North American species. It is grayish to cinnamon on its upper parts and buff underneath, while the **collared pika**, *O. collaris*, is more drab, with grayish patches on the cheeks and around the neck, whitish underparts and a pale gray collar on the neck and shoulders. It occurs farther north than the American pika.

The diminutive harelipped pika—which does not hibernate and must remain active throughout the winter—is one of the few mammals that prepare for the season by cutting, drying and stacking hay gathered within their territory.

AMERICAN PIKA
Ochotona princeps

Mammal: *Ochotona princeps,* American pika

Meaning of Name: *Ochotona,* derived from *ochodona,* a Mongolian name for the pika; *princeps* (chief) refers to an Amerindian name translated as little chief hare

Description: small, stocky, tailless mammal with dense, long, fine pelage; grayish buff or brownish with a mixture of black resulting in a salt-and-pepper look dorsally; grayish underneath; dusky ears are edged with white; small harelipped mouth

Total Length: 7.1 to 8 inches

Weight: 4 to 8.2 ounces

Gestation: 30 days

Offspring: 2 to 5 (average 3); 2 litters per year

Age of Maturity: the year following birth

Longevity: few live for more than 5 years (maximum 7)

Diet: grasses, sedges, herbs and tender flowering plants; engages in reingestion

Habitat: talus, broken rock, rock slides; usually above the tree line; sometimes in rock piles and on lakeshores on the West Coast

Predators: eagles, buteo hawks, fox, marten, fisher, wolverine, lynx, bear and especially ermine, which follow it through its maze of rock tunnels

Dental Formula:
2/1, 0/0, 3/2, 2/3 = 26 teeth

RABBITS & HARES *Leporidae*

"Rabbit" and "hare" are categories that connote two different behavioral and ecological patterns within the family Leporidae. Hares and jackrabbits, which all belong to the genus *Lepus*, are creatures of exposed habitats and are specialized for running. They rarely use burrows except to escape extreme cold or heat. Their young are born fully furred with open eyes and a readiness for activity. By contrast, rabbits are divided into several genera. With shorter hind limbs, they are not as adept at running. They occupy a variety of habitats from marshy areas to heavy forest, where they often dig burrows for nesting and give birth to helpless, almost naked young that are nursed by their mother.

All rabbits and hares are runners, and their bodies reflect their dependence on high speed, leaps and bounds to escape predators. Their limbs are elongated, and the hind feet and legs are much longer than the front, giving them a jacked-up racing-car build. Some of their hind-leg bones are also fused together, allowing them to push off with great force. Their skull is fenestrated; that is, the bones are pitted with cavities that make them lighter, so the rabbit has less weight to carry. The collarbone is also reduced in size and weight as it is in other bounding, running mammals. All these characteristics adapt the rabbit to its special style of movement. It jumps, leaps and spurts, often from side to side. The combination of high acceleration and speed makes pursuit on the ground difficult for most predators.

The extent to which this ability is developed varies with the rabbit species and the habitat it prefers. Rabbits that rely on extensive burrow systems and brushy vegetation for protection have shorter hind legs than jackrabbits do and are thus poorer runners. Jackrabbits live in open habitats, where protective cover is often widely distributed, which increases their dependence on running to escape predators. Of all the rabbits, jackrabbits have the greatest hind-limb development and are capable of bounding across the terrain at 40 miles per hour.

Most rabbits and hares are active at dusk and during the night, a behavioral pattern that reduces their risk of detection by predators. Like other nocturnal mammals, they have relatively large eyes and ears and a good sense of smell. The social behavior of rabbits and hares depends on whether the species lives in burrows and, if it does, how closely the burrows are clustered. Some rabbits, such as the European rabbit, live semicommunally in warrens and many burrows. These burrows are used for generations and are thus an important factor in evolutionary success. Both males and females defend their own burrows. In areas where soils suitable for burrow construction are limited, burrows are a valuable resource, and females may fight to the death for possession of one.

The concentration of many individuals in one area ultimately places some stress on local food resources. Thus, as with other social mammals, such as ground squirrels, whose breeding sites are clumped together, female rabbits form dominance hierarchies. The dominant females suppress the reproduction of subdominant females by denying them access to nest sites and by physical intimidation. Fighting for burrows is less intense in regions where the soil is good and burrows

As nocturnal creatures, rabbits and hares have large eyes and ears to enable them to detect predators. The arctic hare pictured here changes its white winter coat to gray-blue for summer as a means of blending in with its habitat according to season.

can be made easily. It is not reported among cottontail rabbits, perhaps because the females do not dig clustered burrows. Similarly, female hares tend not to fight because they do not dig extensive burrows.

Like the female, the male European rabbit can be intensely territorial when burrows are clumped. In this situation, the females constitute a large defensible resource to which a male can gain exclusive access by fighting and using other forms of dominance signaling. Males of this species pile up their dung pellets to form territorial markers. They also have a chin gland that produces an odorous secretion which they rub

around the warren and onto the fur of females within their territory. In rabbit and hare species with dispersed females, males use a different strategy. They, too, scent-mark a territory, but then they must search for females within it as well as repelling other males.

Most people have heard the phrase "as mad as a March hare," which comes from the springtime mating antics of hares and rabbits. This behavior often involves boxing; individuals stand up on their hind legs and cuff each other in the face and ears. It was once thought that this was a case of male-male competition. However, careful videotaping has revealed that females

A herd of arctic hares takes advantage of the brief northern summer to graze on a lush field of low-growing vegetation.

do most of the cuffing, and the individuals they cuff are courting males. The females appear to be testing male status. In some species, such as the black-tailed jackrabbit, females attack hesitant males, leaping and pawing at them until they are driven off. The females subject persistent males to further tests, leading them on to a series of races and sparring matches.

Female hares and rabbits are usually larger than males, a form of sexual dimorphism that may indicate a history of selection for combative females.

The following report describes the courtship behavior of the snowshoe hare: "The male snowshoe approached the female, sniffed her and jumped into the air. After landing, the male urinated on the female and left. The male reapproached the female, and the female jumped into the air twice, after which the male left. The male returned, jumped into the air and urinated on the female. Both snowshoes then went into the bushes, where more jumping occurred." Males of other species also run or leap past the female, urinating as they go, a behavior also found in some rodents, such as guinea pigs, that may provide the female with pheromonal cues about the physiological and hormonal state of the male. Many mammals assess reproductive maturity and territorial signals from the odor of one another's urine.

Copulation is generally brief and may be accompanied by squeaks and squeals by either sex. After copulation, contact and communication between the male and female generally cease, although males may follow a female around and defend her from other males. Males offer no parental care, however.

Female rabbits become pregnant by induced ovulation; that is, courtship and copulation stimulate the release of eggs for fertilization. Females produce more eggs and implant more embryos than they rear. As pregnancy proceeds, they reabsorb and digest some of the embryos, usually 6 to 30 percent of the fetuses. This may be one means of adjusting the litter size to match the food resources available and the amount of food the female requires for pregnancy and nursing.

Rabbits and hares have a high reproductive rate. Many species are sexually mature when they are just 3 months old. Every year, females may produce several litters of 2 to 12 young each, amounting to a total of 12 to 40 young annually. The number of young depends on species, locality and local conditions. Throughout the animal kingdom, fecundity and mortality generally balance each other, and rabbits are no exception. They are subject to intense predation and low survival rates. The prolific cottontail has a life expectancy of six months. Only a quarter of these rabbits survive for more than a year, and few see their fourth birthday. Hares and rabbits are the major food resource for several large carnivores, including lynx, bobcat, arctic fox and golden eagle.

PRECOCIAL & ALTRICIAL YOUNG

Large, long-lived mammals generally produce precocial young; that is, the young are born already alert, with open eyes, well-developed muscles and a coat of fur. Small mammals, on the other hand, give birth to altricial young—nearly naked babies that have closed eyes and weak muscles. Both strategies have advantages and disadvantages and seem to reflect the animals' differing responses to environmental fluctuations.

Small mammals have a high rate of metabolism, so they grow faster than large mammals. They are also better able to take advantage of sudden increases in food resources. On the other hand, they are more affected by unpredictable environmental changes, such as bad weather, and so hedge their bets against infant mortality by having larger litters, shorter pregnancies and altricial young. The advantage of this system is that the mother can adjust her parental care according to changes in available resources. If food is unavailable, for example, she can abandon her young, and if they are very young, her losses will be slight. If they are large and she is omnivorous or carnivorous, she can eat them, as certain rodents do.

By contrast, a mother with a single large, precocial offspring has put all her eggs into one basket. If the mother is a large grazer, she cannot recoup her investment in offspring by eating it, even if she is starving. Thus her reproductive success depends heavily on the survival of that one offspring. Such a strategy implies a high survival rate for the young. The precocial system also ensures that the offspring will soon be ready to fend for itself, giving both parent and young greater mobility. In addition, a pregnant adult female is far more mobile than one with a nest of altricial young—she can run from predators—while the mother of altricial young must hide her family. Competition among juveniles for food resources may also tip the balance toward the precocial strategy. Fewer but larger and more developed young have a greater chance of survival when food is scarce.

Hares always have precocial young, while rabbits' offspring are more altricial, especially in those species found in northern climates where the weather is unpredictable. Tropical rabbits, however, are more like hares, having smaller litter sizes and precocial young, a pattern that suggests greater predation and more competition among the young. However, lower mortality rates from environmental changes favor the precocial strategy.

Hares, which have no well-developed burrow system for protecting their young and live in exposed habitats, are like the large grazing mammals such as pronghorn antelope, whose habitat they share. The mother hare is usually pregnant for six weeks (cottontail rabbits are pregnant for only four), gives birth in the open, perhaps in a shallow depression, and visits her babies for nursing only once a day for 10 minutes. Her young are soon able to run from predators and move in search of new and shifting food supplies. The mother cottontail, on the other hand, must spend more time and energy nursing her babies, and they are usually not ready to move about and leave the nest until 16 days after their birth.

These different patterns suggest that parental care evolved in response to varying combinations of ecological pressures: predation, competition and unpredictable weather.

EASTERN COTTONTAIL
Sylvilagus floridanus

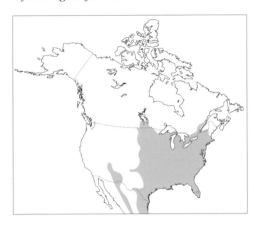

Mammal: *Sylvilagus floridanus*, eastern cottontail

Meaning of Name: *Sylvilagus* (wood hare); *floridanus* (of Florida) refers to Florida, where it was first recognized and named

Description: brownish to gray pelage; prominent rusty patch on nape; legs and throat are buff with dark brown anterior borders and gray posterior borders; tail is brown above and white below

Total Length: 17.5 inches

Tail: 2.4 inches

Weight: 1.8 to 3.3 pounds

Gestation: 25 to 35 days

Offspring: 2 to 12; 3 to 7 litters per year

Age of Maturity: 2 or 3 months

Longevity: approximately 6 to 15 months in the wild, maximum 3 years (due to large number of predators); one lived more than 9 years in captivity

Diet: green vegetation (tender green grasses and herbs) in summer and bark and twigs in winter

Habitat: great diversity of habitats (meadows, orchards, fencerows, edges of swamps and woodlots); also heavy brush and grassland pasture with dense clumps of shrubs and trees

Predators: hawks, owls, red fox, arctic fox, gray fox, long-tailed weasel, marten, raccoon, fisher and coyote; bobcat, lynx, snakes, shrike, golden eagle and crow take the younger ones

Dental Formula:
2/1, 0/0, 3/2, 3/3 = 28 teeth

Cottontail rabbits, such as the eastern cottontail, have thrived in the open-meadow habitats created by the cutting of mature hardwood forests in eastern North America.

EASTERN COTTONTAIL
Sylvilagus floridanus

The eastern cottontail is actually a southern rabbit. Now one of the most common of eastern mammals, it was once a rare beast. It has probably spread north and increased in abundance because of the destruction of mature hardwood forests. The eastern cottontail did not get as far as southern Ontario until the second half of the 19th century, and it did not get up to the Ottawa Valley until 1931.

The cottontail prefers second-growth areas with adjacent meadows. It probably becomes common in its localities after severe forest fires clear mature forests and dense scrub, allowing meadows to grow up. It has the characteristics of a typical "fugitive" species that specializes in short-lived productive habitats, dispersing in search of new areas as older ones decline.

Of the many species of cottontails, the eastern cottontail has the highest reproductive rate. Litter size may be as high as 12, and up to seven litters a year may be born. A female may produce 35 to 38 young per season. More important, cottontails reach reproductive maturity at a young age. Some may breed within two or three months of birth.

Like other rabbits, cottontails give birth to helpless young, almost naked and blind, in a well-constructed nest. The female builds a shallow nest hole in the ground and lines the outside with vegetation and the inside with soft fur that she plucks from her belly. The investment in each offspring is relatively low. The pregnancy is short, only 28 days versus 40 or more in hares, yet the young are free-living within two weeks, and a new litter is already on the way. Few cottontails live more than one or two years.

All of these life-history traits suggest that the eastern cottontail is a rabbit that invests heavily in reproduction and more lightly in competitive ability and predator avoidance. Virtually every raptor and carnivorous mammal will eat cottontails, but there is no evidence that they regulate cottontail density. Before human disturbance, cottontails were probably regulated by the successional loss of habitat and competition for food.

The destruction of forest and predator populations in eastern North America has made the cottontail an extremely abundant animal. It feeds on a tremendous variety of weeds, herbs and shrubs, and its populations now seem limited primarily by human-induced mortality. Road kills and hunting are major controls on cottontails. Indeed, the cottontail is considered the most important game animal in North America.

Little is known about the **mountain cottontail**, *Sylvilagus nuttallii*, found in the west, but biologists suspect its natural history is similar to that of the eastern cottontail.

The mountain, or Nuttall's, cottontail flourishes on the vegetation of the shortgrass and sagebrush plains of western North America, where its population remains stable.

MOUNTAIN COTTONTAIL
Sylvilagus nuttallii

Mammal: *Sylvilagus nuttallii*, mountain cottontail, Nuttall's cottontail
Meaning of Name: *Sylvilagus* (wood hare); *nuttalli* (named after Nuttall, its discoverer)
Description: similar to eastern cottontail, but smaller and paler; grayish brown above with gray flanks and white underneath; buffy brown collar across throat; short ears are black-tipped
Total Length: 13.75 to 15.4 inches
Tail: 1.75 to 2 inches
Weight: 1.5 to 2.25 pounds
Gestation: 25 to 35 days
Offspring: 3 to 8; 2 to 5 litters per year
Age of Maturity: 2 or 3 months
Longevity: 6 months (maximum 3 years)
Diet: prefers grass; also eats sagebrush and juniper berries
Habitat: sagebrush plains, rocky wooded areas or thickets
Predators: bobcat, coyote, fox, badger, owls and hawks
Dental Formula:
2/1, 0/0, 3/2, 3/3 = 28 teeth

SNOWSHOE HARE
Lepus americanus

The snowshoe hare gets its name from its large hind feet, which are thickly padded with coarse hairs and do indeed have the same effect as snowshoes: They distribute the hare's weight over a large surface area, enabling it to run through deep snow. Much of the life of this hare depends on snow. It is a resident of northern temperate forests with long winters and heavy snowfalls. As one of the most abundant of all small game animals, it is sought by a great variety of predators. Its status as a preferred prey item also accounts for another of its common names, the varying hare.

The snowshoe varies its color as a camouflage strategy to conceal itself from predators. In winter, it is snow-white except for its black-tipped ears, and in spring, it turns rusty brown, a pattern that increases its camouflage. The molt follows the normal pattern for temperate mammals. It is triggered in autumn by decreasing day length and in spring by increasing day length. The autumn molt results in the growth of distinctive white guard hairs that replace the brown guard hairs. In spring, the process is reversed. In both seasons, the snowshoe retains a brownish gray underfur that is absent in arctic hares and white-tailed jackrabbits. The white winter coat is also designed to meet winter cold stress and has 27 percent more insulation value than the summer coat.

Snowshoes tolerate others of their own species, and several can often be

Its broad hind feet provide enough surface area for the snowshoe hare to bound easily across the deep snow of the boreal forest.

seen feeding in the same clearing. At mating time, males become more aggressive and may fight over access to a female, wounding each other with their teeth. A male's territory typically overlaps that of several females, and at any one time, a receptive female may be courted by several males. Females are sometimes seen with a train of several males following behind, jumping and drumming with their hind legs. As with other rabbits and hares, snowshoe courtship involves much leaping and urination. The female rears her young without male assistance. She gives birth in a protected spot in brush or grass, stomping the vegetation into a crude nest. The young are well furred, born alert and with their eyes open, and after a week, they are actively feeding and moving around. Within three weeks, they are ready to leave the nest area, which permits the mother to have three or four litters in a season.

The fecundity of snowshoe hares is greater in the northern part of their range, where litter size averages four. In southern areas such as Colorado, it is half as high. As well, northern hares reproduce often enough that their seasonal total of individual young is higher. They produce 10 to 12 offspring per female each year, whereas southern populations, such as those in southern Ontario and Michigan, produce half as many. Even though the northern spring and summer are shorter, it is thought that the longer daylight hours affect the hare's reproductive hormones. While this accounts for the physiological mechanism, the ecological reasons behind the trend may be that competition is more severe in southern populations and that weather-influenced mortality of the young is more severe in the north, favoring larger clutches but smaller offspring. The clutch size also increases and decreases according to population density.

Young hares have an interesting behavior designed to reduce predation. Each day, they separate and move to a sheltered spot by themselves. At feeding time, they return to a central location, where their mother suckles them for 5 to 10 minutes. After feeding, they again disperse. This routine continues until they are all fully weaned. The juvenile hares will not breed until the following spring and summer.

Snowshoe hares are sedentary animals that live in a limited home range the size of which depends on food availability. It is normally less than 25 acres. A limited range enables the animal to become intimately acquainted with the terrain. The territory of a snowshoe hare is crisscrossed with runways between open areas and those with brushy cover that it uses when

pursued by predators. The hares even spend time grooming the trails, clipping away twigs that could impede their movement. In winter, the trails become snow-packed, allowing the hare to use its explosive speed, which may be as fast as 32 miles per hour.

Many raptors catch these hares by surprise attack. Various mammals, including mink, fox, coyote, bobcat and lynx—virtually all the larger predatory animals—use the same technique.

The incidence of predation can be extremely high—up to 40 percent of a hare population is eaten by predators during the winter, which explains why the hare spends large amounts of time motionless and quiet. The hare is also nocturnal, and because its zigzagging trails run through brushy cover, it is likely to escape pursuit if it has advance warning. Much of the time, it simply relies on camouflage, remaining motionless until the danger has passed and breaking into a run only if the predator comes too close. These hares are good swimmers and will plunge into ponds or rivers to escape a predator.

Their preferred habitat is a mixture of dense, brushy cover interspersed with forest, especially conifers and the cedar-alder stands associated with wet soils. During the day, the hares remain in the thickets resting, and at night, they forage along thicket and forest edges. They do not favor mature hardwood forests. Their diet is extremely generalized: dozens of different herbs and tender twigs in summer and bark, buds and twigs in winter. Fast-growing trees such as willow, poplar, alder and young conifers are preferred.

Hares can be tremendously abundant, which affects virtually every major predator and many herbivores in the north-temperate forest community. They may compete with moose and deer for browse. They play a role in the thinning of naturally dense stands of forest, especially after forest fires, and they profoundly affect the density and abundance of some predators, particularly the lynx.

SNOWSHOE HARE
Lepus americanus

Mammal: *Lepus americanus*, snowshoe hare, varying hare

Meaning of Name: *Lepus* (hare); *americanus* (of America)

Description: very broad hind feet; in summer, pelage has three different-colored layers that distinguish it from the other two *Lepus* species; rusty or dark brown pelage with a blackish mid-dorsal line and gray flanks; ventrally, it is white; cinnamon-brown face, legs and throat; brown ears with black tip behind and edged with creamy white; tail is black on top and white below; the soles of the feet are densely furred, and the hind feet are padded with stiff hairs; in winter, pelage changes to varying degrees of white, depending on the amount of daylight, and tips of ears are black

Total Length: 14.3 to 20.5 inches

Tail: 0.9 to 2.2 inches

Weight: male, 3.2 pounds (November); female, 3.4 pounds (November); weight fluctuates, with peaks in December and June

Gestation: 34 to 40 days

Offspring: 1 to 8 (usually 2 to 4); as many as 4 litters per year (first litter is the smallest)

Age of Maturity: the spring following birth

Longevity: 3 to 5 years in the wild; up to 8 years in captivity

Diet: green succulent vegetation (usually clovers, grasses, sedges, ferns and forbs); in winter, buds, twigs, bark and evergreen leaves of woody plants; also frozen meat; can be cannibalistic; coprophagous

Habitat: dense second-growth forests, swamps and thickets

Predators: great horned owl, great gray owl, barred owl, goshawk, lynx, bobcat, red fox, coyote, wolf, black bear, mink and weasel

Dental Formula:
2/1, 0/0, 3/2, 3/3 = 28 teeth

THE 10-YEAR CYCLE

In 1865, the Hudson's Bay Company was flooded with snowshoe hare pelts. By 1870, only a trickle was being offered by trappers. In 1875, snowshoe pelts poured in again in tremendous numbers, hundreds of thousands, and again in 1885, 1895, 1905, 1915 .... Every 10 years, the fur returns peaked and then declined sharply. They stayed low, almost zero, for a couple of years and then grew explosively. These fur returns had nothing to do with fur prices; they reflected tremendous changes in the density of snowshoe hares, estimated to peak in some areas at 10,000 per square mile and then decline to 1 per square mile.

The snowshoe is an important element in the northern coniferous-forest food web, and the cycle has an impact on the populations of lynx, coyote, fox, mink, marten and fisher. The most dramatic effect is on the lynx, which shows the same cyclical change in abundance as the hare population but slightly out of phase with it.

The fact that both lynx and snowshoe

The snowshoe hare, with its great population fluctuations, affects the fortunes of most of the boreal forest's carnivores.

hares show the same periodicity in their cycles and the observation that lynx feed heavily on snowshoe hares gave rise to the suggestion that predation by lynx was responsible for the cycle. The idea was that the lynx are always slightly behind the hare in population growth because they reproduce more slowly and it takes time to convert hares into new lynx. The hare population would peak ahead of the lynx, and then the next generation of lynx would send the hare population crashing down. This has not proved to be the case. The cycle of growth and decline in the lynx population seems to be a product of the hare cycle and not its cause.

Snowshoe hares reach the carrying capacity of the environment and are limited by food before lynx populations are ever large enough to control or over-harvest them. The hare population crashes because of a lack of food and because of diseases that ravage the weakened and overcrowded animals. Aggression among crowded animals lowers the reproductive rate. The lynx and other predators appear to hasten the drop and keep the population low for longer. When the hare population declines and remains at very low densities, other predator populations drop, the thick, brushy herbaceous vegetation rebounds and the hares can then begin an explosive growth phase.

The length of the cycle is not uniform across the entire range of the snowshoe hare, and it is not perfectly regular. Some areas appear to have a 6-year cycle, others a 12-year cycle, which is what one would expect, since food, winter mortality, diseases and a variety of predator populations are all involved. Nevertheless, it is remarkable that the cycle is synchronized over huge areas that involve thousands of square miles. One explanation is that as populations grow, immigration from the choicest dense habitats quickly distributes both hares and predators over a wide area, so a few small local populations are soon converted into a large continuous and synchronous population.

ARCTIC HARE *Lepus arcticus*

The arctic hare is a more northern version of the snowshoe hare. The most northern of all lagomorphs, it extends high into the Arctic archipelago. Accordingly, it is much larger and more thickset than most other hares, with longer, finer fur and shorter ears. It lives on the tundra, which is frozen for much of the year, and it has some adaptations for extracting plants from the hard, dense crust of ice that can cover the low-growing flora. Its incisors are long and shaped differently from those of other hares, and the large claws on all four feet enable it to scrape and chisel away snow and ice to expose its food.

Arctic hares eat a wide variety of

Mammal: *Lepus arcticus*, arctic hare
Meaning of Name: *Lepus* (hare);
arcticus (of the Arctic)
Description: pure white in winter with moderately long, black-tipped ears; summer coat, which is carried for only a short time, varies depending on latitude—can be bluish gray with a frosting of white, white with a cinnamon or gray wash or cinnamon with pinkish buff mottling; tail remains white; undersides of feet are covered with a yellowish brush and have long, strong curved claws
Total Length: male, 23.5 to 31.5 inches; female, 23.8 to 28 inches (female average slightly larger than the male)
Tail: male, 1.6 to 4 inches; female, 1.9 to 2.9 inches
Weight: 6 to 12 pounds
Gestation: 50 days
Offspring: 2 to 8 (average 5); 1 litter per year
Age of Maturity: 1 year
Longevity: not known (probably up to 5 years)
Diet: low-growing tundra plants, twigs and roots of arctic willow and crowberry; meat and seaweed
Habitat: only tundra, beyond the tree line
Predators: arctic fox, wolf, ermine, snowy owl, rough-legged hawk
Dental Formula:
2/1, 0/0, 3/2, 3/3 = 28 teeth

A larger, more thickset version of the snowshoe hare, an arctic hare mother nurses her litter.

plants—herbs in the summer and exposed twigs of shrubs in winter. They will also eat meat given the opportunity. Fox trappers who use meat for bait often catch hares instead of foxes.

Predators such as wolves, arctic foxes, hawks and snowy owls feed on arctic hare, so the hare's tame behavior toward humans seems strange: They show little reaction except to hop away to maintain some distance. Dogs and wolves produce the expected flight, which may involve a strange kangaroo-style hopping on the hind legs. This presumably allows the hare to scan the terrain for wolves that have circled for ambush. Use of the kangaroo hop seems to be correlated with the openness of the terrain. Arctic hares display the sedentary behavior typical of hares, which permits them to build up a series of runways and escape routes.

The short summer of the high Arctic appears to restrict them to a single clutch of up to eight offspring that grow at twice the rate of other hare species, reaching up to 8½ pounds by summer's end.

Arctic hares also undergo population cycles, but these cycles have not been well studied. High populations may account for observations of more than a hundred hares feeding together—they may sometimes act like mildly gregarious grazers, akin to other herbivores that herd together.

WHITE-TAILED JACKRABBIT
Lepus townsendii

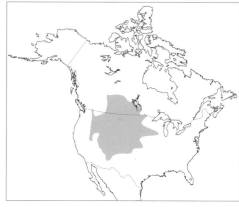

Mammal: *Lepus townsendii*, white-tailed jackrabbit

Meaning of Name: *Lepus* (hare); *townsendii* (named after J.K. Townsend, an ornithologist and author who explored the Rockies in 1834)

Description: uniformly brownish gray with a hoary face; gray ears are rimmed with white and have prominent black tips; gray throat; white underparts and hind feet; buffy forelegs; tail is white above and below; in the southern part of its range, it is more buffy; in winter, coat is white and ears are black-tipped

Total Length: 19.5 to 27.5 inches

Tail: 2.5 to 4.4 inches

Weight: 4.9 to 9.9 pounds

Gestation: 42 days

Offspring: 3 to 6 (usually 4); 1 or possibly 2 litters per year

Age of Maturity: the spring following birth

Longevity: not known (probably up to 5 years)

Diet: grasses, clovers, cultivated grains and alfalfa; in winter, twigs, buds, hay and bark of shrubs and trees

Habitat: open grassland, pastures, cultivated grainfields, sagebrush plains

Predators: coyote, wolf, fox, large hawks and owls, bobcat and eagles

Dental Formula:
2/1, 0/0, 3/2, 3/3 = 28 teeth

A litter of white-tailed jackrabbits, above, shows the white-rimmed ears and browny gray colors of the species' spring, summer and autumn fur. Its winter coat is white, and the ears are tipped with black. Left: With big, long ears for predator detection and huge hind legs for high-speed running, the white-tailed jackrabbit is perfectly designed for wide open spaces.

WHITE-TAILED JACKRABBIT
Lepus townsendii

The white-tailed jackrabbit is a creature of the great plains and prairies. The adaptations that characterize hares are all highly developed in this species. It has powerful hind legs capable of sprinting at speeds of up to 40 miles per hour and of making great 5-yard leaps. This hare's extremely large ears are used to detect predators; when the hare hears something suspicious, it raises and swivels its ears to triangulate and pinpoint the source of the sound.

The ears also serve as heat radiators. During the heat of the prairie summer, jackrabbits can erect their ears and dilate the blood capillaries in them to give off excess body heat. This reduces some of the need for cooling through the evaporation of their perspiration.

Jackrabbits often live in areas where water is usually in short supply. To reduce the amount of water lost by sweating, jackrabbits can let their body temperature rise. Normally, they have a body temperature of 98.6 to 100.4 degrees F, but in the hot noontime part of the day, their temperature may rise to 105.8 degrees. They can also concentrate urine and feces to reduce water loss through excretion.

Jackrabbits follow the typical pattern of grassland animals of having larger home ranges than forest animals. The home range of a jackrabbit has been measured at 220 acres—on average, many times larger than that of a snowshoe hare. They show none of the tendency toward gregariousness that is known in other hares.

RODENTS *Rodentia*

Rodents have chewed, chiseled and gnawed their way to the top of all the mammal orders, so today, they form the most populous mammal group. Nearly 40 percent of all mammalian species are rodents; they are found in almost every terrestrial habitat on every continent. All rodents are similar in design. They have small bodies, but they owe their biological success to their chisel-like, perpetually growing incisors.

Rodent classification is largely based on their gnawing and chewing abilities. Different families of rodents have developed different dental, skull and muscle patterns according to how and what they eat. These animals are basically vegetarians and can gnaw through the toughest tree bark and crack open the hardest nuts with their teeth. The cutting edge of their incisors is sharpened by the chewing motion itself. A hard enamel layer, which is often augmented by red and orange iron compounds, coats the front of these teeth, but the back portion is soft and uncoated. As the rodent gnaws, the back of the tooth wears away faster than the front, a process that shapes the tooth edge into a sharp chisel.

To make gnawing easier, rodents can pull their lips out of the way of their incisors. They have a large gap between their incisors and their molars, and they curl their lips backward into it while chewing. This behavior also permits the rodent to exclude such unwanted debris as wood, nut hulls and soil from its diet.

Rodents' molars are also highly specialized, although the type of specialization varies from one species to another. In some rodents, the molars grind with a complicated but efficient rotary action, enabling them to chew hard plant products. In others, the molars as well as the incisors are renewed by constant growth.

The earliest known rodents were squirrel-like creatures called *sciuromorphs* that lived more than 50 million years ago. They were apparently less efficient at gnawing and chewing than their descendants are. For example, they had weakly developed jaw muscles (known as masseters) and so could not pull the lower jaw forward effectively. By comparison, such rodents as the guinea pig of the Caviidae family have much larger masseters for more efficient gnawing. Mouselike rodents in the suborder Myomorpha have the largest masseters of all and are consequently the most efficient gnawers of the three basic rodent groups.

The fossil record indicates that rodents have recently experienced an explosive diversification and speciation. Unlike many of the large mammal groups, they have suffered few extinctions, and their evolution into different species has been so rapid and extensive that the taxonomic classification of rodents remains unclear.

Like most other squirrels, the Columbian ground squirrel is omnivorous, and when the opportunity presents itself, it will attack and eat such animals as insects, snakes and mice. Its diet also includes all plant parts.

MOUNTAIN BEAVER

Aplodontiidae

MOUNTAIN BEAVER *Aplodontia rufa*

The sole surviving species of an ancient rodent family, the mountain beaver is one of the world's most primitive living rodents. Its family originated some 50 to 65 million years ago in North America and spread to Europe and Asia. At that time, there were several different genera within the family, but all except the mountain beaver became extinct. This may have happened because of the species' need for moist habitats, which became scarce during the dry episodes of the Tertiary period.

Aside from the fact that both are rodents, the mountain beaver and the common beaver are not related. Mountain beavers are terrestrial animals found only in the mild, moist forests of the Pacific coast.

The mountain beaver requires a wet environment because it cannot efficiently regulate its body moisture or its cooling system. At temperatures above 84 degrees F, it begins to suffer heat stress, and if the temperature goes as high as 90 to 95 degrees, it will die within two hours. The mountain beaver cannot cope with drought either. Its kidneys are primitive in design, and as a result, it excretes a large volume of water in its urine.

Aplodontia rufa, however, does have several behaviors that enable it to overcome problems of heat stress and water conservation. For example, it constructs extensive systems of underground burrows and runways that provide it with a cool, stable, humid environment. The tunnels of one individual may occupy an area 100 yards in diameter.

A vegetarian, the mountain beaver meets its water needs through the great variety of succulent plants it consumes. It leaves its tunnel to harvest grasses, twigs and shrubs, then drags them back into its burrow to eat, further reducing possible environmental stress and minimizing the animal's exposure to predators. The mountain beaver climbs trees to clip off branches and twigs, and it also makes hay piles. Both fresh and wilted vegetation are cached in the central feeding chamber, where it stores as much as a bushel of material so that it can spend virtually all of the autumn and winter below ground.

Mountain beavers have a unique defecation system: They extract dung pellets with their teeth as the pellets emerge from the anus, then store them in piles in special chambers. Like rabbits and pikas, they eat some of this dung, presumably to extract nutrients such as the B vitamins produced by microbial fermentation.

The mountain beaver's slow speed makes it easy prey for a wide variety of predators, including wolves, coyotes, weasels, hawks and owls. Given the beaver's penchant for living in loose soils, even bears find them readily available, requiring only a little digging.

One of the world's most primitive rodents, the mountain beaver is found only in the mild, moist forests of the West Coast. A slow-moving animal, it is vulnerable to a wide variety of predators, from eagles to bears.

MOUNTAIN BEAVER
Aplodontia rufa

Mammal: *Aplodontia rufa*, mountain beaver
Meaning of Name: *Aplodontia* refers to simple cheek teeth; *rufa* (red or ruddy)
Description: stout; small, rounded ears, short legs and plantigrade feet with fleshy soles and long claws; coarse, dark blackish brown coat; no apparent tail
Total Length: male, 13.2 to 14.9 inches; female, 13.8 to 14.1 inches
Tail: male, 1.2 to 1.4 inches; female, 0.9 to 1.3 inches
Weight: 2 to 3.3 pounds
Gestation: 28 to 30 days
Offspring: 2 to 6 (usually 3); 1 litter per year
Age of Maturity: 2 years or older
Longevity: 5 to 10 years in the wild
Diet: strictly herbivorous; in summer, forbs and deciduous plants; in winter, bark, twigs, needles and leaves; reingests special green feces
Habitat: dense, wet thickets and moist forests; often found in initial seral stages after a forest has been clear-cut
Predators: puma, lynx, coyote, fox, wolf, bear, skunk, mink, fisher, weasel, eagles, hawks and owls
Dental Formula:
1/1, 0/0, 2/1, 3/3 = 22 teeth

SQUIRRELS *Sciuridae*

Squirrels must count as the most familiar of animals. Every continent except Australia is home to a rich array of squirrels. They are often active in daylight, they frequently live in large, conspicuous colonies, and they are tolerant of the presence of humans. In tropical regions and in the grasslands and open habitats of temperate areas, squirrels are often the dominant mammals. Many people rarely see other common small mammals such as shrews, bats, mice and moles, but almost everyone is acquainted with some kind of squirrel.

Squirrels have very generalized characteristics that have enabled them to spread into a wide variety of habitats and to develop numerous species. They first appeared some 30 million years ago in North America but soon spread to the Old World, where they radiated into Africa and Southeast Asia.

There are three basic groups of squirrels: ground squirrels, arboreal (tree-dwelling) squirrels and nocturnal flying squirrels. Ground squirrels are diurnal and tend to live in colonies that often have highly developed social systems. Almost all of them are seed eaters and grazers. Tree squirrels are also diurnal but usually live solitary territorial lives. They feed largely on nuts and fruit.

Of all the small mammals, squirrels have the largest brains relative to their body size. Their intelligence is reflected in their diverse diets, complicated vocalizations and tendency to develop complex social systems. Squirrels are among the most intelligent of rodents.

TERRITORIAL ECONOMICS

Some species of squirrel are aggressively territorial; others are not. During the breeding season, some males may exclude other males; pregnant and lactating females tend to exclude all intruders. In some species, territorial exclusivity may even extend beyond the reproductive period and is probably related to defending foraging territories and food caches.

Although territoriality has its benefits—a secure food cache and mating area—it also has its costs. As squirrels battle for territory, they expose themselves to predators and expend great amounts of energy. Territoriality can only evolve when the benefits exceed the costs.

Among the western chipmunk species, territoriality depends on such factors as habitat, food supply and climate. The alpine chipmunk is strongly territorial, primarily because the foraging season is short and food is limited. With a territory of boulder fields, where rocks and crevices offer ready refuge from predators, the dangers to an alpine chipmunk defending its territory are relatively low. The yellow-pine chipmunk, which lives lower down in the pine forest, is also strongly territorial and can safely defend a rich nut crop in an area that has abundant cover where it can hide from predators.

By contrast to these species, the least chipmunk is not territorial at all. It lives in hot, dry habitats,

Although the flying squirrel is common in North America, few people ever see one. These shy squirrels shun daylight, preferring to glide through their forest habitat by night, maneuvering around tree trunks and other obstacles in graceful 90-degree turns.

where the cost of territorial chases and disputes is physiologically high. It is active only during the cool of early morning and probably has little time for defensive disputes. The lodgepole-pine chipmunk is also nonterritorial. Presumably, it can defend nut trees the way the yellow-pine chipmunk does, but in its habitat, there is little protective shrubbery for hiding from predators. Defending nut trees would probably result in a high predation rate.

Similar observations about the costs and benefits of territoriality have been made for red squirrels. In the central and northern parts of their range, they are aggressively territorial, but where they overlap in the south with gray squirrels, their system breaks down. The larger gray squirrels do not respond to their aggressive behavior, making territoriality a waste of time and energy for the red squirrel. Douglas' squirrels stop their territorial behavior when the pollen-rich male Douglas fir cones are ready for harvesting. The cones last only a few weeks and do not store well; they are also so plentiful that there is no benefit in defending a tree. The most economical tactic is simply to keep quiet and eat as many of the cones as possible.

One of the three basic groups of squirrels, the ground squirrels, many of which have highly developed social systems, are active by day, when they graze and gather seeds.

YELLOW-PINE CHIPMUNK
Tamias amoenus

YELLOW-PINE CHIPMUNK
Tamias amoenus

The yellow-pine chipmunk is a specialist of the dry, open and rocky habitats that are found in yellow pine and Douglas fir forests. In mountainous areas, this chipmunk ranges widely, from the lowlands all the way to the edge of the tree line.

The burrow system is usually less than a yard long and serves as a storehouse for seeds, especially pine seeds. In the summer, the yellow-pine chipmunk eats fungi, the needles of coniferous trees and the leaves of herbaceous plants, while in winter, it forages more above ground than other chipmunk species do. There is a single spring breeding season, and females produce a single litter per year.

By specializing in dry yellow pine forests, the yellow-pine chipmunk has minimized the amount of competition it faces from the other species of western chipmunk.

Mammal: *Tamias amoenus*, yellow-pine chipmunk

Meaning of Name: *Tamias* (distributor, steward, one who stores and takes care of provisions); *amoenus* (delightful)

Description: ochraceous color with cinnamon flanks and brownish gray rump; ears black dorsally, edged with white posteriorly; buff to white underneath; tail rusty above and tawny underneath; cheeks crossed with three dark stripes, the middle one running through the eye; five dorsal dark stripes with four paler stripes in between

Total Length: 8.4 to 9.1 inches

Tail: 3 to 4.3 inches

Weight: 1.6 to 2.2 ounces

Gestation: 28 days

Offspring: 5 to 7; 1 litter per year

Age of Maturity: the spring following birth

Longevity: at least 5 years in the wild

Diet: primarily a seed eater; nuts are not as important as they are in other chipmunks' diets; eats some insects but less frequently than other chipmunks; fungi

Habitat: open coniferous forests, especially burned-over areas with stumps and brush; also brushy zones on the borders of the open alpine tundra

Predators: long-tailed weasel is the most dangerous predator; also pine marten, rattlesnake, pygmy owl and hawks

Dental Formula:
1/1, 0/0, 2/1, 3/3 = 22 teeth

LEAST CHIPMUNK
Tamias minimus

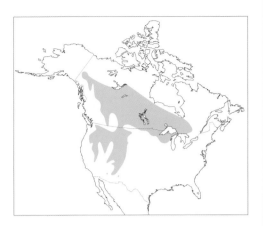

Mammal: *Tamias minimus*, least chipmunk; smallest of chipmunks

Meaning of Name: *Tamias* (distributor, steward, one who stores and takes care of provisions); *minimus* (least)

Description: small with three dark brown stripes crossing the cheeks and two white lines between them which terminate at the ears; five brown-edged black stripes run across the back to the base of the tail, and the medial ones are mixed with gray; ochraceous shoulders, gray rump and legs and white underparts; buffy orange tail; brown ears with pale gray spots behind them; internal cheek pouches

Total Length: male, 8.4 to 12.8 inches; female, 8.9 to 9.4 inches

Tail: male, 3.8 to 4.1 inches; female, 3.9 to 4.2 inches

Weight: 1.2 to 1.9 ounces

Gestation: 28 to 31 days

Offspring: 2 to 7 (usually 5 or 6); 1 litter per year

Age of Maturity: the spring following birth

Longevity: 6 years in captivity

Diet: mostly vegetarian but remains opportunistic and will eat insects and other animal material; seeds, berries, nuts, fruits.

Habitat: alpine tundra; northern mixed hardwood and coniferous forests, especially in open jack pine stands and second growth after fires and forestry programs; shrubby growth, lakeshores, forest edges, brush and log piles

Predators: hawks, owls, snakes, ermine, weasel, mink, grizzly bear, red fox and domestic dog and cat

Dental Formula:
1/1, 0/0, 2/1, 3/3 = 22 teeth

LEAST CHIPMUNK
Tamias minimus

The least chipmunk is the smallest of the western chipmunks, a group of 21 species that are all very similar in appearance. Accurate identification can be difficult, and experts must rely on differences in the size, shape and sculpturing of the penis bone to differentiate among them.

Unlike most other western chipmunks, the least chipmunk occupies many different kinds of habitats and has a broad geographic range. This species is found in every habitat from open

The least chipmunk is able to forage on the tiny grass seeds, small berries and insects ignored by the larger members of its family.

plains to the edge of the tundra, although its prime habitat is the boreal forest, especially in clearings.

Most of its activities are similar to those of the eastern chipmunk. It tends to eat smaller seeds than eastern chipmunks do, even opting for the tiny seeds of blueberries, and many kinds of grasses. It consumes more insects and fewer vertebrates than the eastern chipmunk and normally has only a single litter each year.

RED-TAILED CHIPMUNK
Tamias ruficaudus

The red-tailed chipmunk is one of the larger, more arboreal chipmunks, living in dense coniferous forests where it is active among the lower branches. In regions where the yellow-pine chipmunk and red-tailed chipmunk occur together, the red-tailed chipmunk usually lives at higher altitudes. Although it sometimes nests in tree cavities, the red-tailed chipmunk usually makes summer nests of balls of grass hidden in the dense foliage of trees 15 feet or more above the ground. In winter, it moves to typical chipmunk underground burrows. Its diet is more herbivorous than that of many western chipmunks, consisting mostly of leaves, buds and shoots.

CACHING IN

Many small rodents cannot hibernate, because their metabolism is too high and their body too small to put on enough fat for a northern winter without feeding. Caching food has been their solution. The biggest stashes are built by the biggest rodents. Beavers, for example, may cache a mound of tree branches several yards in diameter. The edible part of the cache is bark, which is available all winter long, but by caching it underwater, the beaver minimizes its predation risk. Another winter bark eater, the porcupine, has not evolved caching behavior—none of its tropical ancestors needed it. Consequently, it must climb trees to keep feeding all winter and is highly exposed to predators. Fishers catch large numbers of winter-foraging porcupines, and horned owls will pluck them from the branches. It would seem that porcupines could profit from a cache, even if it were only at the base of a tree with a rock crevice close at hand.

Predator pressure may favor caching in beavers, but most small rodents cache because of energetic necessity.

Burrowing root feeders such as prairie and woodland voles build large caches of roots and tubers, high-energy foods that store well. One prairie vole cache excavated in Manitoba contained an amazing harvest of 1,176 lily bulbs, 687 onion bulbs, 583 sunflower roots and 417 pasqueflower roots. Such a concentration of resources undoubtedly attracts cache robbers and requires investment in defense. In addition to depredations of other voles, humans often rob caches. Plains Indians sought prairie vole caches and the Inuit those of yellow-cheeked voles. Native peoples are reported to have trained dogs to sniff out the licorice root stashed by tundra rodents.

The risk of theft strongly influences the hoarding strategies of squirrels. *Sciurus* species such as gray squirrels hide each acorn and nut separately to decrease the risk of losing an entire stash. Red squirrels that feed on large piles of conifer seeds, on the other hand, build them into vast central middens containing bushels of cones. Red squirrels can afford to concentrate their food stores, because they normally have to defend them only against other red squirrels. Each cone is a small fraction of the total store, and the territorial owner will detect losses before they become serious. If their territories overlap those of gray squirrels, red squirrels must scatter their hoards, since gray squirrels ignore red squirrels' threats.

Chipmunks also use scatter hoarding to deal with the problem of theft. The burrow serves as a primary storage site, but nearby chipmunks frequently rob their neighbors' burrows. Large cheek pouches enable a chipmunk thief to run in and quickly carry off prized items such as lily bulbs. Thieving chipmunks will make repeated trips to a neighbor's burrow for as long as they can get away with it. The scatter hoards of the chipmunk are smaller and better hidden than the main burrow hoard. When its burrow is robbed, a chipmunk uses the scatter hoards to replace what it lost from the burrow. Scatter hoards are a

RED-TAILED CHIPMUNK
Tamias ruficaudus

Mammal: *Tamias ruficaudus*, red-tailed chipmunk
Meaning of Name: *Tamias* (distributor, steward, one who stores and takes care of provisions); *ruficaudus* (red tail)
Description: large, brightly colored; tawny shoulders and sides, gray rump; three prominent black dorsal stripes, paler side stripes; cheeks have two white stripes and three brown stripes; tail is rufous above and dark red below
Total Length: 8.8 to 9.8 inches
Tail: 4 to 4.8 inches
Weight: 2 ounces
Gestation: 30 days
Offspring: 4 to 6; 1 litter per year
Age of Maturity: the spring following birth
Longevity: not known
Diet: seeds of fir trees; seeds, leaves, buds and shoots of honeysuckle, black locust, cranberries and knotweed
Habitat: spruce-fir, pine-larch-fir or yellow pine coniferous forests; talus slides; mountains up to timberline
Predators: not known
Dental Formula:
1/1, 0/0, 2/1, 3/3 = 22 teeth

kind of theft insurance, and when there is no theft, many are left to rot or sprout if they contain seeds. Chipmunks also place scatter hoards in spots where they can keep an eye on the burrow while they are working and rush back as soon as they spot a thief.

Gray squirrels' scatter hoarding is less easily explained. Flying squirrels in the same forest cache piles of nuts in tree holes. The strategy may be related to the fact that flying squirrels are much poorer

runners on the ground than gray squirrels. Tree holes for caches are limited and must be filled with several nuts. Flying squirrels trade off the risk of theft against greater safety from predators, while the day-active and visually acute gray squirrels may suffer less predation and be more concerned about minimizing robbery.

Lagomorphs such as pikas also store vegetable food. They use a haying technique, as do wood rats, stacking vegeta-

The eastern chipmunk spends most of the daylight hours stuffing its cheek pouches with food in order to build up large caches to tide it over the winter months.

tion to dry to prevent it from composting in the cache. This is clearly a case of convergent behavioral evolution, a phenomenon in which two different and unrelated species confronted with the same problem (a long, barren winter) have evolved the same solution.

EASTERN CHIPMUNK
Tamias striatus

The eastern chipmunk is one of the most beautifully marked and easily identified squirrels. Many of the rural homes and cottages in eastern North America support a resident population of tame chipmunks, as the species is cute and readily taught to beg for food.

The chipmunk's attractive stripes were not developed with people in mind, however, but as a form of camouflage. Chipmunks are most active during the day when the sun is casting strong shadows. As such, they are potential prey for birds, but their striped pattern makes it difficult for aerial predators to spot them among the shadows cast by tree branches and other plants.

The native habitat of the eastern chipmunk is the deciduous hardwood

Harvesting seeds and nuts is only one of the problems an eastern chipmunk must deal with. Theft of its cached winter food supply by neighboring chipmunks is a constant threat.

EASTERN CHIPMUNK
Tamias striatus

Mammal: *Tamias striatus*, eastern chipmunk
Meaning of Name: *Tamias* (distributor, steward, one who stores and takes care of provisions); *striatus* (striped)
Description: tawny stripes from whiskers to below the ear, which distinguish it from all other mammals over most of its range; buff cheeks and eye rings; five dark brown to black stripes down its back, separated by four buff lines from shoulders to rump; reddish hips and rump; buff flanks and forefeet; white underparts; openings in sides of mouth lead to pouches for carrying food (each pouch is almost as large as the head when totally filled)
Total Length: 9.1 to 11.8 inches
Tail: 2.6 to 4.3 inches
Weight: 2.3 to 4.5 ounces
Gestation: 31 days
Offspring: 1 to 9 (usually 4 or 5); 2 litters per year
Age of Maturity: 1 year; occasionally, a female will produce a litter at the age of 3 months
Longevity: 2 to 5 years in the wild; 5 to 12 years in captivity
Diet: major part of diet consists of reproductive parts of plants (bulbs, seeds, fruits and nuts); also green vegetation, mushrooms, fruits, berries, corn, insects, slugs, worms, frogs, mice, snakes, salamanders and eggs
Habitat: deciduous forests with cover and brush; will inhabit more open areas if the earth is porous enough for tunneling
Predators: hawks, fox, raccoon, weasel, domestic cat, snakes, common raven, great blue heron, lynx and coyote
Dental Formula:
1/1, 0/0, 1/1, 3/3 = 20 teeth

Readily tamed and taught to beg for food, the eastern chipmunk is easily identified by its striped markings, which serve as camouflage from aerial predators.

to eat. In mild weather, it may go above ground to forage, but it usually relies on its large food caches.

The chipmunk devotes much of the summer months to storing food in its burrows, acquiring up to 1½ gallons of tree seeds, nuts and plant tubers that store well. In addition, it eats foliage, buds, many kinds of berries and fruit, insects, mice, frogs, slugs and bird eggs. There are even reports of chipmunks attacking and eating garter and red-bellied snakes.

The social life of the eastern chipmunk is territorial and solitary. Males and females have their own separate burrow systems that they defend from other chipmunks of both sexes. Only in mating season will females tolerate the intrusion of a male into their burrows. Their small home ranges are usually less than 2½ acres in size and sometimes overlap with those of other chipmunks; the size of the home range depends on food availability. They defend their burrow systems vigorously—often with a noisy, scolding barrage of chirping and a display of tail-jerking—as there is always the risk of robbery from vital food caches.

Male chipmunks remain sexually active from late winter to autumn, which allows females to give birth twice a year, in early spring and again in late summer. The young, which may number up to nine in a litter, are born blind and naked, the usual pattern for underground mammals. They remain with the mother for six weeks before dispersing to establish their own burrows and food stores. This adolescent period is a time of great danger, as a variety of predatory birds, mammals and snakes feed on the young chipmunks while they build new burrows. Even when established in their burrows, chipmunks must watch for weasels and snakes, which enter the tunnels to prey on them.

Eastern chipmunks climb well and are sometimes seen high up in trees, but they are not as adept as tree squirrels in an arboreal habitat and thus have trouble competing.

forest. It is most abundant in mature stands of beech, maple and other trees that produce large nut crops. The chipmunk eats many other foods, however, and can be found in all stages of forest growth, including mixed coniferous-deciduous stands. Because they spend most of their time on the ground foraging for nuts and other foods, chipmunks prefer areas with rock piles and other forms of protection into which they can easily escape from predators. They rely on vision to detect enemies, so prefer open areas to shade.

Chipmunks have underground nests and only rarely live in tree cavities even though they are agile climbers. They build a twisting system of burrows up to 12 feet long that lead to a nest about 3 feet below the surface. In addition to the nest, the burrow system includes storage tunnels, escape entrances and a work hole. The chipmunk takes care to conceal its burrowing activities, removing the excavated dirt through a work hole (built solely for the purpose) by carrying the soil out in its cheek pouches. It then spreads the soil around the vegetation so that there is no pile of dirt to tell predators where or how fresh the burrow system is. The chipmunk plugs its work hole when not in use and camouflages the regular entrance. It enlarges its tunnel system each year, so by the end of its two-to-five-year life, it has dug an extensive network of side tunnels in addition to the main one. Sometimes, when the original resident of a burrow dies, a new chipmunk takes over and continues to elaborate on the tunnels.

Unlike many other ground-nesting squirrels, the chipmunk does not enter deep hibernation in winter. Instead, it goes into a torpor in which its metabolism is reduced. Periodically, it awakens

Mammal: *Tamias townsendii*, Townsend's chipmunk; largest of western chipmunks
Meaning of Name: *Tamias* (distributor, steward, one who stores and takes care of provisions); *townsendii* (named after J.K. Townsend, its discoverer)
Description: dark brown, which offers little contrast to the dull yellowish or grayish light stripes along its side and back, making it difficult to see; two brown stripes cross buff cheeks; tan underparts; brownish stripe below ear; reddish tail bordered by subterminal black band and gray tips
Total Length: male, 9.7 to 10.4 inches; female, 10.4 to 11 inches
Tail: male, 4.1 to 4.7 inches; female, 4.7 to 5.1 inches
Weight: 2.5 to 4.3 ounces
Gestation: 30 days
Offspring: 2 to 7 (usually 5)
Age of Maturity: the spring following birth
Longevity: 7 years in the wild
Diet: omnivore; diet includes roots, bulbs, grasses, seeds, berries and nuts as well as a substantial amount of animal matter in the form of insects, fledglings and eggs; also cannibalistic
Habitat: dense coniferous forests and coastal lowlands; often lives in subclimax brush and log habitat, since much of its natural habitat has been logged over
Predators: hawks, golden eagle, badger, marten, fox, skunk, wolverine, lynx, coyote, fisher and raccoon; weasel is main predator
Dental Formula:
1/1, 0/0, 2/1, 3/3 = 22 teeth

The largest chipmunk, the Townsend's chipmunk has adapted to life in the tall forests by becoming a climber, building summer tree nests and caching its food high off the ground.

TOWNSEND'S CHIPMUNK
Tamias townsendii

Townsend's chipmunk is the largest species of chipmunk. It favors thick, tangled vegetation and is secretive and shy compared with smaller species. Its coat is darker than other chipmunks', perhaps reflecting its choice of habitat. It is found in the wet, humid Pacific-coast forests, which have far less sunlight than the habitats favored by light-coated species. It is more arboreal than most other chipmunks, climbing trees and shrubs to forage and building summer tree nests for caching food. Its diet is typical of chipmunks and includes a selection of plant parts and insects.

HOARY MARMOT
Marmota caligata

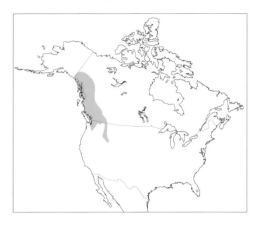

Mammal: *Marmota caligata*, hoary marmot; largest of the Sciuridae

Meaning of Name: *Marmota* (mountain mouse or rat); *caligata* (wearing boots); lower legs and feet are black, giving the appearance of boots; hoary indicates a grayish white coat

Description: head and shoulders are black and white; black "cap"; dark streaks on sides and white patch on muzzle; lower back and rump are grizzled gray washed with yellow; black feet; grayish white underparts

Total Length: 26.8 to 29.5 inches

Tail: 7 to 9.8 inches

Weight: 7.9 to 19.8 pounds; maximum 28.7 pounds

Gestation: 28 to 30 days

Offspring: 4 or 5

Age of Maturity: at least 2 years

Longevity: not known (probably 4 to 6 years)

Diet: herbivore; alpine grasses and forbs, roots, wildflowers and berries

Habitat: subalpine areas with lots of vegetation or rolling alpine meadows, rocky taluses and cliffs; also in the forest edge, where clearings provide food and rock piles provide shelter

Predators: grizzly bear, black bear, wolf and golden eagle; predators must be strong enough to dig a marmot out of its den

Dental Formula:
1/1, 0/0, 2/1, 3/3 = 22 teeth

The largest squirrel in North America, the hoary marmot has a thick silvery fur coat that adapts it for the cold climate of the western mountains.

HOARY MARMOT
Marmota caligata

Marmots are the largest of the North American squirrels. Unlike other groups of squirrels, the five species of marmots are grazers.

The hoary marmot is a huge squirrel, twice as large as a groundhog and the largest of all North American squirrels. Its large size is an adaptation for its life at high altitudes and in the far northern Rockies. The hoary marmot may spend two-thirds of its life hibernating. It pads itself with a layer of fat that may account for 20 percent of its weight and sleeps seven to eight months of the year when the mountain meadows are covered with snow. Like the yellow-bellied marmot, it dens under boulders and rockfalls as protection against digging bears. Hoary marmots are preyed upon by golden eagles, and they are extremely wary, giving a loud police-style whistle whenever they detect a potential predator.

Males establish polygynous harems similar to those of the yellow-bellied marmot. They seem to pursue a mixture of mate guarding and promiscuity that one observer has called "gallivanting." To maximize the number of females inseminated, they leave their core territory and copulate with females associated with other males. Male marmots provide no parental care.

YELLOW-BELLIED MARMOT
Marmota flaviventris

Yellow-bellied marmots live in mountain meadows. They choose a nest site among a pile of boulders at the base of a talus slope or rockfall. They work their nest and burrow system into soil found under and between boulders that prevent badgers and grizzly bears from digging them out. They also excavate a system of auxiliary burrows away from the main burrow system. Shallower and shorter than the main burrow, they run only a yard or two and provide the marmots with temporary refuge.

The yellow-bellied marmot is similar to the groundhog in its diet and deep-winter hibernation but differs in its breeding and social system. Where groundhogs are solitary for most of their adult life, this species has a harem system. A male defends a territory that excludes other males and includes territories of a variable number of females. Some males are unable to acquire a high-quality territory and exist as "satellites" without attracting any females.

In spring, females give birth to a clutch of three to eight altricial offspring. They spend the summer with their mother and may hibernate with her. Yellow-bellied marmots may begin hibernating as early as August in high mountain areas. Early hibernation gives them very little time to deposit the huge fat stores needed for the long winter. The largest old males are usually able to hibernate first, followed by the adult females and finally the young of the year, which begin a month or two after the older males have settled in. Hibernation dens are usually located in areas with heavy snow cover. Adults in a harem hibernate communally.

HAREMS: TO JOIN OR NOT TO JOIN

The breeding system of the yellow-bellied marmot is an example of how male and female reproductive strategies often conflict. Females seek to exclude other females—a strategy that will lower the reproductive success for the resident male. And males seek to increase their mating opportunities through polygyny, which is disadvantageous to the females.

Male yellow-bellied marmots practice resource-defense polygyny: They defend a resource that females find useful and, by excluding other males from the resource, gain exclusive access to the females. One male, for example, may have a territory containing one to four females that he defends and has exclusive sexual access to.

Genetically, the male harem master benefits from polygyny, because the more females he can mate with, the more offspring he will produce. However, the reverse is true for the females. Females must forage within the territory of the male. The more females within a harem, the fewer the food resources per female. This ratio is borne out by birth-rate statistics. As the harem size increases, the male reproductive success rate goes up, but the female reproductive success rate goes down. Marmot females who live monogamously produce several times as many offspring as the average female in a four-member harem, because females must compete for resources within the harem.

Yet there is a 1:1 gender ratio among marmots—just as many males as females. Why, then, do females join harems? Why aren't they all monogamous? Because all males and all male territories are not equal. Prime territory sites with good forage, lookouts for predators and burrow sites are limited, and only some of the males are vigorous enough to control access to them. Females may find it more advantageous to join a harem in a high-quality territory than to join a solitary male in a low-quality territory. Members of a group also benefit from the protection afforded by other members. When a predator is spotted, a marmot will give an alarm whistle that alerts the others. In spite of the added protection, how-

YELLOW-BELLIED MARMOT
Marmota flaviventris

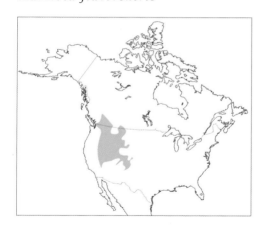

Mammal: *Marmota flaviventris*, yellow-bellied marmot
Meaning of Name: *Marmota* (mountain mouse or rat); *flaviventris* (yellow belly)
Description: heavy-bodied; overall yellowish brown color with buffy yellow neck, hips and belly; yellow patches on each side of neck; creamy-colored bar across bridge of nose and about the lips; pale brown feet; grizzled brown tail
Total Length: male, 18.4 to 26 inches; female, 19.1 to 25 inches
Tail: 5.2 to 7 inches
Weight: male, 4.9 to 11.5 pounds; female, 3.5 to 8.7 pounds
Gestation: 30 days
Offspring: 3 to 8 (usually 5); 1 litter per year
Age of Maturity: 2 years, but most do not mate until their third year
Longevity: at least 3 years
Diet: herbivore; selective with respect to the species of plant and parts of plant consumed; eats native forbs, grasses, sedges, clovers and alfalfa; can be cannibalistic
Habitat: rocky slopes or outcrops; on sides of mountains or other subalpine areas adjacent to lush meadows
Predators: eagle, badger, grizzly bear, wolf and puma (usually take immature animals)
Dental Formula:
1/1, 0/0, 2/1, 3/3 = 22 teeth

ever, it would probably still be better for a female's reproductive success rate if she were the only one in a territory, be it good or bad.

Females are aggressive toward other females from outside the group; within the group, they form dominance hierarchies and harass subordinates. Sometimes, a dominant female will try to bury a subordinate by plugging and stuffing a burrow entrance and may possibly kill the subordinate's offspring. Within the harem, females have a range of territorial strategies. Some females have exclusive territories, while others have overlapping territories. The amount of overlap may reflect status

differences; probably only dominant females are able to have an exclusive territory. Strife between females within a territory is usually lower if they are close genetic relatives such as sisters.

Females compete primarily for good den sites, ones that are well protected and close to prime foraging areas. These are, of course, in short supply. Long-term observations of yellow-bellied marmot colonies have shown that few new burrows are created in any single year. The older, more established burrows usually occupy the prime sites and are improved each year. An individual that chooses to leave the colony or is forced out must build a new burrow,

The yellow-bellied marmot female, like other marmot females, may become part of a harem but will defend its own territory within the larger male territory.

which will usually be in a marginal site, or else undertake a long, dangerous journey to uncolonized areas.

Marmots have a long prereproductive period of two or three years. Year-old males are driven out of the territory by the resident male. Females may drive young females out, but some may remain. Roughly half the females are forced to leave the colony and must try to join another male's harem or set up a den in a single male's territory.

GROUNDHOG *Marmota monax*

The groundhog, or woodchuck, an eastern marmot species, is the most widely distributed and best known of all the marmots. Like other marmots, it has a large, thickset body adapted for digging deep burrows. Its limbs are short and stout, and it has a short tail and a neck that is as thick and wide as its head. Its jaws and incisors are large and powerful, adapted for cutting down large volumes of vegetation. Since woodchucks are grazers, they prefer open areas and forest edges rather than the closed-canopy mature forests that are home to other squirrels. By clearing the eastern forests, humans have turned the woodchuck from a relatively rare animal into one of the most common.

Woodchucks are diurnal, foraging in early morning and late afternoon, especially when the weather is warm and sunny. Colder days find them most active when the sun reaches its peak. Sometimes, they climb fenceposts or small trees, where they sprawl across a high branch to sun themselves. At other times, they sit up at their main burrow entrance, watching alertly for predators and competitor groundhogs.

A groundhog will run for its burrow at the slightest hint of danger. The burrow is a fortress and may have 50 feet of tunnels running as deep as 16 feet underground. Each burrow has a main entrance that the groundhog selects for its view of the surrounding area. There may be three or four alternative entrances that provide both access and exit when it is chased by a predator. One of these entrances is usually a plunge hole with a vertical drop of more than 2 feet. A groundhog that is being chased can drop quickly down this hole and disappear. Normally, the plunge hole is inconspicuous and does not have a large pile of dirt around it— two factors that increase its effectiveness as an unexpected escape route.

All the larger carnivorous mammals and raptors will eat groundhogs if given the opportunity. When cornered, the groundhog is a formidable biter. Its large incisors can slice into flesh with ease, so most predators rely on stalking to catch the groundhog unaware; stealthy hunters such as foxes, coyotes and bobcats take more groundhogs than other predators do. Attempting to dig a groundhog out of its burrow is too dangerous and energy-intensive.

Woodchucks may build two dens: a deep one for overwintering located within the shelter of the forest and a shallow summer one situated in an open area close to foraging. The benefits of having two burrows seem to outweigh the extra energy required to dig them. With its summer home close to forage, the woodchuck expends less energy traveling to and from its food source and also has a quick escape route from predators. Its deep winter burrow keeps it warmer, thus reducing the energy output required for hibernating.

The groundhog is a true deep hibernator. It accumulates fat all summer long until shorter autumn days and foliage-killing frosts send it down into its burrow, where it becomes dormant. It hibernates in a sealed chamber below the frost line. In deep hibernation, its body temperature drops from the normal summer temperature of 95 degrees F to 43 to 46 degrees. Its heart rate slows from 100 beats per minute to 15, and oxygen consumption falls to one-tenth the normal rate. The woodchuck may breathe only once every six minutes when it is in deep hibernation. Hibernating animals lose 30 percent of their weight by burning body fat to keep from freezing. This is a large weight loss, but it is only one-seventh the amount of energy used over the same period by active animals. Hibernation is, therefore, an effective way to pass the winter, and it frees groundhogs from having to store food as nonhibernating squirrels do.

Groundhogs and other marmots are able to hibernate partly because of their large size. They may weigh as much as 14 pounds at full size, which gives them a slower metabolism than that of

GROUNDHOG *Marmota monax*

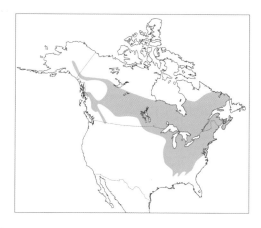

Mammal: *Marmota monax*, groundhog, woodchuck

Meaning of Name: *Marmota* (mountain mouse or rat); *monax* (solitary); "woodchuck" is the corruption of an Indian name used by trappers in northern Canada

Description: heavy-bodied and short-legged; buffy tips on guard hairs give the animal a grizzled appearance; the color is highly variable and contains a number of shades from pale buff to black; bushy dark brown or black tail; black or dark brown feet

Total Length: 18 to 25.7 inches

Tail: 4.1 to 6.4 inches

Weight: 4.9 to 14 pounds

Gestation: 31 to 33 days

Offspring: 1 to 9 (usually 4); 1 litter per year

Age of Maturity: may breed as yearlings, but most breed for the first time as 2-year-olds

Longevity: 4 to 6 years in the wild; 10 years in captivity

Diet: primarily a grazer; eats vegetative parts of plants, bark and twigs if no green leaves available; fond of fruits and vegetables; consumes a few insects and young birds of ground-nesting species

Habitat: well-drained open woods, pastures, fields, clearings and rocky ravines; the deforestation of eastern North America has helped it to prosper

Predators: hawks and rattlesnake eat young; bobcat, coyote, fox and domestic dog are only predators that have not been exterminated in its range

Dental Formula:
1/1, 0/0, 2/1, 3/3 = 22 teeth

smaller rodents. The larger the animal, the longer it can last on the same percentage of body fat. This can be clearly seen by comparing the over-winter weight loss in groundhogs of different ages and sizes. First-year groundhogs normally lose 50 percent of their body weight during hibernation and are probably severely stressed by springtime. Older and larger groundhogs may lose only a quarter of their body weight and so emerge from hibernation in much better condition.

Their large size and their need to endure a long winter hibernation may explain groundhogs' prolonged growth period. Unlike most other squirrels, which reach adult size at the end of their first summer, groundhogs continue to grow for three years and usually do not reproduce until their second year.

The territorial nature of groundhogs may also have contributed to their larger size. Groundhogs defend their burrows and foraging areas from other groundhogs. They are normally solitary creatures except during the spring mating season, when females will tolerate males. Males may fight with other males and often bear head wounds from bites. Groundhogs have a wide range of aggressive signals, including hisses, growls, shrieks and teeth chattering.

Females give birth in spring to a litter of one to nine helpless offspring. They are weaned six weeks later, but they may remain with the mother until late summer, when they disperse to find their own territory. Females may sometimes stay with their mother until the next year, following a pattern similar to that of other ground squirrels. A daughter that inherits the maternal burrow is freed from having to expend the energy required for such extensive excavating.

Empty burrows are quickly occupied by other groundhogs or taken over by rabbits, skunks, foxes and other denning mammals, as well as hibernating snakes, lizards and arthropods.

Heavyset, with strong forelimbs, the groundhog, or woodchuck, is built for digging. Its extensive burrows can be as long as 50 feet.

VANCOUVER MARMOT
Marmota vancouverensis

The Vancouver marmot is a close relative of the hoary marmot. It is restricted to British Columbia's Vancouver Island and probably speciated there when the island population was isolated from the mainland population. Colonies are located in subalpine areas on steep, windswept slopes. In such areas, avalanches clear away the snowpack and open up early-spring grazing areas for hungry marmots.

This marmot is biologically similar to the hoary marmot. It is, however, an endangered species. There are probably fewer than 1,000 individuals, making the Vancouver marmot vulnerable to logging, hunting and other forms of environmental disturbance.

Found only on Vancouver Island off Canada's West Coast, the Vancouver marmot has only a modest population that is highly vulnerable to hunting, logging and other environmental disturbances.

VANCOUVER MARMOT
Marmota vancouverensis

Mammal: *Marmota vancouverensis*, Vancouver marmot

Meaning of Name: *Marmota* (mountain mouse or rat); *vancouverensis* (of Vancouver Island)

Description: glossy chocolate-brown; dirty white ring on muzzle and white patch on forehead; white streaks along chest and abdomen

Total Length: 24.9 to 28 inches

Tail: male, 8.6 inches; female 7.6 inches

Weight: male, 7.7 pounds (may double or even triple its weight from May to September); female, 8.3 pounds

Gestation: not known (probably about 30 days)

Offspring: 3; probably reproduce only every second year

Age of Maturity: female, third year

Longevity: not known (probably 4 to 6 years)

Diet: herbivore; berries, roots and bark in spring and winter; leaves, flowers and berries in summer and fall

Habitat: tree line and beyond in subalpine slopes, meadows or forest openings; favors steep slopes with a southern exposure

Predators: golden eagle, red-tailed hawk, puma and black bear

Dental Formula:
1/1, 0/0, 2/1, 3/3 = 22 teeth

COLUMBIAN GROUND SQUIRREL
Spermophilus columbianus

Mammal: *Spermophilus columbianus,* Columbian ground squirrel
Meaning of Name: *Spermophilus* (seed lover); *columbianus* (part of geographical range includes the basin of the Columbia River)
Description: mottled gray head and neck; pale ginger flanks and underparts; dark reddish feet and legs; bushy tail has a rufous base, a brown brush and a creamy terminal band
Total Length: 12.9 to 14.8 inches
Tail: 3 to 5 inches
Weight: 12 to 28.6 ounces, depending on whether it is entering or emerging from hibernation
Gestation: 24 days
Offspring: 2 to 4; 1 litter per year
Age of Maturity: 2 years
Longevity: 4 to 6 years
Diet: roots, bulbs, stems, leaves and flowers; cultivated crops and some animal food, including insects, dead fish and mice
Habitat: open meadows, sagebrush plains or cultivated fields with a southern exposure and light sandy soil
Predators: diurnal avian predators, weasel, badger, coyote, fox, bobcat, puma, grizzly bear, skunk and wolf
Dental Formula:
1/1, 0/0, 2/1, 3/3 = 22 teeth

The Columbian ground squirrel is a large and slow-to-mature species in which size plays an important role in territorial battles.

COLUMBIAN GROUND SQUIRREL
Spermophilus columbianus

Ground squirrels, like the western chipmunks, are an extremely diverse genus. At least 13 species of ground squirrel inhabit a relatively small geographic range, yet most live within their own specialized habitats.

The Columbian ground squirrel lives in mid- to upper-elevation intermountain basins in open habitats characterized by light soil. Its relatively large size reflects its adaptation to higher elevations. Like the Richardson's ground squirrel, it lives in colonies because of the local soil and habitat conditions. The Columbian ground squirrel is a generalized grazer as well as a predator of insects and possibly mice. It also stores seeds in its burrow system, especially if it is a large, early-emerging male.

Perhaps because of its large physical size and the intensity of its social competition, this ground squirrel has a relatively small litter size. Dominance is achieved by fighting, and a larger squirrel is apt to be a more successful fighter. Litter size declines as altitude increases, suggesting that the squirrels balance their fecundity against the length of the growing season. The survival of juveniles over winter is higher in this species than in other ground squirrels, an indication that their reduced fecundity results in more vigorous offspring.

The Columbian ground squirrel requires two summers to achieve its full body size, whereas Richardson's ground squirrels are fully grown at the end of their first summer. In addition, the young do not disperse until their second summer. Males move away, while females tend to remain near the nest where they were born. Resident females are more likely to vacate their territory if they have a young daughter ready to inherit the site. The clusters of female kin interact in a more amicable manner than female Richardson's ground squirrels do.

Males fight to secure territories that overlap those of several females. After mating, males produce a copulatory plug that ranges from a hard crystalline substance to a white, rubbery one. The plug is anchored firmly in the vagina and prevents other males from inserting sperm for at least a day, minimizing the chance that territorial males will lose paternity rights to intruding males. The thirteen-lined ground squirrel and the prairie dog also form these plugs. Other species of ground squirrels, such as Belding's, have a high rate of multiple paternity—that is, a litter from a single female is fathered by several different males. In these species, males do not form mating plugs, and a receptive female may mate with as many as five different males when she is in heat. As a result, more than three-quarters of the litters have two or more fathers. Such behavior decreases the relatedness of the littermates and also limits the chance for cooperative behavior to develop among offspring. It may be that cooperative interactions between Columbian ground squirrel sisters evolved because of the use of mating plugs by their fathers: The offspring usually have the same father, and they are close genetic relatives.

Sometimes the weaned litters of several female Columbian ground squirrels blend and interact, while the siblings of Richardson's ground squirrels only tolerate each other.

FRANKLIN'S GROUND SQUIRREL *Spermophilus franklinii*

The Franklin's ground squirrel is the largest and darkest ground squirrel in its range. With a long, bushy tail that makes up two-thirds of its total length, it looks more like a tree squirrel than any of the other ground squirrels do. True to its appearance, it is also a much more accomplished climber than other ground squirrels and is often seen high up in trees and bushes.

Secretive by nature, the Franklin's ground squirrel spends up to 90 percent of its life underground, venturing out only on bright, sunny days. It is typically solitary but sometimes gathers in small family groups.

This ground squirrel lives in areas with heavy ground cover that offers some protection from many potential predators. Its extensive burrows, which can be as deep as 8 feet, are fairly well concealed, a result of its practice of scattering most of the soil it excavates at a distance from the entrance.

As this squirrel scurries about on the well-worn runways that radiate out from its burrows, it is very vocal, more so than others of its genus. It produces a remarkably clear whistle and a bird-like twitter. A deep hibernator, the Franklin's accumulates a thick layer of fat, caches a considerable amount of food and insulates the sleeping chamber in its hibernaculum with a layer of grass to prepare for its long winter sleep.

Shy and quick to retreat into the cover of its bushy habitat, the Franklin's ground squirrel is a solitary creature for much of the year except during the mating season.

FRANKLIN'S GROUND SQUIRREL
Spermophilus franklinii

Mammal: *Spermophilus franklinii*, Franklin's ground squirrel, whistling ground squirrel
Meaning of Name: *Spermophilus* (seed lover); *franklinii* (named in honor of Sir John Franklin)
Description: long bushy tail; olive-brown dorsally with gray to white or tawny underparts; gray head with frosting of silver-tipped hairs and a white eye ring; gray feet
Total Length: male, 14.3 to 16.9 inches; female, 14.4 to 16.1 inches
Tail: male, 4.7 to 6.1 inches; female, 5 to 6.1 inches
Weight: male, 1 pound; female, 1.1 pounds
Gestation: 28 days
Offspring: usually 7 to 9 (can be 2 to 12); 1 litter per year
Age of Maturity: after emergence from first hibernation
Longevity: 8 to 10 years
Diet: omnivore
Habitat: transition zone between high coniferous forests and grassy areas; areas with low trees but dense ground cover
Predators: hawks, badger, fox, coyote and weasel
Dental Formula:
1/1, 0/0, 2/1, 3/3 = 22 teeth

GOLDEN-MANTLED GROUND SQUIRREL
Spermophilus lateralis

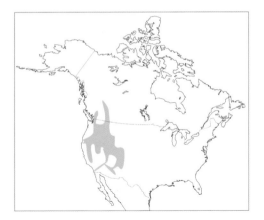

Mammal: *Spermophilus lateralis,* golden-mantled ground squirrel

Meaning of Name: *Spermophilus* (seed lover); *lateralis* (of the side) refers to prominent stripes on each side of body

Description: smaller than closely related Cascade golden-mantled ground squirrel (*Spermophilus saturatus*); ears are quite large for a ground squirrel; diamond-shaped glandular area of thickened skin between the shoulders; two broad white lateral stripes running from shoulders (not cheeks, as in chipmunks) to rump, each side of which is bordered by narrow black stripes; a mantle that varies from tawny to russet-brown covers head, neck and shoulders; white crescents above and below eyes; buff underparts, feet and legs

Total Length: 10.6 to 12.4 inches

Tail: 2.5 to 4.7 inches

Weight: 5.8 to 9.7 ounces

Gestation: 28 days

Offspring: 2 to 8 (usually 4); 1 litter per year

Age of Maturity: the spring following birth

Longevity: 11 years in captivity (probably less in the wild)

Diet: omnivore; seeds, fungus, leaves, flowers, fruits, roots, eggs and arthropods

Habitat: mountain slopes and foothills; in alpine tundra beyond tree line

Predators: hawks, golden eagle, bobcat, fox, coyote, weasel, skunk and grizzly bear

Dental Formula:
1/1, 0/0, 2/1, 3/3 = 22 teeth

The golden-mantled ground squirrel is known for its coloration and its attitude. The "big chipmunk" makes its home at the very edge of the tree line in the western mountain ranges.

GOLDEN-MANTLED GROUND SQUIRREL
Spermophilus lateralis

Striking coloration and a bold disposition have earned the golden-mantled ground squirrel the nickname "big chipmunk." Extremely independent, with no family ties whatsoever, this ground squirrel has a variety of calls, including sharp chirps and chitters that it uses in conjunction with tail twitches when it senses danger nearby.

Like its relatives, the golden-mantled ground squirrel is diurnal and remains sheltered in its burrow during inclement weather. When it scampers from place to place, it holds its tail at a 45-degree angle to the ground. In another familiar pose, it sits alertly upright on its haunches, surveying its domain. Its grooming regime includes a dust bath followed by a thorough combing with teeth and claws.

The short, simple burrows have openings at the base of trees or stumps, beneath fallen logs or among loose rocks. All traces of soil are carted away from the entrances. In late summer, a strong hoarding instinct sets in, and the squirrel busily packs its cheek pouches to capacity and transports its booty to its burrow or to storage holes. During hibernation, it wakes up briefly every two weeks or so but eats little in these short periods. The food cache probably serves as a food reserve for spring when snow still covers much of its food supply. When it hibernates, the golden-mantled ground squirrel sleeps rolled tightly into a ball, nose to toes, its tail curled up over its head and shoulders.

The **Cascade golden-mantled ground squirrel,** *Spermophilus saturatus,* is closely related to the golden-mantled ground squirrel but is smaller and confined to the slopes of British Columbia's Cascade Mountains (see page 104).

ARCTIC GROUND SQUIRREL
Spermophilus parryii

The arctic ground squirrel is the largest species in this genus, and it also occurs the farthest north. It has a large litter size, usually six young, which is typical of animals adapted to Arctic habitats.

Arctic ground squirrels dig burrows, but permafrost limits the depth of these to less than 3 feet. They form colonies, and their mazes of burrows and tunnels often intersect those of other squirrels. Females disperse less than males, and sisters often live adjacent to one another, a behavior that results in the formation of female kin clusters. The closely related females interact in a relatively friendly manner with each other but are hostile to unrelated females.

Males are polygynous and attempt to control an area that contains more than one female. Males will also kill young arctic ground squirrels. When the males disperse, they move into areas inhabited by nonrelatives, so infanticide costs them little. Indeed, besides providing them with food, it may increase their future daughters' opportunities of finding territories. Females may form kin clusters in response to infanticide by the males—a group of females is better able to defend its young than several single, uncooperative females would be.

Males continue to defend their territories even after the mating season is finished and often do so with increased vigor—perhaps in an effort to defend their young against the cannibalistic tendencies of intruding males. As a result, unlike other male ground squirrels, those of the Arctic go into hibernation after the females.

The young disperse during the season in which they are born. They are nearly full-grown before autumn, and after their winter hibernation, they are ready for mating. Such rapid maturation reflects the tremendous productivity of the Arctic in summer.

These squirrels feed on a wide variety of plants as well as fruit, carrion, eggs and nesting birds.

In the brief summer of the far north, the arctic ground squirrel must grow from infancy to a size larger than any other species of ground squirrel attains. By fall, it is nearly full-grown.

ARCTIC GROUND SQUIRREL *Spermophilus parryii*

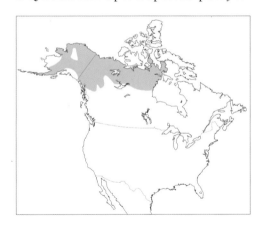

Mammal: *Spermophilus parryii*, arctic ground squirrel; largest of the ground squirrels

Meaning of Name: *Spermophilus* (seed lover); *parryii* (named by Sir John Richardson after American botanist and explorer Dr. C.C. Parry, 1823-90)

Description: cinnamon and tawny head, cheeks and shoulders; buff eye ring; grayish to buffy brown nape and back flecked with white spots; tawny flanks, legs and underparts; tail is a combination of browns and black-tipped hairs, tawny below; black terminal brush

Total Length: male, 14.8 to 17.1 inches; female, 13.7 to 16.7 inches

Tail: male, 4.1 to 5 inches; female, 3.5 to 5.3 inches

Weight: male, 1.7 to 2 pounds; female, 1.5 pounds

Gestation: 25 days

Offspring: 4 to 8 (usually 6); 1 litter per year

Age of Maturity: the spring following birth (approximately 11 months)

Longevity: maximum 8 to 10 years in the wild

Diet: tundra vegetation such as leaves, seeds, stems, flowers and roots of grasses, forbs and woody species; also fruit, carrion, eggs and nesting birds

Habitat: tundra regions beyond the tree line and clearings within northern forests; usually beside water on eskers, moraines and in brushy meadows

Predators: Arctic carnivores (ermine, wolf, arctic fox and grizzly bear) as well as some airborne predators (rough-legged hawk, peregrine falcon, gyrfalcon and snowy owl)

Dental Formula:
1/1, 0/0, 2/1, 3/3 = 22 teeth

RICHARDSON'S GROUND SQUIRREL
Spermophilus richardsonii

....

Richardson's ground squirrels are prairie specialists. They form colonies not because they are social but because they inhabit areas with short vegetation, easily worked soils and good drainage. Colonies are densest in virgin prairie areas, with about eight individuals per acre living together. Each adult digs its own burrow system. These consist of an extensive system of tunnels and storage, nesting and hibernation chambers as well as up to eight entrances. The tunnels may run for 15 yards and extend to a depth of 6 feet. The ground squirrels pile the excavated

earth outside their burrows to form observation mounds. Despite their tendency to live in dense colonies, Richardson's ground squirrels are solitary animals, and each adult defends his or her own burrow.

These squirrels are diurnal and omnivorous. Their diet consists mainly of herbaceous prairie plants, but they also eat large numbers of insects such as grasshoppers and will eat carrion when they get the chance. They cache seeds in their burrows to eat when their fat stores are depleted at the end of their seven-month hibernation. They hibernate in one of their deepest chambers, which they plug and seal with soil to reduce the risk of being dug up by a predator. They also insulate the cham-

In the dry North American Midwest, ground squirrels such as the Richardson's—a prairie specialist that survives as an omnivore—are among the most diverse groups of mammals.

ber with a lining of dried plants. Males begin and end their hibernation before females. They may begin hibernating as early as July and emerge in January in an attempt to mate with as many females as possible. Although the earliest emergent males may increase the number of potential matings, they risk being weakened by cold weather and limited foraging opportunities. Thus when the peak of the female emergence occurs, they may be less successful in vying with other males for mates. Males fight and wound each other in their battles over females and sometimes die from their wounds. They also lose weight during the mating season, while females gain weight—another indicator of the high cost of the males' wide-ranging combative activities.

During the breeding phase, males intrude on female territories, but when the mating season is finished, females oppose and exclude them, as they do other females. Males are passive while the females are bearing their young. Females give birth to a single litter in spring after a short 24-day pregnancy. The young are weaned and active outside the nest five weeks after birth. They remain with their mother for several more months and participate in defending the territory from intrusions by other colony members. By late summer, they reach adult size and disperse. The young of a given year can identify their siblings after they emerge from hibernation, an important mechanism for avoiding inbreeding.

Ground squirrel burrows interfere with agriculture, and wide-scale poisoning and bounty programs have been sponsored to reduce the species. As well, ground squirrels carry ticks and fleas that harbor Rocky Mountain spotted fever and a type of bubonic plague. At least one squirrel bounty hunter has died of the plague, presumably from handling dead squirrels.

WHAT'S IN A WARNING?

A colony of ground squirrels has a predator warning system. The squirrel that sees a hawk, for example, whistles loudly, alerting other squirrels in the area to take cover in their burrows. This sounds simple and straightforward, but it is not.

A social group is rife with conflicting interests. Kin groups, which ought to cooperate closely, live side by side with unrelated, competing individuals as well as other individuals that represent an entire set of intermediate degrees of relationship. Thus an alarm call will affect the survival not only of the caller but of all the variously related squirrels that hear the call.

A successful behavior increases the reproductive success of the individual exhibiting the behavior, thus passing that behavior along to future generations. At the same time, the success of a particular individual is measured by his or her reproductive rate, successful individuals reproducing at a higher rate than average. So why should a squirrel give an alarm call that alerts other squirrels?

There is, after all, a risk that the call will attract the predator's attention to the caller, which would directly lower the caller's reproductive success. Furthermore, the call may increase the survival rate of unrelated squirrels. In that case, it will lower the relative reproductive success of the caller. Biologists do not expect alarm calls to benefit a group of random individuals.

There are, then, two different ways of looking at alarm calls. One view argues that alarm calls are a form of manipulation and selfishness: The caller causes other individuals to respond to a warning by running or otherwise escaping, creating a diversion so that the caller is less likely to be selected by the predator. The caller, it is believed, has the advantage of knowing where the predator is and can then take advantage of the action and confusion created by the call to make its escape.

The alternative and competing hypothesis is that alarm calls benefit relatives in the vicinity of the caller. By increasing the survival and reproductive success of close kin, the caller increases the spread of the genes that control alarm-calling behavior.

Ground squirrels are the ideal organisms with which to test these two views, both because they make alarm calls frequently and because their social system and dispersal behaviors produce an asymmetric pattern of genetic relatedness. Sons disperse and generally end up in areas surrounded by nonrelatives, but daughters often set up near their

RICHARDSON'S GROUND SQUIRREL
Spermophilus richardsonii

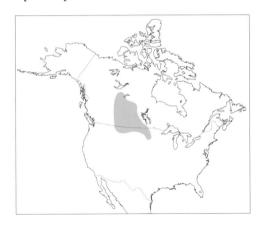

Mammal: *Spermophilus richardsonii,* Richardson's ground squirrel
Meaning of Name: *Spermophilus* (seed lover); *richardsonii* (named after Sir John Richardson, who discovered the species in 1820)
Description: plump squirrel with long tail and small internal cheek pouches; smoky gray dorsally with yellowish cheeks, shoulders, flanks and thighs; cinnamon-buff head; brown transverse bars on rump; submarginal black band on tail, which is bordered with white or buff; eyes set high in skull to permit it to spot airborne predators with only the crown of its head protruding from burrow
Total Length: 10.9 to 12 inches
Tail: 2.6 to 3.3 inches
Weight: 14.2 ounces in spring; increases to 17.1 ounces in autumn prior to hibernation
Gestation: 22.5 to 28 days
Offspring: usually 6 to 8, but 2 and 11 have occurred; 1 litter per year
Age of Maturity: 11 months
Longevity: 3 to 4 years
Diet: mainly herbivorous; roots, leaves and seeds of native grasses and forbs as well as crop plants; also carnivorous, eating insects and carrion; partly cannibalistic
Habitat: open prairie and plains with gravelly and sandy soils; also sagebrush grassland near water
Predators: hawks, burrowing owl, weasel, ferret, badger, fox and coyote
Dental Formula:
1/1, 0/0, 2/1, 3/3 = 22 teeth

CASCADE GOLDEN-MANTLED GROUND SQUIRREL
Spermophilus saturatus

Mammal: *Spermophilus saturatus*, Cascade golden-mantled ground squirrel
Meaning of Name: *Spermophilus* (seed lover); *saturatus* (full, filled)
Description: larger than closely related golden-mantled ground squirrel (*Spermophilus lateralis*); dark brown back; russet head and shoulders; single white stripe on sides, bordered with black
Total Length: 11.5 to 12.4 inches
Tail: 3.6 to 4.6 inches
Weight: 6.0 to 9.8 ounces
Gestation: 28 days
Offspring: 1 to 5 (usually 4); 1 litter per year
Age of Maturity: the spring following birth
Longevity: at least 4 years
Diet: plant material, especially vetch leaves, bark, huckleberries, grass seeds and leaves, berries, seeds of lupine and pine; subterranean fungi
Habitat: coniferous forests, meadows and cleared areas
Predators: owls, hawks, coyote, fox and bobcat
Dental Formula:
1/1, 0/0, 2/1, 3/3 = 22 teeth

Ground squirrels such as the Richardson's greet intruders with a loud, shrill whistle. When relatives are nearby, these squirrels are more likely to give the warning call.

mothers, producing clusters of closely related female kin.

Studies of Richardson's, Belding's and thirteen-lined ground squirrels have all ended up supporting the kin-selection explanation of alarm calls. The individuals that call the most are female. Most often, they are mothers with offspring or closely related kin nearby.

Furthermore, the studies of Belding's ground squirrels revealed that there was a real cost to alarm calling. The Belding's ground squirrels that called were more frequently attacked by predators than were noncallers. Females with relatives nearby, however, called in spite of this. They were also more likely to call than either males or females with no close kin nearby. This provides strong evidence that nepotism—the favoring of kin—has been the selective force behind alarm calling.

THIRTEEN-LINED GROUND SQUIRREL
Spermophilus tridecemlineatus

The 13 alternating light and dark stripes gracing the back of the thirteen-lined ground squirrel make it easy to distinguish from any other mammal. More solitary than most ground squirrels, it lives alone or in small family groups, preferring open habitats with little vegetation, where it constructs a shallow burrow a foot or two below the surface with a deeper nesting chamber. Shorter burrows throughout its home range that serve as hiding places are connected by well-traveled runways radiating out over the surface. It is believed that this squirrel does not stray far from its burrow.

It assumes an upright position so that it can keep a vigilant eye out for any of a host of predators. If danger is sighted, it sounds an alarm call, either a short, sharp whistle or a trill it can "throw" as a ventriloquist does so that it does not expose itself.

The thirteen-lined ground squirrel hibernates from September to April, curled up into a stiff, cold ball. Studies have documented that its respiration rate drops to one breath every five minutes from its usual 100 to 200 breaths per minute.

One of the most beautifully patterned of all the mammals, the thirteen-lined ground squirrel is well camouflaged amidst the sun and shadow of grassland vegetation.

THIRTEEN-LINED GROUND SQUIRREL
Spermophilus tridecemlineatus

Mammal: *Spermophilus tridecemlineatus,* thirteen-lined ground squirrel
Meaning of Name: *Spermophilus* (seed lover); *tridecemlineatus* (thirteen-lined) refers to the dorsal stripes characteristic of this species
Description: seven dark brown stripes separated by six narrow buff stripes on back; each brown stripe is enclosed by a row of buff squares; brown and buff specks on top of head; cinnamon nose, eye ring, cheeks, feet and underparts; yellowish brown tail has submarginal black band tipped with beige hairs; cheek pouches open into the sides of the mouth
Total Length: male, 10.1 to 11.7 inches; female, 8.9 to 10.7 inches
Tail: male, 3.6 to 4.4 inches; female, 3.5 to 3.9 inches
Weight: male, 5.8 ounces (maximum 8.8 ounces); female, 4.9 ounces
Gestation: 27 or 28 days
Offspring: 3 to 13 (usually 8); possibly a second litter if first one is lost
Age of Maturity: 11 months
Longevity: maximum 8 to 10 years in the wild
Diet: true omnivore; consumes more insects than most other ground squirrels; fresh green foliage and seeds, berries, domestic grain and garden produce; occasionally eats meat and carrion and even its own young
Habitat: transitional zone between grassland and forest with low grass, weeds or shrubby vegetation; also golf courses, abandoned overgrown fields, meadows and along fencelines between cultivated fields
Predators: hawks, shrike, crow, badger, weasel, coyote, fox, skunk and domestic cat
Dental Formula:
1/1, 0/0, 2/1, 3/3 = 22 teeth

BLACK-TAILED PRAIRIE
DOG *Cynomys ludovicianus*

Prairie dogs are among the most social of North American squirrels, and their behavior is the most elaborate of all. One prairie dog town in Texas contained an estimated 400 million inhabitants and covered an area that extended 25,000 square miles.

Named for their barklike warning call, black-tailed prairie dogs are at the extreme end of the scale of ground squirrel evolutionary tendencies. They are stouter than their cousins, they remain active except during the very coldest winter weather, and instead of using cheek pouches to carry and cache seeds, they eat large quantities of leafy vegetation and have evolved

bigger incisors and molars for the job.

The densely packed "towns" in which they live alter the landscape of western grasslands. Before poisoning campaigns exterminated wholesale numbers of prairie dogs, their towns used to reach staggering sizes. Such large colonies may have had a mutually beneficial relationship with the vast bison and pronghorn antelope herds that ranged the same areas. The herds are thought to have grazed plants that the prairie dogs shunned, and the buffalo wallows encouraged the grassy and herbaceous vegetation favored by the prairie dogs.

Prairie dogs' feeding habits and mound building leave their mark on the landscape. Their selective grazing favors the growth of certain species of woody shrubs, and sometimes a town

Extended families cooperate to outcompete other prairie dogs for grazing and burrowing territory, the key to success for squirrels such as the black-tailed prairie dog.

can be spotted from miles away by the silvery blue shine of the sage growing in the colony. Grass and broad-leafed herbs are so heavily cropped that towns are often depleted of favored foods. When this happens, prairie dogs will dig roots and eat insects.

The entrance to the burrow of a prairie dog is unmistakable. It is in the crater of a volcano-shaped cone built of soil removed from the tunnel system. The cone serves as both a lookout perch and a dike to prevent surface water from pouring down through the entrance. The burrow is a remarkable excavation that begins with a straight plunge of 9 to 15 feet, a depth requiring that towns be located in areas of deep and malleable soils. The burrow then turns and runs horizontally for 50 feet or more. Short side tunnels lead to nesting chambers or tunnels used for defecation, and there may be multiple exits. Burrow systems are usually 25 to 50 yards apart.

Towns are organized into extended female kin groups called coteries. A coterie typically consists of a single adult male, three to four adult females (often sisters or cousins) and larger numbers of juveniles of both sexes. A male maintains more or less exclusive sexual access to the breeding females in one coterie, but his territory may expand to include a second. In this case, the females of one coterie remain loyal to their own and are hostile to females of the other. A male's behavior is thus subject to the outcome of female-female interactions.

Cooperation, sociability and egalitarianism are the most striking features of a coterie. The members usually sleep communally. They greet each other with a hug, placing their forepaws around each other. Their social gestures also include nose or teeth touching and tail flicking. And they all give alarm calls, defend their territory and build the burrow system. Neither males nor females in a single coterie dominate relationships with one another through violence or threats. However, as in any group, there is a mix of cooperation and competitiveness. Some subtle forms of competition may exist among females, because not all females within a group breed and because the average reproductive success per female declines as the size of the group increases. If competition does exist, more obvious cooperative behavior generally overshadows it. For example, nonbreeding females assume more than their share of colony defense, and mothers may also feed infants that are not direct descendants. On the other hand, pregnant and lactating females defend their nests

against other members of the group, and females may kill the offspring of other females within the group.

Both males and females breed at 2 years of age. Breeding occurs in late winter. The litter size is small as ground squirrels go—an average of three pups weaned per female. The pups first emerge above ground in May and June. Female pups will remain in the group for life, and males will disperse the next summer at the age of 12 to 14 months. Why males disperse is not clear. It may be because the residents evict them, because females refuse to breed with closely related males or because the males are genetically encoded to disperse to avoid inbreeding.

After dispersing, a male must set up his own burrow system and attract females. Only the largest coteries have more than one breeding male. They will tolerate and may even groom each other and share burrows, but one male fathers the bulk of the offspring.

Colonies expand as mature males move to the periphery. Food depletion is lower there, but pioneering males and the females that they attract face a greater risk from predators such as coyotes and hawks than the centrally located residents do. Like all ground squirrels, prairie dogs give alarm calls, providing advance warning to interior residents. The warning call is one of at least nine vocalizations that the black-tailed prairie dog uses. Among its other greetings, threats and social signals is the territorial "bark," from which it derives its common name.

Many carnivorous mammals and raptors feed on prairie dogs. Badgers are sometimes able to excavate them, and coyotes working in pairs can sometimes catch them. The endangered black-footed ferret used to feed mainly on prairie dogs, but the poisoning campaigns that eradicated most prairie dog towns destroyed most of the ferrets as well. Rattlesnakes and burrowing owls also eat prairie dogs and use their burrows. The owls nest in them, and the snakes den and overwinter in them.

BLACK-TAILED PRAIRIE DOG *Cynomys ludovicianus*

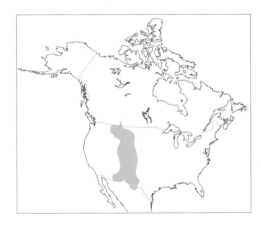

Mammal: *Cynomys ludovicianus*, black-tailed prairie dog
Meaning of Name: *Cynomys* (dog mouse); *ludovicianus* indicates that it was found in Louisiana; known as prairie dog because of its sharp, barking alarm call
Description: pinkish tan dorsally; whitish or pale buff underparts and lower part of face; short ears may be hidden in fur; larger and stouter and has a shorter tail than squirrels
Total Length: 14.2 to 16.3 inches
Tail: 3 to 4 inches
Weight: male, 3 pounds; female, 2.5 to 2.8 pounds
Gestation: 30 to 35 days
Offspring: 2 to 8 (usually 5)
Age of Maturity: 2 years; some mature as yearlings but have smaller litters
Longevity: 3 years in the wild; 7 to 8.5 years in captivity
Diet: primarily forbs and grasses; some animal matter; opportunistic but does select for certain plants according to nutritional requirements
Habitat: dry, open upland prairies and shortgrass plains; likes river flats and coulee bottomlands
Predators: rattlesnake, burrowing owl, eagles, hawks, badger, coyote and black-footed ferret
Dental Formula:
1/1, 0/0, 2/1, 3/3 = 22 teeth

Because prairie dogs live in large, dense colonies containing many closely related individuals, incest could become a problem. Special behavioral adaptations have evolved to prevent it.

The black-tailed prairie dog does not hibernate, although it sometimes becomes inactive during very cold spells. This is attributed to its ability to meet all its water needs from grazing plants. By contrast, the white-tailed prairie dog, which has a relatively high water requirement, is an obligate hibernator. In winter, it minimizes its water needs by turning its metabolism down and sleeping the season away.

INCEST: HOW TO AVOID IT

Animals that live in dense colonies run a high risk of incest: mating with a close relative. In most animals, incest results in a phenomenon that geneticists call inbreeding repression.

Every mammal has two sets of genes, one set from each parent. Some of these genes may be defective, but if the copy from either parent is functional, it can mask the effect of the defective gene. For example, an animal might inherit from its father a defective skin-pigment gene, but if the copy of the gene it receives from its mother is functional, the animal will grow up to be normally pigmented.

Defective genes that are not expressed when a functional copy of the gene exists in the same body are called deleterious recessives. They are hidden, transmitted from generation to generation, and are exposed and removed by natural selection only when an individual receives two identical copies, one from each parent. An albino organism might be the result of such a pairing.

Mammals carry large numbers of deleterious recessives, and their effects on an individual's fitness vary. A gene that reduces fitness and reproductive success by 50 percent is half a lethal equivalent. Humans carry an average of two lethal equivalents, and if expressed, they could cause death. Other species have been shown to have similar numbers of deleterious genes hidden in their gene pool, and virtually every study of every mammal subject to inbreeding has shown severe costs when these genes are expressed.

Inbreeding increases the chance that both copies of a gene are identical. If an animal carrying a defective gene breeds with a brother or sister or one of its parents, the chances are 50-50 that the mate carries the same defective gene. Simple laws of probability predict that

the resulting offspring are highly likely to express a defective trait. For example, a deleterious recessive gene in humans can produce a genetic disease called phenylketonuria, which suppresses production of a metabolic enzyme and can cause severe mental retardation and grave illness. The gene occurs in 1 person in 100, but it is carried and transmitted from generation to generation mostly in the recessive state. Individuals who carry the defective gene are unaware of its presence, because they usually also carry a working copy of the gene that produces the necessary enzyme. Under the laws of probability, the chance that an individual will inherit two copies of the gene from parents who are not related is 1-in-100 times 1-in-100, or 1 in 10,000. Inbreeding between brothers and sisters increases 500-fold the chance that their offspring will receive a defective copy from each parent and express the disease.

How can prairie dogs living in such densely populated towns avoid inbreeding? One study found several answers. Newborn males disperse from their coterie before they reach breeding age, and their sisters and female cousins remain behind. This eliminates incest between siblings of the same age. A father also usually leaves the coterie before his daughters begin mating. If a father remains, the daughters tend not to come into estrus. (Nine percent of the offspring in this study were sired by a male from outside the coterie, so females do have some chance of recruiting an unrelated mate if necessary.) And finally, if a female does come into estrus when one of her close male relatives is around, she will avoid mating with him. This avoidance is based on the ability to distinguish kin from nonkin by their scent—which may explain why prairie dogs spend so much time hugging and grooming each other.

Two cases of inbreeding did occur in this study. No birth occurred in one instance. In the second, the litter died shortly after weaning. The avoidance of incest, then, appears worthwhile.

EASTERN GRAY SQUIRREL
Sciurus carolinensis

The eastern gray squirrel, which is now so common in eastern cities, was once a creature of the virgin hardwood forests of the eastern part of North America. It was most common in large stands along rich river valleys, while relatives such as the fox squirrel were more abundant in upland areas, and red squirrels occupied the coniferous forests.

Since it is an arboreal (tree) squirrel, the eastern gray squirrel spends most of its time above ground. It has strong, fixed claws designed for gripping bark and a large, fluffy tail that provides insulation and gives it balance as it leaps from branch to branch.

Eastern gray squirrels feed primarily on nuts. They eat the large seeds of maples, oaks, hickories and beeches and cache large numbers of nuts, not in piles but singly, in holes in the ground. They have an amazing ability to relocate their stores, which they disperse throughout their territory. They can smell a nut that is buried in soil and covered by a foot of snow, but they also find many nuts simply by looking in the likely places. They miss some 10 to 20 percent of their nuts, which then grow into trees. Their nut-burying behavior thus influences the rate and pattern of forest regeneration.

Besides nuts, eastern gray squirrels eat large amounts of tree buds and flowers in spring, and in summer, they add leaves, fruit, insects and bird eggs to their diet. They strip the bark off young trees such as the sugar maple and can distinguish which trees have the thickest sap. In some areas, their bark stripping kills many trees. They eat deer antlers, bones and turtle shells to obtain calcium. In autumn, they eat fungi, including some *Amanita* mushrooms, which are fatal to humans. Presumably, the eastern gray squirrel's liver and digestive system have some unusual detoxifying capabilities.

Tree squirrels have a simple social system. The home range of a male overlaps that of several females. During the mating season, males exclude other males from their territory, and breeding females exclude other squirrels from the vicinity of their nest. Squirrels may also be territorial and aggressive around concentrated food resources, but normally, they are spaced out and have few interactions. As population densities increase, they establish dominance relationships by teeth-chattering threats and chases. Eastern gray squirrels are highly vocal and have a rich repertoire of sounds they use in communication. In winter, territoriality is less intense, and several squirrels may nest in the same den to keep warm.

Eastern gray squirrels use two types of nests. In summer, they build leaf nests in tree crowns. An individual may build several nests at different locations and move to them as food distribution shifts. Their winter nests are more protected and are typically found high above ground in a tree hollow, which they line with vegetation. They favor large, overmature and slightly rotten trees. Foresters and woodlot owners who cut down such trees probably contribute to the overwintering deaths of eastern gray squirrels and thus help to set limits on the overall eastern gray squirrel population. Female eastern gray squirrels also select this sort of den for raising their offspring. Pregnant or nursing females vigorously defend these trees against other squirrels.

This squirrel does not hibernate but remains active during winter. Courtship begins in the second half of winter. Females make a quacking call to announce that they are in heat. This attracts large numbers of males who then chase them through the trees. Many squirrels are probably killed at this time by such aerial predators as hawks and owls. Females can produce two litters, one at the end of spring and one in late summer, but only 20 to 40 percent of the females produce a second litter. Each litter averages two to four young, which are born blind, naked and helpless. The

EASTERN GRAY SQUIRREL
Sciurus carolinensis

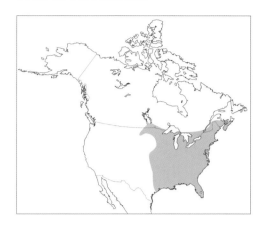

Mammal: *Sciurus carolinensis*, eastern gray or black squirrel

Meaning of Name: *Sciurus* (shade tail), from habit of lying sprawled on a horizontal limb with tail held over its back as a sun shade; *carolinensis* (of Carolina) indicates that it was first described in Carolina

Description: soft, dense pelage is grizzled gray with yellowish brown tones on head, midback, sides and upper feet; whitish to brownish yellow underparts; whitish eye ring and spot behind ears; long, thick pelage in winter; upper parts are washed with silver; ears are silver-tipped; other color phases are common: black, red and mixtures of these; some albinos have been reported

Total Length: 16.5 to 21.1 inches

Tail: 7.9 to 9.8 inches

Weight: 11.9 to 23.8 ounces

Gestation: 40 to 44 days

Offspring: 1 to 6 (usually 2 to 4); 2 litters per year (only 20 to 40 percent have 2 litters)

Age of Maturity: female, 30 to 36 weeks (only females over 2 years old will breed in both breeding seasons)

Longevity: 3 to 6 years in the wild (some have been found to be 13 years); 15 to 20 years in captivity (maximum 23.5 years)

Diet: buds, flowers, seeds, nuts, fruits, fungi, some insects and occasionally bird eggs; deer antlers, bones and turtle shells for calcium

Habitat: forest stands of eastern hardwoods or mixed forests; beech/maple, hemlock hardwoods, red and white pine; along streams (especially where there is a wide river-bottom habitat) and in suburban areas

Predators: hawks, weasel, mink, raccoon, skunk, snakes, gray wolf, owls and raven

Dental Formula:
1/1, 0/0, 2/1, 3/3 = 22 teeth

The gray squirrel's natural haunt was once the tall trees of virgin eastern forests, but it is one of the few wild mammals that have thrived in the large cities of eastern North America.

mother may continue to nurse the first litter even while she is pregnant with the second litter. She will also move her young from nest to nest if she is disturbed. The father provides no parental care. Both sexes disperse in the autumn.

A black form of this squirrel is more common in the north. Its darker coat possibly acts as a kind of solar heater on sunny days.

North American hunters shoot more than 40 million eastern gray squirrels a year. Eastern gray squirrel populations fluctuate wildly because they depend on the unpredictable fruitings of nut trees. They have also been periodically depleted by mass dispersals, starvation and devastation by mange mites.

ESCAPE IN A TIME WARP

Squirrels have created several kinds of problems for nut growers. The most obvious one is that of sharing the harvest, and it is usually dealt with in a straightforward manner: The squirrels are removed. This does not, however, remove the influence of squirrels. Their impact has been etched deeply into the genetic programs of the nut trees, and as a result, nut trees have an ingrained tendency toward irregular bearing, a trait that has become the bane of plant

breeders. Some years, the trees in a forest or orchard all set a heavy crop; other years, there is nothing.

The years in which a heavy crop is set are known as mast years and are spaced at irregular intervals, sometimes one, two, three or even seven years apart. In some localities, almost all reproductive trees, regardless of age or location, are synchronized and in phase. The cues that synchronize them are not well known, although weather is important. Low rainfall in early summer stimulates the formation of reproductive buds and controls the potential for seed production the next year. This potential can be altered by hard spring frosts. And if the previous year was a heavy mast year, the trees lack the resources to produce a large crop no matter how favorable the environment. The result is a highly erratic pattern that seed-eating squirrels have not yet been able to track closely.

Trees bear erratically, not because they are unable to cope with unpredictable weather but to thwart nut-eating squirrels. Trees have evolved to make use of the unpredictable nature of the weather to reduce the number of rodents that prey upon their offspring.

By interspersing the mast years with barren, nutless years, the trees subject the squirrels to feast-and-famine cycles. Rodent populations decline when there

is no nut crop, but when there is a crop, the rodent population is swamped with seeds. There are literally more than they can eat. In mast years, seed predators take only 1 to 10 percent of the nut crop. In off years, rodents harvest almost 100 percent of the crop.

Predator swamping, or satiation, is thought to be the explanation for a number of strange animal and plant cycles. Some bamboos fruit together at intervals of more than 100 years and then die off, causing starvation among bamboo-eating pandas. Cicadas tend to emerge en masse every 13 to 17 years, and sea turtles also have massive, unpredictable egg-laying sessions. The mast fruiting of nut trees may be one reason that so many tree squirrels include a wide variety of alternatives in their diet.

The feast-and-famine cycle of nut production no doubt produced the spectacular migrations of eastern gray squirrels in the last century and the first part of this century. The continent then retained more of the eastern gray squirrels' native habitat, and consequently, the squirrels were more abundant. In some years, observers reported thousands of squirrels on the move and many diving into rivers. Ernest Thompson Seton, whose estimates of animal numbers have generally been supported by later observers, calculated that some of the mass migrations in the early part of the century involved more than a billion squirrels moving in a wave across the countryside.

The most recent documented massive migration of eastern gray squirrels occurred in the southern Appalachians in 1968. Thousands of squirrels moved in the autumn, drowning in reservoirs and being crushed on the highways. The year before had been a mast year, and this had produced an abundance of young squirrels that overwintered with low mortality. The next spring, a frost destroyed the flower and fruit buds of the nut trees. There was no nut crop, and the large squirrel population had no food to store for the winter. Chalk one up for the trees.

EASTERN FOX SQUIRREL
Sciurus niger

The eastern fox squirrel is a solitary animal most of the time, even though the home ranges of several squirrels may overlap; it will sometimes share a den in winter with several others.

The eastern fox squirrel is most active in the morning and afternoon. When it sprawls on a limb in midday, its long, bushy tail functions as a sunshade.

Like other tree squirrels, the eastern fox squirrel hoards nuts, burying each one singly in the forest earth. Sometimes it retrieves almost all of its nuts, even from under the snow, thanks mainly to its acute sense of smell, but aided to some degree by its memory.

This species has two different types of home. Its winter residence and natal den are usually located in a cavity in the trunk of a tree. In summer (and in winter, if tree holes are scarce), the eastern fox squirrel fashions a nest in the fork of a tree limb from leaves and twigs cut from the tree.

EASTERN FOX SQUIRREL
Sciurus niger

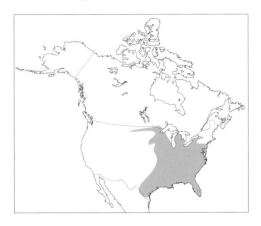

Mammal: *Sciurus niger*, eastern fox squirrel
Meaning of Name: *Sciurus* (shade tail), from habit of lying sprawled on a horizontal limb with tail held over its back as a sun shade; *niger* (black), based on black color phase
Description: soft, dense pelage with heavy underfur and long, coarse guard hairs; three color phases (black, gray and red) have a geographical pattern of distribution; gray phase is dominant in the northern population (each hair is tricolored, giving a grizzled effect); pale fulvous to buffy ears, cheeks, feet and underparts; reddish bushy tail with a subterminal black border and cinnamon tips; no cheek pouches
Total Length: 19.7 to 22.4 inches
Tail: 8.3 to 10.6 inches
Weight: 1.6 to 1.8 pounds
Gestation: 44 days
Offspring: 1 to 6 (usually 3 or 4); 2 litters per year
Age of Maturity: female, 1 litter as yearling; male, matures more slowly
Longevity: 6 to 10 years in the wild
Diet: omnivore; nuts, acorns, seeds, buds, flowers, catkins, fleshy fruits, insects, fungi, bird eggs and cambium beneath the bark of small branches
Habitat: suburbs; open hardwood woodlots with clearings interspersed; along shrubby fencerows
Predators: red-tailed hawk, great blue heron, owls, osprey, coyote, gray fox, weasel, raccoon and domestic dog
Dental Formula:
1/1, 0/0, 1/1, 4/3 = 20 teeth

DOUGLAS' SQUIRREL
Tamiasciurus douglasii

Mammal: *Tamiasciurus douglasii*, Douglas' squirrel
Meaning of Name: *Tamiasciurus* (one who stores, hoarder + shade tail); *douglasii* (named after David Douglas, botanist and explorer of North America—same Douglas as Douglas fir)
Description: dark reddish pelage in summer with blackish ear tufts; black flank stripe; rust feet, eye ring and underparts; chestnut tail with black subterminal band and prominent buff-white tip; more grayish in winter, and underparts turn pale yellowish gray
Total Length: 11.4 to 12.5 inches
Tail: 4.4 to 5.4 inches
Weight: 6 to 8.1 ounces
Gestation: 35 days
Offspring: 4 to 8 (usually 4); 1 litter per year
Age of Maturity: the spring following birth
Longevity: up to 7 years in the wild, but probably less than 3 is more usual; 10 years in captivity
Diet: more vegetarian than red squirrel; primarily conifer cones; also fungi, seeds, nuts, fruits, catkins and ferns
Habitat: dense coniferous forests as well as logged-over areas
Predators: pine marten is major predator; also fisher, lynx, weasel, mink, bobcat, goshawk, red-shouldered hawk, sharp-shinned hawk and sparrow hawk
Dental Formula:
1/1, 0/0, 2/1, 3/3 = 22 teeth

RED SQUIRREL
Tamiasciurus hudsonicus

The red squirrel's thickly furred tail provides balance as it races energetically through the forest along tree branches.

Squirrels in this genus are abundant and conspicuous—two characteristics that have earned them many common names such as chickaree and fairy-diddle. More often, they are called pine squirrels or simply pineys because they make their home in the northern coniferous forests.

The red squirrel is a small, highly arboreal species that inhabits the northern boreal forest. It lives in a range of woody environments from coniferous forests, especially spruce, pine and

hemlock, to mixed hardwood deciduous stands, where it prefers maple and elm. At the southern edge of its range, the red squirrel is found in the same areas as gray squirrels.

Red squirrels are high-energy animals. They are noisy and seem to be constantly active during daylight hours. Where some squirrels are shy and secretive, these are bold and aggressive. They scold intruders, including people, with a vigorous display of foot stamping, tail flicking and chattering. They run through the trees at high speeds, leap into space spread-eagled and drop tens of yards to other trees or to the ground. Even falls from the treetops all the way to the ground do not seem to harm this small squirrel.

Red squirrels have a generalized diet. They will eat insects and mice and can be major predators on bird eggs and nestlings. As well, they heavily crop young conifer sprouts and flowers, eat berries and mushrooms and gnaw holes in bark or use the holes of sapsuckers to lap up tree sap. In short, red squirrels will eat virtually all the items that other tree squirrels eat except for low-energy leafy vegetation.

Because of their high metabolism, they require a diet with a high energy content. While they obtain some of this energy from being more carnivorous than other tree squirrels, they get most of it from their distinctive diet of pine, hemlock and other conifer cones. When the cones bear maturing seeds, these squirrels cut virtually every cone from the branches and let them fall to the ground. They then gather the cones into huge piles. The seed middens may be 3 feet deep and several yards across and contain bushels of cones. They prefer shady and humid sites that prevent the cones from drying out and dropping their seeds. These sites and nearby refuse piles of emptied cones are often used year after year and develop into large, conspicuous piles. The squirrels also store seeds in tree hollows and hang fungi among the tree branches to dry; later, they

cache these in a protected dry spot.

Both sexes are territorial and defend their territories against intruders of their own and other squirrel species. At least four different vocalizations are used during territorial encounters.

Females can have two litters a season but usually have time to rear only one. Receptive to males for only a single day, females advertise their availability with an odoriferous vaginal secretion. A group of males collects, and the dominant male mates repeatedly with the female. Males must chase and vocalize at other males to keep them away.

The female red squirrels have an unusual coiled vagina that seems to be unique among squirrels. This structure is matched by the male's long, threadlike penis and loose penis bone. Their reproductive anatomy is so different that it was once suggested that red squirrels be considered a separate family.

They make their nests in tree hollows and also build leaf-and-twig nests. They may adapt the abandoned nests of large birds, such as crows, hawks and owls, for nesting. Before weaning her young, the mother moves them to a nest at the edge of her territory and begins to exclude them from the rest of it. Daughters are more likely than sons to inherit territory at the edge of their mother's. Territories vary in size, depending on the abundance of food.

These squirrels do not hibernate, but they spend little time in the trees in winter. Instead, they build an extensive system of runways through the snow.

Red squirrels are eaten by hawks, owls and predatory mammals such as fishers, badgers, bobcats, red foxes, wolves and pine martens. The pine marten, a large, fast arboreal weasel, is one of the few predators that succeeds in pursuing these squirrels through the trees. Before pine martens were depleted by trapping, they may have been the red squirrels' major predator.

Several million red squirrels are trapped each year for the fur trade, making them one of the more economically valuable fur bearers.

RED SQUIRREL
Tamiasciurus hudsonicus

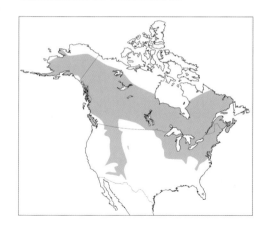

Mammal: *Tamiasciurus hudsonicus*, red squirrel, chickaree, fairydiddle, pine squirrel

Meaning of Name: *Tamiasciurus* (one who stores, hoarder + shade tail); *hudsonicus* (refers to Hudson Bay region, where type specimen was derived); chickaree is said to be an imitation of its cry

Description: soft, dense pelage, glossy olive-brown dorsally, flecked with black; limbs and backs of ears are cinnamon; winter pelage is thicker, brighter and more reddish; red or black tufts on ears; white eye ring that, along with the tawny tail, is the only constant coloration

Total Length: 11 to 13.4 inches

Tail: 3.9 to 5.7 inches

Weight: 4.7 to 8.8 ounces

Gestation: 35 to 40 days

Offspring: 2 to 7 (usually 4); 1 litter per year (2 in southern part of range)

Age of Maturity: 1 year

Longevity: probably less than 3 years in the wild; 9 to 12 years in captivity

Diet: opportunist; primarily seeds, nuts and cones of conifers; also buds, flowers, fruits, bark, mushrooms and sap; will eat insects, bird eggs, fledglings and mice (more carnivorous than other tree squirrels)

Habitat: assorted woody environments from coniferous forests, especially spruce, pine and hemlock, to mixed hardwood deciduous trees (maple and elm, in particular); may also be found in swamps

Predators: hawks, owls, marten, fisher, badger, bobcat, red fox, wolf and domestic cat

Dental Formula:
1/1, 0/0, 1-2/1, 3/3 = 20 or 22 teeth

NORTHERN FLYING SQUIRREL *Glaucomys sabrinus*

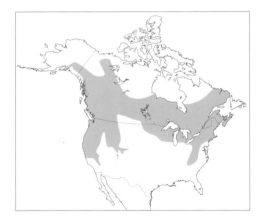

Mammal: *Glaucomys sabrinus*,
northern flying squirrel

Meaning of Name: *Glaucomys* (gray mouse); *sabrinus* (river nymph) refers to Severn River on the west coast of Hudson Bay, where species was first identified

Description: slightly larger than the southern flying squirrel; back is cinnamon-brown, individual hairs are slate-colored and light yellowish brown at tips; light buff underparts with lead-colored hairs at the base; broad, flattened tail, gray above, paler below and darker toward the tip

Total Length: 9.6 to 14.4 inches

Tail: 4.3 to 7.1 inches

Weight: 2.5 to 4.9 ounces

Gestation: 37 days

Offspring: 2 to 6 (usually 3); 2 litters per year

Age of Maturity: female can give birth at 9 months; the spring following birth

Longevity: 3 to 4 years in the wild; 10 years in captivity

Diet: prefers seeds; also tree buds, bark, leaves, lichens, fruits, nuts, tiny soil fungi, maple sap, insects, bird eggs and fledglings

Habitat: heavily wooded areas primarily composed of coniferous species and northern hardwoods such as spruce and cedar or hemlock/yellow birch habitats

Predators: owls, goshawk, gray fox, weasel, marten, gray wolf, bobcat, lynx and domestic cat

Dental Formula:
1/1, 0/0, 2/1, 3/3 = 22 teeth

The southern flying squirrel, whose huge eyes enable it to leap and glide though the forest at night, thereby avoiding predators, is able to travel through the air for some 260 feet.

SOUTHERN FLYING SQUIRREL *Glaucomys volans*

Flying squirrels occupy the nighttime nut-eating niche in the eastern and northern forests. They are the only nocturnal gliding North American squirrels. Flying squirrels glide by extending a fold of skin that runs from the wrist of the forearm along the side of the body and out to the ankle of the leg. Their wrist has a cartilage spur that extends outward, further increasing the spread of the membrane. They have a flattened tail and a lighter, more delicate body structure than other tree squirrels.

By gliding, they move rapidly from tree to tree, both to forage and to escape predators. A squirrel may start a glide from a running leap, or it may sit motionless on a trunk or limb with its head down in a crouch and then leap outward. They glide at an angle of 30 to 40 degrees and can maneuver around tree limbs and other obstacles, even making 90-degree turns. At the end of a glide, they pull up sharply to check their speed and to soften the landing. The length of a glide depends on the height of the launching point. They can glide more than 260 feet, not as impressive a distance as the 1,500-foot glides of the larger Asian flying squirrels but nonetheless graceful and beautiful.

Although flying squirrels can soar easily among the trees, they are inept when on the ground and are very slow runners. A human can easily run one down. If a flying squirrel is surprised on the ground, it will try to hide if it is not near a tree.

The southern flying squirrel lives in mature hickory, oak and beech forests, where it eats the nuts of these trees in addition to bird eggs, nestlings and insects. Unlike squirrels in the genus *Sciurus*, they cache their nuts above ground in tree hollows.

During the day, flying squirrels den in hollow trees and cavities made by woodpeckers. Sometimes they use nests of leaves. In winter, as many as 20 squirrels may den together to increase heat retention. Females are territorial in summer and exclude other squirrels of both sexes from their area. Males are less territorial and have broadly overlapping ranges. Females have the potential to breed twice, but whether most of them do is not certain.

SOCIAL LIFE OF SQUIRRELS

Some squirrel species are social; others are solitary. As social creatures, people are understandably interested in what ecological and evolutionary forces cause an animal to be social. Studying animals such as the squirrel family, in which species vary considerably in degree of sociality, has helped us understand the factors that contribute to their behavior. Such studies must use closely related organisms, ones that have not had a very long genetic separation. Animals that are related but have lengthy evolutionary histories may be social or not social for different reasons, a

problem that is minimized in the study of such closely related species as the squirrels. For example, the woodchuck is a solitary creature, while the prairie dog is highly gregarious. What factors cause these differences? How much does sociality depend on genetics, and how much of it is caused by the environment?

Of course, no species is always antisocial or always gregarious; there is a continuum of behavior between the two extremes for every species. Ground squirrels have such a variety of social systems that scientists have classified them into five grades representing transitions along the solitary/social continuum. They have created the classifications from observations of the animals' family life, the basic unit of sociality in mammals. How long do family members remain together, do they cooperate, do they pass on and inherit resources, do they defend a territory together, and do their descendants continue to associate? Such analyses are also concerned with territoriality, because all ground squirrels are territorial. Who, then, shares a territory, and who has to leave at maturity?

Gail Mitchener, a devoted student of ground squirrels, proposes this classification of their social systems from her observations:

1. **ASOCIAL:** In this system, there is no sharing of territories by males and females. The young disperse soon after weaning. Family members defend their territories and are as antagonistic toward one another as they are to unrelated individuals. In short, it is everyone for him- or herself. Social interactions and cooperation are limited to mating and rearing infants. This kind of system is typical of groundhogs and Franklin's ground squirrels.

2. **SINGLE-FAMILY FEMALE KIN CLUSTERS:** In this system, males and females also have separate ranges and territories, but mothers and daughters live near each other and may share

SOUTHERN FLYING SQUIRREL *Glaucomys volans*

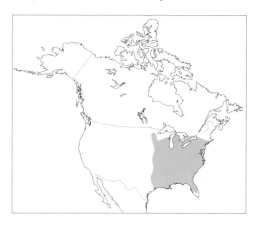

Mammal: *Glaucomys volans,* southern flying squirrel
Meaning of Name:
Glaucomys (gray mouse); *volans* (flying)
Description: soft, silky pelage is pale olive-brown, and ventral hairs are white from base to tip (different from the northern flying squirrel); tail is gray, ventrally flattened and densely haired; eyes are large, black and luminous; skin of flank extends between wrist and ankle and is supported by cartilaginous spur
Total Length: 8.3 to 10.1 inches
Tail: 3.1 to 4.7 inches
Weight: 1.8 to 2.8 ounces
Gestation: 40 days
Offspring: 1 to 6 (usually 2 or 3); 2 litters per year
Age of Maturity: usually 1 year; possibly 9 months
Longevity: 4 to 5 years in the wild; 8 to 13 years in captivity
Diet: omnivore; nuts, acorns, seeds, berries, fruits, moths, June bugs, trees, buds, bark, eggs and young birds (one of the most carnivorous of sciurids)
Habitat: woodlots, prefers seed-producing hardwoods, especially maple/beech stands or poplar stands; also mixed deciduous/coniferous forests
Predators: night-flying owls are major predators; also hawks, raccoon, weasel, fox and domestic cat
Dental Formula:
1/1, 0/0, 2/1, 3/3 = 22 teeth

a home range. Daughters often remain close to their mothers for life. The kin group consisting of mother and daughters is hostile to other groups of females. The sons leave home at maturity, and each establishes his own territory. Belding's ground squirrels, Richardson's ground squirrels and white-tailed prairie dogs use this system.

There is an interesting asymmetry between the sexes in this system. Males, because they disperse widely, are rarely closely related to the individuals around them. Females, on the other hand, live in closely related groups. The territory that a male defends is used only during the mating season, so the resources within his territory are of little long-term value to the females.

3. FEMALE KIN CLUSTERS WITH MALE TERRITORIALITY: In this system, the males' territories overlap those of several females and their daughters, and males defend their territories past the mating season. Such behaviors are typical of arctic ground squirrels and Columbian ground squirrels and lead to more cooperation and interaction. Females rear their litters alone in their own burrows, but they all defend a part of their area included in the large territory of the male.

Nevertheless, they have separate breeding areas and do not all live entirely within a single male territory, nor do they cooperate in defending the male's territory as a whole. There are more interactions among juveniles from several different litters, and as in the other systems, males disperse, while females remain near their mother.

4. POLYGYNOUS HAREMS WITH MALE DOMINANCE: In this system, which is practiced by marmots, males are territorial, and their territory contains one to four females. (Polygyny is the practice in which a male has more than one mate.) Again, females have daughters that tend to stay near them, while their sons disperse. Males must patrol their territory to keep rival males

from their harem, and fights between males are common. As a result, harem masters are short-lived. They are evicted or eaten by competitors every two to three years. Females, by contrast, live as long as 11 years, usually in the same harem as their sisters or close cousins. Yet they do not assist the male in defending his territory as a whole, since they have their own activity areas and interact more with females. They are subordinate to the male.

5. EGALITARIAN POLYGYNOUS HAREMS: Olympic marmots and black-tailed prairie dogs are among the most social of rodents. They have few aggressive dominance interactions. Females are not subordinate to males. Males maintain harems in which the juvenile offspring—both males and females—may reside for as long as two years. Harem masters are not aggressive toward young males after the mating season has passed and do not mind their associating with the harem. All members of the extended-family group defend the family's territorial boundaries against the incursions of other families. This behavior is different from that of yellow-bellied marmots, where a single male is charged with excluding other males. These marmots and prairie dogs do share the same dispersal pattern, however: The daughters remain in the family unit when the mating season begins, whereas the sons disperse to found their own unit or perhaps to invade an established unit.

Ground squirrels' social systems thus range from completely separate male and female territories to male territories that include some females and then to a system of an extended family in which the territory of a male and some females is identical and defended in an egalitarian manner. In other words, as social complexity increases, male-female cooperation and especially female-female (mother-daughter-sister) cooperation increases. This latter feature is due to the asymmetrical dispersal of the sons and the daughters and the resulting

advantages and disadvantages to each.

Dispersal is a risky business. It increases one's chances of being eaten by a predator or damaged in a fight for territory. The mortality rates for females are thus lower because they typically do not have to disperse. A daughter also benefits because she inherits the extensive burrow system controlled by her female ancestors. Burrow sites are often limited and require a great deal of energy to dig. Because they raise the young, females also need a more extensive burrow system than males do.

Yet there are benefits to dispersing, the chief one being that the males are placed in a population of genetically unrelated individuals. A male that remains at home would end up mating with sisters or other close relatives, which would increase the chances of genetic defects within the population. Thus it is to the parents' advantage to pass their territory and burrows along to their daughters while encouraging their sons to disperse.

This does not, however, answer the question of why woodchucks are nonsocial while prairie dogs congregate in dense colonies. Congregating has a cost. It increases the spread of disease and causes local food shortages and competition for space. Probably the key benefit is that many eyes are better than two. Social rodents are much more effective at spotting predators and warning each other of the danger. There appears to be a relationship between such social systems and habitat. Social squirrels typically live in exposed, open habitats that are highly vulnerable to visual predators. The less social woodchuck and tree squirrels are forest species and thus may benefit less from a predator-lookout system. There would also be more competition for food resources from a larger local population.

Many pressures can destabilize the social system. Female competition within a male's territory could drive other females out, reduce cooperation and raise the cost of territory maintenance, which might, in turn, make it

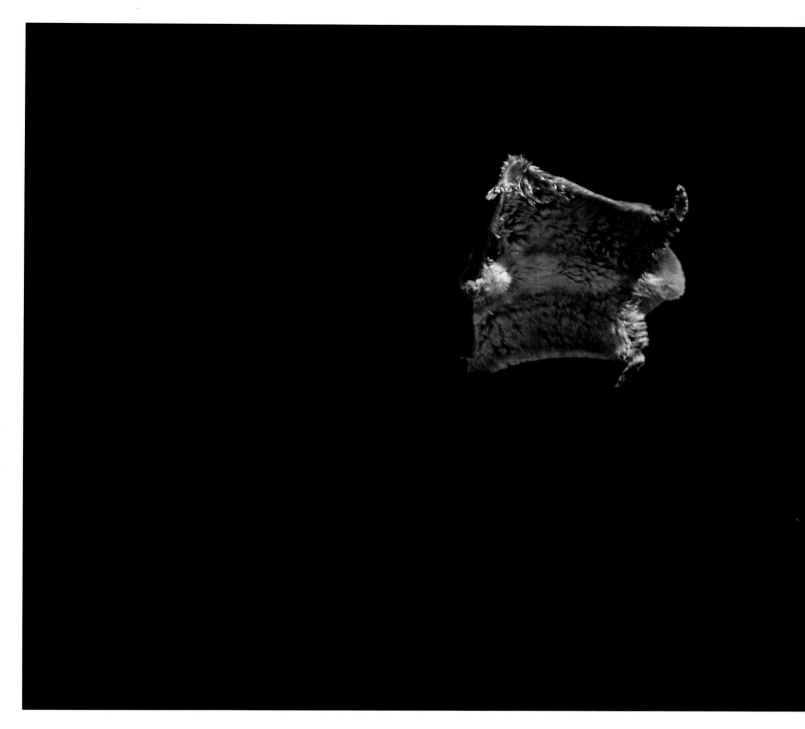

The flying squirrel does not fly but glides by extending a fold of skin that runs from its wrist to its ankle. Other adaptations for gliding include a flattened tail and a lighter body than other squirrels have.

more likely that both female and male young would disperse. A male might aggressively persecute his male relatives if they are potential competitors for mates within his territory. At high alti-tudes and in northern latitudes, animals may grow larger because a large body is more efficient at storing fat needed for overwintering. This means large off-spring, but large offspring require a longer time at home before they dis-perse to fend for themselves, so parents will have a reduced reproductive rate.

There are thus many trade-offs in the sociality equation. The costs and bene-fits of sociality differ for every species according to environment, food re-sources, predators, dispersal problems and nest-site requirements. The ultimate denominator, however, is the behavior that contributes most to the spread of an individual's genes, either directly through his or her own mating or indi-rectly through the reproductive success of relatives who share a portion of their genes. This is the final determinant of which forms of social behavior succeed.

POCKET GOPHERS *Geomyidae*

Pocket gophers are underground specialists. Their large front feet, short ears, small eyes and reduced ear flaps are reminiscent of moles' and provide suitable protection for a life in tunnels. Their eyelids clamp shut so tightly that even the finest dust grains cannot penetrate them, and their ears have valves to close off the outer opening. Special hairs on the tail and on the loose-fitting skin are equipped with mechanoreceptors, cells that are sensitive to touch and help gophers orient themselves in the dark. Like moles, they have stout, powerful forelimbs with large scraping claws for digging. Some species, especially those living in hard soil, also appear to use their large projecting incisors in digging.

Gophers are small enough to fit in a coat pocket, but their common name actually comes from their fur-lined cheek pouches, which they use to transport food. Presumably, the fur lining is an adaptation to cope with hauling gritty soil-coated roots around in the mouth. Like pants pockets, gophers' cheek pockets can be turned inside out for food removal and cleaning.

Gophers' teeth and foreclaws grow continuously and rapidly. One study estimates that over the course of a year, their total tooth growth would measure 1½ feet longer than a gopher's entire body. Of course, the tooth growth is constantly eroded by digging and their gritty diet.

Pocket gophers consume only plant matter, primarily grasses, herbs, limited amounts of shrubbery and great quantities of roots and bulbs, which they drag into their burrows to eat. They build up large caches of roots in autumn for use during winter, when the upper soil layers are frozen solid. Pocket gophers are generalists, shifting their diet according to plant availability and their need for water, vitamins and plants to store for winter. Rapidly growing legumes, for example, contain the high levels of protein required by young growing gophers, whereas roots are rich in carbohydrate energy and overwinter well in the storage chambers.

Tunneling is an energy-expensive way to forage. Studies indicate that a gopher's foraging strategy is to reduce this cost by keeping the tunnel radius to the absolute minimum required for passage. Gophers dispose of excavated soil by piling it in mounds, an activity that attracts predators. Since large mounds must increase mortality rates, smaller gophers that make smaller mounds are more successful. The gopher's size is also influenced by the strength required to excavate soils of different textures. Harder soils demand greater effort, so the gopher is likely to be larger. The combination of predator pressure and soil texture may have led to the evolution of different body sizes in various pocket gopher species and races.

The herbivorous diet of pocket gophers makes them pests in agricultural situations. In addition to the damage they do to root crops, their extensive burrows cause many problems. One gopher

The northern pocket gopher, like all geomyids, uses its powerful forepaws to excavate its tunnels and harvest plant roots. In so doing, it churns and aerates the layers of soil, improving its texture and its capacity for holding water.

dug 478 feet of tunnel in five months. It has been estimated that a gopher excavates more than 1 ton of soil every year. Thus in a field occupied by a colony of gophers, as much as 6 tons of earth per acre may be moved yearly. Much of the soil is pushed up to the surface and left in mounds that interfere with the operation of agricultural machinery. As a result of these problems, farmers poison vast numbers of pocket gophers every year.

Gopher mounds can be distinguished from molehills by the fan shape created when the gopher turns around and kicks the dirt out with his hind feet. The soil plug is located to one side rather than in the center as it is in molehills. Gophers also fill in tunnels that have been harvested of roots, whereas moles use them as pitfalls to trap mobile worms and insects.

The tunnel system provides gophers with a stable environment as well as protection from many predators. Gophers have two types of tunnel: a shallow set less than 20 inches below the surface for eating, traveling and collecting roots, and a deeper set for breeding and for refuge from digging predators and excessively hot or cold weather. The nest chamber lies well below the frost line, keeping the gopher warm during harsh winters. Likewise, the nest remains cool and humid in the heat of summer. Pocket gophers, like mountain beavers, have a limited tolerance for high temperatures. A pocket gopher will die within an hour if it is exposed to a temperature of 100 degrees F. Cold temperatures are less of a problem. Gophers remain active in the winter and extend their burrow system under the snow.

Soil characteristics are a large factor in controlling the density and distribution of territories of underground animals. Pocket gophers seal their burrows with a firm plug of soil when they are inside. This keeps out flash-flooding rains, predators and flies. However, it also makes the gopher dependent on the soil's gas exchange to provide oxygen. Thus gophers cannot live in clay or wet

soils, which have poor gas exchange. They also avoid very shallow soils and excessively rocky or hard soils. Gophers often prefer friable, deep loam with good drainage. Wherever such soils occur, pocket gophers of one species or another will be found. They occur in a wide range of habitats in western, northern and central North America, although not in the boreal forest and tundra. Even in porous soils, the concentration of carbon dioxide in burrows is high. As a result, pocket gophers have evolved a physiological tolerance for high carbon dioxide and low oxygen. Their metabolism is also slower than expected for animals of that size.

Different species of pocket gophers do not normally live in the same area. The range of one species extends until it abruptly ends and a new species occurs. These contiguous but nonoverlapping distributions suggest that competition between the different species is affected by soil types. It may be that certain species can live only in a particular type of soil, and this would limit the range of each species.

Population density is related to the amount of forage available and the size of individual territories. An individual may range over 200 square yards. Like most burrowing mammals, pocket gophers are intensely territorial. Neither males nor females tolerate intruders, and both sexes will fight fiercely. A burrow represents a large investment in time and energy and is thus a valuable resource. If a gopher is trapped and removed from its burrow, the burrow is soon reoccupied. During one study on trapping, 18 gophers were consecutively removed from a single burrow. Gophers only cohabit during the mating season. Some species appear to have a social system in which adjacent males and females share a common nesting burrow but have separate sets of shallow tunnels as their territories. Males are polygynous and often have territories that overlap those of several females. Their polygyny is reflected in their size. In some species, the males grow twice

as large as the females, suggesting that males are selected for fighting ability and territoriality.

Most species of pocket gopher appear to have similar life cycles. Mating takes place in winter or early spring, according to species and habitat. Northern and high-altitude populations have one litter per year, while southern populations may breed several times in the same period, especially if they inhabit rich agricultural areas. Females may mature in their first year, males in their second. Later maturation is likely part of the

Spring thaw reveals the extensive labyrinth of burrows built by pocket gophers to aid them in their search for the plant roots and tubers they need for nourishment.

male reproductive strategy, which requires a large body size for polygynous territorial defense. A large body may also be necessary because of the costs of finding a mate. Males find their mates by digging underground and constructing long, straight-line burrows, a transect approach that maximizes the number of other burrows the males'

intersect. Straight-line runs of 150 yards have been reported. After mating, females and males reseal their burrows to separate them.

Pocket gophers have relatively small litters, often averaging only three offspring. Their closed-burrow system protects their young, so infant mortality is low and they do not need to produce large litters. The young, like most burrowing mammals, are born in a totally helpless altricial state, with their eyes, ears and cheek pouches completely closed. Their eyes and ears do not open

until they are almost 4 weeks old, and they are weaned after five to six weeks, which is a long time given the small size and short lifespan of these animals. When the young gophers are 2 months old, they disperse to set up their own burrow systems. Their chances of success are low. Males have an expected lifetime of little more than a year, females a year and a half. A wide variety of predatory mammals, snakes and birds eats pocket gophers.

Pocket gophers' burrows bring many ecological benefits to natural habitats. They are havens for a wide range of animals, including tiger salamanders, box turtles, burrowing owls, toads, lizards and many mammals such as skunks, weasels and rabbits. One survey of southern pocket gophers revealed that 15 different species of animals, all highly adapted for a subterranean existence, were found only in pocket gopher burrows.

In addition, gophers' digging improves soil aeration and texture and increases the percolation of water into the ground. Their mounds provide germination sites for rare plant species that rely on quick colonization and dispersal to survive competition from larger and longer-lived herbs and shrubs. It has been suggested that the interaction of the great herds of bison—which once grazed western North America—with pocket gophers and prairie dogs helped build the deep grassland soils. The bison created many wallows, trampling and denuding areas that were then colonized by the plants gophers prefer. In turn, the plants attracted larger populations of gophers, whose deep burrowing brought new mineral soil to the surface, where it mixed with plant humus and animal dung to produce the deep loams of the grassland prairies.

Similarly, today's overgrazing by domestic livestock removes vegetative cover and usually results in an increase in pocket gopher populations. The gophers' cropping activities will then keep the area open for decades, even if the livestock is removed.

NORTHERN POCKET GOPHER *Thomomys talpoides*

Mammal: *Thomomys talpoides,*
northern pocket gopher
Meaning of Name: *Thomomys* (heap +
mouse) refers to the heaps of earth thrown at
frequent intervals along the line of the burrows;
talpoides (molelike) refers to its burrowing habits
Description: gray washed with brown;
thick, stubby tail sparsely covered with short,
stiff white hairs; soles of feet are naked except
for a row of short bristles surrounding them;
large fur-lined cheek pouches open on the side
of the face; furred lips can close behind projecting incisors, enabling the gopher to cut roots
and dig without eating dirt
Total Length: male, 7.5 to 10.1 inches;
female, 8.7 inches
Tail: male, 1.9 to 3 inches;
female, 2.6 inches
Weight: male, 5.3 ounces;
female, 4.5 ounces
Gestation: 18 days
Offspring: 1 to 8 (average of 3);
1 or 2 litters per year
Age of Maturity: male, in its second year;
female, 11 to 12 months
Longevity: can live 4 to 5 years in the wild,
but most do not live beyond their second year;
6 years in captivity
Diet: primarily roots of perennial forbs as well
as green parts of plants
Habitat: grassy prairies, mountain meadows,
fields, brushy areas, riverbanks and open
pine forests; broad range of soil tolerance
but prefers moist, not wet, soils
Predators: owls, badger, weasel, skunk,
coyote, fox and snakes
Dental Formula:
1/1, 0/0, 1/1, 3/3 = 20 teeth

NORTHERN POCKET GOPHER *Thomomys talpoides*

The northern pocket gopher inhabits the deep soils of the northern prairies and the meadows of the western mountains. It is the northernmost species of pocket gopher. It prefers moist rather than wet soils and will tolerate heavy soil. In the summer months, these gophers may move from drier soils to damper ones. Also, during the summer nights, they make brief, above-ground foraging trips to cut herbaceous plants, which they drag down into their burrows. Weasels, badgers and gopher snakes are their main predators.

The **plains pocket gopher**, *Geomys bursarius*, is one of the largest pocket gophers. It inhabits sandy soils in the central prairies and avoids clay and gravelly soils.

THE VARIABLE GOPHER

Pocket gophers are an exclusively North American group. They are not particularly ancient; in fact, modern genera began to appear only four million years ago. Yet within that time, the group has diversified into some

35 different species and 300 subspecies.

A subspecies is a race or variety of the main species—a group of populations that is physically different from other populations of the species and inhabits a distinct geographical area. There are several difficulties with subspecific description. It is more arbitrary than description of true species. Species are usually genetically, physically and otherwise distinct entities, but subspecies intergrade. Clear-cut boundaries between sub-

An escaping pocket gopher seems to dive literally headfirst into the soil, clearing its way with strong forelimbs.

species often do not exist, and only sophisticated statistical analysis can distinguish differences between populations. However, members of a species do vary in appearance, and the subspecific category is a useful way of documenting that variation. The variation is interesting because it demonstrates how subdivided and plastic some species are.

Biologically, a species is defined as a population of individuals that can interbreed. The mixing of genes during sexual reproduction makes every member of the species part of a common gene pool that is distinct and separate from the gene pool of other species. Sometimes, however, members of one population may cross a geographical barrier, such as a river, and interbreed with a different population. Over time, the genetic composition of the two populations may diverge through mutation or localized selection. A gopher population living in a high-altitude region, for example, is under different environmental pressures than one living in a low-altitude region, and localized differences will develop within the same species, and this will create subspecies. If the differences and the isolation are reinforced, the subspecies may become so different that they are no longer capable of interbreeding and must be considered separate species.

Pocket gophers represent an extreme case of species subdivision. Because the animals are quite sedentary, rates of interbreeding between various populations may be low. Yet there is great variety within a species, making the taxonomy of pocket gophers exceedingly difficult. Geographically separate populations of some species look as different from each other as members of other species do. Traditional taxonomy relies on physical characteristics to determine an animal's species. With gophers, however, this is often not sufficient, and taxonomists must use genetic techniques to make an absolute identification. All of this suggests that the speciation process is still active in pocket gophers.

PLAINS POCKET GOPHER
Geomys bursarius

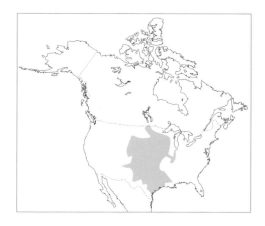

Mammal: *Geomys bursarius,* plains pocket gopher
Meaning of Name: *Geomys* (earth + mouse); *bursarius* (purse), probably refers to large, external fur-lined cheek pouches
Description: much larger than northern pocket gopher; pelage is slate-gray underneath and brown- tipped; rich brown hair on back, lighter on belly; white forefeet, dirty white hind feet; long tail sparsely covered with white hair
Total Length: male, 9.8 to 12.8 inches; female, 8.3 to 11.5 inches
Tail: male, 2.6 to 4.1 inches; female, 2.0 to 3.9 inches
Weight: male, 6.9 to 13.5 ounces; female, 3.8 to 11.4 ounces
Gestation: at least 51 days
Offspring: 1 to 7 (average of 2 to 4); 1 to 3 litters per year
Age of Maturity: not known
Longevity: average at least 2 years
Diet: primarily roots, bulbs and tender green plants
Habitat: grassland, pastures, lawns, prairie areas with sandy loam
Predators: king snake, great horned owl, weasel, skunk, badger
Dental Formula:
1/1, 0/0, 1/1, 3/3 = 20 teeth

KANGAROO RATS & POCKET MICE *Heteromyidae*

Kangaroo rats and pocket mice are close relatives of pocket gophers, but they have evolved in a different direction. While pocket gophers went underground and evolved a long, squat body with powerful forelimbs, kangaroo rats became upright animals with small, weak forelimbs and large hind limbs designed for bouncing across arid open habitats. Like kangaroos, they have a long tail for balance when they hop, and elongated hind feet for a base. Their neck is short, which keeps the head stable when they hop. They share with the pocket gophers fur-lined mouth pockets for transporting seeds; they also have similar teeth.

The heteromyid rodents are delicate mice with thin bones and a narrow, mouselike skull with a huge enlargement at the ear bones, an adaptation that allows them to detect the sound of approaching predators. The family is confined to the Americas and contains 75 species.

Pocket mice are bounders. They have enlarged hind feet that propel them along in leaps of a yard or more. But unlike kangaroo rats, pocket mice stand in a horizontal bipedal posture rather than upright. Their tail is about one body length long, shorter than and not as bushy as the kangaroo rat's.

ORD'S KANGAROO RAT
Dipodomys ordii

Ord's is the most generalized and wide-ranging kangaroo rat. Like all members of the genus, it is a bipedal hopper, living in dry, sandy areas. Its tail and hind legs are large and are used for locomotion, for dodging predators and for communicating and fighting with other kangaroo rats.

This kangaroo rat, like the others, is not a strong digger, but it makes burrows in the sand where it hides during the day. The burrows, less than 3 feet deep, lead to a grass-lined nest and side chambers for seed storage as well as some surface branching tunnels. The nest is usually built into the side of a bank or mound. A series of well-worn trails used in foraging extends from the entrance. This rat also constructs shallow funk holes, which it uses to avoid predators temporarily.

The Ord's kangaroo rat eats most kinds of seeds found in the areas where it lives. It will also eat grasshoppers, moths and other insects along with some roots and green leafy material. It may depend on succulent legumes with fleshy tubers for much of its water requirement in dry periods.

The breeding system of the Ord's kangaroo rat is tied to the rains. Few females come into estrus

Like the kangaroo, the kangaroo rat has a long, balancing tail and large hind limbs for hopping. Its ear bones—enlarged, as are those of the other heteromyid rodents—are adapted for detecting the sound of approaching predators.

ORD'S KANGAROO RAT
Dipodomys ordii

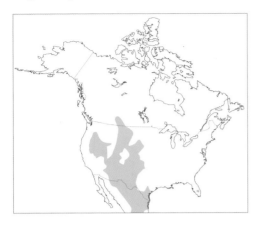

Mammal: *Dipodomys ordii*,
Ord's kangaroo rat

Meaning of Name: *Dipodomys*
(two-footed mouse); *ordii* (named after pioneer
American zoologist George Ord)

Description: upper parts are tawny with a
few black hairs along the mid-dorsal line; white
underparts; white spot over each eye; white
lines across the hips; ventral stripe tapers to a
point near the tip of the tail; two gray lines
above and below tail and gray terminal
tuft; furred cheek pouches; large, luminous
dorsal eyes

Total Length: 10.4 to 11.1 inches

Tail: 5.6 to 6.2 inches

Weight: 1.9 to 3.4 ounces
(peaks in breeding season)

Gestation: 29 to 30 days

Offspring: 1 to 6; may be 2 litters per year

Age of Maturity: may be capable
of breeding at 2 months

Longevity: at least 2 years in the wild

Diet: seeds, grasses and forbs form most
of the diet; also some fruits, leaves, stems,
buds and insects

Habitat: sandy soils in open areas
with sparse brush or grass

Predators: rattlesnake, burrowing short-eared
owl, horned owl, badger, black-footed ferret,
skunk, fox, coyote and weasel

Dental Formula:
1/1, 0/0, 1/1, 3/3 = 20 teeth

during dry times, whereas rains will stimulate breeding. This corresponds to a similar behavior on the part of the plants. Many plant species in arid areas adjust their flowering and seed production to the abundance of winter rain. Kangaroo rats can adjust their reproduction to match the expected seed crop. There may be a breeding period following each of the winter and summer rainy seasons.

Kangaroo rats are solitary and territorial. Individuals fight by jumping in the air and slashing at each other with their clawed hind legs. They also turn backward and kick sand at enemies, including rattlesnakes.

Snakes are prominent nocturnal predators in the hot, arid open habitat of the kangaroo rat, and some of the rat's sensory physiology is designed to match the physical features of this environment. Kangaroo rats have large dorsally placed eyes that give them excellent night vision and a view of aerial predators such as owls. Their hugely enlarged eardrums are sensitive to very low-frequency sounds, which enables them to hear the wing beat of an approaching owl and detect the air-pressure wave of a striking rattlesnake. Because of this ability, kangaroo rats are often able to leap out of the way of a striking snake. A kangaroo rat can leap 6 feet in one hop.

Low-frequency sound transmits well in open areas and through the ground. Accordingly, kangaroo rats can pick up the footsteps of approaching predators, and they drum their own feet to communicate with other kangaroo rats. Both the distress call of the young kangaroo rat and the threat growl are sent out at low frequencies. This is at the opposite end of the spectrum from mice and small insectivores such as shrews, moles and bats, which use high-frequency ultrasound in their communication.

Heteromyids such as kangaroo rats can live in the driest habitats, obtaining all the water they need from dried plant seeds.

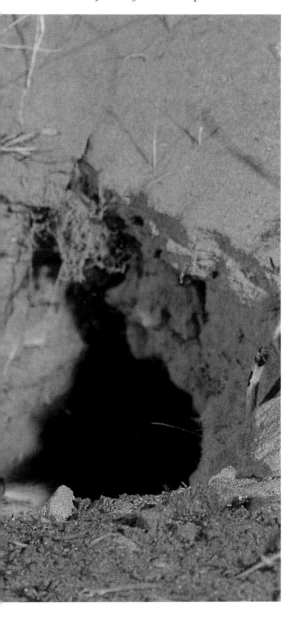

OLIVE-BACKED POCKET MOUSE *Perognathus fasciatus*

Weighing only one-quarter to one-third of an ounce, the olive-backed pocket mouse is one of the smallest North American rodents. It is a resident of dry shortgrass prairie, especially where the soil is sandy and there are bare areas. It is a solitary species and makes shallow burrows through the light sand, avoiding heavy and humus-rich soils. The forepaws are used in digging, something that kangaroo rats are unable or unwilling to do. The pocket mouse often takes sand baths, which may reduce its skin-parasite load and help keep it clean. Sand-bathing is also thought to be a form of scent-marking that declares territorial presence. The sand piles that result from burrowing and the subsequent use of these piles for bathing may be forms of chemical communication among pocket mice and other heteromyids.

The olive-backed pocket mouse and other pocket mouse species build summer nests roughly 1 to 2 feet below the surface and winter nests 6 feet deep. They go into a torpor during cold weather but are not deep hibernators and rely on caches of stored seeds to get through the winter. They obtain all their water from these seeds.

Pocket mice breed twice in a season, in spring and summer, producing a litter of about four. Owls, snakes and predatory mammals such as weasels and skunks prey on pocket mice.

The **Great Basin pocket mouse**, *Perognathus parvus*, has a biology similar to that of the olive-backed pocket mouse, except that instead of seeds, it eats significant numbers of insects in summer. The habitat of this mouse is the shrubby plains of the Great Basin in the western United States.

OLIVE-BACKED POCKET MOUSE *Perognathus fasciatus*

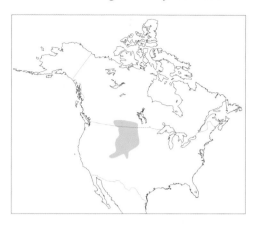

Mammal: *Perognathus fasciatus*, olive-backed pocket mouse
Meaning of Name: *Perognathus* refers to the fur-lined pockets on the outside of the cheeks, where it stores and carries food; *fasciatus* (from *fascia*, band or girdle)
Description: stiff but silky pelage; external fur-lined cheek pouches can be turned inside out for washing; olive-gray dorsally, white underparts bordered by a buffy yellow stripe that runs from the cheek to the thigh
Total Length: 4.5 to 5.7 inches
Tail: 2.2 to 2.6 inches
Weight: 0.25 to 0.35 ounce
Gestation: not known (probably 3 to 4 weeks)
Offspring: 4 to 6; 1 litter per year (may have 2)
Age of Maturity: if born early in the season, can breed by late summer
Longevity: 2 years
Diet: major food is weed seeds but will also eat insects
Habitat: open grasslands with sandy loam; also found on the edge of aspen parklands
Predators: rattlesnake, owls, weasel, badger, skunk, fox, coyote, deer mouse and grasshopper mouse
Dental Formula:
1/1, 0/0, 1/1, 3/3 = 20 teeth

BEAVER *Castoridae*

The Castoridae are a declining lineage. They once ranged throughout the northern hemisphere and included terrestrial as well as aquatic species. One extinct group constructed deep, spiraling burrows. Another evolved into a gigantic muskratlike animal the size of a black bear that fed on marshy vegetation. The family seems to have originated in North America as a group of digging rodents and eventually spread to Asia. Modern semiaquatic beavers arose in Asia and then emigrated to North America. Now, only a single North American beaver species remains, and the populations of its Eurasian counterpart are reduced to tiny remnants. Nevertheless, the North American beaver is among the most successful of the continent's mammals.

BEAVER *Castor canadensis*

The beaver is not simply a creature of northern forests but ranges from northern Mexico to the southwestern deserts of the United States, from Rocky Mountain meadows to the very edge of the Arctic tundra. Beavers appear to live almost anywhere in the temperate region where there are trees to eat and water to live in. Most of their adaptations involve these two necessities.

The beaver is the second-largest rodent in the world. Only the South American capybara, which can weigh up to 150 pounds, surpasses it in size. The beaver has a sturdy skeleton to support the strong muscles it uses for dragging trees and building dams. Its skull is massive, supporting a bite capable of slicing into large hardwood trees, and its teeth are as wide and stout as wood chisels. Its large, webbed hind feet make it a powerful swimmer. The beaver has nostrils that can close, valves to shut the ears, lips that seal the mouth for chewing underwater and a membrane to protect the open eye. Its fur is dense and sleek, and it possesses a special split toenail on the hind foot for grooming. The large, flattened tail serves as a rudder that allows the beaver to swim and steer efficiently while towing branches and logs. The tail is muscular and can be used to produce a burst of speed underwater. On land, it props the beaver into an upright position for cutting trees. The beaver has a well-developed diving reflex that slows the heart, reduces blood circulation to the extremities and conserves enough oxygen for it to remain submerged for 15 minutes.

The most remarkable adaptations of the beaver are behavioral ones. Beavers build dams, lodges and food caches. When they move into a new area along an unoccupied stream, the first thing they build is a dam. Normally, a dam is placed at a narrow spot in a valley, which minimizes the amount of material needed for construction, but in a flat habitat, a dam may extend for hundreds of yards. The dam is a composite of logs, sticks, rocks and muck that impedes but does not halt the flow of water. Most of the outflow percolates through the dam rather than over it so that the current does not continually erode the dam. The dam serves several purposes. It backs up water, giving the

The beaver is a selective forager, gathering only specific sizes and species of trees. Inefficient on land, the beaver conserves energy by cutting large trees only when they are close to the water. The farther the beaver must travel to drag new building materials back to its lodge, the smaller the tree.

BEAVER *Castor canadensis*

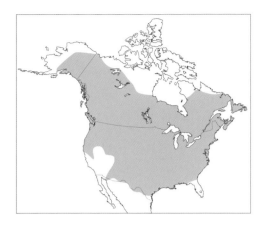

Mammal: *Castor canadensis*, beaver; largest rodent in North America

Meaning of Name: *Castor* (beaver); *canadensis* (of Canada)

Description: unique tail is well furred at the thick base but only sparsely haired on its paddle; rich glossy brown or yellowish brown pelage with chestnut-brown to tawny underparts; black tail and feet; horny pads underneath the first two claws (claws have serrated edges for combing and grooming); lips meet behind incisors, enabling beaver to cut branches underwater

Total Length: male, 39 to 44 inches; female, 37 to 45 inches

Tail: male, 15 to 21 inches; female, 16 to 20 inches

Weight: 28.7 to 77.1 pounds

Gestation: 90 to 110 days

Offspring: 1 to 9 (usually 2 to 4); 1 litter per year

Age of Maturity: 1.5 to 3 years (sometimes 4, depending on exploitation and environmental factors)

Longevity: 10 to 15 years in the wild; one lived 24 years in captivity

Diet: nonwoody vegetation in the summer and woody vegetation in the winter; bark cut from soft cambium layer, leaves, twigs, buds, water vegetation and submerged roots; has been known to exhibit coprophagy

Habitat: forested areas (prefers stands in early successional stages) associated with ponds, lakes and slow-flowing rivers and streams; occasionally in streams on the prairies, muskegs, tundra and alpine meadows

Predators: coyote, timber wolf, domestic dog, red fox, eagle, black bear, lynx, bobcat, fisher and mink

Dental Formula:
1/1, 0/0, 1/1, 3/3 = 20 teeth

beaver easy access to trees and reducing its need to travel over land, where it is vulnerable to predators. Beavers will also build canals that run for hundreds of feet. They may divert other streams into the canal system and build smaller dams, all to create water access to stands of food. It is much easier for them to tow branches through water than to transport them overland. The dam may be 10 feet high or more to provide adequate water depth to build a secure lodge.

A lodge typically has an underwater entrance near the pond or stream bottom, making entry difficult for all predators but otters. The interior has a dry raised platform consisting of a previously emergent streambank or constructed of enough layers of woody debris and mud to be above water level. The roof of the lodge is a thick weave of intermeshed twigs, and before winter, when the lodge will be occupied, the roof is layered and smeared with muck and mud that freeze into a hard, virtually impenetrable roof. Much of the material used in lodge construction comes from branches the beavers have already cut and eaten the bark from.

For winter, beavers build food caches —piles of interwoven branches and sticks placed in the water—to which they gain access by swimming under the ice from the lodge. Their food caching is an adaptation to the ice cover inherent in northern winters; southern beaver populations do not cache food.

Beavers will excavate bank burrows for summer use where soil conditions permit. Bank dens may or may not be covered with branches and mud.

Lodge construction requires much of the beavers' time and involves continuous maintenance. The value of the territory they create is high, so they need to be vigilant in defending it against other beavers. They have developed a cooperative, territorial family unit that maintains its lodges, dams and feeding areas and excludes unrelated beavers. All members of the colony scent-mark around the water's edge and along the dam with a musky secretion from the

castoreum gland as well as with urine and possibly oil. They also scent-mark special foot-high mounds that they build of vegetation and debris. The castoreum scent gland produces a complex pheromonal mixture of more than 50 different kinds of molecules, enough complexity to give each beaver its own unique chemical signature. It is not known how much individual recognition exists in beavers, but it is clear that colony members can smell and distinguish one another's scent from that of outsiders. The dominant male beaver, in particular, becomes highly aggressive if he smells foreign castoreum. The beavers will hiss and slap their tails when they smell the scent and then investigate it. Trappers take advantage of scent-marking behavior by rubbing beaver castoreum on beaver traps; they never fail to attract the resident beaver. Under normal conditions, a foreign beaver detected in this way will be attacked and driven out. Beavers can inflict formidable gouges and bites and have been known to kill intruding beavers in territorial disputes.

The social structure of a beaver colony is based on a monogamous mating pair. They share a lodge and cooperate in sharing building duties and territorial defense. The female normally selects the home site and generates the social stability of the family unit. If her mate dies, she will remain in the territory and accept a new male. If the female dies, however, the territory may be abandoned.

The pair produces one litter each year and tolerates the presence of previous offspring. How many offspring remain in the colony and for how long apparently varies according to the quality of the habitat. Typically, the male and female pair is accompanied by the immature young of the year and several other juveniles that may be as old as 2½ years. The presence of an extended family of closely related kin explains the use of the tail slap on the water as a warning signal. Even though the slapping draws a predator's attention to the beaver issuing the warning, the benefi-

The dams and lodges built by the beaver can radically alter the surrounding landscape. The underwater entrance of the lodge keeps out almost every predator.

ciaries of this warning will, in most cases, be close relatives.

Most colonies include 5 or 6 individuals, 12 being a reported maximum. Twelve adult beavers would weigh close to half a ton and would place severe grazing pressure on the surrounding trees. Pressure on the local food resource seems to select for juvenile dispersal, which appears to be instinctive in 2-year-old beavers and not necessarily the result of eviction by the parents. Low-quality habitats have the highest rate of juvenile dispersal. Most beavers move only a few miles during the dis-

persal phase, but one tagged animal is known to have moved 150 miles. It is also possible that one of the juvenile beavers may ultimately inherit the lodge and territory of its parents.

In any case, all juveniles acquire a considerable amount of knowledge and experience from their residency in the parental colony. Young beavers are born in spring in the lodge, usually in a clutch of two to four. They are furred but remain in the lodge, where they are breast-fed for a full month or more. All members of the colony cooperate in bringing food to the young, but the parental male does most of the work, a highly unusual pattern in mammals. The year or more that young beavers spend as members of the parental colony is devoted not just to growth but

also to learning and polishing the techniques of construction and tree felling. Experience and strength appear to be necessary for a beaver to be successful. Reproduction is usually physiologically impossible until the animal is 2 years of age, quite old for rodents. Beavers continue to grow for four or five years in the extreme parts of their range and up to nine years in more central regions.

Beavers eat shrubs and weedy vegetation in the summer months, but their tree cutting gives them a unique resource base. Beavers have felled trees almost 4 feet in diameter. Cutting and harvesting a tree this size requires some special techniques. Beavers are not able to fell trees with any great directional precision, but they may not need to. The direction in which a tree falls

depends on its lean, the wind and the presence of obstructions. The trees they cut are near the water's edge and naturally tend to lean toward the open area above the pond or stream and usually away from a downhill slope. Thus, on average, trees fall toward the water. Beavers trim off smaller limbs to take away, normally leaving the heavy trunk behind. Most of the nutrients they need are in the young bark and leaves. The felling of large trees allows sun-loving pioneer trees such as willow and aspen to sprout. They are trees that coppice easily, and many generations of quickly harvested stump sprouts can be taken before the tree dies. Thus the beaver often modifies mature stands of unpalatable hardwoods and conifers to create faster-growing stands of palatable species that are easily harvested.

Few other wild animals, except possibly elephants, modify the landscape as much as beavers do. Prior to the European colonization of North America, an estimated 60 million beavers existed. Colonies need about a mile to a mile and a half of stream or pond shoreline, so many millions of acres of forest and wetland wildlife were under the consid-

The low energy cost and the relative safety of water transport explain why the beaver builds dams and canals.

erable influence of beavers. Although beavers were decimated and entirely trapped out in many regions, they have been restored to most of their former range. Much of the habitat previously dominated by beavers is now occupied by humans, who have also eliminated many of the large carnivores that once preyed on beavers. As a result, beavers frequently come into conflict with farmers and other landowners.

Beavers are still heavily trapped in many areas, but in semiurban and farming regions, trapping is often economically and aesthetically unattractive, so beavers may become a problem, flooding land, plugging culverts and irrigation canals and cutting valuable trees. Without some form of regulation, populations grow until the beavers deplete their food resources and become susceptible to epidemic diseases such as tularemia. However, where beaver populations are regulated by natural predation and management plans, they bring innumerable benefits.

In addition to their high-quality fur, beavers provide significant ecological advantages. The wetlands they create are breeding and feeding habitats for waterfowl, frogs, salamanders, fish and mammals such as otters, muskrats and water shrews. Not only that, but the beavers' dams provide erosion control, conserve water and increase the water quality of large rivers by reducing the amount of silt introduced into them. The open areas that beavers create and then abandon support a distinctive set of plants that depend on disturbance for continued existence.

The impact of the beaver is so great that many of the ecological dependencies that have developed in its presence remain to be discovered. A recent example concerns a group of fruit flies that are heavily dependent on the presence of beavers. These fruit flies breed under the rotting bark and sapwood of cut willows and aspens and are never found more than a few dozen yards from water except during very wet periods. It is likely that the flies are highly dependent on beavers, whose activities create the flies' breeding sites. Thus when the beavers were threatened with extinction by overtrapping, the flies were equally threatened. This may seem insignificant, but it is worthwhile recalling that fruit flies, including those associated with beavers, have been the laboratory organisms and tools with which major insights into the genetic basis of life have been gained.

THE JUGGLING BEAVER: THE TACTICS OF OPTIMAL FORAGING

A beaver is confronted with a complicated foraging problem. It eats plants, usually trees that grow on land, but its home and refuge is in the water. It is well adapted for tree cutting but poorly adapted for moving trees overland and escaping land predators. It must assess whether it is more profitable to expend time cutting through a large tree with a huge crown of branches or to move from small tree to small tree, cutting quickly but getting little yield per tree and spending more time waddling along the ground. How far should it go from the safety of the water to get how large a tree? Some trees are more nutritious, some are hard to cut, some are better for storage, while others make better building material. Should the beaver cut in the daytime, when it is hotter and more costly, or at night, when it is cooler but predators such as bears and wolves are more active?

These are some of the difficult trade-offs that the foraging beaver faces. This kind of problem is one of optimal foraging, a branch of ecological study that addresses how animals solve these complicated questions and what constraints have influenced the design of foraging behavior by natural selection. No one believes that an individual beaver consciously assesses the pros and cons of foraging. However, the way in which its behavior has evolved should reflect the relative intensity of the different constraints. For example, if beavers spent long periods away from water, one could infer that predation pressure is relatively insignificant. On the other hand, if many animals are known to attack beavers, biologists might expect to see beavers restrict the distance they move from the water and to venture far away only for particularly valuable food items. In the end, the best foraging strategy will not be the one that yields the most food but the one that yields the most descendants. There have been several studies to investigate the way beavers solve their foraging problems.

The most obvious relationship is between the size of the tree and the distance a beaver will go to cut it. One might think that beavers would be willing to walk a long way to cut a large tree that has many leaves and branches. But the reverse is true. The larger the tree, the closer it must be to the edge of the pond. Beavers will usually go only 40 to 50 yards from water to cut, and the farther they go, the smaller the tree. This reflects the inefficiency of a beaver on land and the high cost of dragging logs across the ground. Only small trees that can be quickly cut and dragged are taken far from water. Although wolves and bears often kill them, beavers are formidable opponents of most animals. The evidence indicates that when foraging, the beaver is not trying to minimize time or exposure to predators but aiming to maximize energy by reducing the cost of the harvest.

The size of a tree and its distance from water are not the only factors in the calculation. It is also affected by tree type. A comparison study of the beavers' ash- and aspen-cutting behavior is a good illustration. Beavers would cut aspen, peel it to eat the bark or store it in a food cache and then use the remaining branches in construction. Ash, however, was used only in construction. Accordingly, they would travel farther to cut an aspen than an ash. Size selectivity, as we have seen, is influenced by distance. Thus when trees were more than 40 yards from the water's edge, the beavers were much more selective about its size. There was also a size distinction based on tree type: Of the aspens and ashes cut at the same distance from the pond, the aspens were bigger, which reflected their greater value to the beavers. The foraging strategy of the beaver is indeed a sophisticated juggling act.

MICE, RATS & VOLES *Muridae*

At one time, the Muridae family included only Old World rats and mice and was considered separate from the New World mice, known as Cricetidae. Today, however, the New and Old World species are lumped together in the family Muridae and divided into three subfamilies. Together, they make up the largest, most successful and most adaptable family of mammals. As it now stands, 78 species ranging in size from the harvest mouse to the muskrat find their home in North America.

The subfamilies, in North America at least, are quite distinct. Voles, lemmings and the muskrat form the subfamily Arvicolinae, while deer mice, harvest mice and wood rats fall into Sigmodontinae. The Sigmodontinae tend to be mouselike, with a pointed muzzle and a long, naked tail. Their natural history and generic classification are diverse, as are their habits, and they are discussed separately in the species accounts. The third subfamily is the Murinae, which includes the introduced house mouse and two introduced rat species.

As a whole, the Muridae family is usually nocturnal and omnivorous, has multiple litters and does not hibernate.

The arvicolines—voles, lemmings and the muskrat—are compact, with a shortened tail and round muzzle and head. Both groups originated in the Tertiary period (70 million years ago), but it was only relatively recently, especially in the Pleistocene epoch (1 million years ago), that their explosive and rich speciation took place.

Voles and lemmings are the dominant small mammals of the far north and are an important source of food for predatory mammals and raptors. There is little physical variation among the arvicoline species. They are all stocky and have blunt noses, small eyes and ears and short tails; they run low to the ground, their legs almost hidden beneath the body. The largest species, such as Richardson's water vole and the yellow-cheeked vole, weigh about 4 ounces and the smallest, the creeping vole, less than 1 ounce.

All species are herbivores with teeth adapted for grinding vegetation very finely, and they have an enlarged intestinal chamber in which the ground plant material is fermented. Some species cache food stores, and others do not. Most of them, however, eat a significant proportion of their feces in the same manner as rabbits. Voles and lemmings depend on plant material to supply their water, and as their kidneys are not efficient in water conservation, only a few species are found in arid habitats.

Voles and lemmings have a high reproductive rate. Males are capable of breeding two months after birth, but females may mature only three weeks afterward. Pregnancy is short and usually lasts less than three weeks.

Most species have eight mammary glands and can feed that many young when the food supply is adequate. The young, born in a well-insulated nest, are naked, blind and helpless. They develop rapidly and are weaned within three weeks. The mothers can become pregnant immediately after

Members of the Muridae family such as this diminutive deer mouse may look unassuming, but they are among the most successful of all mammals and comprise dozens of species.

giving birth and while they are still lactating. This gives them a phenomenal reproductive potential—in captivity, one meadow vole female produced 17 consecutive litters within a year, resulting in 83 offspring and 78 grandchildren before she reached her first birthday.

The high birth rate is accompanied by a high mortality rate. Average life expectancy in the field is often only a month; under ideal conditions, they may live for roughly a year, and a rare few make it to two years. Their populations fluctuate wildly from less than one animal to thousands per acre in three- to four-year cycles. When vole and lemming populations peak, many mammal and bird predators eat nothing else.

In most species, females are aggres-

sive and territorial; males are sometimes territorial and fight for access to females. Females take an active role in courtship, following the male and investigating his scent, sometimes attacking and killing strange males. Males taking over a territory may kill the offspring of a female and, when mating, produce a mating plug to prevent other males from mating with her. Home ranges of polygynous males tend to be larger than those of females and take in several burrows. Mature males use scent glands along the sides of their bodies to mark their territories. The marked area changes radically with population density but usually measures a little over an acre. An acre will normally accommodate dozens of voles or lemmings.

The highly prolific meadow vole, whose average lifespan in the wild is less than a year, begins to breed at the age of three weeks.

For the western harvest mouse, the advantages of being light and small include the ability to climb small plants in search of seeds and other foods such as grasshoppers and moths.

Mammal: *Reithrodontomys megalotis,* western harvest mouse

Meaning of Name: *Reithrodontomys* (groove-toothed mouse) refers to grooves on upper incisor teeth; *megalotis* (large + ear)

Description: pale gray to brown above; dark mid-dorsal stripe runs from forehead to tail; brown flanks and cheeks; underparts and feet vary from white to deep gray

Total Length: 4.7 to 6 inches

Tail: 2.3 to 3.2 inches

Weight: 0.32 to 0.60 ounce

Gestation: 23 to 24 days

Offspring: 1 to 9 (usually 2 to 4); several litters per year (up to 14 in captivity)

Age of Maturity: 4.5 months

Longevity: few live more than 1 year in the wild (maximum 18 months)

Diet: primarily seeds of grasses and forbs as well as green shoots of vegetation; insects (moths and grasshoppers)

Habitat: stands of shortgrass with clumps of forbs and small shrubs scattered throughout; dense vegetation near water

Predators: snakes, squirrels, owls, shrikes, weasel, skunk, fox and larger shrews and mice

Dental Formula:
1/1, 0/0, 0/0, 3/3 = 16 teeth

WESTERN HARVEST MOUSE
Reithrodontomys megalotis

The western harvest mouse is one of the tiniest mice in North America, weighing roughly four-tenths of an ounce. It is a grassland species that lives in areas with a mixture of open and shrubby vegetation. Mainly a herbivore, it feeds on leaves, grass and herbs in summer and switches to seeds in autumn and winter. It caches both leaves and seeds. The western harvest mouse will also eat insects, especially lepidopterous larvae. It often uses the runways of other rodents, especially those of meadow voles, and it builds fist-sized grass nests in vegetation clumps and other protected spots, where it rests during daylight hours. A harvest mouse's light weight enables it to climb around shrubbery and other vegetation in search of food. Except in the winter months, these mice appear to be continually reproductive, females producing several litters of one to nine offspring a year. Harvest mice rarely live for more than a year.

WHITE-FOOTED MOUSE
Peromyscus leucopus

Mammal: *Peromyscus leucopus*, white-footed mouse

Meaning of Name: *Peromyscus* (little pouched mouse); may also be from Latin *pero* (pointed), which refers to the characteristic pointed nose; *leucopus* (white foot)

Description: short, soft, dense pelage; light brown in color with dark dorsal stripe; white underparts with gray base; white throat; black spot at base of whiskers; ears outlined in white but no preorbital tuft of white hair; indistinctly bicolored tail is paler below

Total Length: 5.7 to 7.7 inches

Tail: 2.4 to 3.7 inches

Weight: 0.53 to 1.1 ounces

Gestation: 22 to 25 days

Offspring: 1 to 9 (usually 4); 2 to 4 litters per year

Age of Maturity: male, 7 to 11 weeks; female, as early as 4 weeks

Longevity: usually do not survive into second year in the wild; can survive 5 years or more in captivity

Diet: primarily seeds of grasses, weeds, clover, fungi, fruits and nuts; also larvae and cocoons of beetles, moths, butterflies and other invertebrates

Habitat: primarily associated with deciduous woodland and shrubby habitat; sometimes occur in open areas

Predators: snakes, owls, weasel, mink, fox, skunk, raccoon and domestic cat

Dental Formula:
1/1, 0/0, 0/0, 3/3 = 16 teeth

The white-footed mouse looks like the deer mouse and shares its habitat but is more arboreal than its ground-bound counterpart.

WHITE-FOOTED MOUSE
Peromyscus leucopus

The white-footed mouse looks so much like the deer mouse that the two species can be very difficult to distinguish from each other. The white-footed mouse is generally smaller, has less contrast in its bicolored tail and also lacks the white ear tufts characteristic of deer mice.

Large, shining eyes, long, sensitive whiskers and large ears are indicators of its nocturnal existence. Most white-footed mice are active year-round, even in the most inclement weather. Others become torpid in winter, and some huddle in communal nests below ground, strategies that help them conserve energy. The communal nests even have a social structure in that the dominant mouse usually nestles snugly in the middle, leaving the colder outside areas for lower-ranking individuals.

When the breeding season arrives in March, these aggregations split up and the females establish nonoverlapping home ranges that they defend aggressively. The white-footed mouse is prolific, a necessity given its short lifespan in the wild, which averages less than five months. The female produces several litters in quick succession, and the young are ready to breed when they are about 2 months old. It is not surprising that the white-footed mouse is usually the most abundant small mammal in its range.

DEER MOUSE
Peromyscus maniculatus

The deer mouse is extremely common and widespread. A habitat generalist, it lives in areas ranging from mature deciduous and boreal forests to dry grasslands, and in rural areas, it is often a common resident of human habitations. The deer mouse is the only native rodent that seems to prefer houses as a place to live. Of all non-commercial mammals, this species is the most studied. Almost any North American mammalogist can find a nearby population to observe.

The diet of deer mice is as general as its choice of habitat. It eats and stores many kinds of seeds (especially wild-cherry pits and hickory nuts), flowers, berries and insects, and it will even eat salamanders and bird eggs when given the chance. Deer mice cache large volumes of seeds for winter use, up to almost a gallon in each cache. Generally, these seeds are smaller than those selected by squirrels and include species such as ragweed, tick trefoil and grasses. Seed abundance is the most critical part of the deer mouse's feeding requirements.

Deer mice are sedentary and have well-defined home ranges of 3 acres or less in size. They use clearly defined trails and build well-insulated nests of fine, dry vegetation in protected spots such as hollow logs and under rocks. They have a strong homing tendency and will return to the home range even after being moved 2 miles away. Home ranges overlap, and there is little aggressive territoriality except for breeding purposes. A female will repel intruders from the vicinity of her breeding nest.

Females can breed several times in a season. They usually mate and give birth in spring to a litter of one to eleven, then mate and become pregnant again almost immediately. Gestation lasts three weeks to a month, depending on whether the female is breast-feeding another litter. The young are born helpless and take roughly a month to be weaned. As weaning time approaches,

DEER MOUSE
Peromyscus maniculatus

Life in the wild for the deer mouse is filled with challenges. While 95 percent of wild mice do not survive their first year, the deer mouse can live for eight years in captivity.

the pregnant mother will usually move to a new nest to give birth.

One important aspect of the breeding biology of the deer mouse may be male parental care. Few mammals have male parental care, but deer mice do. The female excludes the male from the nest when the young are born but later accepts his presence. He assists in grooming his offspring, maintaining the nest and accompanying the young weaned mice on foraging trips. When juveniles mature, the adult male is thought to expel them aggressively from his territory. Whether males provide parental care or not may depend on the density of females. Males can sometimes exclude other males and mate with several different females, which may reduce the opportunity for and the value of parental care for the male. On the other hand, if male parental care increases the female reproductive rate and juvenile survival, it might pay females to tolerate the presence of other females. There are some reports of communal broods consisting of two females.

Deer mouse densities vary greatly from season to season and year to year. The abundance of the year's seed crop may greatly affect overwintering mortality. Captive deer mice live as long as eight years, but in the wild, few of them ever see their first birthday. Densities at

the start of spring are often a tenth of what they were the previous autumn. Population turnover—the replacement of older individuals by new individuals—has been measured at 95 percent per year. In other words, only 5 percent of deer mice survive more than a year.

To conserve heat during winter, deer mice may huddle in groups. They enter a daily torpor, allowing their body temperature to drop, and then they heat up again for an active feeding and foraging period in the evening.

Owls and carnivorous mammals feed heavily on deer mice, especially in winter when the mice travel over snowfields and there is little protective cover. Deer mice wisely avoid travel on moonlit nights. It has been shown that the success of short-eared owls hunting for deer mice increases as the moon waxes.

The **Keen's mouse**, *Peromyscus keeni*, is a close relative of the deer mouse. It inhabits the damp West Coast forest of Englemann spruce and other conifers and the coastal islands of British Columbia. It is not known how different this species' life history is from that of the more common deer mouse, but where the deer mouse is found, the Keen's mouse seems to disappear even though it is larger. The more generalized deer mouse probably outcompetes the Keen's mouse.

Mammal: *Peromyscus maniculatus,* deer mouse

Meaning of Name: *Peromyscus* (little pouched mouse); *maniculatus* (small-handed)

Description: pale grayish buff to deep reddish brown dorsally with white flanks and underparts; tail is always sharply bicolored, black above and white below; ears are covered in fine gray hair with tufts of whitish hair at the anterior base

Total Length: 4.8 inches

Tail: 1.8 to 5 inches

Weight: 0.42 to 1.2 ounces

Gestation: 22 to 35 days

Offspring: 1 to 11 (usually 4 to 6); 2 to 4 litters per year (can have up to 14)

Age of Maturity: male, 40 to 45 days; female, 32 to 35 days

Longevity: few survive past 1 year in the wild (maximum 32 months); have lived as long as 8 years in captivity

Diet: primarily a seed eater; also nuts, acorns, fruits, mushrooms, flowers and berries as well as insects and their eggs and larvae, caterpillars and spiders

Habitat: broad tolerance; occurs in almost every dryland habitat within its range (not found in moist areas); alpine areas, boreal forests, woodlands, grasslands, brushlands, meadowlands and cultivated fields

Predators: owls, weasel and fox are probably its most important predators; also snakes, short-tailed shrew, squirrels, skunk, mink, raccoon, bear, coyote, wolf and large fish

Dental Formula:
1/1, 0/0, 0/0, 3/3 = 16 teeth

NORTHERN GRASSHOPPER MOUSE *Onychomys leucogaster*

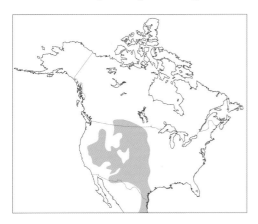

Mammal: *Onychomys leucogaster*, northern grasshopper mouse
Meaning of Name: *Onychomys* (claw-mouse) because of its large claws; *leucogaster* (white belly)
Description: short, fleshy tapering tail; stomach has specialized brown glandular swelling midway along the greater curvature; no cheek pouches; ruffled-looking pelage is long, fine and oily; brownish gray to pinkish cinnamon or buff upper parts; grayish white cheeks, nose and feet; underparts are pure white; tail is grayish white below and gray above and has white tip; whitish tufts around ears
Total Length: 5.6 to 6.3 inches
Tail: 1 to 2.4 inches
Weight: 0.9 to 1.8 ounces
Gestation: 26 to 37 days for nonlactating females; 32 to 47 days for lactating females
Offspring: 1 to 6 (average of 4); several litters per year (up to 12 in captivity)
Age of Maturity: 2 to 5 months
Longevity: not known (probably 1 year in the wild)
Diet: primarily an insectivore (grasshoppers, beetles, caterpillars, moths, ants, flies); also other invertebrates such as spiders and small vertebrates (mice and voles); seeds of wild forbs and other plants in summer
Habitat: shortgrass prairies and desert scrub
Predators: rattlesnake, ground squirrel, weasel, ferret, badger, fox, coyote and owls
Dental Formula:
1/1, 0/0, 0/0, 3/3 =16 teeth

NORTHERN GRASSHOPPER MOUSE *Onychomys leucogaster*

Although most mice feed primarily on plants, the grasshopper mouse thrives on meat. It has a stout body, large claws, heavy forepaws, a strong set of jaws, a sturdy head and no cheek pouches, all of which are related to its diet. Grasshopper mice do, in fact, eat grasshoppers and many other invertebrates, including scorpions, caterpillars and even groups with hard bodies such as dung beetles. Grasshopper mice will corner and kill other species of mice with a bite to the base of the skull, the same technique used by carnivores such as weasels and cats.

The grasshopper mouse is a slow runner. Its short, stubby limbs seem designed more for digging. In its native desert and grassland habitat, it builds an extensive system of burrows at the soil surface and will use the runways of other small mammals. The burrows have sections for food caches, an underground nest to retreat to during the day, sanitation burrows and short segments at the edge of the territory that are scent-marked and used to declare territorial perimeters. Like other carnivores, this mouse has a relatively large home range and is intensely territorial. The grasshopper mouse emits a loud wolf-style "howl." It rears up on its hind legs with its head back and utters a high-pitched shriek that sounds like a whistle. The howl is thought to be a declaration of territoriality. Grasshopper mice also use other vocal calls, including a repeated barking squeak.

In winter, when insect numbers are reduced, the grasshopper mouse relies on seeds for food. It is possible that this mouse competes more with shrews than with other species of mice.

SEX-RATIO MANIPULATION

Most mammals have close to a 1:1 sex ratio at birth, which maximizes the reproductive success of the average mother. Since every individual is derived from a male parent and a female parent, the average genetic value of a son will equal that of a daughter. They both have the same opportunity to contribute genes to the next generation. That is what a mother is selected to do —to maximize the number of genes that her sons and daughters will contribute to future generations. What happens if she produces only sons or only daughters instead of a 1:1 mixture?

When a population produces an excess of females, selection will favor the female that produces plenty of sons, since their mating success will be higher than that of daughters. There will be a large number of females to mate and few male competitors, so the sons will produce more offspring than the average daughters. The reverse situation also holds: When there is an excess of males, producing daughters is the best strategy. Thus the population converges to the 1:1 sex-ratio strategy.

The best strategy is for females to produce a litter of half males and half females. Nature, however, is more complicated than this. Sons and daughters are not equally valuable. Their value— the benefits they will yield in grandchildren minus the costs of producing them—ought to influence the parent. Normally, parents give birth to equal numbers of males and females, but if one sex costs more than the other to produce, then relatively few of the more expensive sex will be produced. Thus, on average, the total resources invested in males will equal the amount invested in females.

A further complication is that the reproductive success of sons and daughters depends on the breeding system of the population, on whether the population is growing, stable or declining and on the condition of the mother and how it affects the condition of her offspring. If the mating system is a harem system, where only a few males control access to the females, there may be intense selection for producing large, high-quality sons. A large, competitive son may mate

Unlike most mice, the slow-moving northern grasshopper mouse flourishes on a diet of meat—including grasshoppers, scorpions and caterpillars—rather than plants.

with many females, while a low-quality son will have almost no chance to fight for and obtain a harem.

By contrast, virtually all daughters, whether they are fit or not, will be mated and included in a harem. In this situation, a mother in less than prime physiological condition ought to produce more daughters than sons. Her daughters may be somewhat less than prime, but they will all get mated, whereas less-than-prime sons have almost no chance of breeding. The reverse strategy should hold for females in excellent condition. They can get the most return by producing sons whose prime condition ensures that they will gain

a harem and will sire many offspring.

The same pattern may also operate within the lifetime of a single female. When a female is young and has few resources to invest, she might produce more daughters and shift toward producing sons as she grows older and acquires more resources for rearing better-quality offspring. When mice are fed a deficient diet, for instance, they produce smaller litters than adequately fed mice, and the reduction in litter size is due almost entirely to the selective reabsorption of male embryos by the mother. The hungry mother diverts investment away from her embryonic sons and shunts it into producing daughters. Similarly, in wood rats, mothers that had a deficient diet selectively starved their sons and concentrated on feeding their daughters. In all of these cases, the results depend on the mating system. If

the mating system is polygynous, with intense competition and selection for high-quality males, biologists expect this pattern. But in a monogamous system, with low male-male competition, biologists do not expect it.

A different social and mating system may favor a different strategy of sex-ratio manipulation. If, for example, most of the social competition is between females, not males, biologists would expect the reverse pattern. In rhesus monkeys, where females compete for dominance status, a mother's rank will influence her daughter's. Dominant females suppress the reproduction of subdominants, and their daughters are more likely to become dominant breeders. Accordingly, it has been found that dominant females produce an excess of daughters. By contrast, the success of a son is not influenced by the rank of a mother, so sub-dominant females may increase their reproductive success by producing sons, not daughters.

To understand the pattern of sex ratio in a population, one must know what the costs of producing sons and daughters are. Even though one might expect females to bias their investment toward males or females according to their age, status or health, one still expects to see the population exhibit a 1:1 ratio of investment in the two sexes—for every female that overproduces sons, there will be a corresponding advantage for a female that produces more daughters. To know whether this argument holds, it is necessary to count the number of sons produced and the cost of producing them, total it and compare it with the number of daughters and the cost per daughter. If the theory holds, biologists expect that the more costly sex will be the less common.

Red deer, which are close relatives of North American elk, provide a bizarre variation on this theme. Male red deer would seem to cost more to produce than female red deer. Sons suckle more than daughters and are weaned at a heavier weight. This makes sense because red deer are a harem-breeding species with intense male-male competition and a selective demand for large, fit sons. If a female produces a son, the high cost of rearing him apparently so depletes her that she is much less likely to breed the next season than if she had reared a daughter. Given that males cost much more to produce, the population should contain more females than males. It does not. This shows the difficulty of measuring costs. It turns out that part of the cost of a daughter lies in sharing the foraging range with her. Males move away from the area where they were born; females tend to stay and forage in their mother's home range. Evidence indicates that they compete with her and with one another for food, and the more daughters a female has near her, the lower her reproductive rate is.

In this sense, red deer are like honeybees. A queen produces only a few daughters and thousands of sons even though daughters and sons are roughly the same size. A daughter, however, will assume control of her mother's hive, and the mother will leave, so the cost of each daughter is high compared with the cost of a son. Those thousands of sons probably cost the mother the same as a single daughter.

INFANTICIDE

Rodents commit infanticide, killing both their own offspring and those of other members of their species. Biologists have known about this for at least two centuries, but until recently, they gave it little attention. Darwin, for instance, noted that in our species, abortion and infanticide have traditionally been the most widespread form of birth and population control. "But," he claimed, "the instincts of the lower animals are never so perverted as to lead them regularly to destroy their own offspring." In this case, Darwin was wrong. Biologists are discovering that infanticide is a conspicuous part of the biology of rodents and other mammals and that it is not perverted but makes sense as a reproductive strategy.

It is hard to imagine how killing one's own offspring could be favored by natural selection, and perhaps that is the reason why infanticide was long considered an expression of social pathology. Overcrowding, stress and hunger were thought to lead to cannibalism, abortion and infanticide, as indeed they do, but it may also be that the individuals who commit infanticide are actually increasing their reproductive success.

There are several distinct forms of infanticide. A female may kill some of her own offspring as a means of adjusting her litter size to match her resources. Experimental manipulations in which mouse pups are added to the litter of a mother mouse show that a female with a limited amount of food and teats will eat some of the offspring, reducing the clutch size to a normal level. Under conditions of food stress, it has been shown, for example, that a female who raises seven offspring will actually have an overall higher reproductive success than a female who attempts to rear eight. The offspring from the smaller clutch are larger and have a higher survival rate, and the mother may have increased her chances of rearing another litter in the future. This form of infanticide regulates the quality of surviving offspring and increases the total lifetime production of the female.

A different form of infanticide is directed against the offspring of other parents. Both males and females may practice this, the most overt expression of reproductive competition. Since natural selection favors individuals who leave the most descendants, killing the offspring of a competitor is one of the most direct ways of raising one's reproductive success. This practice is carried out by several rodents. Female muskrats apparently kill the offspring of other females when taking over their burrows. It has also been documented in Belding's and arctic ground squirrels. So intense is the competition for burrows that many students of colonial squirrels and rodents believe female infanticide and competition for burrows to be a driving force which favors social groupings and extended families. The closely related females of extended families cooperate to repel intruders.

Another form of genetic competition appears to influence male infanticide. Male rodents and several kinds of monkeys, lions, horses and other mammals often kill the offspring of a female after they have taken control of a territory or harem and evicted the previous resident male. They are disposing of offspring with which they have no close genetic relationship and also returning the female to reproductive readiness sooner. If a nursing female kept her offspring, the intruding male would ordinarily have to wait until the litter was weaned before he could father his own. Without

her young, the female is ready to breed within days, thus increasing the number of offspring the new male can sire within his lifetime. At the same time, he disposes of individuals that will compete with his own heirs.

Some females have probably evolved ways of countering the infanticidal male. Pregnant females may enter into a fake estrus and copulate with the new resident male, allowing him to believe that her offspring resulted from mating with him. Males must have some mechanisms designed to prevent them from killing their own offspring. Copulation with the mother may be the best means they have of assessing their paternity. Females may also simply be more aggressive. Lactating female arvicoline rodents are more aggressive than males and nonbreeding females and will physically drive intruders away.

If a female has little opportunity for preventing male infanticide, she may evolve a physiology that minimizes her losses: the strange Bruce effect. A pregnant mouse female may spontaneously abort her embryos if she is exposed to the urine of a strange male. The new smell may signal to her that her mate has been displaced, and if the new male is likely to kill her newborn pups, she would be better off aborting them as soon as possible and starting over.

Infanticide studies are difficult to conduct. Laboratory work is full of artificialities, and field observations are hard to come by. However, the patterns of infanticide that have been recorded suggest that the behavior is not simply the social pathology of individuals too stressed and starved to behave in a biologically adaptive manner but rather a behavior molded by natural selection.

The future of these newborn collared lemmings is not necessarily secure. Biologists have determined that infanticide among rodents is practiced as a reproductive strategy.

BUSHY-TAILED WOOD RAT
Neotoma cinerea

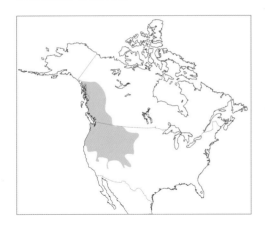

Mammal: *Neotoma cinerea,*
bushy-tailed wood rat, packrat

Meaning of Name: *Neotoma* (new +
sharp, cutting), an allusion to the teeth
indicating a new genus of rodent; *cinerea*
refers to ash color

Description: squirrel-like tail covered with
long fur; soft, dense pelage; varies in color
from pale gray washed with tawny to black;
grayish white with creamy patches ventrally;
tail is dark gray above and white below

Total Length: 15 to 17 inches

Tail: 5.2 to 8.7 inches

Weight: 7.5 to 10.5 ounces

Gestation: 27 to 32 days

Offspring: 1 to 6 (usually 2 to 4);
1 litter per year

Age of Maturity: 11 months

Longevity: at least 4 years

Diet: roots, stems, leaves and seeds of trees,
shrubs and forbs; needles of conifers and
berries; does not eat grass

Habitat: Arctic alpine to desert areas,
prefers transitional zones; found on cliffs,
rock slides, caves, river canyons and rock
outcrops in pine forests

Predators: great horned owl, rattlesnake,
weasel, skunk, marten, wolverine, fox,
coyote and wolf

Dental Formula:
1/1, 0/0, 0/0, 3/3 = 16 teeth

The bushy-tailed wood rat uses twigs and debris of all kinds—including the litter left by humans at campsites and cabins—and incorporates them into its large woven nests.

BUSHY-TAILED WOOD RAT
Neotoma cinerea

The bushy-tailed wood rat is also known as the packrat, a name it earned for its habit of carrying shiny objects—spoons, cigarette lighters, matches and other human debris—away from cabins and campsites. It incorporates these objects into its jumbled nest of sticks, bones and foliage. The tangled pile of debris, built in a rock crevice or other protected spot, may be 3 feet in circumference. In forested areas without rocky outcrops, the nest may be located high in the branches of a large coniferous tree. Inside a coarse outer pile of debris lies a compact nest of fine, dry, shredded plant material. The coarse outer pile is a form of protection from predators and is also used as a place to dry food caches and to sit and eat. Sometimes a packrat will build a debris nest for use as a food cache only and will use a rock crevice for its resting nest. A wood rat will find a cabin a convenient den spot and, within a few days, will have coated it with urine and musk and shredded and disturbed the entire contents.

The bushy-tailed wood rat is a herbivore of the western mountain coniferous forest and grazes on the leaves of shrubs and conifers. In the autumn, it caches large piles of twigs and dried vegetation, a behavior similar to that of pikas, which also live in mountainous talus areas, except that the wood rat is able to use coarser woody vegetation in its caches.

Wood rats of both sexes are territorial. Males fight for access to female territories and do much scent-marking with musk glands and urine.

SOUTHERN RED-BACKED VOLE *Clethrionomys gapperi*

The southern red-backed vole is a hyperactive, nervous animal found in a variety of forested and shrubby habitats. It uses the runways of other small mammals in its excursions across the forest floor. It will also climb and forage in shrubbery and trees. In winter, it builds tunnels through the snow.

This species has sometimes been found nesting in tree hollows, but normally, it builds a round ball of shredded plants under a stump or fallen log. Females are aggressively territorial, more so than males, whose ranges often overlap. Its diet is a mixture of leaf stems, berries, nuts, tree sprouts, bark, fungi and any young mouse nestlings it happens to find. Red-backed voles grind their food very finely and probably digest it more efficiently than the deer mice that share the same habitats.

Females have multiple litters from spring through autumn. The young are born helpless after a three-week pregnancy. Weaning and dispersal occur after another three weeks.

Closely related species are the **western red-backed vole**, *Clethrionomys californicus*, and the **northern red-backed vole**, *C. rutilus*. The former is found in the thick damp West Coast forest, and the latter is a tundra species.

Red-backed voles are a good indicator of environmental disturbance. Clear-cut logging and land development normally render them extinct locally, perhaps because of a high food dependence on fungi such as bolete mushrooms that live in symbiosis with tree roots. When the trees disappear, so do the mushrooms and the voles. These voles also eat lichens that grow on trees and may depend on them. Deer mice, which do not feed heavily on these items, often increase with logging and development.

All voles are eaten by predatory birds and mammals.

The population of the red-backed vole is an indicator of ecological disruption. When an area is logged-out, the mushrooms on which the voles thrive disappear, as do the voles.

SOUTHERN RED-BACKED VOLE *Clethrionomys gapperi*

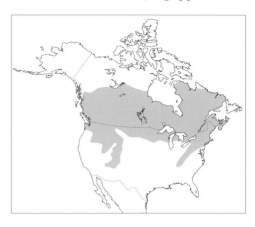

Mammal: *Clethrionomys gapperi*, southern red-backed vole, boreal redback vole, Gapper's redback vole

Meaning of Name: *Clethrionomys* (bolt-toothed mouse) refers to rounded enamel ridges on teeth or to the fact that molars are rooted; *gapperi* (named after naturalist W. Gapper)

Description: bright reddish dorsal stripe runs from forehead to base of tail; gray face, flanks and rump; whitish or buff feet and underparts; brown ears; bicolored tail; during gray phase, a sooty dorsal stripe replaces the reddish one

Total Length: 4.7 to 6.5 inches

Tail: 1.2 to 2.3 inches

Weight: 0.5 to 1.4 ounces

Gestation: 17 to 19 days

Offspring: 2 to 8 (usually 4 to 6, but size increases with latitude); 3 or 4 litters per year

Age of Maturity: female has first litter at 4 months

Longevity: usually 1 year in the wild, but some have lived 20 to 36 months

Diet: omnivore; prefers petioles of broad-leafed forbs and shrubs and other growing vegetative parts of weeds and some grasses; also large quantities of conifer seeds, nuts, bark, roots, insects, centipedes, spiders and snails as well as fungal materials

Habitat: both coniferous and mixed forests close to springs and bogs; around mossy decaying stumps, scattered shrubs and leaf litter

Predators: hawks, owls, raccoon, weasel, red fox, coyote, skunk, marten, mink, short-tailed shrew, red squirrel and domestic cat

Dental Formula:
1/1, 0/0, 0/0, 3/3 = 16 teeth

WESTERN HEATHER VOLE
Phenacomys intermedius

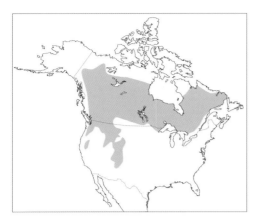

Mammal: *Phenacomys intermedius,* western heather vole

Meaning of Name: *Phenacomys* (cheat or deceiver mouse) refers to the fact that the external appearance gives no clue to its real affinities; *intermedius* (between, intermediate) probably refers to medium-length tail

Description: fairly loose, thin skin; long, fine-textured pelage; varies from grayish brown to dark brown; nose also varies from yellowish to orange-brown to gray; bicolored tail; silvery gray underparts; white feet

Total Length: 4.8 to 6.1 inches

Tail: 1 to 1.6 inches

Weight: 0.9 to 1.4 ounces

Gestation: 19 to 24 days

Offspring: 2 to 8 (average 5); 2 or more litters per season

Age of Maturity: female, 4 to 6 weeks; male, not until the following spring

Longevity: not known (probably 1 to 2 years)

Diet: bark and buds of shrubs and heaths; forbs, berries, seeds and lichens

Habitat: dry open stands of pine or spruce; usually near water; also near forest edges in shrubby vegetation; open, moist, grassy areas near mountaintops and rocky slopes

Predators: hawks, owls, weasel and marten

Dental Formula:
1/1, 0/0, 0/0, 3/3 = 16 teeth

WESTERN HEATHER VOLE
Phenacomys intermedius

The western heather vole is a creature of the boreal forest, a habitat it shares with the red-backed vole. Red-backed voles are often day-active, while western heather voles are mainly nocturnal. Western heather voles store food in caches. In summer, they browse the foliage of shrubs and herbs, and in winter, they eat twig buds and bark. The western heather vole does not eat the grasses and sedges that some voles and lemmings specialize in. A completely docile animal, it does well in captivity. In winter, it nests on the ground surface in snow-covered runways, but in summer, it has burrows up to 8 inches deep and uses runways through the litter.

ROCK VOLE
Microtus chrotorrhinus

The rock vole occurs in colonies associated with rocky talus areas in the eastern coniferous forests of Canada and the upper elevations of the northern Appalachians. It is a shy, secretive species that is day-active but rarely seen. Colonies seem to be associated with small clearings in moist forested areas with water nearby.

PRAIRIE VOLE
Microtus ochrogaster

Prairie voles live in grassland areas with light soils and have one of the most interesting social biologies of all voles. Both sexes cooperate in caring for the young, and families may remain together after the young mature. They share the same burrow and food caches. The burrow systems are shallow but extensive—some runs extend more than 325 feet—and these voles will also use the tunnels of moles. The food caches contain up to 7 pounds of plant roots for winter provisions.

ROCK VOLE
Microtus chrotorrhinus

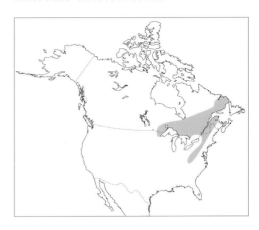

Mammal: *Microtus chrotorrhinus,* rock vole, yellownose vole

Meaning of Name: *Microtus* (small ears); *chrotorrhinus* (color + nose) refers to yellow nose

Description: grayish brown back and dull to silvery gray ventrally; orange or rufous face with rich yellow around the nose spreading backward to include the ears; winter coat is longer and glossier

Total Length: 6 to 7.3 inches

Tail: 1.7 to 2.1 inches

Weight: 1 to 2 ounces

Gestation: not known (probably 20 to 21 days)

Offspring: 2 to 5; 2 or more litters per year

Age of Maturity: not known (probably 25 to 45 days)

Longevity: not known (probably less than 1 year)

Diet: stems and leaves of forbs and other green plants (false mitrewort, violet, bunchberry and mayflower)

Habitat: cool, moist, rocky woodlands under cliffs or rock outcrops; usually found near forest springs or among the bracken in small clearings in spruce/birch/balsam fir forests

Predators: hawks, owls, gulls, snakes and small carnivores

Dental Formula:
1/1, 0/0, 0/0, 3/3 = 16 teeth

PRAIRIE VOLE
Microtus ochrogaster

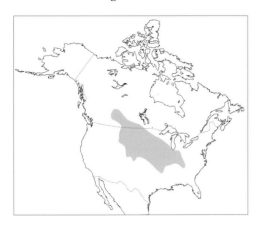

Mammal: *Microtus ochrogaster*, prairie vole
Meaning of Name: *Microtus* (small ears); *ochrogaster* (yellow belly)
Description: grayish to dark brown with a mixture of buff and black hairs; buffy gray underparts tipped with light cinnamon to buff; tail is dark brown above and light gray beneath
Total Length: male, 4.8 to 6.6 inches; female, 5.2 to 6.7 inches
Tail: male, 1 to 1.7 inches; female, 1.2 to 1.6 inches
Weight: male, 1.3 to 1.9 ounces; female, 1.3 to 2 ounces
Gestation: 21 days
Offspring: 2 to 6 (usually 3 or 4); up to 5 litters per year
Age of Maturity: female breeds at 30 days
Longevity: usually less than 1 year in the wild but can live up to 22 months; approximately 35 months in captivity
Diet: varies with season; green forbs, grasses, bulbs, rhizomes, seeds, acorns, grains, fruits, tree bark, insects, invertebrates, small vertebrates and each other
Habitat: open habitats (grassland plains, fencerows and prairies) with lots of vegetation for cover; not usually found in wooded or damp areas but does occur in hayfields and along field borders
Predators: diurnal and nocturnal predators; fish, frogs, snakes, owls, hawks, opossum, short-tailed shrew, coyote, fox, mink, least weasel, domestic cat
Dental Formula:
1/1, 0/0, 0/0, 3/3 = 16 teeth

SINGING VOLE
Microtus miurus

The song of the singing vole is a high-pitched trill that may act as an alarm call. The species is colonial and exhibits some of the same communal warning systems that ground squirrels use. The song may also be a territorial call uttered to discourage intruders. This species inhabits the tundra of the west, and like pikas, it collects huge hay piles for winter, up to half a bushel in a pile. It also caches large stores of tubers, valuable resources which Indians and Inuit used to rob and which other voles likely still do. The singing vole makes an underground nest and storage chamber, is active climbing in shrubbery and swims well.

SINGING VOLE
Microtus miurus

Mammal: *Microtus miurus*, singing vole, Alaska vole
Meaning of Name: *Microtus* (small ears); *miurus* (small + wild ox) or could be derived from Latin word *miurus*, meaning "wonderful"; also called singing vole because of its habit of coming to the entrance of its burrow and uttering a high-pitched trill
Description: small vole with short tail; color varies with range; buff or tawny ear spot; bi-colored tail tipped with stiff buff or tawny hairs; grayish flanks and feet; gray underparts with an ochraceous tint; may have buff patch at base of whiskers
Total Length: male, 5.8 to 6.3 inches; female, 5.3 to 6.3 inches
Tail: male, 0.8 to 1.4 inches; female, 1 to 1.3 inches
Weight: male, 1.4 to 2.1 ounces; female, 1.1 to 1.8 ounces
Gestation: not known (probably 20 or 21 days)
Offspring: 4 to 12; up to 3 litters per year
Age of Maturity: not known (probably 25 to 45 days)
Longevity: not known (probably less than 1 year)
Diet: Arctic forbs and leaves and twigs of dwarf arctic willow
Habitat: alpine tundra, willow thickets; along riverbanks, lakeshores and gravel beds; high, well-drained slopes
Predators: gull, gray jay, jaeger, short-eared owl, grizzly bear, wolf, red fox, arctic fox, ermine and least weasel
Dental Formula:
1/1, 0/0, 0/0, 3/3 = 16 teeth

LONG-TAILED VOLE
Microtus longicaudus

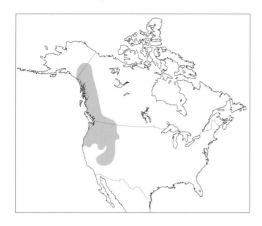

Mammal: *Microtus longicaudus,*
long-tailed vole
Meaning of Name: *Microtus* (small ears);
longicaudus (long tail)
Description: large vole; dark gray with
brown or blackish overtones; gray underparts
and dirty whitish feet; bicolored tail, slightly
paler underneath; relatively long tail for a vole;
winter pelage is longer and grayer
Total Length: 6.6 to 7.6 inches
Tail: 2 to 3.5 inches
Weight: male, 1.4 to 2.1 ounces;
female, 1.3 to 2 ounces
Gestation: not known
(probably 20 or 21 days)
Offspring: 2 to 8; more than 1 litter per year
Age of Maturity: not known
(probably 25 to 45 days)
Longevity: not known
(probably less than 1 year)
Diet: grasses, bulbs, bark of small twigs
Habitat: grassy areas in forests, alpine stream-
banks and meadows, marshes, grasslands
and sagebrush plains; brushy areas in winter
Predators: hawks, owls, gulls, snakes
and small carnivores
Dental Formula:
1/1, 0/0, 0/0, 3/3 = 16 teeth

WOODLAND VOLE
Microtus pinetorum

Woodland voles live in deciduous
eastern forests. They are subterranean and usually do not come above
ground except for brief periods at night.
Their eyes and ears are reduced. Tunnels of the woodland vole are shallow
and run through the leaf litter, so this
vole favors well-drained mature forests
with light soils and a thick leaf mulch.
It feeds heavily on the roots and underground tubers of perennial wildflowers,
which are cached in underground storage chambers. Leafy material and seeds
are also eaten. Females aggressively defend their nests.

WOODLAND VOLE
Microtus pinetorum

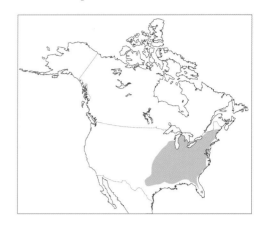

Mammal: *Microtus pinetorum,* woodland vole,
pine vole
Meaning of Name: *Microtus* (small ears);
pinetorum (of the pines); the name pine vole
is misleading, since the species actually prefers
areas of deciduous woods
Description: very small eyes and ears; dull,
reddish brown, plush, thick molelike fur; soft
individual hairs; no scattered long guard hairs
as found in most other voles; silvery or buffy
gray ventrally; bicolored tail, brown above
and gray below
Total Length: 4.3 to 5.2 inches
Tail: 0.7 to 0.9 inch
Weight: 0.7 to 1.3 ounces
Gestation: 20 to 24 days
Offspring: 1 to 6; 1 to 4 litters per year
Age of Maturity: male, 48 to 56 days;
female, 70 to 84 days
Longevity: 1 year in the wild, but usually
less than a few months
Diet: nuts, seeds, bark from roots, bulbs,
tubers, rhizomes and green leaves; also a
variety of ground-living insects, their larvae
and other invertebrates; can be cannibalistic
Habitat: deciduous forests with loose sandy
soils and a thick layer of humus for burrowing;
occasionally found in grassy areas in orchards,
sand dunes, hillsides and along fencerows
Predators: snakes and short-tailed shrew are
main enemies; also fox, raccoon, opossum,
skunk, mink, weasel, coyote, domestic dog and
domestic cat
Dental Formula:
1/1, 0/0, 0/0, 3/3 = 16 teeth

WATER VOLE
Microtus richardsoni

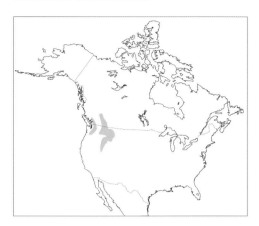

Mammal: *Microtus richardsoni*, water vole, Richardson's water vole
Meaning of Name: *Microtus* (small ears); *richardsoni*, likely after discoverer of species
Description: largest vole within its range; amphibious adaptations include a fusiform body, dense underfur and fringes of stiff hairs on the edges of the hind feet; combination of reddish brown and black-tipped hairs dorsally; smoky to pale gray ventrally; bicolored tail is brown above and light gray beneath
Total Length: 9.2 to 10.8 inches
Tail: 2.6 to 3.9 inches
Weight: 2.5 to 3.5 ounces
Gestation: not known
Offspring: 2 to 8 (average of 5); 2 litters per year
Age of Maturity: female can mature in 5 weeks (has smaller litters)
Longevity: not known (probably 1 or 2 years)
Diet: herbs, twigs and buds of willows
Habitat: alpine meadows; along mountain streams, creek banks and marshes; occasionally found along streambanks in alpine forests or in forest glades
Predators: probably hawks, owls, gulls, small carnivores and possibly large fish
Dental Formula:
1/1, 0/0, 0/0, 3/3 = 16 teeth

WATER VOLE
Microtus richardsoni

The water vole has a tiny geographic distribution and a specific habitat. It is found in Rocky Mountain meadows and alongside mountain streams and ponds, where it builds extensive burrow systems. One of the largest of North American voles, it has large feet that are relatively powerful and adapted for digging. Most of its food is herbaceous vegetation gathered above ground. It dives and swims well and takes to water when pursued.

TUNDRA VOLE
Microtus oeconomus

The tundra vole is found in the tundra of the far northwestern Arctic and in northern Russia and Scandinavia. It often makes shallow burrows in moist habitats, feeds heavily on grasses and sedges and caches roots, seeds and grass for winter use.

TUNDRA VOLE
Microtus oeconomus

Mammal: *Microtus oeconomus*, tundra vole, root vole
Meaning of Name: *Microtus* (small ears); *oeconomus* (economic) refers to its habit of storing grass seeds and forb rhizomes in its burrow in the fall
Description: grizzled brown washed with buff or fulvous; gray feet; heels and wrists are well covered with stiff, silvery hairs in winter; bicolored tail
Total Length: 6 to 7.4 inches
Tail: 1.4 to 2.1 inches
Weight: male, 1.2 to 1.6 ounces; female, 0.9 to 2.8 ounces
Gestation: not known (probably 20 to 21 days)
Offspring: 5 to 11
Age of Maturity: not known (probably 25 to 45 days)
Longevity: not known (probably less than 1 year)
Diet: sedges, grasses, seeds and rhizomes
Habitat: tundra in close association with water; sedge and cottongrass marshes
Predators: owls, hawks, gyrfalcon, jaeger, gull, shrike, ermine, arctic fox, wolverine and even lake trout
Dental Formula:
1/1, 0/0, 0/0, 3/3 = 16 teeth

CREEPING VOLE
Microtus oregoni

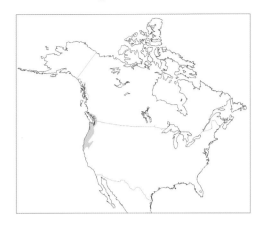

Mammal: *Microtus oregoni*, creeping vole, Oregon vole; the smallest species of the genus
Meaning of Name: *Microtus* (small ears); *oregoni* (of Oregon)
Description: dusky brown above, silvery ventrally; black-tipped ears; gray feet; bicolored tail
Total Length: 4.9 to 6 inches
Tail: 1.1 to 1.5 inches
Weight: 0.6 to 0.7 ounce
Gestation: 23 or 24 days
Offspring: 1 to 5; usually 3 litters per year (maximum 5 or 6)
Age of Maturity: male, 40 to 50 days; female, 22 to 27 days
Longevity: 320 days in captivity
Diet: underground rootstocks and green forage
Habitat: coniferous forest edges or bushy grassy areas; prefers relatively dry conditions
Predators: hawks, owls, snakes and small carnivores
Dental Formula:
1/1, 0/0, 0/0, 3/3 = 16 teeth

CREEPING VOLE
Microtus oregoni

The creeping vole has a narrow distribution along the West Coast. It inhabits most coniferous forests but favors forest-edge situations and locally dry conditions where it burrows extensively just below the surface. It feeds generally on leaves and berries of shrubs and herbs but derives most of its food from underground roots and tubers. The mild coastal climate allows creeping voles to reproduce year-round.

MEADOW VOLE
Microtus pennsylvanicus

Although the meadow vole prefers wet, grassy fields and meadows, it thrives in a vast array of habitats. The most widespread species of *Microtus* in North America, it is active all year, usually early in the morning and just before sunset. It constructs a labyrinth of runways that crisscross through the grass and lead to shallow burrows. Nests woven from dried grasses are located either at the ends of the burrows or on the surface. Winter nests are constructed beneath a blanket of snow for protection. Well away from the nest, large piles of greenish brown pellets dot the runways—the communal toilet areas of these clean creatures.

The meadow vole subsists almost exclusively on tubers and green vegetation, including grasses and sedges. To reach seed heads, it gnaws grass stems into match-sized cuttings that it leaves in piles on runways. It can eat in excess of its own weight daily and reingests its feces to maximize vitamin intake.

A prolific breeder, the meadow vole produces litter after litter throughout a long breeding season lasting from April to October and, under ideal conditions, all winter as well. The meadow vole vocalizes to threaten other voles, and its young produce ultrasonic calls to elicit their parents' attention. If alarmed, it stamps its hind feet.

MEADOW VOLE
Microtus pennsylvanicus

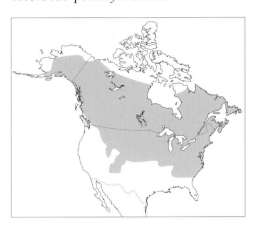

Mammal: *Microtus pennsylvanicus*, meadow vole, field mouse
Meaning of Name: *Microtus* (small ears); *pennsylvanicus* (of Pennsylvania)
Description: long, soft, dense fur; coat varies from grizzled rusty brown to dark brown above and dusky gray below; winter coat is longer and grayer
Total Length: male, 5.9 to 7.8 inches; female, 5.7 to 7 inches
Tail: male, 1.6 to 1.8 inches; female, 1.6 to 2 inches
Weight: male, 1.1 to 1.6 ounces; female, 1.1 to 1.8 ounces (maximum 2.5 ounces)
Gestation: 20 to 21 days
Offspring: 1 to 11 (usually 3 to 5); average of 4 litters per year (17 litters were born to one animal in captivity)
Age of Maturity: male, 45 days (if born in midsummer, probably not until the following season); female, 25 days
Longevity: usually less than 1 year in the wild; can survive several years in captivity
Diet: primarily herbaceous vegetation; seeds, grain, bark, fruits, insects, snails and other invertebrates and small vertebrates
Habitat: wet meadows and open grassland; near water; overhead grass cover is essential
Predators: owls, snakes, fish, carnivores and birds
Dental Formula:
1/1, 0/0, 0/0, 3/3 = 16 teeth

TOWNSEND'S VOLE
Microtus townsendii

Townsend's vole is a large West Coast vole. A good swimmer, it is often associated with water in summer. It digs long, shallow runways in light soil and may place the entrance to its nest underwater. Its winter nest is on drier ground, where soil freezing is less of a problem. It cuts a variety of green vegetation and tubers as food.

VOLES AS VECTORS

Plagues such as the black death and the typhus epidemics that have periodically decimated the human inhabitants of Asia and Europe have relied on rodents to carry them: Mice and rats adapted to human environments are convenient vectors for the bacteria involved. They do a good job of spreading them, introducing them to new hosts such as urban humans, mammals whose bodies have not evolved the biochemistry or developed the immune reactions needed to fight off the disease.

In the New World, lemmings and voles are also convenient hosts for many parasites of mammals. Fortunately, voles and lemmings have remained creatures of the wild and do not pose a threat to urban North Americans. Every year, however, humans contact some of the pathogens carried by wild voles and lemmings. A common affliction known as backpacker's disease—a kind of diarrhea caused by the protozoan *Giardia lamblia*—infects the gastrointestinal tract and can be severe if not treated. Normally, *Giardia* is thought of as a disease of polluted Third World cities with poor sanitation, but backpackers who drink from crystal-clear mountain streams and seemingly pure Arctic lakes hundreds of miles from the nearest city can pick up *Giardia*. The protozoan is found in several species of vole, and when their feces wash into a water supply, humans can be infected.

In the far north and the west, voles are implicated as vectors of tularemia, a bacterial disease that causes a severe inflammation of the lymphatic system and can be fatal to humans. Voles may spread the disease among themselves through cannibalism at high population densities and introduce it into water sources used by humans. In Asia, the clearing of forests and the subsequent rise in the vole population are credited with increasing human tularemia infections. Trappers who handle wild animals are constantly at risk of contracting tularemia.

Voles are strongly implicated as reservoirs of *Babesia microti*, a parasite of the mammalian bloodstream. It is transmitted by tick bites in animals such as voles. A recent survey of New Englanders bitten by ticks or suffering from a fever showed that 7.5 percent had had contact with *Babesia*. The disease can kill people whose spleen has been removed or who are using chemotherapeutic drugs that depress the body's immune response.

Voles are also vectors for many kinds of parasitic worms that complete their final stages of development in large mammalian carnivores and predatory birds. There is a cestode worm parasite transmitted from voles to arctic foxes that also finds its way into human populations in Siberia and Alaska. This worm can destroy the liver and cause death if the person is not treated.

The catalog of vole pathogens is a long one and includes many species that are not human health threats. The ones that do affect us, though, are a clear reminder of the benefits humans acquired when we began to associate disease with biological vectors instead of supernatural causes and learned to wash, to disinfect with soap and to cook meat before eating it.

TOWNSEND'S VOLE
Microtus townsendii

Mammal: *Microtus townsendii*, Townsend's vole
Meaning of Name: *Microtus* (small ears); *townsendii* (named for its discoverer, J.K. Townsend)
Description: blackish brown dorsum, grayish underneath; black tail; winter coat is longer with underparts more silvery
Total Length: 6.7 to 8.7 inches
Tail: 1.9 to 2.8 inches
Weight: approximately 0.6 to 0.7 ounce
Gestation: 21 to 24 days
Offspring: 1 to 9 (usually 4 or 5)
Age of Maturity: not known (probably 25 to 45 days)
Longevity: not known (probably less than 1 year)
Diet: underground rootstocks
Habitat: moist fields and meadows; marshes and mountain slopes; usually near water
Predators: hawks, owls, gulls, snakes and small carnivores such as the short-tailed shrew, badger, coyote, fox, skunk and weasel
Dental Formula:
1/1, 0/0, 0/0, 3/3 = 16 teeth

YELLOW-CHEEKED VOLE
Microtus xanthognathus

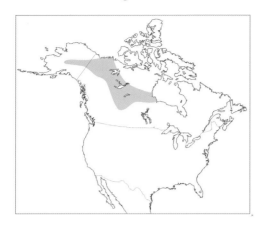

Mammal: *Microtus xanthognathus*, yellow-cheeked vole, taiga vole, chestnut-cheeked vole
Meaning of Name: *Microtus* (small ears); *xanthognathus* refers to yellow cheek patch
Description: dull brown above, gray below; ears have rusty edges; prominent chestnut to rusty yellow cheek patch
Total Length: 7.3 to 8.9 inches
Tail: 1.8 to 2.1 inches
Weight: 4 to 6 ounces
Gestation: not known (probably 20 to 21 days)
Offspring: 7 to 11
Age of Maturity: the year following birth
Longevity: not past second winter
Diet: opportunistic feeder, with horsetails, grasses and berries predominating in summer and stored rhizomes in winter
Habitat: riparian forest edge; lightly burned forest; bordering tundra and sphagnum bogs
Predators: marten, great gray owl
Dental Formula:
1/1, 0/0, 0/0, 3/3 = 16 teeth

The sagebrush vole, like all voles, is an important food for birds such as owls and hawks as well as weasels, foxes and snakes.

YELLOW-CHEEKED VOLE
Microtus xanthognathus

The yellow-cheeked vole is found in western boreal forests, often near bogs and other wet areas. It constructs runways through the litter on the forest floor. The runways are relatively deep and marked by dirt piles that suggest the activity of moles rather than voles. The yellow-cheeked vole is colonial. It eats large quantities of lichen and horse-tail, foods favored by few other species.

SAGEBRUSH VOLE
Lemmiscus curtatus

The sagebrush vole specializes in dry habitats with open areas and scattered shrubbery. It builds underground nests at the base of shrubs and constructs shallow runways to adjacent shrubs. It is active during the day as well as at night.

SAGEBRUSH VOLE
Lemmiscus curtatus

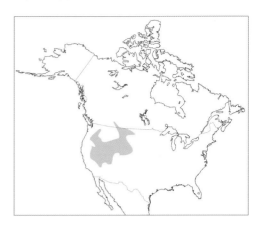

Mammal: *Lemmiscus curtatus*, sagebrush vole
Meaning of Name: *Lemmiscus* (lemming); *curtatus* (shortened) probably refers to short legs and tail
Description: has modifications for burrowing in sand, including small ears, short tail, stout claws and haired palms and soles; palest of voles, with buffy or ash-gray back, paler sides, dirty white underparts and whitish feet; clear buffy areas on nose, ears and flanks; whitish tail with a dark gray dorsal stripe and terminal "pencil" of hairs
Total Length: 4.4 to 5.1 inches
Tail: 0.7 to 0.8 inch
Weight: 0.8 to 1.3 ounces
Gestation: 24 or 25 days
Offspring: 1 to 13 (usually 5); more than 1 litter per year (14 litters per year in captivity)
Age of Maturity: male, 60 to 75 days; female, 60 days
Longevity: not known (probably 1 or 2 years)
Diet: in summer, green vegetation (especially sagebrush) rather than seeds, seeds in autumn and bark and twigs in winter
Habitat: high, dry sagebrush steppes; semiarid prairies; rolling hills or brushy canyons; prefers loose soil (found in driest places of all voles)
Predators: short-eared owl, snakes, hawks, weasel, ferret, badger, fox and coyote
Dental Formula:
1/1, 0/0, 0/0, 3/3 = 16 teeth

MUSKRAT *Ondatra zibethicus*

The muskrat is a giant among arvicolines, the largest of the North American species. It has an extensive range, from the north of Mexico to the very northern edge of the Canadian mainland far above the tree line. It is also the most valuable North American species in the modern fur trade. The annual harvest of 4 to 8 million muskrats is worth many millions of dollars.

The tremendous value of muskrats is due to their wide distribution and their adaptation to highly productive aquatic habitats—ponds, lakes, streams, canals, reservoirs and marshy areas which are deep enough that the water does not freeze in the winter.

They share many similarities with the beaver: a coat designed for activity in the water that consists of a thick, waterproof underfur overlaid with long, glossy guard hairs; hind feet that are partially webbed and sport large claws; and a long, vertically flattened tail used in swimming. Like the beaver, the muskrat also has a high tolerance for carbon dioxide in its blood and can swim at least 100 yards underwater and stay submerged for as long as 17 minutes.

Another similarity between muskrats and beavers is their ability to build houses and canals. Muskrats nest in a wide variety of habitats, ranging from large lakes and rivers to small ponds and marshes. Where a solid bank is available, a muskrat will construct a burrow with an underwater entrance connecting to a nesting chamber, usually with more than one exit tunnel, that sits above the water level. When water levels decline during dry spells, muskrats extend their entrance tunnels to deeper water. In areas without raised banks, they build lodges out of cattails, bulrushes and other vegetation, piling it into a mound and then plastering it with mud and muck. The lodge is roughly 3 feet above the water level. Inside, the muskrat constructs a dry, grass-lined nest. These huts are normally built in autumn and are designed to last only through the winter months.

In open water, muskrats will also build feeding platforms of organic debris and vegetation so that they can bring their food up out of the water and eat it without losing body heat. The muskrat is a small mammal with naked feet and tail, and it loses considerable heat when in the water.

In winter, in areas where the water surface freezes, muskrats build "push-ups," domes of roots and vegetation over a hole in the ice where they can emerge to breathe and feed. The insulating quality of the push-up, especially when snow-covered, prevents a thick ice cover from forming and enables the muskrat to keep its breathing holes open all winter.

The construction and feeding activities of muskrats have considerable ecological impact on marshes. Muskrats are credited with creating the large, open-water areas that attract waterfowl. Their lodges, abandoned in summer, provide nesting sites for waterbirds and also support rare and diverse miniature communities of marsh plants that do not occur in thick stands of cattail and bulrushes.

Muskrats are mostly herbivorous, eating the roots, tubers, stems and leaves of many aquatic and terrestrial plants. Like beavers, they are able to pull their lips in behind their incisors when they gnaw underwater. Given the opportunity, muskrats will eat frogs, crayfish, clams and young waterbirds. When food is abundant, muskrat populations can soar to densities of 12 to 36 per acre of marsh.

The density of muskrat populations fluctuates cyclically in some areas. In northern Canada, it appears to follow a 6-year cycle, and in other areas, a 10-year cycle. The factors driving the cycle are unknown, but along with food depletion, water fluctuations seem to affect populations adversely. The highest populations usually occur after wet years, while droughts cause high dispersal and mortality. Wildlife managers sometimes encourage muskrat populations to explode by reducing trapping in densely

MUSKRAT
Ondatra zibethicus

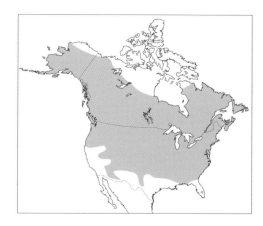

Mammal: *Ondatra zibethicus*, muskrat; the largest of North American murids
Meaning of Name: *Ondatra* is the Iroquois name for this animal; *zibethicus* refers to its two anal glands
Description: waterproof fur is composed of dense, soft underfur and long, coarser, shiny guard hairs; pelage is silvery brown to glossy dark brown with chestnut- to hazel-colored flanks; gray underparts are paler; scaly, black, naked tail is flattened from side to side; small spot on chin; blackish nasal pads and soles of feet; partially webbed toes, strong claws and large hind feet that are slightly rotated
Total Length: male, 19.3 to 24.3 inches; female, 20.2 to 23.5 inches
Tail: male, 8.7 to 11.1 inches; female, 7.6 to 10.9 inches
Weight: male, 1.7 to 2.6 pounds; female, 1.8 to 3 pounds
Gestation: 22 to 30 days
Offspring: 1 to 12 (usually 6 to 8); 2 or 3 litters per year
Age of Maturity: 6 months in the south; 1 year in the north
Longevity: 3 or 4 years in the wild; 10 years in captivity
Diet: primarily a herbivore that eats aquatic vegetation; cattail is one of the most important plant foods; also eats frogs, clams, crayfish, mussels, small turtles and young waterbirds
Habitat: ponds, lakes, streams, canals and reservoirs (deep enough that water will not freeze); freshwater marshes
Predators: mink is the most serious; also fox, coyote, wolf, weasel, raccoon, black bear, lynx, bobcat, otter, owls, hawks, raven, pike and snapping turtle (preys on young)
Dental Formula:
1/1, 0/0, 0/0, 3/3 = 16 teeth

Well adapted for wetland living, muskrats are able swimmers and eat both land and aquatic plants. To preserve body heat, however, they prefer not to eat in the water.

Mink are the most serious predators. With their aquatic ability and streamlined bodies, they can catch muskrats in their burrows.

None of these predators appears to cause decline in muskrat populations, however. It may be that changes in breeding biology and aggression between muskrats influence population cycles the same way they are thought to affect vole and lemming populations. The fact that their cycles are longer may be due to their lower reproductive rate, which increases the time the population needs to reach peak densities. The longer 10-year cycle occurs farther north, suggesting that the shorter breeding season and slower growth rate influence the length of the cycle.

Muskrats are territorial. Females will kill other females and their offspring to gain control of a burrow, and there is considerable fighting among muskrats at high population densities. A monogamous pair bond appears to exist during the breeding season, females aggressively defending their nest against other females and males fighting with other males. Males, however, do not seem to offer much, if any, parental care.

Young muskrats are altricial, born blind and virtually naked. They are usually weaned after a month, and the female will then breed again. Litters are larger in the north than in the south, and large females may bear up to 12 young per litter. Compared with other arvicolines, the muskrat matures late, which is to be expected because of its large size and territorial nature. In northern areas, muskrats seem to take a full year to reach maturity.

Males advertise their maturity and territorial status with excretions from a pair of glands in the anal region. Females have a less-developed set. During the mating season, these glands enlarge and leak an oily, musky secretion through pores in the male's foreskin. The secretion mixes with the urine and is deposited around the territory, a musky advertisement that gives the muskrat its name.

vegetated marshes. Eventually, an "eat-out" results in which almost all the vegetation is consumed. The large areas of open water that remain make perfect waterfowl habitats.

Many animals prey regularly on muskrats—large raptors such as great horned owls and marsh hawks and mammals such as foxes, raccoons, weasels, otters, mink and coyotes.

BROWN LEMMING
Lemmus trimucronatus

The brown lemming is a tundra species that favors damp meadows and the edges of watercourses and lakes. Although its major foods are the shoots of grasses and sedges, it will browse in winter on shrubs such as dwarf willow that lie beneath the snow. In suitable habitats, lemmings often cluster and build extensive networks of runways just under the soil surface and through the tangled vegetation. Nests are balls of grass on the soil surface.

Although lemmings are densely packed, they are not sociable. They fight with one another in breeding season and when populations become dense. Arctic lemmings follow a three-to-four-year cycle and, when abundant, are an important food item for many Arctic mammals. The breeding success of predatory birds such as jaegers is closely tied to the lemming population.

Lemming populations may exhaust their food resources and remove 95 percent of the vegetation cover in peak years. Dense populations result in reduced reproduction and mass migrations that lead to the death of many lemmings by drowning and starvation and allow predators to eat large numbers.

The brown lemming occurs in the same geographic area as the **Peary Land collared lemming**, *Dicrostonyx groenlandicus*. The two species differ in the plants they eat. Brown lemmings prefer grasses, sedges and mosses, while collared lemmings feed primarily on willow leaves and forbs. Also, collared lemmings turn white in winter, while brown lemmings do not.

Both the **southern bog lemming**, *Synaptomys cooperi*, and the **northern bog lemming**, *S. borealis*, are found in eastern forest areas where marshes and other wet habitats such as sphagnum bogs occur. In appearance, they resemble the common meadow vole, but have long, shaggy fur and a delicate skull. They have a more specialized diet than the vole, feeding mainly on grass and sedges. Southern bog lemmings build shallow runways, while nests of northern bog lemmings are underground in summer and above ground in winter, perhaps to take advantage of the insulating value of snow in areas where the soil is wet and freezes solid.

Brown lemmings undergo cyclic population explosions that subside only after they have grazed away most of the tundra vegetation and exhausted their food supply.

BROWN LEMMING
Lemmus trimucronatus

Mammal: *Lemmus trimucronatus*, brown lemming

Meaning of Name: *Lemmus* (lemming), derived from the Norwegian word for lemming; *trimucronatus* (three + sharp point)

Description: large head with no apparent neck, fat body, short, furry feet, stubby tail; claws are specialized for digging, and soles and toes are covered with long, stiff bristles; reddish brown back and rump; grayish head and shoulders; winter coat is longer and grayer

Total Length: male, 5.2 to 6.6 inches; female, 5.2 to 6.3 inches

Tail: male, 0.6 to 1 inch; female, 0.7 to 1 inch

Weight: male, 1.7 to 4 ounces; female, 1.4 to 3.7 ounces

Gestation: 16 to 23 days

Offspring: 1 to 13 (usually 4 to 8); 1 to 3 litters per year

Age of Maturity: male, 4 to 5 weeks; female, 3 to 4 weeks (delayed until 6 to 9 months if population is too high)

Longevity: 1 or 2 years in the wild; up to 3 years in captivity

Diet: primarily grasses and sedges; monocotyledons; tundra grass and cottongrass sedge are among the most important; also mosses, bark and twigs of willows and dwarf birch, berries, lichens and roots

Habitat: wet tundra areas covered with grasses and sedges, streambanks, lakeshores, grassy slopes, alpine meadows and rock talus

Predators: owls, glaucous gull, raven, gyrfalcon, hawks, jaeger, least weasel, ermine, arctic fox, wolf, wolverine, grizzly bear and even caribou

Dental Formula:
1/1, 0/0, 0/0, 3/3 = 16 teeth

NORTHERN BOG LEMMING
Synaptomys borealis

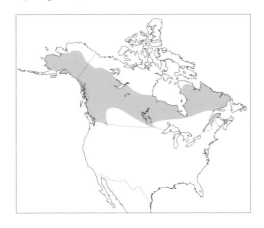

Mammal: *Synaptomys borealis*, northern bog lemming

Meaning of Name: *Synaptomys* (joined together + mouse) refers to these animals as a connecting link between lemmings and field mice; *borealis* (of the north)

Description: brownish gray above, silver below; buffy orange hairs at base of ears; flank glands of male often marked with white hair patches; upper incisors slightly grooved

Total Length: 4.6 to 5.5 inches

Tail: .75 to 1.0 inch

Weight: .75 to 1.13 ounces

Gestation: 21 to 23 days

Offspring: 2 to 6; 2 to 8 litters (average 4) per year

Age of Maturity: male, 4 to 5 weeks; female, 3 to 4 weeks

Diet: primarily green vegetation such as grass, sedges and leafy plants; leaves small piles of plant cuttings along runways

Habitat: alpine and subalpine meadows; bogs, muskeg

Predators: owls, hawks, fox and wolf

Dental Formula:
1/1, 0/0, 0/0, 3/3 = 16 teeth

SOUTHERN BOG LEMMING
Synaptomys cooperi

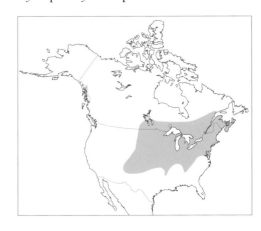

Mammal: *Synaptomys cooperi*, southern bog lemming

Meaning of Name: *Synaptomys* (joined together + mouse) refers to these animals as a connecting link between lemmings and field mice; *cooperi* (named after Cooper, its discoverer)

Description: brownish gray above, silver below; ears and eyes almost invisible; short tail; buffy patch at the base of each ear; upper incisors bear shallow groove

Total Length: 4.6 to 6.1 inches

Tail: .5 to .9 inch

Weight: .75 to 1.75 ounces

Gestation: 23 to 26 days

Offspring: 1 to 8; 2 to 3 litters per year

Age of Maturity: male, 4 to 5 weeks; female, 3 to 4 weeks

Diet: primarily green vegetation such as grass, sedges and clover; also fungi, algae, blueberries and huckleberries

Habitat: grassy meadows, damp mixed forests, sphagnum and heath bogs

Predators: opossum, short-tailed shrew, raccoon, fox, weasel, skunks, hawks, owls and snakes

Dental Formula:
1/1, 0/0, 0/0, 3/3 = 16 teeth

The northern bog lemming shares many characteristics with its relative Synaptomys cooperi, including brownish gray fur on top and silvery-colored fur below, a dietary preference for green vegetation and a damp habitat near marshes, bogs and muskeg.

PEARY LAND COLLARED LEMMING
Dicrostonyx groenlandicus

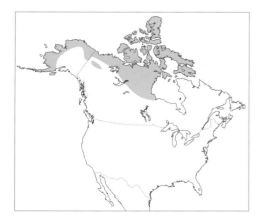

Mammal: *Dicrostonyx groenlandicus*, Peary Land collared lemming, Greenland collared lemming

Meaning of Name: *Dicrostonyx* (forked + sharp point + claw) refers to the two claws on forefeet that develop secondary hooks in winter and look like a double forked claw; *groenlandicus* (of Greenland)

Description: the only rodent that turns white in winter; feet are broad and heavily furred on the soles for life in the Arctic; shoulders, chest and flanks are tawny to chestnut; gray back with black median stripe; tawny flanks and belly; tawny or chestnut ear spots with gray crescent behind

Total Length: 5.2 to 6.4 inches

Tail: 0.4 to 0.8 inch

Weight: 1.6 to 4 ounces

Gestation: 19 to 21 days (may extend to 22 to 26 days because of delayed implantation as a result of lactation)

Offspring: 1 to 7 (usually 5); 2 or 3 litters per year

Age of Maturity: male, 46 days; female, 27 to 30 days

Longevity: few live beyond 1 year in the wild; just over 3 years in captivity (maximum)

Diet: primarily willow leaves and forbs; also sedges, cottongrass, grasses, bearberries, buds and twigs

Habitat: Arctic tundra zone

Predators: raptors and carnivores

Dental Formula:
1/1, 0/0, 0/0, 3/3 = 16 teeth

LABRADOR COLLARED LEMMING
Dicrostonyx hudsonius

Mammal: *Dicrostonyx hudsonius*, Labrador collared lemming, Ungava lemming, Hudson Bay collared lemming

Meaning of Name: *Dicrostonyx* (forked + sharp point + claw) refers to the two claws on forefeet that develop secondary hooks in winter and look like a double forked claw; *hudsonius* (of Hudson), from Hudson Bay

Description: grizzled gray with dark stripe running along middle of back; tawny ear spots and pale collar; tawny flanks and tawny band runs across the throat in summer; white in winter; develops characteristic winter claws on the third and fourth digits

Total Length: 5.3 to 6.6 inches

Tail: 0.4 to 0.9 inch

Weight: 1.6 to 2.4 ounces

Gestation: 19 to 21 days (longer if female is still nursing a litter)

Offspring: 1 to 11 (usually 3 or 4); 1 or 2 litters per year

Age of Maturity: not known

Longevity: some have lived longer than 2 years in captivity

Diet: any available vegetation

Habitat: tundra of Ungava and islands in Hudson Bay

Predators: not recorded, but probably include owls, hawks and carnivores such as fox, weasel and wolf

Dental Formula:
1/1, 0/0, 0/0, 3/3 = 16 teeth

As winter approaches, the Peary Land collared lemming turns white, which allows it to forage above the snow without being conspicuous to predators such as raptors.

JUMPING MICE *Dipodidae*

Only four species of this small family exist in North America. They are specialized for jumping and, like kangaroo rats, have large hind limbs and long tails. Jumps are usually no longer than a yard and are normally much shorter. When the animal is startled, it makes a large jump first, then rapidly hops away in foot-long jumps. The short forelimbs are used to hold and manipulate food as the mouse eats, which it does in an upright position. Unlike kangaroo rats, jumping mice prefer wet areas and are adept at swimming and even diving. They are capable of hibernation for seven to eight months of the year, and they store large quantities of fat. They do not build up winter food caches, and they lack cheek pouches. Insects, spiders, seeds and fungi form their diet. They are most active at night.

They build their nests in fallen rotted logs and grass clumps. Pregnancy lasts about three weeks, and the young, which are born helpless, are weaned in four weeks. Females may breed up to three times in the spring-to-late-summer breeding season. All species appear to have similar natural histories, and they seem to differ primarily in geographic range and habitat.

The **meadow jumping mouse**, *Zapus hudsonius*, is found in damp meadows across the continent. Its range includes northern hardwood forests in the east and coniferous forests in the north and west. The **Pacific jumping mouse**, *Z. trinotatus*, is a resident of moist habitats of the West Coast. The **western jumping mouse**, *Z. princeps*, lives in the western mountain region. The **woodland jumping mouse**, *Napaeozapus insignis*, is an eastern species that overlaps the eastern range of the meadow jumping mouse. As their common names imply, these species are separated by different habitat preferences.

The meadow jumping mouse uses its large hind feet to propel itself with kangaroo-style hops through the damp meadows and woodlands it inhabits.

MEADOW JUMPING MOUSE
Zapus hudsonius

Mammal: *Zapus hudsonius*, meadow jumping mouse

Meaning of Name: *Zapus* (strong or big feet); *hudsonius* refers to Hudson Bay area, where the first described specimen was obtained

Description: coarse, wiry pelage; back is olive-brown because of mixture of black and buff hairs; flanks are paler, underparts are buffy white; belly and back are distinctly separated by clear, pale yellow stripes; sharply bicolored tail, brown above and white below

Total Length: 7.1 to 9.3 inches

Tail: 4.3 to 5.5 inches

Weight: 0.42 to 0.53 ounce in spring and early summer; 0.99 ounce prior to hibernation

Gestation: 17 to 21 days

Offspring: 2 to 8 (usually 4 to 6); 2 or 3 litters per year

Age of Maturity: male, if born early in season, may breed the same year; female, 2 months

Longevity: 1 to 2 years in the wild; 5 years in captivity

Diet: omnivore, but primarily seed eater; also fungi, fruit, insects and their larvae

Habitat: various habitats, including grassland, low meadows, edges of forests and fencerows; also along grassy streambanks

Predators: owls, hawks, raven, red fox, gray fox, wolf, mink, long-tailed weasel, domestic cat, snakes, frogs and pika

Dental Formula:
1/1, 0/0, 1/0, 3/3 = 18 teeth

WOODLAND JUMPING MOUSE *Napaeozapus insignis*

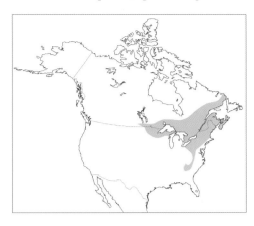

Mammal: *Napaeozapus insignis*, woodland jumping mouse

Meaning of Name: *Napaeozapus* (glen or wooded dell + strong or big feet); *insignis* (a distinguishing mark)

Description: brightly colored with golden yellow sides streaked with black hairs, brownish back, white belly; very long white-tipped tail

Total Length: 8.0 to 10.5 inches

Tail: 4.5 to 6.4 inches

Weight: 0.63 to 0.88 ounce

Gestation: 23 days

Offspring: 4 to 6; possibly 2 litters per year

Age of Maturity: about 1 year

Longevity: 1 to 2 years in the wild

Diet: subterranean fungus *Endogone*; seeds; caterpillars, beetle larvae, grasshoppers, dragonflies and fly grubs; fruit

Habitat: hardwood and coniferous forests, near water

Predators: skunk, weasel, mink, bobcat, owls and rattlesnake

Dental Formula:
1/1, 0/0, 0/0, 3/3 = 16 teeth

PORCUPINE *Erethizontidae*

New World porcupines, Erethizontidae, evolved in South America as forest animals. Like many other South American animals, this family is adapted for life in the trees. The large pads and claws of their hind feet act as clamps when they climb tree trunks, and their stiff belly hairs give them a firm grip on the bark. One South American genus even has a naked, muscular prehensile tail used in tree climbing.

PORCUPINE *Erethizon dorsatum*

The North American porcupine is a recent offshoot of the South American stock. Porcupines first moved into North America when a land bridge formed several million years ago and connected the two previously separate Americas. The porcupine found a ready niche in North American forests, as no large grazer then existed that could feed on the bark and twigs of trees as well as their leaves. Thus the porcupine became an abundant arboreal animal in North America. It is, in fact, far more common than South American porcupines, which face stiff competition from leaf-eating squirrels, monkeys and other mammals.

The porcupine's most striking feature is its hair, which has been modified into barbed quills. Designed to penetrate and work into the skin and flesh of a would-be predator, each quill has a sharply pointed end with a series of overlapping shinglelike barbs. When the quill penetrates flesh, the shingles expand, and the muscles of the victim draw the quill in deeper as they shift and contract.

Porcupines do not throw their quills, as is commonly believed. They have muscles in their skin that cause the quills to stand erect and detach easily when the animals are threatened. Usually, however, it is the action of the attacker or the swinging tail of the porcupine that delivers a load of quills. Because of their barbs, the quills are difficult to remove, which often causes festering and may result in death. If the animal does not die, it learns a powerful lesson about porcupines that may contribute to the porcupines' continued survival. They are sedentary creatures and may occupy the same territory for years. Raccoons, foxes and other animals that share their territory likely only harass a porcupine once.

Porcupines are not, however, invincible. Their large size makes them a valuable prey item, and some animals have developed techniques for killing them without being badly quilled. Fishers are the most famous enemies of porcupines. Fast-moving predators, they can rush in on the clumsy and myopic porcupine and bite it in the face until it is dead or helpless. They then turn it over, exposing its quill-less belly, and eat through its gut until only the outer skin of quills remains. Great horned owls also kill porcupines by driving a talon through the eye and into the brain. Large carnivores such as pumas also eat porcupines. The porcupine defends itself from such predators by climbing a tree and placing its back to the attacker so that its strong, flailing tail lies between the two.

Porcupines are generalized herbivores that eat a wide variety of plants. They feed on almost every kind of tree they encounter. In winter, the bark,

The porcupine is the only animal adapted for grazing the upper reaches of northern forests. Its long fur enables it to forage even in the dead of winter.

PORCUPINE *Erethizon dorsatum*

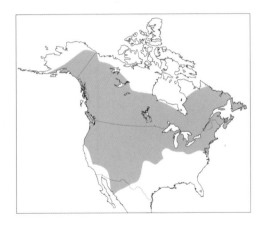

Mammal: *Erethizon dorsatum*, porcupine; the second-largest rodent (next to the beaver)
Meaning of Name: *Erethizon* alludes to the porcupine's ability to excite or irritate; *dorsatum* (pertaining to the back) refers to the spines
Description: first digit on hind feet is replaced with a broad, movable pad, allowing a firmer grasp on branches; adult coat is glossy brown to black above; individual hairs are often tipped with white or yellow-white; approximately 30,000 quills with brown tips and hollow shafts; coarse, dark brown ventral hair contains no quills
Total Length: 25.5 to 35.5 inches
Tail: 5.7 to 11.8 inches
Weight: 7.3 to 30.2 pounds; large males may be 39.7 pounds
Gestation: 205 to 217 days
Offspring: 1 (twins are rare)
Age of Maturity: 1.5 to 2.5 years
Longevity: 6 to 11 years
Diet: primarily vegetarian; green leaves of forbs, shrubs and trees; clovers, alfalfa, corn; cambium layer, inner bark, needles and barbs of trees (especially yellow and white pine); in summer and late winter, they crave sodium and gnaw on bones and antlers or ax handles, oars, utensils—anything with salt from the kitchen or perspiring humans
Habitat: forests with mixed deciduous and coniferous trees but prefers hemlock and pine habitats; sometimes found on prairies and in eastern farmland and aspen swamps; makes use of rocky talus slopes, quarries and caves
Predators: fisher is most successful; also wolverine, bobcat and occasionally wolf, coyote, fox and great horned owl
Dental Formula:
1/1, 0/0, 1/1, 3/3 = 20 teeth

sapwood and buds of trees make up the bulk of their diet, especially in areas with heavy snow cover. During the summer, they feed mainly on the ground, eating shrubs and herbaceous plants. Sometimes they even wade into ponds to eat waterlilies, possibly because of the high sodium content of many aquatic plants. A taste for salt also accounts for the porcupine's habit of eating plywood, outhouses and boat seats, virtually anything that has an elevated salt content. When given a choice, they prefer alkaline to acidic foods.

The porcupine, a powerful gnawing animal, is equipped with large, protruding incisors and strong jaw muscles. Its gut, like that of most herbivores, is long, nearly 21 feet, and is designed to ferment and extract nutrients from a large volume of plant material. Bacterial fermentation of plant-cellulose molecules contributes to a third of the porcupine's energy requirements.

The porcupine is usually a solitary animal that feeds by itself. It is not, however, territorial. Often, two animals can be seen feeding amicably in the same tree or pasture. In winter, several porcupines may share the same rocky den, hollow tree or cabin crawl space. Each porcupine's home territory shifts with the season. In winter, they rarely move more than a few hundred yards from their den site. In summer, however, they may range over 250 acres. They also disperse in early and late summer, some individuals moving as far away as 20 miles; a 6-mile dispersal is not uncommon. The reasons for such dispersals are unknown but may be related to depletion of food resources around dens as well as the need to mate with unrelated individuals.

The only intense social interactions seem to occur during the breeding season in the late summer and autumn. Females come into heat for only 12 hours, and they mate only once. During the rest of the year, it is thought that a membrane seals the vagina. As a result, there is intense male-male competition for mating opportunities. Males are

highly aggressive to other males and will engage in fierce battles during which they bite and drive hundreds of quills into each other (porcupines are adept at pulling quills out of themselves). They also scream loudly and utter a variety of grunts, whines and screeches while chattering their teeth threateningly. There is usually a high proportion of females in any porcupine population, indicating that male-male combat may lead to relatively high male mortality rates.

In the mating season, males search for females and declare their presence by urinating in the area. They also search for female urination sites; urine probably contains hormones that indicate an animal's gender and reproductive state. When a male does find a female's urination site, he rubs his genital region over the area, possibly marking it with a glandular signal.

Chemical communication plays a large role in porcupine courtship. Here is one account of a process many people have wondered about: "The male usually coaxes the female to the ground, where he will rear on hind legs and tail while emitting low vocal 'grunts.' He then proceeds to spray the female with bursts of urine from a rapidly erecting penis, and after wrestling, chases, vocalization and more urine showers, a coitus is effected. It is performed, as in most mammals, with the male taking the active role and, contrary to folklore, mounting from the rear. The receptive female elevates her hindquarters and arches her tail over her back, providing the male with a platform for his forepaws or chest. The male then permits his forepaws to hang free. Coital contact is brief, with a violent ejaculation, and afterward, the male drops back to groom and clean. Further matings may ensue until one of the pair climbs a tree and ends the contact by hostile screaming. A vaginal plug is formed shortly after mating, and the female is no longer receptive."

Porcupine males have very large Cowper's and prostate glands, which

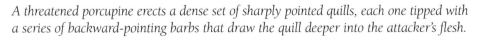
A threatened porcupine erects a dense set of sharply pointed quills, each one tipped with a series of backward-pointing barbs that draw the quill deeper into the attacker's flesh.

may produce a secretion that creates the mating plug. The design of their penis is unique. It lies in a sheath pointing backward, and a complex set of muscles, not blood pressure, causes an erection. The reason for this design is unknown, but it may help the porcupine climb up and down trees rapidly.

Porcupines invest a great deal of energy in rearing their offspring. The litter size is low as rodents go—one offspring per year—and the pregnancy period is long, 205 to 217 days, which is as long a gestation as large grazing herbivores such as moose have. The young are born in dens in spring and early summer and are quite precocial. At birth, their eyes are open, their quills are functional, and they are mobile. They are even able to eat vegetation within a

week. Nevertheless, the mothers remain close to their young and feed them milk for much of the summer. It is not known why porcupines put such a heavy investment in so few young. Possibly, it is because, compared with other rodents, they have a low mortality rate and stable populations. Their large size may give offspring a competitive advantage and enable them to ward off big predators.

It is difficult to say how long porcupines live, but in captivity, they are known to survive for more than 10 years. Their longevity means that in spite of the low birth rate, populations can become very dense—and a dense porcupine population can result in considerable tree mortality. Porcupines are not prudent harvesters. Rather than browsing from tree to tree, a porcupine will sit in one mature tree for days, completely girdling it, eating the top into a gaunt white skeleton and eventually killing it. As a result, it is necessary to control porcupines, particularly since their natural control, the fisher, has been extinguished by trapping in much of its former range. Ideally, the reintroduction of such natural predators as the fisher should be encouraged and a moratorium on or better control of fisher trapping be promoted.

MEAT EATERS *Carnivora*

Carnivores are hunters. Most of the species in this order live by killing and eating other mammals, their predilection for red meat reflected in a unique kind of teeth. All carnivores, from the giant grizzly bear to the smallest weasel, have four teeth specially adapted for eating meat—an upper and lower pair of premolars and molars. Called carnassials, they act as shearing blades that cut against each other as the mouth opens and closes. This slicing mechanism evolved more than 50 million years ago, when a group of primitive insectivores began to eat fewer insects and more mammalian meat.

By the time the first carnivores appeared, mammals had already existed for more than 100 million years and evolved into three groups known as herbivores, omnivores and insectivores. The new specialization of meat-eating predators was a successful evolutionary innovation, and the group proliferated and radiated explosively into the diversity of forms we now recognize as bears, weasels, cats, raccoons, mongooses, dogs, seals, sea lions and walruses. It is hard to believe that animals so different in size, body form and behavior could all have descended from the same ancestor. Yet this common ancestry is reflected in many adaptations, the most important of which—like the carnassial teeth—relate to their lives as predators.

In addition to slicing and shearing meat, carnivores must be able to deliver a killing bite, usually with large incisor teeth. The powerful movement of the mouth as it opens to deliver that bite is unlike the one used for closed-mouth chewing, so carnivores have two entirely different sets of muscles to deliver biting power, one for when the mouth is open (the temporalis) and the other for when the mouth is closed (the masseter). Because large expanses of bone are needed to anchor these muscles, most carnivores have several bone ridges running along the skull. They are especially well developed in the largest carnivores such as pumas and grizzly bears.

The bodies of carnivores have adapted to their predatory lifestyle in several ways. Because they must be flexible enough to roll, twist and contort while making a kill, they have evolved a body plan with little fusion of bones except in the feet. In most species, the bones in the wrist and ankle are fused to strengthen the feet for rough-terrain running. Likewise, the clavicles, or collarbones, of carnivores are drastically reduced in comparison with other orders because of their method of running down prey with a straight forward and backward stride. With little need for tight control of the forelimbs' side-to-side movement, a well-developed clavicle is not necessary.

While the meat of vertebrates is a much more concentrated source of energy than plant or insect material, it is relatively hard to acquire. Therefore, carnivores have developed prey-sensing mechanisms, investing heavily in the senses of sight, hearing and smell. As a corollary, their well-developed senses have predisposed them to make use of a rich array of sensory communication devices, including complicated chemical signals, vocalizations and facial expressions. Only primates exceed carnivores in the sophistication of their communication systems.

The mountain lion is a meat specialist. Its sharp teeth and claws make it a capable predator, and its speedy digestive system allows it to handle the up to 18 pounds of meat it is able to eat in one meal.

FOXES & WOLVES *Canidae*

Canids are long-distance runners. More than 50 million years ago, when the family began to evolve in North America, its members had short, stubby legs, broad five-toed forepaws and long, thin bodies; they looked more like weasels than wolves. Subsequently, their legs became longer, compact toes and toe pads developed to absorb the shock of running, and bones in the forelegs fused to keep them from twisting as they ran.

The incisors—front teeth adapted for cutting—grew larger, and the muzzle lengthened so that the canid could slash open-mouthed at running prey and deliver a penetrating bite when it fell. The long muzzle also featured enlarged and highly convoluted spiral bones, coiled like turbines to filter air as it passed through the nose and provide a huge sensory surface for smelling prey. More important, the turbinate bones enabled the long-distance runner to conserve moisture lost through high ventilation rates and, in extreme weather, to warm or cool the air before it reached the lungs. The development of carnassial teeth (adapted for tearing flesh) and crushing molars allowed canids to eat a more varied diet than that of families with reduced molars.

These adaptations were most useful on open grasslands, and the fossil record indicates that the family diversified on the dry plains of North America, reaching a zenith there some 20 million years ago with 42 different genera. Some of these canids were extremely large and muscular. For example, the bone-eating dogs of the genus *Borophagus* were sometimes as large as bears and had huge, crushing jaws. Paleontologists think that they were the North American equivalent of hyenas, scavenging much of their food and cracking the bones left from the kills of other carnivores.

Today, only 10 to 15 genera and 35 species of canid remain. Nevertheless, they are a tremendously successful family that thrives on every continent except Antarctica. The wolf, dingo, African wild dog and coyote are still dominant mammals in their respective habitats, ranging over vast expanses of open country.

The family displays great adaptability in body form—witness the wide variety of shapes and sizes of domestic dogs. Canids also have a broad range of hunting strategies. For example, although most canids belong to the open country, roaming grasslands, tundra, dry mountains and deserts, there are certain foxes, bush dogs and raccoon dogs that have a lower body form and hunt alone, often in forested habitats, in search of small prey.

None of the canids is very large. The fennec, a small Saharan fox, weighs only 2 pounds; at the other extreme is the largest species, the timber wolf, that weighs a maximum of 176 pounds. Yet the social flexibility of canids allows them a great breadth of diet, some of them hunting mammals as large as moose and buffalo and others consuming rodents and insects. The small African hunting dog weighs only 55 pounds, but by hunting in a group, it is able to prey on adult lions. In general, the pack hunters are highly carnivorous and prey on large mammals, while solitary species, especially the smaller ones, are omnivorous and may eat large amounts of vegetable matter.

Canids depend heavily on their vision, and many species hunt during the day. Also, most members of the family have big bushy tails and

The arctic fox is well adapted to life in the extreme north and capable of enduring temperatures of minus 70 degrees F without seeking shelter. Its camouflage coat grows more dense during the winter months, and its thickly furred feet are protected against frostbite by a countercurrent blood-circulation mechanism.

large erect ears that they use to communicate with other members of their species. The face itself is highly flexible and expressive of emotional states. Wolves, for example, are able to display at least 13 facial expressions, many of which resemble those of the even more expressive primates—including monkeys, apes and human beings. Back arching, paw raising and groin presentation are also used socially.

The canids have excellent hearing and a rich vocal repertoire consisting of as many as eight kinds of signals. The nose of a dog is estimated to be 100 times more sensitive than a human being's, and canids are also able to communicate by smell. Thus sniffing genitals and scent-marking with urine are important means of receiving and giving information. The dog that urinates on a fire hydrant leaves a signature that indicates identity, sex, reproductive state and possibly other information. Urine is also used to mark territorial boundaries.

Howling is one way wolves send and receive information about territory boundaries, pack size and location of competing wolf packs. A deep-toned howl is a warning to would-be intruders, while a high-pitched howl can be a summons to other members of the pack.

HOWLING & SCOWLING

The sound of howling wolves and coyotes is a wild one that sends a shiver down the spine. One longtime student of wolves described it thus: "The cry of the lobo is entirely unlike that made by any other living creature—it is a prolonged, deep, wailing howl, perhaps the most dismal sound ever heard by man. The best comparison I can give would be to take a dozen railroad whistles, braid them together and then let one strand after another drop off, the last peal so frightfully piercing as to go through your heart and soul."

Wolves do not howl at the moon, and their howling is not some canine expression of melancholy. They howl at each other as a way of scowling—a canine kind of warning.

Wolves and coyotes kill members of their own species. Often, the victim is a lone individual killed by a group of strangers whose realm he has invaded,

but even full-fledged packs may fight each other, especially if food is scarce. (There is, however, a well-documented case from Riding Mountain National Park, Manitoba, of one pack displacing another even though there was enough food in the area for both packs.)

A conflict between two wolf packs is similar in some ways to a conflict between two nations armed with nuclear weapons. If they are to avoid mutually fatal conflicts, they must maintain communication so that they will have advance warning of each other's intentions. Such communication springs not from concern for the other group but from the need for self-protection, because lethal fights may be detrimental to both parties.

Wolves scent-mark the borders of their territories to warn wanderers that if they trespass, they can expect to be attacked. Howling is another way of establishing territoriality and sending out long-distance signals about location. Wolves howl all through their own territory, not just at the borders, to define

their space to surrounding wolf packs.

When wolves hear other wolves howling, they usually reciprocate, for howling is an expression of strength and silence an admission of weakness that could invite intrusions. Wolves guarding a kill howl to protect their meal. Breeding wolves at their dens almost always respond to the howling of distant packs. When one member of a pack howls, all the rest join in to indicate not only the location of the pack but its strength as well. A medium-sized pack will howl 50 percent more than a small pack, but lone wolves on the move rarely howl because it would broadcast their location and vulnerability.

In Superior National Forest in northeastern Minnesota, intruding packs have made direct forays into the home sites of others, killing some individuals and, in one case, forcing the victimized pack to disband and disperse. It may be that the amount of howling and its strength enabled intruders to assess the weakness of their neighbors before they made their move.

COYOTE *Canis latrans*

A natural target of the gray wolf, the coyote has historically tended to populate areas beyond the wolf's range, opting for the arid grasslands and deserts of North America while the wolf prospered to the north. Wolves are known to kill coyotes, but with the gradual extermination of wolf populations, the coyote has steadily expanded its range to the north and east from its original distribution in western North America. Human activity, while tending to eliminate the wolf and big game, has unwittingly enhanced the populations of smaller mammals, providing coyotes with a steady food supply.

Coyotes do not hunt big game. They have smaller bodies and smaller social units than wolves do and are far more catholic in their feeding habits, eating anything they can get—usually ground squirrels, rabbits and, more rarely, deer, but also mice, voles, fruits and insects.

The male-female pair is the coyotes' basic social unit, although they often operate within a pack made up of other males and females, probably siblings or offspring, when range and prey are adequate. The breeding biology of coyotes

With the help of other members of the pack, a breeding pair raises its offspring to about the age of one year, when young coyotes begin to adapt to life on their own.

is similar to that of wolves. Both parents—a pack's sole breeding pair—care for the pups with the assistance of other pack members. The young usually disperse at the age of 1 year, especially in habitats that do not support large game animals. The social flexibility of coyotes enables them to survive both in virgin wilderness and on the outskirts of large cities, where they kill rodents and scavenge for garbage.

Coyotes are adept at solving unusual foraging problems, and their reputation for wiliness is well deserved. They have been seen fishing, wading out into the water, plunging their heads below the surface and emerging with carp gripped between their teeth. They also catch crayfish that crawl along the bottom of streams, and on Pacific coast beaches, they search for and excavate sea turtle eggs. Coyotes often follow a badger around as it searches for ground squirrels. When the badger digs into the burrow, the coyote positions itself at one of the side entrances, ready to pounce on any squirrels that take the emergency exit.

Coyotes work in pairs to sneak up on prairie dogs and other rodents. While one approaches conspicuously to attract the attention of the prairie dog, the other stalks it from behind. They also follow vultures and ravens in search of carrion, and they prey on domestic sheep.

Farmers' efforts to control coyotes have usually been fruitless, as the coyote can climb fences 6 feet high and burrow under electric fences, and poisoning programs have often resulted in killing other species. The coyote continues to flourish despite intensive efforts to reduce its numbers.

SOCIAL ECONOMICS

Students of social behavior among animals have long been fascinated by the coyote and the gray wolf. Sometimes coyotes live in packs, sometimes in pairs and often alone. Gray wolves are more social, but the size of the pack ranges from three or four to as many as

COYOTE *Canis latrans*

Mammal: *Canis latrans*, coyote
Meaning of Name: *Canis* (dog); *latrans* (barking); coyote is from the Aztec name *coyoti*
Description: color varies from grizzled gray to rufous; dark vertical lines on lower forelegs; muzzle, outside of ears, forelegs and feet are reddish brown to yellow; white throat and belly; prominent dorsal stripe and a dark cross on shoulders formed by black-tipped guard hairs; fawn-colored tail (lighter underneath) has black tip; scent gland above base of tail; tracks similar to domestic dog's, but in a straight line
Total Length: 3.4 to 4.5 feet
Tail: 11.4 to 15.7 inches
Weight: male, 18 to 51 pounds; female, 15 to 40 pounds
Gestation: 60 to 63 days
Offspring: 1 to 9 (usually 6)
Age of Maturity: female, 1 year; male, slightly older
Longevity: usually 6 to 8 years in the wild (maximum 14.5 years); one animal lived almost 22 years in captivity
Diet: opportunistic feeder, but small rodents and lagomorphs, along with carrion, form a major part of diet; also white-tailed deer, birds, eggs, insects, snakes, turtles, frogs, fish, acorns, fruits and plants
Habitat: open grasslands and plains, mixed forest and cleared environments, agricultural areas, burned-over woodlands, lowland conifers and brush and occasionally upland hardwood forests
Predators: man, wolf, lynx, puma, black bear, grizzly bear, golden eagle and domestic dog
Dental Formula:
3/3, 1/1, 4/4, 2/3 = 42 teeth

A coyote possesses great stamina and is able to run for hours in search of prey, which may include fare that ranges from small rodents and rabbits to birds, insects, acorns and fruit.

twenty. The conventional explanation is that the degree of sociality in canids is related to the size and abundance of the prey that they hunt.

Small canids such as foxes always eat small mammals, insects or fruits; they hunt alone and are not social. This same lack of sociality is seen in arid-grassland coyotes, which feed on rodents, probably because the rodents could more easily see and avoid a large group of predators than they could the more efficient individual or pair. An individual or pair,

however, would be unable to catch and kill a larger animal such as a white-tailed deer. In some areas, coyotes appear to subsist on the carcasses of large mammals that they do not kill but find as carrion. Here, a large group can defend the meat against other coyotes and scavengers.

There is clearly a general correlation between canids' group size and the size of their prey. But among coyotes and perhaps wolves, the correlation may be the *result* of social behavior rather than

a cause of it. If pack size is determined by foraging efficiency, then the amount of meat caught by each individual should increase with the size of the pack. The size of the pack should, therefore, stabilize at the point of maximum meat yield per capita. In fact, though, packs are usually larger than simple efficiency would dictate. In other words, there are more animals in the pack than are needed to handle the kill. There is also evidence that when food is limited, the birth rate declines as the group size increases.

Cooperative hunting efficiency may not be the only factor controlling group size. Individual resistance to leaving the pack may be just as important. Increases in pack size are usually the result of delayed dispersal of younger wolves or coyotes. Young canids may delay dispersing to help raise their young kin and acquire much-needed breeding skills at the same time. Also, membership in an existing pack brings the benefits of access to an established territory. If the habitat is saturated and prospects for establishing a new territory are slight, the individual is faced with a long, hazardous journey away from its pack.

Saturation of the habitat and competition between packs may contribute to the development of groups that are larger than the optimum foraging size. The threat of annihilation by competing wolves may encourage packs to prolong their association with unnecessary members even though the pack would eat better if it were smaller. If this is true, then pack size should increase as competition between groups increases.

The social economics of coyotes and wolves depends on more than just the size of their prey. Competition within and between groups, the genetic relationship of members, the longevity of individuals and groups, the cost of dispersal and the difficulty of establishing new groups are all part of a complex equation. That complexity may be the reason for so much variation in the sociality of coyotes and wolves.

GRAY WOLF *Canis lupus*

The gray wolf is the largest of the dogs, and a pack of wolves is the continent's most formidable predatory apparatus, capable of hunting down even the largest mammals.

For hundreds of years, gray wolves ranged over the entire northern hemisphere, from the farthest reaches of Siberia south to China, from Lapland to Spain, from Greenland to Mexico. But as agriculture spread, their southern ranges disappeared. Humans' hatred of the wolf has ancient roots and is mainly due to the wolf's competition with rural humans in the pursuit of big game. When humans began to keep livestock within the wolf's range, the antipathy intensified. Although there is good evidence that European wolves sometimes preyed on humans, it is competition, not fear, that best explains the widespread aversion. Wolves that have attacked humans were almost certainly suffering from rabies, because healthy wolves, made cautious by centuries of being hunted, tend to avoid people.

Individual wolves are not physically formidable. They rarely stand more than 3 feet high at the shoulder, weigh less than the average adult human and have neither great speed nor stamina. This means that although wolves can sprint faster and bite harder, humans are, surprisingly, the more dangerous long-distance predator. Wolves normally pursue their prey at less than 25 miles per hour, and since they rarely run for more than 20 minutes at a time, they do not cover great distances (the longest chase on record is 13 miles). Humans can run as fast and can often go farther. Plains Indians used to make a sport of running down wolves on foot, and a white Canadian, Thomas Kessick, is credited with running one down in 1865 between Fort Pelly and the Touchwood Hills in Saskatchewan. The 100-mile chase came to an end when Kessick killed the exhausted wolf with his knife.

The success of the wolf as a large-game predator is a factor in its social re-lationships. Almost 80 percent of gray wolves belong to packs that travel, hunt and den together; only a few individuals live largely solitary lives. The pack is a kind of extended family centered on a breeding pair that produces an annual litter of some half-dozen young. The pups may stay with their parents as they grow older to form the basis of an average eight-member pack, although at maturity, some may be forced to leave to seek breeding partners. Wolves mature at almost 2 years of age and usually breed in their third year.

Wolves have a well-developed hierarchy that affects breeding privileges, and normally, only the dominant male and female breed. Eventually, one of the breeding pair will be challenged by a stronger wolf in a courtship that may extend for months or even a year and ends with the establishment of dominance. Fighting may be part of the process, but often, more subtle behavior is involved. Aggressive males with designs on leadership may, for example, tackle dangerous prey or an intruder such as a grizzly, or they may stand guard while other pack members rest.

Females often take the active part in courtship. In one recorded case of a wild female courting a tame male that was already paired with a tame female, the wild female killed her rival and mated with the tame male.

Breeding takes place in the winter. One baffling aspect of the breeding of wolves and close relatives such as the domestic dog is the copulatory tie. During copulation, the male's penis becomes locked in the female vagina, and he is held in a seemingly awkward position, straddling the female for as long as half an hour. Some biologists claim that this is a way of cementing the pair bond. Others hold that since the male is putting himself in a very vulnerable position, the tie effectively ensures that the dominant male is the only one that will risk copulation.

The mother seeks out a rocky, protected den before the birth of her altricial (helpless) pups. They take 10

GRAY WOLF *Canis lupus*

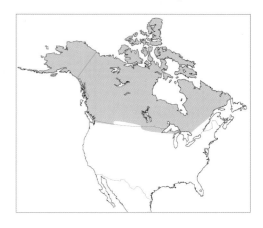

Mammal: *Canis lupus*, gray wolf, timber wolf
Meaning of Name: *Canis* (dog); *lupus* (wolf)
Description: covered with bristly hair; color is extremely variable, from white to black and all intermediate degrees of cream, gray, brown and orangey black; gray tones are the most common (with yellow and reddish hues usually lacking); similar to coyote but much larger; wolf holds tail straight out, while coyote points tail down at an angle
Total Length: 4.9 to 6.7 feet
Tail: 13.8 to 23.6 inches
Weight: male, 44 to 176 pounds; female, 40 to 121 pounds
Gestation: 63 days
Offspring: 1 to 11 (usually 6 or 7)
Age of Maturity: male, 3 years; female, 2 years
Longevity: may live 16 years, but usually not more than 10 in the wild; 18 years is the record in captivity
Diet: carnivore; primarily big game (moose, caribou, deer, wapiti, bison, muskox and mountain sheep); also smaller game (rabbits, shrews, voles, mice, squirrels, beaver, muskrat), birds, fish, berries, fruits, insects, grass and crayfish
Habitat: shows little preference for special habitats; frequents all habitats and travels along game trails, forest edges and lake shorelines
Predators: man, grizzly bear; eagle, black bear, bobcat and lynx may eat unattended pups, but this is probably unusual
Dental Formula:
3/3, 1/1, 4/4, 2/3 = 42 teeth

months to reach adult size. During the first few months, when the pups are unable to hunt and forage, other members of the pack help the mother feed and care for them.

Being at the top of the predatory chain, wolves are not subject to predation (except by man), but they are food-limited, meaning that the size of litters and packs and the overall population density are clearly tied to the abundance of game. To obtain enough food, packs range over wide areas, and hunting grounds may cover anywhere from 400 to 5,000 square miles, depending on the availability of food. Wolves tend to move along a circuit, covering as much as 50 miles in a day.

Packs are territorial and hostile to nonmembers—lone wolves are usually attacked and killed. Wolves are also hostile to other large carnivores and have often been known to tree mountain lions, harass bears and kill wolverines and coyotes.

The prey of the wolf is as varied as the habitat it occupies. It feeds heavily on arctic hare on Ellesmere Island, caribou in the barren grounds, moose in the boreal forest, deer in deciduous forests and, in earlier times, buffalo on the plains. They also consume smaller animals occasionally—beaver, foxes, ground squirrels and rodents. Wolves suffer a perpetual cycle of feast and famine and can go for two weeks or more without feeding. When a kill is finally made, a wolf can eat as much as 20 pounds of meat, swallowing huge chunks with virtually no chewing.

Biologists disagree as to whether wolf predation seriously affects the abundance of big game, but it is reasonable to assume that the effect on populations of slow-growing herbivores such as moose and elk could be significant. This assumption has led many governments to embark on campaigns that have seen wolf populations hunted and poisoned into extermination throughout most of their former range. Only in Canada and Alaska do large wolf populations still exist.

TACTICS

Wolves are not invincible predators. The deer and moose they feed on have developed ways of protecting themselves from attackers, and in response, wolves have developed countermeasures to increase their effectiveness. Both the hunter and the hunted have learned tactics that play on the weakness of their adversary.

Wolves are not fast runners. Over the long haul and under favorable ground conditions, deer and moose can outrun them, and moose can outswim them. Wolves have responded by relying heavily on the value of surprise. They stalk their prey, approaching from the upwind side so that their quarry is not warned by their scent. When they have managed to creep close to the unsuspecting deer or moose, they rush to the attack.

Small, agile prey, such as the white-tailed deer, may respond by bounding rapidly away. They are capable of simply outrunning the wolf. They can also leap through the low brush that impedes their pursuer, and in winter, the long-legged deer plunge easily through the soft snow, while their enemies bog down behind them. Wolves may respond to the superior agility and speed of the deer by setting up an ambush and driving the prey toward hidden members of the pack. This behavior has not been rigorously studied, but it is certainly possible in rolling, open terrain. Wolves can live for nearly two decades, often remaining in a single area, and may learn enough of the topography and the behavior of their prey to predict the probable course of a chase.

Not all prey run from wolves. Muskox will stand and fight as a group, and so will individual moose. The way wolves tackle a moose seems to depend on the moose's reaction. A well-documented study on the outcome of moose-wolf encounters in Isle Royale National Park in northern Michigan found some clear patterns. Of 131 moose discovered by wolves, only 6 were killed. Sometimes the moose became aware of approaching

Female wolves find a protected den where they give birth to their pups, which will take 10 months to grow to adult size. Other pack members take part in their care.

wolves before being spotted and was able to avoid them. Even when the wolves saw the moose and pursued it, in half the cases, the moose simply outran them. Sometimes, however, the moose was surprised and stood at bay or turned and faced its attackers after an initial chase.

Most moose that turned to fight were successful. In all of the 36 recorded cases in which the moose decided to fight, the wolves gave up very quickly.

Fights were brief—the longest battle was over in only five minutes. The principal weapons of the moose and other hoofed animals are not the antlers but the forefeet. The moose whirls and lashes out with bone-breaking blows. It only takes a few minutes for the wolves to get an idea of their quarry's abilities. If it appears strong and able to mete out punishment, they abandon the attack and move off in search of easier prey. On the other hand, if they can panic the moose into bolting, they have an advantage and will run alongside, ripping at its belly and legs. Often, one wolf will attempt to clamp its teeth onto the moose's nose while the others attack its body.

White-tailed deer lack the strength and ferocity of the moose, so are forced to protect themselves by strategy, using the territorial nature of wolves to their own advantage. Wolf packs defend their territories against other wolves, and trespass is severely punished, so there is often a kind of buffer zone, a "no-wolf's-land," between adjacent territories. Neither pack tends to hunt close to the territory of another because of the threat of aggression, and deer tend to establish their yards in this neutral ground. Such deeryards usually last until there is a shift in the wolf population. Wolves in the surrounding territories feed on surplus deer that may be forced out of the buffer zone by competition.

The buffer zones have been compared to the no-man's-land that once existed between hostile tribes of native people. Such areas supported relatively high densities of game and were a source of replenishment for areas cropped by hunting and predation. Similarly, modern-day moose gravitate to camping and recreational areas in national parks, which the wolves avoid. Wolves leave a buffer zone around their main competitors—humans—and the moose use it.

ARCTIC FOX *Alopex lagopus*

The arctic fox lives at the top of the world in a ring of tundra that circles the northern parts of Russia, Alaska and Canada. This small carnivore is superbly designed for northern conditions, with a compact body, furry feet and a huge bushy tail.

In extremely cold weather, the arctic fox can maintain its body temperature at up to 200 Fahrenheit degrees above the ambient temperature. Thus even when Arctic winters bring temperatures approaching minus 80 degrees, the fox keeps itself at a steady 104, its normal temperature. A thick, insulating coat and the ability to increase its metabolic rate when temperatures drop below minus 60 degrees mean that the fox can function effectively during even the most severe northern winters.

The feet of the arctic fox are warmed by a countercurrent blood-circulation mechanism. As cool blood returns to the body from the capillaries in the toes and feet, it picks up heat from the fresh warm blood that is being pumped from the heart and warm body core. This warm blood is then carried back into the feet, keeping them just a degree or two above freezing, despite the fact that the fox is standing on ice or snow.

The arctic fox, like many northern animals, turns white in winter. This is a form of camouflage that varies with the environment: On islands or along the open coast—in Iceland, for example—the coat of the arctic fox usually has a bluish gray cast.

A solitary hunter, Alopex lagopus *relies on its acute hearing to track down meals on the move. This arctic fox has successfully targeted a rodent's runway beneath the snow.*

The breeding biology of the arctic fox has also been modified for life in harsh weather. For example, in years of abundant food, litter sizes average 20, which is two to four times the size of red or gray fox litters. Average arctic fox litters contain 6 to 12 offspring; the largest have 25. Large litters allow the fox to exploit years when lemmings are plentiful and to protect the family from extinction in years when the weather is severe and food is scarce.

Arctic foxes are monogamous and breed once a year in the spring. After the female gives birth, she remains in the den with her pups for the first few days while the male brings food. Almost from the beginning, the pups tend toward strong sibling rivalry, and when food is scarce, the weaker members of the litter may be killed by the stronger. Although they are altricial—born blind, naked and helpless—the pups develop rapidly, and by the time they are 2 weeks old, they have been weaned and are ready to venture outside the den. By late summer, the male stops caring for them; very soon, the female follows suit. The young then disperse, leaving the male and most females ready to breed again by the next spring.

Arctic foxes are not extremely territorial, although males tend to exclude other males from their den sites during breeding season. Thus although the dens may be scattered far and wide— as few as one in every 22 miles—they may also be clumped together in good sheltered spots.

Dens remain in use for long periods, and some are known to have been inhabited for up to 60 years. Foxes avoid areas of permafrost for their dens, aiming for high, well-drained areas where the soil is light and easily excavated. More rarely, they burrow into rock piles. Their dens are a system of tunnels with many entrances and exits—usually a dozen or so but sometimes up to 100. In low years in the population cycle, many dens may be empty; in years of high population density, good dens may be hard to come by.

Dens are often recognizable from afar as islands of lush grass among the shrubs and mosses. The foxes' digging stimulates the growth of vegetation, which is also enriched by the nutrients excreted near the entrance of the den.

Small rodents, particularly lemmings and voles, are the most important food of the arctic fox. Breeding pairs with pups may eat as many as 4,000 lemmings in the denning season. Populations of small mammals on the tundra tend to wax and wane every three to five years, however, and the foxes are tied to the same wheel. Like lemmings, foxes often migrate in huge numbers when their food source disappears. Some amazing journeys have resulted: One fox was tagged in Russia and caught in Alaska; another, tagged and released in Ontario, was caught two years later 700 miles away.

The hunting success of the arctic fox depends on its keen sense of smell, which it uses to locate lemmings in their burrows under the snow. Foxes have been known to venture out onto the pack ice, where they are able to sniff out the presence of seal pups under 2 feet of snow. Arctic foxes forage within a 1-to-8-mile radius of the den, depending on the abundance of prey. When small mammals such as lemmings, voles and ground squirrels are scarce, the foxes feed on nesting birds; in winter, they trail wolves and polar bears and feed on the remains of their kills. They must, of course, be very cautious, since wolves and bears are—along with humans— the major predators of the arctic fox.

Some of the Inuit depend heavily for their livelihood on trapping the arctic fox. Other predators are the snowy owl, large hawks and, in the southern part of the range, wolverine, weasel and red fox. In recent years, red foxes have been moving farther into the range of the arctic fox and have inflicted increasing damage.

Like the red fox, the arctic fox is subject to rabies, and in epidemic years, up to 20 percent of the population may succumb to the disease.

ARCTIC FOX *Alopex lagopus*

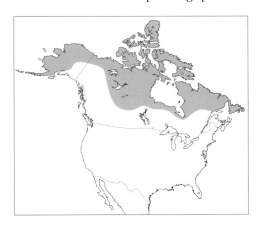

Mammal: *Alopex lagopus*, arctic fox
Meaning of Name: *Alopex* (fox); *lagopus* (hare + foot) refers to hair on the soles of its feet, probably for traction on ice
Description: soles of feet are well furred; two color phases in winter—white and blue (varies from blue-black to pearl-gray; populations in marine areas have more blue foxes; in summer, both phases are dark brown on the back, tail and outer sides of the legs and yellow-white to buff on belly and flanks; compact body, short legs and less pointed ears than other foxes
Total Length: male, 2.9 to 3.9 feet; female, 2.5 to 2.8 feet
Tail: male, 11 to 13.4 inches; female, 10.4 to 12.6 inches
Weight: male, 7.1 to 8.8 pounds; female, 5.5 to 7.3 pounds (can reach 19.8 pounds)
Gestation: 49 to 57 days
Offspring: 1 to 14 (usually 5 or 6); up to 25 have been recorded
Age of Maturity: 9 to 10 months
Longevity: one captive lived 15 years, but many young do not survive first 6 months; few live more than several years in the wild (can live 8 to 10 years)
Diet: scavenger; prefers lemmings, Arctic voles and ground squirrels; also ground-nesting birds, carrion (follows wolves and polar bears to clean up their prey carcasses as well as eating stranded marine mammals), fish, mollusks, crabs and sea urchins
Habitat: primarily in Arctic and alpine tundra, usually in coastal area; can be found in the boreal forest border during winter and will venture onto frozen seas
Predators: besides man, wolf is chief predator; also polar bear, grizzly bear, snowy owl, peregrine falcon, golden eagle, wolverine, weasel and red fox
Dental Formula:
3/3, 1/1, 4/4, 2/3 = 42 teeth

Large-eared and small-bodied, the swift fox relies on a single food source—grasshoppers—for up to half its summer diet. Other staples include jackrabbits, rodents and birds.

SWIFT FOX *Vulpes velox*

The swift fox has adapted to life on the dry prairies. Like other desert foxes, it is small, only half the weight of a red fox. It has large ears. Many large-eared foxes are insectivores, and indeed, often half the swift fox's summer diet consists of grasshoppers. It is also a competent predator on mammals, taking its name from the speed with which it runs down rabbits. The swift fox has been clocked at 37 miles per hour, the speed of the very fast jackrabbit.

The swift fox lives primarily in the shortgrass prairie and desert, where it preys on small mammals, principally jackrabbits, rodents and some ground-nesting birds.

The swift fox is too small to be a threat to livestock. Nevertheless, it was poisoned almost to extinction in Canada in the 1930s, along with many other grassland predators and rodents. Habitat destruction also played a part in wiping it out as the prairie was gradually plowed under. In the United States, however, the swift fox survived, and it is now being reintroduced into Canada.

SWIFT FOX *Vulpes velox*

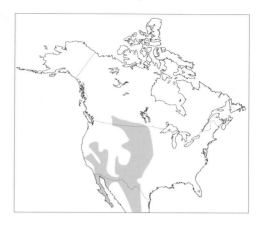

Mammal: *Vulpes velox*, swift fox
Meaning of Name: *Vulpes* (fox); *velox* (quick, swift); called swift fox because of its speed
Description: in winter, pelage is long and dense; mainly buffy gray above and orange-tan on the sides and legs; the cylindrical tail is also tan and is tipped with black; the throat, chest, underparts and inside of the ears are creamy white; there are two prominent black spots on each side of the snout below the eyes; in summer, the fur is short, coarse and more reddish; red fox has white tail tip, and gray fox is larger and darker
Total Length: 2.8 feet
Tail: 8.9 to 13.8 inches
Weight: male, 3.7 to 6.6 pounds; female, 3.5 to 4.6 pounds
Gestation: 50 to 60 days
Offspring: 1 to 8 (usually 4 or 5); 1 litter per year
Age of Maturity: male, first year; female, 10 months (not all females breed the first year)
Longevity: 8 to 10 years in the wild; have lived up to 12 years, 9 months in captivity
Diet: omnivore; however, jackrabbits, cottontails and carrion are the most important food items; also rodents, birds, insects and a few lizards and fish; some vegetable matter, including grasses and berries
Habitat: open plains and prairies and shrubby deserts with sparse grasses of short and medium height
Predators: coyote, wolf, eagle, red-tailed hawk and rough-legged hawk
Dental Formula:
3/3, 1/1, 4/4, 2/3 = 42 teeth

RED FOX *Vulpes vulpes*

The red fox enjoys the largest geographic range of any living carnivore. It is widely distributed throughout the northern parts of both the Old and New Worlds wherever the habitat is relatively undisturbed.

The red fox has only recently become common throughout North America. It is now found everywhere from the high Arctic to the deep south, except in dry plains and deserts. The fox may not be native to the continent, however. Some scientists believe that North American red foxes are descended from the European species introduced into New England in 1750, but fossil skeletons have been found that predate that import, so other scientists argue for a relatively rare breed of native red fox that may have interbred with the European import. The resulting hybrid may have then proliferated; alternatively, the formerly rare native fox may have spread in the wake of increased human activity.

The diet of the red fox is limited only by what it can find or catch. Scientists prodded by hunters suspicious of fox depredations of game birds and small animals have learned much about the fox's diet, discovering, for instance, that most foxes are omnivorous: When wild grapes, blueberries, cherries and other small fruits are in season, they may eat only fruit; at other times, they feed primarily on small mammals up to the size of cottontails and groundhogs. Their diet is supplemented with insects, frogs, snakes, birds and bird eggs. Red foxes also scavenge the carcasses of large animals that they cannot kill themselves.

The red fox's habitat ranges from tundra and boreal forest all the way to prairie. It is rarely found deep in mature forests, however, preferring to roam the open country and live at forest edges.

Red foxes breed as monogamous

Sharp vision, acute hearing and a keen sense of smell are essential senses for this hunter of small mammals. Extended whiskers orient the red fox and help it deliver a deadly bite.

pairs once a year, appropriating the burrows of other small mammals such as groundhogs for dens where their pups can be born. In spring, the females give birth to a litter of about five. Much variation in social and breeding behavior exists, but in some areas, the male stays with the family and assists in rearing the young. When many den sites are clumped together, though, males may mate with more than one female and neglect to provide parental care.

As the pups grow older, the parents bring them half-dead animals to play with to begin their education as hunters. Soon, the young accompany their parents on foraging trips during which they acquire the skills they will need for survival. By the end of summer, the new generation disperses, and by spring, they are themselves ready to breed.

Except during the reproductive season, foxes are solitary and hunt alone. They stay in one home range, marking the boundaries with scent and urine. Although they are not overtly territorial, males may exclude other males during the breeding season.

In habitats shared with coyotes, there may be antagonism between the two species. An adult fox will approach and bark at coyotes that come too close to its breeding den; coyotes respond by chasing the agile fox, but they are seldom able to catch it. Pressure from coyotes, however, does cause foxes to favor denning near human habitation, since foxes tolerate human disturbance much better than coyotes do.

Red foxes are the main carriers of rabies in eastern North America, and their population periodically suffers epidemic outbreaks of the disease. Rabies is often transmitted to livestock or attacking dogs and thus to humans. Recent attempts to inoculate wild foxes against the disease have involved dropping medicated meatballs from airplanes. Experiments have shown that most foxes in a given area will come across one of these meatballs and eat it. This has made it possible, for the first time, to control the scale of rabies epidemics.

RED FOX *Vulpes vulpes*

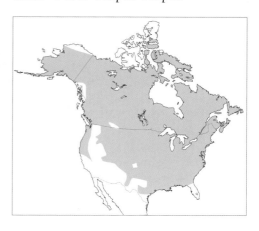

Mammal: *Vulpes vulpes*, red fox
Meaning of Name: *Vulpes* (fox)
Description: long, silky fur; three distinct color phases: **1.** red fox: face, top of head and nape are yellow to rusty red; back is yellowish red or fulvous; lips, chest, abdomen, inside of ears and tip of tail are creamy white; back of ears and anterior portions of legs are black; **2.** cross fox: grayish brown, long black guard hairs form a cross from shoulder to shoulder; **3.** silver fox: totally black except for white tip on tail and a variable amount of frosting; also a black phase, which is entirely black; all other North American canids lack white tail tip
Total Length: 3 to 3.6 feet
Tail: 13.8 to 16.5 inches
Weight: 7.9 to 15 pounds (up to 30.9 pounds)
Gestation: 51 to 53 days
Offspring: 1 to 10 (usually 5 to 7); 1 litter per year
Age of Maturity: 10 months
Longevity: few live more than 3 to 4 years; has potential to live 12 years
Diet: omnivore, but more of a carnivore, as it prefers animal matter; small rodents, frogs, insects, birds, snakes and plant material such as acorns, grasses, corn, fruits
Habitat: open regions such as farming areas, prairie, alpine and Arctic tundra, meadows, bushy fencelines, woody stream borders and forest clearings, low shrub cover and along beaches bordering larger lakes
Predators: man is chief predator; also wolf, coyote, dog, lynx, bobcat; occasionally bear and wolverine, as well as hawks and owls
Dental Formula:
3/3, 1/1, 4/4, 2/3 = 42 teeth

GRAY FOX
Urocyon cinereoargenteus

The gray fox is roughly the same size as the red fox, and it shares much of the same geographic range. The two species are separated, however, by their distinct habitat preferences and behavior. Gray foxes seem to avoid the open agricultural land that red foxes thrive on, preferring to range through shrubby woodland with hilly and rocky terrain. Like the red fox, gray foxes are omnivorous, but they tend to eat more plants and many more insects than other foxes in the same area.

The biggest and most obvious difference between the two species is the ability and inclination of the gray fox to run up trees and even to jump from the branches of one tree to another—possibly a survival mechanism favored by long interaction with predatory coyotes. That is part of the reason why 18th-century colonists in New England, frustrated to find that their hounds could not follow the trail of the gray fox, decided to import the more convenient European fox.

Gray foxes sometimes establish their dens in animal burrows and rocky cavities, but more often, they nest in thick brush or high up in hollow trees. This habit may limit the animal's northern distribution, although it extends well into South America. In fact, the gray fox may have originated in the warm habitats of the south.

The reproductive and social behavior of this fox appear to be similar to those of its red cousin. However, few detailed studies of gray foxes in the wild have been carried out.

OLFACTORY SOPHISTICATION

Carnivores—including domestic cats and dogs—have the most highly developed noses of all mammals. They make use of their sense of smell not only to find food but also to communicate with one another.

Humans are probably most familiar

The highly developed sense of smell of canids such as this gray fox enables them to locate prey that is still out of sight and to follow it unerringly, even when the trail is hours old.

The gray fox prefers shrubby woodland, avoiding the open habitat of the red fox.

with the dog's remarkable sense of smell. Dogs have been observed to recognize members of a family by smell alone and are able to distinguish even genetically identical twins. They can recognize the smell of human fingerprints that have been left on a glass slide for six weeks. They can trail a human on the run even when the person wears rubber boots or rides a bicycle. Dogs can even follow odors left scattered on vegetation or trailing in the air. That is why they have been used to track escaped prisoners and search for contraband and bombs.

Since the domestic dog is a very recent descendant of the gray wolf, it is likely that wolves and other canids have a sense of smell at least as acute as the dog's, and possibly more so. In the wild, this sensitivity allows canids and other carnivores to locate prey that is out of sight and to follow it unerringly.

Carnivores' highly developed sense of smell also plays an important social role, as their noses register signs left by other members of their own species. Most carnivores scent-mark with urine and glandular secretions, often as a way of setting territorial limits. Recent studies show that breeding wolves, both male and female and especially newly formed pairs, scent-mark their territory, a procedure that is likely an important

part of establishing dominance. Lone wolves do not scent-mark.

Carnivores have a pouch of receptor cells called the Jacobson's organ on the roof of the mouth that sometimes connects with the nasal passages. The function of the pouch is unclear, but it may be used in analyzing hormones excreted in the urine of other individuals. It is thought that when a male tastes the urine of a female, pulling his lips back from his gums in a prolonged grimace as he does so, he is activating these sensitive cells to identify females that are in a reproductively receptive state.

Wolf urine is made up of a mixture of volatile compounds called ketones and sulfides. They vary in type and proportion according to the sex of the wolf and the time of year, and each compound has a distinctive smell. Also present in the urine is a series of long-chain aldehyde molecules that change according to the hormonal state of the animal. That is why wolves are probably able to read a great deal in the smell of urine. The arctic fox, a much less social animal, has, predictably, a simpler set of compounds in its urine.

Cats mark their territory by spraying urine widely over vegetation rather than marking a series of single spots. This increases the effect of the scent and improves the status of the individual. Cats also rub their cheeks against the ground to leave a trail of glandular secretion, but it is not known what information they are conveying.

Urine may also be used as a reminder. Recent studies of fox and coyote food caches show that the animals will not urinate in the area until the food has been entirely consumed. Then they deliberately urinate on the cache site, perhaps to serve notice that the cache is exhausted of usable food even though the area still reeks of good meat.

So insensitive is the human nose that we have been slow to recognize the importance of smell in the lives of the carnivores. It may be that even more olfactory sophistication lies undiscovered, right under our noses.

GRAY FOX
Urocyon cinereoargenteus

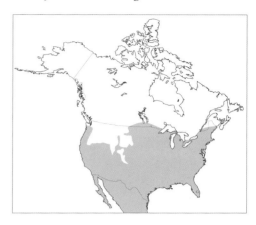

Mammal: *Urocyon cinereoargenteus*, gray fox
Meaning of Name: *Urocyon* (tailed dog); *cinereoargenteus* (silvery gray)
Description: pelage is denser and coarser than that of the red fox; the upper pelage is pepper-and-salt due to white bands and black tips on guard hairs; underfur is buffy; legs, cheeks and chest are ochraceous; upper lip, throat and belly are whitish; black nose with a muzzle patch forming a black line extending to and around each eye; long, thick brush; tail has a black tip
Total Length: 2.5 to 3.5 feet
Tail: 10.8 to 17.5 inches
Weight: male, 8 to 13 pounds; female, 7.5 to 11.9 pounds
Gestation: 51 to 63 days
Offspring: 1 to 7 (usually 4)
Age of Maturity: male, unknown; female, usually in first year
Longevity: 6 to 10 years in the wild; over 13 years in captivity
Diet: omnivore; small mammals (especially cottontails), birds, insects, fish, fruits, nuts and grains; takes more plant food than other foxes do
Habitat: primarily wooded and brushy country in rocky or broken terrain; also marshes
Predators: bobcat and coyote; great horned owl may eat young
Dental Formula:
3/3, 1/1, 4/4, 2/3 = 42 teeth

BEARS *Ursidae*

Bears, the largest terrestrial carnivores, are very unlike their agile, fleet-footed relatives among the cats and dogs. Large and ponderous, with a heavy, flat-footed gait and teeth more suited to crunching and grinding than to stabbing and biting, they have tended to turn from meat as a primary source of food.

The Indian sloth bear, *Melursus ursinus*, has become virtually an anteater and is one of the more extreme examples of the bear's movement away from meat. In order to feed on termites and ants, it has developed specialized teeth, none of which are incisors. It also has naked, flexible lips and a long, thin tongue for sucking up insects. At the other end of the spectrum is the polar bear, the most carnivorous of all, with well-developed carnassial teeth for slicing meat. Grizzly and black bears take the middle ground with an intermediate tooth structure, some generalized incisors, well-developed canines and large molars for masticating vegetable matter.

The largest bears are those found in the north—the black, grizzly and polar bears. The large size of northern species is an adaptation to winter, when the bears den up and spend months in dormancy without eating. The low metabolic rate associated with their large size means they can live for long periods on stored body fat. One of the costs of being so large is having to patrol a large feeding territory. Northern bears require hundreds of square miles to support themselves. Bears are territorial and rarely congregate except at particularly rich feeding grounds such as salmon runs and garbage dumps.

In spite of their large size, bears often eat small food items. Their strength enables them to flip boulders over and tear logs apart to get at ants and insect larvae denied to other mammals. Their large size also renders them immune to predation. Grizzlies and polar bears appear to have no natural enemies aside from man. Black bears are rarely killed, but accounts of predation by wolves and grizzly bears exist.

The ancestor of the modern bear was a small foxlike animal related to the dog, a form that gave way quite recently to the larger bears we know today. Grizzly and polar bears, for example, evolved only in the past two million years. The grizzly, or brown, bear developed in Asia and spread to North America less than 70,000 years ago. The polar bear is an even more recent development and is thought to have split off from the brown bear in the middle of the last ice age, about 10,000 years ago.

Despite their massive skulls and heavy bones, all bears are fast sprinters, able to keep pace with a horse and outrun a man, at least over a short distance. Many are good tree climbers even though their short tails are of little use for balance—or, incidentally, for social signaling. Some tropical bears such as the sun bear forage extensively in the trees of Southeast Asia, and they all have large nonretractable claws that they use as foraging tools. On the whole, bears tend to have smaller eyes and ears than other carnivores do, and they depend less on sight and hearing for communication and hunting. A keen sense of smell is vital, however, since much of their foraging is done at night.

Up until 10,000 years ago, the most powerful

An adult grizzly keeps its eyes peeled for one of the thousands of spawning salmon making their way upstream. Although it is an omnivore and a dedicated eater of vegetation such as grasses and sedges, the brown bear relies on these fat-rich fish to put on much-needed weight in preparation for its winter hibernation.

land predator in North America was a giant long-legged bear called *Arctodus simus*, built for speed and equipped with the large canines and carnassials associated with big-game predation. When the large grazing animals disappeared, this great killer was also doomed to extinction. The bears that survived were the smaller, more flexible omnivorous bears, the black, the brown and the polar bear, which had adapted for unrivaled dominance in the Arctic habitat.

Bears never penetrated south of the Sahara into the African continent, a failure that may have had a positive effect on human evolution. Some scientists argue that it was the lack of competition from large, intelligent and omnivorous bears that allowed the tree-dwelling primates to evolve into large, intelligent and omnivorous terrestrial apes—a group that includes humans.

BLACK BEAR *Ursus americanus*

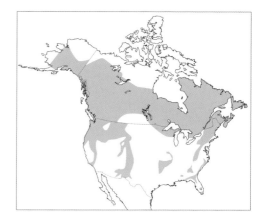

BLACK BEAR *Ursus americanus*

The black bear is the success story of its kind. Less spectacular than the polar bear or the grizzly, it is undeniably more prosperous. While strict controls have been needed to prevent the threatened grizzly and polar bear populations from being harvested out of existence, the black bear puts up with an annual hunting toll of 30,000 without significant effect. The black bear's secret is its wide-ranging tastes in food and its ability to thrive in virtually any kind of forest habitat. In both deciduous and coniferous forests, from the tundra tree line all the way into Mexico, wherever there is enough natural forest to sustain it, the black bear continues to inhabit almost all of its former range. Only in the densely settled eastern part of North America has it disappeared.

The black bear is the most omnivorous of all bears and, indeed, of all carnivores. For much of the year, it browses on twigs, buds and berries, switching to nuts and roots in the autumn. Three-quarters of its food consists of vegetable matter. It makes up the rest of the menu by finding grubs and worms under rocks and rotting logs, and it will not turn up its nose at carrion. The bear also hunts mice, birds and other small mammals. By feeding

The most omnivorous of all carnivores, the vegetation-loving black bear can exist at much higher densities than the more meat-dependent bear species.

lower on the food chain, the black bear has freed itself from a dependence on big game. The result is that forests can support a much higher density of black bears than of other large carnivores such as the puma or even the grizzly.

Black bears are mainly nocturnal and begin to forage at dusk, although as winter approaches, they may spend more time feeding, both in the daytime and at night. Because they are mainly vegetarian, most of their food disappears with the first snowfall. It is crucial, therefore, that they accumulate sufficient fat during the late summer and fall to support them through a winter-long period of hibernation.

The bear's dormant state causes a reduction in metabolic rate so that the animal burns less fuel than it does when active. Despite the fuel savings, the long fast—in some areas, lasting almost half a year—uses up great reserves of fat, sometimes as much as 40 percent of the bear's autumn body weight.

Females begin to breed between the ages of 3½ and 5 years every other year. They usually give birth to two cubs—occasionally three or four—during the denning period. The young bears stay with the mother when she leaves the den and return with her to spend the next winter in her den. They disperse the following summer, and the female breeds again. In northern areas, the den can be a sheltered cave, a hollow tree or an excavated hole that is often lined with vegetation.

Black bears have few natural enemies,

Mammal: *Ursus americanus*, black bear
Meaning of Name: *Ursus* (bear); *americanus* (of America)
Description: dense, coarse pelage; usually black with cinnamon-brown muzzle and white V on chest; cinnamon-colored bears occur in the west; other color phases include white and blue and are restricted to locations on the Pacific coast.
Total Length: male, 4.5 to 5.9 feet; female, 3.9 to 4.9 feet
Tail: male, 3.5 to 4.9 inches; female, 3.1 to 4.5 inches
Weight: male, 249 to 595 pounds; female, 203 to 449 pounds
Gestation: 210 to 220 days (including a period of delayed implantation)
Offspring: 1 to 5 (usually 2); 1 litter every other year (sometimes every 3 or 4 years)
Age of Maturity: male, 5 to 6 years; female, 3.5 to 5 years
Longevity: 25 to 30 years in the wild, but usually less than 10; up to 30 years in captivity
Diet: omnivore; berries, fruits, nuts, twigs, leaves, tubers, roots, insects and their larvae, eggs, carrion, honey and small mammals; also garbage (garbage eating is a fixation with many bears, and natural-food foraging becomes secondary)
Habitat: mainly forested areas; also swamps, marshes and thickets in several successional stages; may occur on tundra and in mountainous areas
Predators: man, grizzly bear; gray wolf may attack young, or a pack of wolves may kill a female
Dental Formula:
3/3, 1/1, 2-4/2-4, 2/3 = 34 to 42 teeth

Black bear cubs are typically born in January or February, and the number of cubs in a litter depends on the food supply available to the mother. At birth, a cub is completely helpless.

although grizzlies will charge and kill them on occasion, and gray wolves will attack weakened adults or young cubs if they find them alone. The black bear might have been much more vulnerable in the past, however, as it evolved with the giant bears and canids of the Pleistocene. Its fast and skillful tree climbing may have been a protective strategy developed in that era.

Black bears are solitary creatures, marking out their territories with excretions. The bears leave deep claw marks high on scattered trees to show their size and strength and perhaps to mark territory as well.

Bears use a wide range of vocalizations, moaning, teeth chattering and posturing to threaten members of their own species. Females with cubs are notably aggressive, but otherwise, few black bears attack people. Populations of bears growing up around campgrounds and garbage dumps, however, have learned to associate humans with food, mostly as competitors but sometimes as prey. The consequences can be fatal.

EMBRYOS ON HOLD

A black bear sow may mate, ovulate and fertilize her eggs in June. The fertilized egg begins to divide and grow into a fetus. Then, suddenly, progress stops. At this stage, in most mammals, the fetus would implant itself in the wall of the mother's uterus, where it would absorb nutrients from the mother through the placental membranes. Over the gestation period, it would grow and develop into the form of a new animal. In the black bear, however, the embryo may be held in limbo without any development at all for as long as half a year.

Black bears and many of their close relatives are not the only mammals able to delay implantation. Weasels, deer, seals, the armadillo and a few other unrelated species seem to have evolved this ability independently. Though the groups are unrelated, it is probable that each was subject to similar ecological conditions favoring this strategy.

For some species, the delay is obligatory, while for others, it is facultative (dependent on circumstances). The facultative delay is believed to be used by some rabbits and rodents when excessive nursing demands are already being made on the mother by an existing litter. If she has a large family that is literally draining her nutritional reserves, she may delay implantation and even abort the embryo. In the obligatory delay, the hiatus occurs regardless of the mother's nutritional state and may be an

adaptation to allow a period of physiological assessment.

In bears, implantation is likely delayed until the summer and autumn fattening period has passed. If it has been a year of scarce food, with few acorns and fruits, most females do not bear young, even if they have mated and are carrying embryos. The female must have enough fat not only to sustain herself during the winter but also to produce milk for the cubs. Delayed implantation prevents her from investing in a pregnancy before her food reserves are established. Once that is done, implantation occurs, and the pregnancy proceeds. Similarly, in weasels, most of which stay active over the winter, implantation is delayed until the end of winter, when female fat reserves have met the test of the most severe winter conditions.

But why not simply delay mating and fertilization to eliminate the loss of even partially developed embryos? Many female bats store sperm for the entire winter, allowing their eggs to be fertilized only when spring has clearly arrived. For them, it seems to be more convenient and efficient to mate in autumn than in spring.

That is not true of bears. For them, autumn is a crucial time for the laying on of winter fat. Courtship and mating at that time would deplete their physical resources disastrously and impinge on their winter survival. Also, when females have an extended period of estrus—in grizzlies, for example, it is two to five weeks in duration—the time of their mating may result in giving birth at a time that is far from optimal. If sperm do not store well, then delayed implantation is a solution.

The phenomenon of delayed implantation is, at least in some species, widely variable. Most weasels, for example, delay the development of their embryos, although some do not. The delay may be the female's attempt to time the birth of her young; it may equally well relate to the level of nutrient reserves. No widely accepted theory exists to explain it, and more study is needed.

GRIZZLY OR BROWN BEAR
Ursus arctos

In terms of size, range and diet, the grizzly bear stands midway between the black and polar bears. It is larger and more carnivorous than the black bear but smaller and with a more varied diet than the polar bear; it has a narrower distribution than the black but ranges more widely than its Arctic cousin. Yet in terms of range, the grizzly is not what it was: This bear used to roam throughout the Great Plains and prairies of North America and all along the western coast of the United States but now survives only in the western mountains and the tundra of the north.

Like the black bear, the grizzly is highly omnivorous, but there are times of the year when its diet is mainly meat. During the spring calving season, for example, it eats young elk, deer and caribou. All summer, it digs for rodent species, and during the salmon runs, it turns into an effective fisherman. In late summer, berries are the most important food, along with nuts, herbs and grasses. It feeds selectively, but some 200 different species of plants make up roughly half its yearly food intake.

The size of the grizzly's home range has been found to vary from 10,000 to 27,000 square miles, depending on the abundance of food and probably on the character of the individual bear. Males

The brown bear's identifying characteristics are its broad face, its powerful long claws and its massive build, especially the sizable shoulder hump that sets it apart from other bears.

GRIZZLY OR BROWN BEAR
Ursus arctos

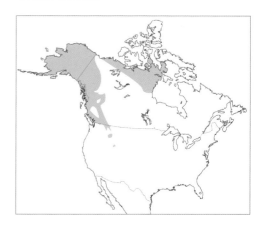

Mammal: *Ursus arctos*, grizzly bear, brown bear

Meaning of Name: *Ursus* (classical Latin word for bear); *arctos* (classical Greek word for bear)

Description: prominent hump on shoulders is formed by muscles of massive forelegs; face is dish-shaped; very long claws; pelage varies from pale yellowish to dark brown or almost black; white tips on hairs produce a frosted or grizzled effect

Total Length: 8.5 feet

Tail: 2.4 to 8.3 inches

Weight: 322 to 842 pounds

Gestation: 180 to 266 days

Offspring: 1 to 4 (average 2); every third year

Age of Maturity: can breed at 3 years; continues to grow for 5 or 6 years, sometimes longer

Longevity: about 25 years in the wild, possibly up to 50 years

Diet: omnivore, but plants and vegetation make up most of the diet; new grass, sedges, roots of legume *Hedysarum* (probably the most important food in much of the range), fruits, salmon, insects, fungi, roots, moss, mice, marmots, ground squirrels, newborn elk, moose, deer and caribou

Habitat: variety of habitats; prefers open areas; alpine tundra, high mountains, subalpine forests, alpine meadows and along coastlines; requires some areas with dense cover

Predators: no natural enemies apart from man

Dental Formula:
3/3, 1/1, 2-4/2-4, 2/3 = 34 to 42 teeth

typically roam farther than females do. They also emerge from dormancy (not true hibernation) much earlier in the year than the females and tend to remain active much later.

In late summer, grizzlies begin to fatten up, preparing for denning-up. Like black bears, they spend the entire winter holed up in protected dens that they dig into well-drained slopes where drifting snow accumulates and acts as insulation. They can easily be awakened. While living in their winter dens, females may give birth to one to four cubs (usually two). Females can begin to breed at 3 years of age, but they do not normally reproduce until their fifth year. The father provides no parental

Brown bears have perfected the art of salmon fishing and have a reputation for choosing productive fishing spots such as those beneath waterfalls or in shallow rapids. Its jaws agape, a bear literally waits for a salmon to hurl itself upstream into its mouth. Once it catches a fish, a bear is likely to leave the stream to eat it, away from other bears and scavengers.

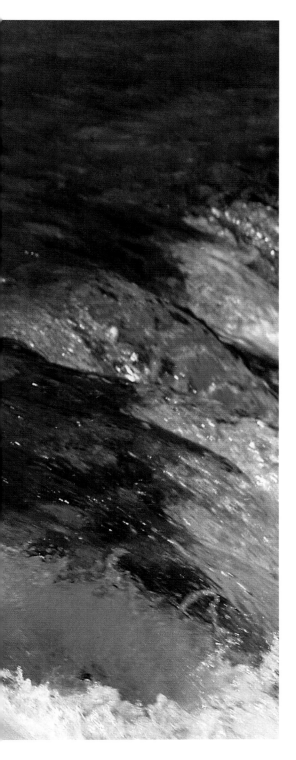

over a two-day period, while males will copulate with as many females as they can gain access to. Ovulation is induced by copulation. As with other bears, the mating success of the male depends on establishing a territory that overlaps those of several females.

Adult males are territorial and will fight to gain or defend a home range. Young bears that still have to win a territory are particularly likely to engage in fierce mauling fights, although mature males in established ranges tend to leave one another alone. Females with cubs are extremely dangerous and likely to attack anything that threatens them. A black bear, if startled, may climb a tree or disappear under cover when it feels itself to be in danger; a grizzly, however, seems to believe that the best defense is a good offense.

Sport hunting has accounted for the death of many grizzlies, and increasingly, food-laden campers and backpackers who trespass on a bear's territory and leave a trail of garbage behind them are leading to the shooting of many more grizzlies. Grizzlies have a strong homing instinct and are difficult to transplant from areas the public wishes to enjoy in its pursuit of wilderness. People must realize, however, that the grizzly, with all its ferocity and power, is the epitome of the wilderness. Campers and hikers need to learn to move safely through the wild parts of this continent without attempting to destroy the animals that make it what it is.

BEAR ATTACKS

Bear attacks human! Such headlines, evoking the terror and pain of the victim, horrify the public from time to time. The usual result is the shooting of one or more bears. Conflict with humans now constitutes one of the major pressures on grizzly populations. Painfully little is known about the cause of attacks, although one authority writes: "Such improbable stimuli as severe thunderstorms, forest fires, perfume, cosmetics and menstruating women have been suggested."

More probably, aggression is simply a normal part of the lives of most bears. Bears are not always aggressive toward humans or other bears. Their reactions likely depend on many factors—health, sex, whether it is breeding season, whether young cubs or a source of food are present and, indeed, on the personality of the bear. The context of the encounter is also important: Was the bear surprised? Was it hungry and following the scent of food?

Bears must defend their territories from other bears. Males must fight rivals for food and the right to breed. Females must defend their cubs. Unfortunately, bears and humans do not understand each other's signals. Humans are roughly the same size as bears, and they hold themselves in an upright posture, which is threatening to bears because it conveys aggression and readiness to fight. And humans fail to recognize a bear's hostile postures and sounds; if frightened, a person may run, taking on the vulnerable appearance of a subordinate bear or a prey item. Even if the bear is merely irritated and intends only to discourage this strange competitor, the moderate bite or blow it delivers may be enough to seriously wound or kill a human.

Attacks on humans by wild bears are exceedingly rare and usually happen in campgrounds, where bears are conditioned to eating garbage and food that reeks of human scent. Campground bears have lost their fear of humans and when hungry may treat them as competitors or, indeed, as items of prey. It is public ignorance, not the bear, that is at fault. A failure to respect potentially dangerous animals combined with poor management of human recreation results in more injured humans and more dead bears every year. It may be in the course of nature that bears and people cannot coexist without conflict. It is clear, however, that proper management of human-bear interactions would eliminate the vast majority of attacks.

care, and the cubs remain with their mother until the second summer.

Many males and females may congregate during the breeding season. Mating is entirely promiscuous. Copulation, according to one observer, is "prolonged and vigorous," lasting for 10 to 60 minutes. Females may mate many times with as many as four males

POLAR BEAR *Ursus maritimus*

The polar bear, which can weigh as much as 1,760 pounds, is the largest terrestrial carnivore. Yet although it is larger than the grizzly, its long legs and neck and lean body make it look much less massive. Even the polar bear's muzzle is long and pointed.

The polar bear is designed for operating in snow and ice. The long legs and neck permit the wide-reaching blows and bites the bear uses to capture seals. Its legs also allow it to rear up high in the deep snow. The thick white coat is another Arctic adaptation, and one that goes far beyond camouflage. Mixed with the deep fur are many hollow hairs that trap warm, insulating air and act as solar collectors. The ears of the polar bear are relatively small, and its hearing

is poor. However, it has much better eyesight than most bears, since good vision is vital in the open Arctic habitat. Polar bears are often seen standing high on their hind legs, obviously scanning the landscape. And, like all carnivores, they have a keen sense of smell.

In fact, the polar bear's sense of smell is crucial to its success as a hunter. In the spring seal-breeding season, for example, polar bears forage on both land-fast pack ice and ice floes surrounded by open water. On land-fast ice, they sniff out the dens of ringed seals hidden beneath the ice and eat the seal pups.

The bears also stalk the ringed and bearded seals that haul themselves up onto the ice. Sometimes swimming underwater, the bear works its way through a mix of ice and open water

Capable of charging across the frozen tundra at 30 miles per hour, the adult polar bear is a formidable adversary of other polar bears as well as beluga whales and walruses. Equipped with excellent senses of smell, hearing and vision, the polar bear is a specialized hunter that can sniff out a seal beneath its snow-covered breathing hole.

until it is close enough to a seal to make the final rush. Polar bears also search out the breathing holes of seals and wait, ready to hook the seal out with long, sharp, curving claws that seem custom-made for the task. The seals' breathing holes are usually covered by a thin layer of ice or snow with just a tiny airhole exposed, so the bears have to excavate them, running the risk that the seals will be warned off by increasing light at the hole. But the polar bear has learned to fool the seal by leaning its head over the hole to darken it.

Stalking bears rely on their white coloration for camouflage. They seem to be aware of its value and have even stooped to trickery to take advantage of it. Some bears have been seen covering their black noses with a paw while hunting. A seal can easily outswim a bear, but the bears have developed countermeasures. Although seals' eyes function well underwater, they do not have good visual judgment when they surface. One polar bear was seen pretending to be an ice chunk while he stalked an adult ringed seal in open water. First observed about 230 feet from a seal resting on the ice, the bear began swimming strongly toward it. Whenever the seal went underwater, the bear immediately stopped swimming and floated motionless; when the seal surfaced, the bear resumed its swim, gradually closing the distance between them. Finally, the seal surfaced right beside the bear, apparently mistaking it for floating ice. The bear killed it with a sudden lunge and a single bite.

When polar bears kill a seal, they often eat only the skin and a layer of blubber, leaving the meat virtually untouched, a windfall for the ravens and arctic foxes that follow the bears. Many of these animals subsist entirely on scavenged leftovers.

Polar bears also sniff out and eat the carcasses of dead whales and walruses, and as many as a dozen bears may congregate around a dead sea mammal. In a similar way, the bears also gather at garbage dumps to pick over the bones of civilized life, bringing them into direct conflict with northerners who have established dumps in bear country. Moving the bears provides only temporary relief, since they seem to have a strong homing instinct. Bears relocated 300 miles away from Churchill, Manitoba, have returned within weeks.

Polar bears will eat almost any meat for which they can profitably forage. They have been known to attack anything from beluga whales that venture into shallow water to seabirds and small mammals. They eat some berries and a little grass and seaweed when the season allows, a small vegetable component of their diet that supplies important vitamins and trace elements.

Polar bears do not always, or even ordinarily, hibernate in winter—especially the males—although their degree of inactivity may depend on the weather, the state of the ice pack and the fat reserves of the bear. However, in November and December, pregnant females consistently retreat to their dens, which are deep hollows dug into snowdrifts, to give birth to their cubs. The purpose of denning seems to be more to protect the young bears than to conserve the energy of adults. Unlike black bears, the meat-eating polar bears can hunt all winter long, and thus they do not need to conserve energy while waiting for the return of vegetable life.

Females breed between the ages of 3 and 7 at two- to four-year intervals. In the fall, when they come into estrus, their scent is likely to attract a number of males. After mating, the females retreat to their snowy dens to give birth to one or two cubs. The mother and cubs will break out of the den in March and will stay together for the next two years.

Animals as large and thickly furred as the polar bear tend to suffer in the warm Arctic summers. Some summer dens have been found around the southern end of Hudson Bay, where bears have dug burrows up to 20 feet long into the permafrost in search of coolness. Some of these dens appear to have been in use for hundreds of years.

Polar bears are dangerous animals. As solitary hunters stalking and killing large mammals for their subsistence, they are prepared to fight members of their own species to protect or gain access to a kill. Also, polar bears do kill people. The killers are often young bears—aggressive male youngsters that ritualistically spar with each other during the autumn. Any one of their playful bites or irritable blows would be enough to kill a human.

POLAR BEAR *Ursus maritimus*

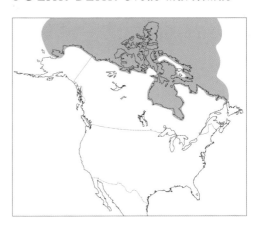

Mammal: *Ursus maritimus*, polar bear
Meaning of Name: *Ursus* (bear); *maritimus* (of the sea)
Description: pure white in winter; in summer and autumn, the coat is thinner and has a yellow wash or is almost golden; soles of the feet are bordered with dense fur for insulation
Total Length: 6.5 to 9.8 feet
Tail: 3 to 5 inches
Weight: male, 660 to 1,760 pounds; female, 330 to 660 pounds
Gestation: 195 to 265 days (including a period of delayed implantation)
Offspring: 1 to 4 (usually 2); every 2 to 4 years
Age of Maturity: male, 4 years; female, 3 to 7 years
Longevity: 20 to 35 years in the wild; up to 40 years in captivity
Diet: primarily the ringed seal (also harp, bladdernose and bearded seals and young walrus); also seabirds, eggs, carcasses of stranded marine mammals and other carrion; fish, mussels, crabs, grasses, seaweed, lichens, mosses and sedges
Habitat: prefers pack ice that is subject to periodic fracturing in combination with open water and land (barren rocky shores and islands)
Predators: man is major predator; occasionally, a male walrus, a killer whale or wolves may kill one, but this is probably rare
Dental Formula:
3/3, 1/1, 2-4/2-4, 2/3 = 32 to 42 teeth

RULES OF THE NORTH

If one examines the locations of the largest individuals of a species—the biggest gray wolves, brown bears, moose or deer—a pattern emerges. The biggest animals seem to come from the extreme northern limit of their ranges. The same is true of closely related species. Wood rats that live in the north or at high altitudes are 300 percent larger than species from hot desert areas. This pattern is known as Bergmann's rule, which states that the average size of a mammal increases with the coldness of the climate.

One explanation for this pattern is that larger mammals have a slower rate of heat loss relative to body weight than smaller ones do. However, the total amount of heat lost still increases with the animal's body size. So even if it is more efficient at heating itself, a larger animal will require and burn more food than a smaller one. To explain Bergmann's rule, it is necessary to find some absolute advantage rather than the relative one of large body size.

One possibility is that larger animals can fast and hibernate, living off stored body fat for longer periods than small ones. This effect becomes greater as the average temperature drops. A large mammal, then, can wait out a week-long northern blizzard or an extended period of hibernation better than a small mammal—but it will still have to consume more food to acquire the fat stores needed to do it.

Another possibility is that a larger body size may enable an animal to feed on a wider variety of food sources, but it is difficult to see how this correlates with latitude. Certainly there is no evidence that the larger wolves and bears in the north are more efficient hunters than those in the south.

A larger body size could also be an adaptation to permit the larger litter sizes of the north that are a hedge against unpredictable weather. However, this idea is ruled out too, because it would be reflected only in larger females, but in fact, both sexes exhibit the tendency toward large size.

A survey of 47 different mammal species showed that only 32 percent followed the trend predicted by Bergmann's rule. In other words, most species do not follow Bergmann's rule. The records of huge northern mammals may be more a measure of the health and the size of wilderness mammal populations than of Bergmann's rule.

Another rule that has been applied to northern mammals is Allen's rule, which states that as one moves north, the size of the extremities, such as ears, feet and other exposed areas, is reduced. The explanation is that animals can reduce heat losses by reducing unnecessary body surface area. Gray wolves in the north have such shortened muzzles that their teeth grow cramped together. This may reflect a compromise between the need for long turbinate bones to warm incoming air in the nasal passages and the need to reduce heat loss through the facial area.

Arctic foxes are also cited as examples of the effect of Allen's rule. They have short, stubby legs, a reduced muzzle and short ears. But again, the validity of this generalization is open to question: The body form of bush dogs in the South American tropics is not unlike the arctic fox's. Allen's rule, like Bergmann's, has yet to be tested and demonstrated with convincing data. It may be that adaptive forces other than minimizing heat radiation have shaped the mammals of the north.

ENERGY CONSERVATION

One of the ecological advantages that mammals enjoy is the ability to maintain a high body temperature that enables them to stay active in extremely cold environments. Animals such as reptiles, whose body temperature fluctuates with the environment, are forced into inactivity by cold weather. In the north, snakes and lizards spend more than half their lives doing nothing because they are too cold to move. By contrast, many mammals can boost their metabolic rate to compensate for increased cold and can thus stay active, which is why mammals, not reptiles or amphibians, have colonized the cold regions of the Earth.

But mammals pay a high cost for maintaining their body temperature. A mammal at rest burns three times the number of calories that a lizard does, and during the winter, an active mammal expends far more energy. This is no problem for mammals that have a constant supply of food; rodents that burrow beneath the snow can feed on grasses and sedges, making use of the insulating properties of the snow, and the weasels that eat those rodents can likewise stay active. But mammals that feed on herbaceous forbs or berries and fruits may find it impossible to get enough food to meet their heating costs. Some, such as the pika and the mountain beaver and other rodents, must build up a winter food store, while others have evolved the ability to hibernate or go torpid.

Deep hibernation is the most extreme energy-conservation strategy, as it involves profound changes in the metabolism. As the deep hibernator settles into its winter sleep, its heartbeat slows. The jumping mouse's heart beats at a rate of 500 to 600 times per minute when it is active, but in deep hibernation, it slows to 30 beats per minute or less. Similarly, its oxygen consumption drops to a level that is only 5 percent of the active mouse's rate. The body temperature falls until it is just 4 degrees above freezing to further reduce the amount of heat burned by the body. Some mammals such as the red bat may even lower their body temperature to 23 degrees F without sustaining frost damage. Some mammals simply rely on torpor, a less extreme slowing of the metabolism. For example, a bat's body temperature may decline from close to 104 degrees F to around 77 degrees each day after it finishes foraging, then as the evening's activity period approaches,

Deploying their mighty jaws, snowshoe-sized paws and boundless energy, young and old male polar bears pass the time leading up to the winter freeze with endless hours of wrestling. These mock fights allow the younger bears to rehearse skills essential for survival later in life.

its temperature rises again. This sort of torpor is used by many smaller mammals such as chipmunks, which may remain torpid for periods of up to five days.

Small mammals that stay active during winter can use other adaptations to reduce heat loss. Rodents that eat bark and dried stems and seeds in winter are forced to eat snow as a water supply. The energy cost of melting snow in the body is substantial, so some small northern rodents such as the red-backed vole concentrate their urine in winter to reduce water loss. This reduces two types of energy expenditure: the heat in the body being carried away when the warm urine is excreted and the melting of the snow required to replace it.

The deepest hibernators are small rodents with a high surface area in relation to their body mass and the quantity of fat they have stored. Larger animals do not need such a radical lowering of body temperature. Black bears, for example, den up for the winter, but their reduction in body temperature is less extreme. The body temperature of a denning bear may be only a few degrees lower than when it is active. For years, this led some researchers to claim that bears were not deep hibernators. The distinction is somewhat misleading. Black bears are extremely efficient hibernators; their higher body temperature simply reflects a lower rate of heat radiation in relation to their size and fat stores. They do not need to be cooler.

One advantage to the bear of staying closer to the active state is that it is more easily aroused and ready to move if necessary. The black bear's heartbeat drops from 40 to 10 beats per minute, and its oxygen consumption is cut by half, but a disturbed bear can make a coordinated response, something deep hibernators are incapable of doing.

As large mammals that evolved in the tropics, humans have no hibernating abilities, although some of us do seem to get fatter and sleepier in winter. Hibernators such as the black bear may provide us with valuable medical insights, however. Bears burning their winter fat have blood-cholesterol levels that are twice as high as when they are active. These levels are also twice as high as the normal human level. Yet black bears do not suffer from the heart and circulatory diseases that many doctors believe are linked to high cholesterol in the human bloodstream.

Bears can also go without urinating for as long as 100 days. Researchers interested in kidney disease are studying the mechanisms bears use to avoid the buildup of too much urea and urine. Apparently, some hormones may cause the urea in the urine to be reabsorbed and converted back into protein to rebuild muscles and other tissues. This is the way science progresses. An interest in the energy-conservation adaptations of mammals may one day lead to a treatment for gout or kidney disease in humans.

EARED SEALS, WALRUS & HAIR SEALS

Until recently, pinnipeds were classified in their own order, Pinnipedia, but they are now considered part of the same ancestral group from which other Carnivora arose. Pinnipeds lead a double life. Seals and sea lions live part of their lives in the water and part on land or ice. Most species court, mate and give birth out of the water, and all of them swim and dive for their food. Their dual existence means that they must cope with two very different sets of environmental problems.

The most obvious adaptation to aquatic life is streamlining. The penis, testes and nipples have moved inside the body, and the ears have become very small, providing the pinniped with a smooth, obstruction-free shape. The limbs have been greatly reduced and converted into flippers, and the tail is shortened. The neck is long and the spine flexible, which allows for undulating swimming motions and agile underwater turns. Maneuverability is also enhanced by the lack of a collarbone and a very small pelvis. The fur of the true seals and the walrus has been trimmed. Instead of fur, they depend on a thick layer of blubber for insulation from the cold seawater. The skin is rich in oil glands.

Pinnipeds are active mammals. Northern species maintain a body temperature that is 11 Fahrenheit degrees warmer than the aquatic environment for much of the year. This requires rapid food digestion. Seals can pass a meal through the digestive tract in as little as six hours. This is not to suggest any wasteful haste. Indeed, they may be extremely efficient digesters, since their intestines are among the longest in the world relative to their body length. One Steller sea lion's intestine measured 264 feet, a remarkable 38 times its body length.

Feeding underwater has required special design features for vision. The large rounded eye is shaped like that of a fish. It features a well-developed tapetum lucidum, a mirrorlike membrane that runs along the back of the eye. This increases visual sensitivity in the low light conditions underwater. The receptor cells in the mammalian eye consist of cones that detect colors in bright light and rods that are sensitive to the difference between dark and light. Scientists believe the eye has a switch system that uses cone vision in bright light and rod vision as the light dims.

The pinnipeds' double life also requires a good thermostat. In cold water, the animals need to conserve heat. While they are on land—whether they are lazing in the hot summer sun or fighting or breeding in the local rookery—the problem is staying cool. Seals use their flippers as heat radiators. The blood system is designed like a countercurrent heat exchanger. The hot seal can shunt blood in the flippers that has been cooled by the environment back into the body. Alternatively, to conserve heat while the seal is underwater, the flippers absorb heat from arterial blood before it returns to the body.

The pinnipeds—including eared seals, the walrus and hair seals—have a distinctive look. True seals, the hair seals, developed from a separate carnivore ancestor, probably an ancient relative of the sea otter. This lineage is different from the one

The evolutionary history of pinnipeds such as these Steller sea lions is one of compromise between adaptations for a life on land, where they mate and give birth, and for a life in the sea, where they feed. The pinnipeds are now considered part of the same ancestral group from which other Carnivora arose.

that gave rise to the walrus and eared seals. Moreover, seals are more recent, having originated 15 million years ago. By contrast, walruses and eared seals emerged about 25 million years ago.

EARED SEALS

The eared seals, or Otariidae—a group that includes fur seals and sea lions—are the most recent offshoot of the enaliarctids, extinct doglike carnivores. Unlike most of the walrus family, which also arose from this stock, the eared seals have not suffered extinction. Indeed, the group is more diverse than ever. The fact that they retain external ear flaps and have a face that is less telescoped than that of true seals also indicates that this group is a recent arrival in the marine environment. Eared seals are considered conservatives in evolutionary terms, most species having the same body plan and life-history pattern. Their hind limbs point forward. They use their front flippers for swimming and moving around on land, where they are able to amble and scrabble about in a way that true seals would find impossible.

In comparison with true seals, whose sleek, streamlined bodies are insulated with a thick layer of blubber, eared seals keep warm with a coat of thick fur. The lack of blubber may mean that otariids are less well adapted to cold ocean waters. They must keep swimming to maintain their body temperature in frigid conditions that would find some phocid seals able to loll about comfortably motionless without cooling off. Otariids are extremely vulnerable to oil spills, which reduce the insulating properties of their fur.

WALRUS

Twenty million years ago, a family of large, bearlike carnivores ambled into the shallow bay waters of the northern Pacific Ocean. Eventually,

they diverged from their now extinct ancestral family, the Enaliarctidae, and gave rise to the walruses and fur seals. Early walruses speciated widely and once dominated the warm coastal and temperate waters of the Pacific, but they gradually became extinct, leaving the modern walrus, *Odobenus rosmarus*, as the sole surviving member of the family Odobenidae.

HAIR SEALS

Hair seals, the Phocidae, are the most aquatic of the pinnipeds. Absence of an external ear is evidence of how completely they have evolved for life in the water. For swimming, they use primarily their rear flippers and the undulation of the hind end of the body. To reduce drag, their forelimbs are kept close to the body except when they are maneuvering. Hair seals are ungainly on land. The specialized forelimbs and backward-pointing hind flippers are of little use for locomotion.

On land, the forelimbs serve mostly for heat radiation and social gesturing. Some hair seals are so streamlined that their fusiform cigar shape is similar to that of fast-swimming animals such as tuna and dolphins. Certain species are able to use their speed to propel themselves several yards out of the water, then land on the ice to bask. To move around on land, the hair seals use a caterpillarlike undulation that clearly distinguishes their family from the eared seals, which use their front flippers for both swimming and walking.

Among the pinnipeds, the hair seal is the richest family, with 19 species found along the coastlines of the northern and southern hemispheres. They have the greatest variation in body size, breeding biology and ecology. The elephant seal may reach a weight of 3 tons, while the ringed seal weighs only 100 pounds. Some hair seals are polygynous, while others are monogamous breeders. Some species are specific to freshwater lakes or Caribbean islands. Most hair seals

are equipped with simple cheek teeth for feeding on fish, squid and mollusks. Two species are filter feeders and have highly complicated cheek teeth, while most species have peglike teeth that are adapted for catching and killing fish. The leopard seal of Antarctica has huge, sharklike teeth adapted for its predatory life, which includes eating penguins and other seals.

Most phocid species are long-lived, usually attaining 30 years and, in some cases, up to 56 years. Their reproductive rate is low, and their single-pup litters are born on ice or land. Females mate soon after giving birth, but implantation is delayed. Many Arctic phocid species spend months on the ice, fasting during unfavorable weather and feeding at other times to accumulate large stores of blubber.

Evolved from land mammals, eared seals such as these northern fur seals lack insulating blubber layers and must keep warm with thick coats of fur.

Mammal: *Callorhinus ursinus*, northern fur seal, Alaska fur seal
Meaning of Name: *Callorhinus* (beautiful hide); *ursinus* (bearlike)
Description: large hind flippers that are turned forward for moving on land; thick underfur, unlike the true seals; bulls are black dorsally and brownish red ventrally, with a grizzled gray mantle on neck and shoulders; cows are gray above and reddish below, but pelage looks darker in the water; pups are born with a shiny black pelage that is shed and replaced with a silver coat
Total Length: male, 6.2 to 7 feet; female, 3.5 to 4.5 feet
Tail: 2 inches
Weight: male, 330 to 600 pounds; female, 84 to 119 pounds
Gestation: 1 year (including a 4-month period of delayed implantation)
Offspring: 1 (there is one case on record of twins)
Age of Maturity: male, 4 to 5 years, but does not breed until 10 years of age; female, 3 to 5 years
Longevity: male, 15 years; female, 22 years
Diet: squid and fish (capelin, herring, anchovy, salmon, sand lance, rockfish) are major food; sometimes eats birds; stomach often contains rocks
Habitat: mostly pelagic; spends six to eight months of the year at sea; young animals are found in coastal waters in the winter; rookeries are formed on rocky beaches
Predators: large sharks, killer whale and man
Dental Formula:
3/2, 1/1, 4/4, 2/1 = 36 teeth

EARED SEALS *Otariidae*

NORTHERN FUR SEAL
Callorhinus ursinus

The northern fur seal is highly pe- lagic, a creature of the open ocean. It fishes at dusk and at night and rests on the surface during the day. Its aquatic life is made possible by its dense fur, which traps air bubbles, adding buoyancy as well as insulation. Fur seals are migratory, moving south along the coast to California in North America and to Japan in Asia. It is likely that their distribution changes according to the movements of fish.

At sea, fur seals are largely solitary. Only during the summer breeding sea- son do they congregate at rookeries on islands along the coast of Alaska. Fur seals have a typical harem system of mat- ing, with a large bull defending a group of females. Females mate again a week after giving birth, then return to the sea to feed for five or six days, leaving the pup to survive on the fat it accumulated from the previous week's suckling. Pups disperse at the end of summer.

Although fur seals have endured cen- turies of harvesting because of their rich coats, populations are currently healthy. Increased oil-spill pollution and Arctic fishing may place them at risk.

STELLER SEA LION
Eumetopias jubatus

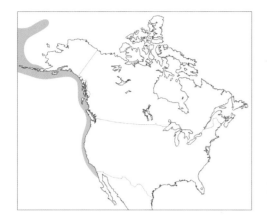

Mammal: *Eumetopias jubatus*, Steller sea lion, northern sea lion; largest of the eared seals
Meaning of Name: *Eumetopias* refers to broad forehead; *jubatus* (having a mane) refers to the male's shaggy mane
Description: largest of the eared seals; the cow is slim, but the bull has massive forequarters and a swollen neck; whiskers are approximately 20 inches long and are stiff, pale and mystacial; large flippers; pelage lacks an undercoat; bulls have a mane and dark brown flippers and are buffy above, reddish brown below; cows are uniformly brown
Total Length: male, 8.8 to 10.5 feet; female, 6.1 to 7.8 feet
Weight: male, up to 2,000 pounds; female, 606 to 805 pounds
Gestation: 1 year (including a 4-month period of delayed implantation)
Offspring: 1
Age of Maturity: male, 4 to 6 years, but not an effective breeder until 9 to 15 years; female, 3 to 6 years
Longevity: 17 years
Diet: wide variety of invertebrate marine life, especially squid
Habitat: chiefly marine but sometimes goes up rivers; spends most of its life in a narrow belt of coastal water; breeds on islands, rocky outcrops, boulders, cobblestone and coarse sand beaches
Predators: man, killer whale and large sharks
Dental Formula:
3/2, 1/1, 4/4, 1/1 = 34 teeth

Weighing up to one ton, massive male Steller sea lions, like the bull shown at center, above, may each guard a harem that contains as many as 30 females within a breeding colony.

EARED SEALS *Otariidae*

STELLER SEA LION
Eumetopias jubatus

Weighing in at a ton, a male Steller seal lion is the heaviest of all the eared seals. Steller sea lions are slightly less gregarious than other otariids. They feed in inshore waters on fish and bottom invertebrates, possibly causing local depletions of fish. This is certainly the opinion of West Coast fishermen, who periodically call for bounties on these animals. Considering the variety of the Stellers' diet, though, it is questionable how much they will reduce a particular fish population when other more common foods are available. In one case, two sea lions that were killed in the midst of a salmon run proved to have only lampreys in their stomachs.

A more important problem may be the effect these large, powerful animals have on fishing gear. Sea lions rip great holes in gill nets as they pillage them for fish. Fishermen complain about sea lion damage all along the British Columbia coast. In response, the government has sponsored programs to reduce sea lion populations to a few thousand. Only in

the northern limits of their range—the ice-free Alaskan islands and coast—are there large populations of approximately 200,000 individuals.

Steller sea lions form dense breeding colonies. Males control territories in summer, a task that precludes feeding for several months. They occupy rocky areas along the seashore, where females come to give birth. A male may guard up to 30 females. Females, however, may move from one harem to another. They mate again only a week after giving birth to a single pup, although the pups may be suckled for as long as a year. They leave the rookery at the end of the summer.

Females mature at 3 to 6 years. Males mature at 6 years but require at least a decade to attain the huge size of a typical harem bull.

Killer whales have been observed preying on Steller sea lions. In one case, wildlife biologists watched as a pod of orcas penned a pair of sea lions in by encircling them. The sea lions were helpless, unable to escape. Eventually, a large male orca swam into the circle, approached them and swatted them with its flukes hard enough to knock one of them into the air. Neither sea lion escaped.

CALIFORNIA SEA LION
Zalophus californianus

As the name suggests, this is a more southerly sea lion than the Steller. The California sea lion is smaller and more graceful, sociable and playful than the Steller, making it the usual choice of aquarium trainers. Being eared seals, they are highly adept with their flippers, but why they are so willing to catch thrown objects in their mouths is unknown. The movement may mimic an action they use underwater for grabbing fish that swim by. In fact, most of their performing behavior—flipper slapping and even trumpet blowing—appears to re-create many of the actions used in normal sea lion life.

The California sea lion's breeding traits are very similar to the Steller's, except that the large males are constrained by overheating problems. California sea lions breed as far south as Mexico. During the summer breeding season, males are exposed to the hot sun and must make frequent dives into the water to cool off, leaving the female vulnerable to the intrusions of nonterritorial males who may try to sneak a copulation. A prime territory, then, is one that allows quick entry to and exit from the water. Sleeping lowers California sea lions' heat production by 25 percent, which is still not adequate protection in bright sunlight. They try to stay in areas where breaking waves and wind will increase evaporation. When necessary, they may urinate on themselves and wave their flippers to hasten the process. Sweating accounts for only 12 percent of their heat loss.

The breeding season of the California sea lion is shorter than that of the Steller, perhaps as a consequence of the male's smaller body size and reduced capacity to rely solely on stored body fat.

The California sea lion has the same diet as the Steller. The two species would probably compete if their ranges were not for the most part separate. Lately, there has been a rise in the number of California sea lions moving into British Columbia waters for winter feeding. This may be a result of reduced populations of Steller sea lions.

A familiar sight to anyone who has watched a seal show at a public aquarium, the California sea lion is both social and playful, making it a favorite of aquarium trainers.

CALIFORNIA SEA LION
Zalophus californianus

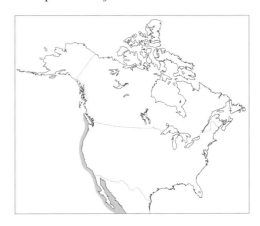

Mammal: *Zalophus californianus*, California sea lion

Meaning of Name: *Zalophus* (high crest) refers to the high sagittal crest on the male's skull; *californianus* (of California)

Description: fusiform body; hind flippers trail when swimming, but rotate forward when resting on land; has a high forehead, small pointed ears and long, stiff mystacial whiskers; bulls have a bony crest on the crown of the head; pelage does not have an undercoat; looks black when wet and buff to brown when dry

Total Length: male, 6.5 to 8.2 feet; female, 4.9 to 6.5 feet

Tail: male, 4.5 inches; female, 3 inches

Weight: male, 441 to 661 pounds; female, 110 to 220 pounds

Gestation: 11.5 to 12 months (including a 3.5-month period of delayed implantation)

Offspring: 1

Age of Maturity: male, 5 years; female, 3 years

Longevity: 18 to 25 years in captivity

Diet: mainly squid, octopus and a variety of fish such as herring, sardines, rockfish, hake and ratfish

Habitat: rookeries and hauling-out spots are usually sandy or boulder beaches backed by cliffs and sometimes sea caverns; shore-living and coastal, not usually more than 100 miles out to sea

Predators: man, killer whale and large sharks

Dental Formula:
3/2, 1/1, 4/4, 1-2/1 = 34-36 teeth

WALRUS Odobenidae

WALRUS *Odobenus rosmarus*

The walrus cannot be mistaken for other pinnipeds. Its upper canines are stretched into huge, ever-growing tusks up to 3 feet long in males and 2 feet in females. The walrus has a small head with a dense set of facial whiskers set on a swollen, wrinkly body that is virtually naked of fur.

The body of the walrus is adapted for grazing along the bottom of cold northern oceans. It uses its tusks less for clam digging than for dragging itself around when laboring on the bottom or hauling out onto ice floes. The generic name, in fact, means "tooth walker." The walrus is able to blow powerful jets of water out of its mouth. One way it may feed is to use its tusks to anchor itself head-first in the sediments and then expose nearby clams by blowing away the

mud. The walrus seems to plow and root in a piglike fashion, leaving a messy trail of churned mud and debris behind it across the ocean floor. Occasionally, when a male decides to dine on a seal or a beluga whale, its tusks are used as weapons.

The walrus's weak cheek teeth are unable to crush mollusk shells efficiently. Instead, it is believed that the walrus holds the shell in its lips and moves its powerful tongue up and down like a piston in its cylinder-shaped mouth. This creates a strong suction that is capable of extracting the clam or snail from its shell.

The tusks are probably most often used to deliver social signals in disputes over status and mating. This would explain why males have larger tusks than females. Walruses are gregarious animals. They haul out on ice or shore in dense packs. During the winter breeding season, females form small bands

To keep warm during dives, the walrus shunts blood away from its skin, which causes a distinct white coloration.

roughly a dozen strong. The males follow them and energetically advertise their presence with underwater sounds and specific calls. Some of the noises, produced with a special throat sac, have a bell-like quality different from the usual barking walrus voice.

Males use their tusks to establish dominance over other males. The tusks are displayed in threat encounters similar to those enacted by bighorn sheep. Since the size of the tusks increases with the age and weight of the male, they are probably a reliable signal of fighting ability. If the rival male is not convinced (and effectively discouraged) just by looking, the tusks may be used as weapons in an escalated fight. The male's swollen neck is covered with a thick, lumpy hide that seems to be a form of protection against rivals' jabs and stabs.

Females may use their tusks to protect their offspring from predators and to establish a position within the herd. The only animals that pose a threat to the adult walrus are polar bears and killer whales. Sometimes, the role changes. Groups of walruses have been seen threatening a polar bear, slapping their flippers as they advance toward it. In the water, a milling herd of agile walruses could easily damage a bear. As well, groups of walruses are known to attack Inuit boats. The Inuit claim that walruses will also attack the killer whale. When Inuit in boats are approached by killer whales, they cup their hands and bellow into the water, imitating the sound of an enraged bull walrus, which drives the killer whales away.

The walrus shows an interesting adaptation to Arctic waters. Its skin functions as a heat sink and radiator. During a cold-water dive, the walrus is able to maintain a stable internal temperature almost 100 Fahrenheit degrees warmer than the surrounding water by shunting blood away from the skin and blubber layer. When the walrus hauls out and basks in the sun, it faces a serious overheating problem, so it shunts blood back to the surface layer and turns a bright reddish brown. Its hairless, corrugated skin acts as a radiator, releasing excess body heat.

Unlike many Arctic mammals, the walrus has an extremely low reproductive rate. Females give birth to a single calf—rarely, two—in spring. The calf is relatively helpless, suckling for half a year and dependent on contact with its mother for warmth. The calf will remain with its mother for two years. This means that females breed only every two to three years or at even greater intervals. Juveniles disperse and segregate with others of the same sex and age. Females may be ready to reproduce at age 4 to 7, but males usually need 10 to 15 years to reach the size of a harem-controlling bull.

Walruses are migratory. Like most Arctic marine mammals, they must move with the ice. Different populations move at different times and over varying distances depending on the pattern of freezing and thawing. Some walrus populations were once resident as far south as the Magdalen Islands, Sable Island and possibly into New England. These were wiped out by overhunting. Walruses now number 200,000 or less in the Pacific Ocean and 25,000 in the Atlantic, a small fraction of their previous numbers. Although the Inuit continue to depend on the walrus as a source of meat, oil, leather and ivory tusks for use in carving, Arctic oil development and the possibility of massive clam-dredging operations are now the greatest threats to the walrus.

PINNIPED POLYGYNY

Pinnipeds exhibit some of the most extreme cases of sexual dimorphism in the animal kingdom. Males of some pinniped species may be three times the size of females and display strange protuberances on their noses, utter violent roars and comport themselves in a ferocious manner. On the other hand, the males of some seal species look much like females and are fairly quiet and mild-mannered, even at breeding time. The degree of dimorphism is closely correlated to the kind of breeding systems the different species have developed.

The largest, most ferocious and most vocal males are in the harem-breeding species such as sea lions, fur seals, walruses and elephant seals. Some males have harems that contain as many as 100 breeding females. The benefit to harem masters is obvious: They have a much higher reproductive rate than monogamous males do. This raises the question as to why other pinnipeds, especially the true seals, lack harem-breeding behavior. Similarly, why do some pinnipeds such as ringed seals have a reduced form of polygyny?

The presence or absence of harem polygyny appears to depend on the dispersion of females. In species such as

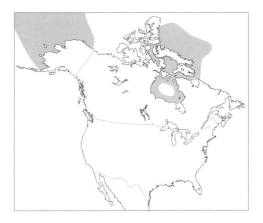

Mammal: *Odobenus rosmarus*, walrus
Meaning of Name: *Odobenus* (tooth + walk) refers to the walrus dragging itself along the ice using its tusks; *rosmarus*, from Norwegian and earlier Scandinavian words meaning whale horse or walrus
Description: largest North Atlantic pinniped; skin is beige-brown in color, very thick and wrinkled and sparsely covered with short, wiry, reddish brown hairs; color changes to reddish brown at the belly and the base of the flippers; has quill-like whiskers set in two well-developed pads on the upper lip; the long tusks are actually enormously elongated canine teeth; limbs are short; the tail is enclosed in a fold of skin
Total Length: male, 8.3 to 12.1 feet; female, 7.5 to 9.6 feet
Weight: male, 2,000 to 2,432 pounds; female, 1,250 to 1,629 pounds
Gestation: 15 months (including a 3-month period of delayed implantation)
Offspring: 1 (rarely 2) every 2 or 3 years
Age of Maturity: male, may mature at 6 years but usually 9 to 10; female, 4 to 7 years
Longevity: 16 to 35 years, possibly up to 40 years in the wild
Diet: clams are the principal food; also eats whelks, sea cucumbers, crustaceans, worms and small polar cod
Habitat: open northern waters near the edge of the polar pack ice; finds shelter on isolated rocky coasts, islands and ice floes (especially those floating over shallow shellfish beds)
Predators: primarily man; killer whale and polar bear may prey on the young or infirm
Dental Formula:
1/0, 1/1, 3/3, 0/0 = 18 teeth

the ringed and bearded seals, females do not tolerate the near presence of other females, and their birthing dens or sites are dispersed. From the male standpoint, dispersed females are not a defensible resource. The females of harem-breeding species, however, are usually forced to come to a crowded space for giving birth. Species that give birth on beaches or rocky shores have a limited number of sites available to them. The location must have good water access and be difficult for terrestrial predators such as bears to reach. Whenever females concentrate, there is potential for males to evolve harem-breeding behavior, meaning that they attempt to gain exclusive access to a group of females. In the highly mobile fur seal, this may involve actively herding and controlling the movement of the females. In heavy and less mobile species such as elephant seals and Steller sea lions, the male may simply defend a prime piece of real estate from other males and mate with whichever females decide to use the area.

The eared seals and the walrus are highly polygynous harem breeders. This may have resulted from their dependence on dry land, which in turn stems from their use of fur rather than blubber for insulation. A young otariid cannot leave the rookery to nurse in the water until its fur molt is complete. This means that a male otariid can economically defend a harem of females who are forced to stay in one area with their pups. If the females were free to come and go at the time they come back into estrus, it would be more difficult for a single male to defend them. By contrast, most true seals nurse their pups for short periods and tend not to be harem breeders. The exception is the elephant seal, an extreme harem breeder. Female elephant seals nurse their young for about a month, somewhat longer than most other true seals.

Seals that are not harem breeders are not necessarily monogamous in the conventional sense. The males do not remain with a single mate, nor do they provide parental care. They are like the displaying bird species whose males sing and dance for the approval of the females. Males are chosen or rejected according to the effectiveness of their courtship. Species such as the harbor seal use a variety of twisting jumps, splashes and complex vocalizations to pay court to the females. Male-male competition also plays a role in this system: Dominant males may intimidate smaller, younger males and prevent them from displaying.

The pinniped breeding system depends strongly on the actions of the females. Either they control the degree of harem formation by their level of tolerance for other females, or they control the amount of polygyny by choosing the most effective suitors over others.

The largest and most ferocious male pinnipeds occur in harem-breeding species such as the walrus. Tusks up to a yard long are a signal of dominance over females and other males.

A harbor seal pup, above, is weaned after four weeks. A streamlined body and the absence of an external ear are evidence of this seal's extreme adaptation to aquatic life, overleaf.

HAIR SEALS *Phocidae*

HARBOR SEAL *Phoca vitulina*

Harbor seals range the coasts of the northern hemisphere from the southern edge of the temperate zone to the high Arctic. They are the most widespread seal in northern waters and tolerate a broad range of water salinity and temperature. Harbor seals swim up large rivers such as the St. Lawrence and have traveled as far inland as Lake Ontario. There are also several landlocked harbor seal populations in lakes in British Columbia and Quebec.

Harbor seals are wary animals and require secure haul-outs (onshore gathering places) on rocks, sandbars and mudflats with easy access to deep water. Hauling out in groups permits a bit more relaxation. Studies have shown that harbor seals spend less time scouting for predators when they are in a group than when they are alone. Usually, they haul out and rest at low tide then reenter the water to feed as the tide comes in. In winter and during stormy weather, harbor seals spend most of their time in the water.

Harbor seals are extremely common but rarely occur in groups of more than a hundred. Larger gatherings may have difficulty finding enough food. They are generalized fish eaters, feeding on a broad spectrum of species. They will dive to 980 feet and remain submerged for up to 23 minutes. They eat smaller fish while they swim underwater, but larger catches are brought to the surface.

The harbor seal's appetite can lead to conflict with humans, as a seal can eat 9 pounds of fish daily. There may be hundreds of harbor seals along certain bays, and their catch can total several tons a day in an area where humans are also competing for fish. Sometimes harbor seals feed heavily on the salmon runs, and they may foul fishing gear or rob fish traps. This has led to the harbor seal's extermination along parts of the coastline. Human vengeance is often unjustified, though—for much of the year, harbor seals have little impact on fishing profits, since they feed on noncommercial fish species.

The breeding system of the harbor seal is poorly understood. Most reports indicate that mating is promiscuous and is conducted in shallow water near haul-out spots in late summer and autumn. Males perform jumps and flips

HARBOR SEAL *Phoca vitulina*

Mammal: *Phoca vitulina*, harbor seal
Meaning of Name: *Phoca* (seal); *vitulina* (sea calf)
Description: profile resembles a dog's; large convex eyes are dorsally placed to provide good underwater vision; from the front, the nostrils form a broad V, almost meeting at the bottom; mystacial whiskers; color is extremely variable but is essentially bluish gray on the back with irregular dark brown spots, streaks or blotches; silver-white belly with scattered dark spots
Total Length: male, 4 to 6 feet; female, 4.5 to 5.5 feet
Weight: male, 160 to 200 pounds (maximum 249 pounds); female, 128 to 200 pounds (maximum 245 pounds)
Gestation: 10 to 11 months (including a period of delayed implantation)
Offspring: 1 (rarely 2)
Age of Maturity: male, 3 to 6 years (usually 5); female, 2 to 5 years (usually 3 or 4)
Longevity: probably 40 years
Diet: primarily fish (herring, alewife, flounder, hake, smelt, cod); also mollusks such as squid, octopus and clams and sometimes crayfish, crab and shrimp
Habitat: coastal waters of the northern oceans in bays, harbors, estuaries, mudflats and even some accessible lakes if certain features are present
Predators: polar bear, walrus, killer whale and sharks; golden eagle may prey on young
Dental Formula:
3/2, 1/1, 4/4, 1/1 = 34 teeth

for females. Females delay implantation for several months and give birth in early summer to a single pup or, rarely, twins. Harbor seal pups, born on the shore or in the water, are fairly precocious, able to dive after a week and crawl when on land. Pups are weaned at only 4 weeks, although for the next few months, the mothers accompany and care for them. Maturity is not reached until 5 to 6 years, and the harbor seal may live to be 40.

MAMMALS & MILK

Breasts, which are unique to mammals, are modified sweat glands. The advantages of liquid milk help explain the marvelous success enjoyed by mammals. The mother is often more

The fat-rich milk of a mother seal ensures that seal pups such as the hooded seal pup, below, grow at an accelerated rate.

mobile and a better feeder than her offspring. She can store up nutrients and feed them to her young as milk, which allows them to grow faster than if they had to find their own food. As well, because the young have milk, the eruption and development of teeth can be postponed until later.

Mammalian teeth are encased in rigid enamel, so they cannot continue to grow as the rest of the animal does. Milk feeding enables tooth development to be postponed. In some cases, the teeth emerge when the jaws reach adult size; in others, they emerge in a sequence as the animal grows.

Mammals are able to adjust the nutritive quality of their milk according to their particular life history. Seals, whose pups are subjected to extreme cold stress, have placed a premium on rapid development. Half the seal's milk may be fat, while the butterfat content in the milk of a dairy cow is only 4 to 10 percent. Large grazers, whose young need

to develop muscles and be highly mobile soon after birth, produce milk that contains less fat and more protein.

Besides being nutritious, milk is an important source of antibodies—a means by which mothers can transfer resistance to infection to their young. Many antibody molecules are too large to cross the uterine membrane that links the mother and fetus.

The breast-feeding of a young mammal makes extreme demands on the mother. In small rodents, a lactating female must eat 240 to 330 percent more food than normal. A mother may lose up to half of her skeletal calcium while lactating unless she has a rich supply of calcium in her food. The mother who is trying to maximize her lifetime reproduction often engages in weaning conflict with offspring that would prefer to suckle longer. While individual offspring would benefit from longer feeding, the mother's chance of having future offspring would eventually decrease.

RINGED SEAL *Pusa hispida*

The most abundant marine mammal in the Arctic, the ringed seal is popular with predators because of its thick layer of blubber and is a critical part of the Arctic coastal ecosystem.

Mammal: *Pusa hispida*, ringed seal; the smallest of the pinnipeds

Meaning of Name: *Pusa* (seal); *hispida* (rough, hairy or bristly) could refer to either the coarse hair texture or the whiskers

Description: resembles a small harbor seal; pelage color is quite variable; dorsally, it is brown to bluish black in the background with irregular creamy rings with dark centers; silver belly; pups have a soft, crinkly white coat

Total Length: 4 to 5.5 feet

Weight: 110 to 249 pounds

Gestation: 10.5 to 11 months (including a 3.5-month period of delayed implantation)

Offspring: 1

Age of Maturity: male, 5 to 7 years; female, 4 to 6 years

Longevity: up to 43 years, but 20 to 25 years is more usual

Diet: primarily shrimplike organisms and, to a lesser degree, small fish such as polar cod, herring, whiting, eulachon and smelt; also a few crabs and prawns and, in deeper water, krill

Habitat: land-fast ice or the solid ice cover of the Arctic Ocean, where it occurs in the shifting leads and pressure ridges; usually in fiords and bays but also in some lakes and estuaries; infrequently on drifting ice floes of open seas

Predators: man, polar bear, sharks, killer whale and occasionally walrus

Dental Formula:
3/2, 1/1, 4/4, 1/1 = 34 teeth

HAIR SEALS *Phocidae*

RINGED SEAL *Pusa hispida*

Usually less than 5 feet long and weighing under 225 pounds, the ringed seal is the smallest pinniped. Even so, it has been important prey for both Inuit and polar bears. Populations are estimated at close to five million, making it the most abundant marine mammal in the North American Arctic and one of the most important elements in the high-Arctic coastal ecosystem.

Ringed seals restrict their range to the Arctic ice packs. Their adaptations to this habitat include strong claws on their front flippers for scraping breathing holes through the ice. In winter, the ringed seal's blubber layer accounts for 40 percent of its body weight, which explains its popularity with predators.

The ringed seal's diet changes with the seasons and its travels on the pack ice. Such crustaceans as krill, shrimp and larger planktonic organisms make up its main diet. It also eats smaller fish such as arctic cod and capelin. In midsummer, ringed seals enter a curious period of fasting when they haul out on the ice for a couple of months to laze in the sun and shed their coats.

The ringed seal's mating system is poorly understood, although it seems to be monogamous or weakly polygynous. Mating occurs under the ice, and males may protect underwater territories. In the spring breeding season, males are sometimes scarred, possibly from fighting. Still, dispersed distribution of females may prevent much harem building. If monogamy exists, it does not include male parental care.

The denning of female ringed seals is unique. In spring, they excavate tunnels and chambers in the snow on the pack ice, where they give birth to their pups. When the thick winter ice begins to buckle and form pressure ridges, the females swim underneath, searching for a crevice that will lead through the ice into the snow and become the single underwater entrance to the den. Dens are usually about 10 feet long and 2 feet high. For safety, they may build multiple dens to reduce the chances of a bear or arctic fox excavating the one containing their pup. The males' dens are safe from predators because of a musky smell that polar bears, sled dogs and Inuit all find unpleasant.

Ringed seal pups are less precocial than those of the slightly larger harbor seal. They stay in the den until they are weaned, at least two months. As the pup grows, it builds itself numerous tunnels under the snow to increase its chances of escaping predators. Pups are born with a snow-white coat that is difficult for an animal peering into a tunnel to detect. Despite these precautions, polar bears may find half a year's crop of pups. Ringed seals fortunate enough to survive to maturity may live for 43 years.

GRAY SEAL *Halichoerus grypus*

The gray seal has a relatively limited range, generally staying north of Cape Cod and south of the Arctic. It is an inshore fish eater and frequents the same areas as the harbor seal. One of the larger seals along the Atlantic coast, the gray probably takes bigger fish than its cousins the harbor seals do, feeding on large flatfish and crabs as well as migratory schools of herring, mackerel and salmon. The gray seal is a more accomplished walker than the harbor seal and will breed farther from water. Where the two species occur together, the gray seal displaces the harbor seal from haul-outs.

Gray seals breed in dense, noisy aggregations and have evolved a polygynous breeding system. A male can guard a group of up to 10 females. The polygynous nature of males is reflected in their larger body size and possibly in their longer snout, which may be used in aggressive vocalizations. Female gray seals are aggressive to other females and repel them during the breeding season, a behavior that sometimes forces males into monogamy. The origin of the females' territoriality could be their tendency to return year after year to the same spot to give birth This suggests that females are competing for nesting spots of varying quality.

Females give birth to a single precocial white pup that is weaned after three weeks and then deserted.

Gray seals have been observed napping on the bottom of the ocean floor, occasionally rising to breathe while still asleep, then gently sliding back down.

An inshore fish eater, the gray seal has been observed napping on the ocean bed, occasionally rising to the surface to breathe and sinking back down while still slumbering.

GRAY SEAL *Halichoerus grypus*

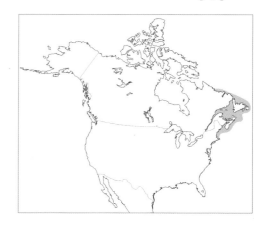

Mammal: *Halichoerus grypus*, gray seal
Meaning of Name: *Halichoerus* (sea pig); *grypus* (hooked nose)
Description: flexible forelimbs and long, slender claws increase its mobility on land; bulls have swollen, scarred, wrinkled necks and broad, distinctive "Roman" noses; male pelage has overall brownish gray or black tone with obscure lighter marks on neck and flanks; female's pelage is a lighter gray to tan color and silver or whitish underneath; pups have a long, crinkly white coat that they molt at the age of 3 or 4 weeks to a dark gray, spotted juvenile coat
Total Length: male, 8 to 9.8 feet; female, 7 to 7.5 feet
Weight: male, 617 to 798 pounds; female, 400 to 551 pounds
Gestation: 11.5 months (including a 3-month period of delayed implantation)
Offspring: 1
Age of Maturity: male, 3 to 7 years; female, 3 to 4 years
Longevity: male, 35 years; female, 45 years
Diet: primarily a coastal feeder, eating whatever is abundant and available; cod, flounder, skate, pollock, mackerel, whiting and rockfish, as well as squid and pelagic crustaceans
Habitat: along exposed rocky coasts, cliffs and caves of remote islands, reefs and shoals
Predators: man and killer whale
Dental Formula:
3/2, 1/1, 4/4, 1/1 = 34 teeth

HARP SEAL *Pagophilus groenlandicus*

The harp seal is a controversial pinniped. The merits and demerits of the commercial harvest of the harp are fiercely disputed on an international scale. The harp seal is specialized to live on the unstable edge of the North Atlantic ice pack. Females about to give birth gather at special haul-out sites on the ice sheets. Though aggregations numbering in the thousands are common, losses to natural predators are very low. Harp seals appear to whelp out of the usual range of polar bears. But since the ice sheets drift as far south as Newfoundland and the Magdalen Islands, the remarkable density of harp seal aggregations makes them highly attractive to the sealing industry.

Harp seals have a migratory lifestyle determined by the ice and the season. In late September, as the bays of the high Arctic begin to freeze, they commence the southward migration. Harp seals stream out of Hudson Bay and from around Greenland and the Arctic archipelago, moving through Hudson and Baffin straits and south along the coast of Labrador. Some harp seals travel into the Gulf of St. Lawrence, while others head for the Grand Banks. They feed through the winter until the ice sheets have reached their southernmost extension, becoming very fat from a rich diet of oceanic fish and larger crustaceans such as krill. In spring, they haul out to give birth and then breed.

The haul-out sites are located along particular channels and holes that provide inroads through the ice. The seals often choose rough, hummocky ice, and the large aggregations may help keep the holes open. Females defend a small patch of ice adjacent to where they whelp, while males haul out and wait for females to wean their pups and begin the new year's mating. Fasting during the haul-out period results in a stoppage of growth that leaves annual rings on the teeth, providing, like tree rings, a convenient way to determine the age of harp seals.

In the whelping grounds, up to 6,000 females per square mile each give birth to a single snow-white pup. Doing virtually nothing but nurse, the precocious harp seal pups grow rapidly, from a birth weight of 7 to 9 pounds to 90 to 105 pounds within two weeks. They are then weaned, an expedient aimed at getting the pups into the safety of the water as soon as possible. Their weight gain seriously depletes the mother's nutrient reserves. A harp seal mother can recognize her own offspring by its smell, and if orphaned or abandoned pups attempt to nurse, she will repel them.

Being born onto the ice is a shock for the pups. Extensive shivering and brown fat tissue specialized for producing heat from fatty compounds combat hypother-

This adult harp seal has survived the vulnerable pup stage, when snow-white fur makes pups a popular target of hunters.

mia, while the white coat acts like greenhouse glazing, allowing the pup's body to soak up and retain solar energy.

Weaned pups are deserted by their mother about the time they begin to molt, losing their white coat and growing the mottled juvenile version. Juveniles move to the ice edge and begin feeding on krill and other animals when they are a month old. By that time, their weight has fallen by 50 percent, forcing them to fend for themselves or starve. The harp seal matures within 3 to 10 years and lives as long as 30 years.

Once they have weaned their pups, female harp seals are ready to breed. Males compete for their attentions by putting on swimming and jumping displays and waving their flippers. The males vocalize underwater using 16 different calls. Copulation takes place in the water. Mating seems to be promiscuous, with no pair-bonding, mate-guarding or harem formation. It is probable that the female's choice of mates is based on the quality of the male's courtship.

CONSERVING THE CUTE

Animal conservationists appear to have their favorites. The World Wildlife Fund uses a panda for its logo. Greenpeace spends money to prevent the clubbing and skinning of undeniably cute harp seal pups. Burros receive a very expensive helicopter airlift out of canyon country they are destroying by overgrazing. There is public outrage over the harvesting of wild horses.

This concern for the welfare of wildlife, even for species introduced by humans in the first place, is heartening. However, it is interesting and perhaps shortsighted that there is little public concern for rare shrews, a species with limited distribution, or for threatened species of bat. Nor is the public clamoring for wolverines to be reestablished in their former haunts. There may be a pattern to the expression of popular interest. This is of great concern to scientists, because it means that conservation

decisions are made and funding becomes available for reasons that are often more emotional than biological.

Konrad Lorenz, the famous German student of animal behavior, suggested a reason that might explain why the public worries intensely about harp seals, which are not at all endangered, and yet cares virtually nothing about the fortunes of small rodents and shrews whose biology remains almost unknown. Lorenz noted that there is an "infant schema" that instinctively tugs emotional strings in the human observer. Large rounded heads, receding chins and big eyes are the signals that evoke human sympathies and make puppies irresistible. Many people get the same kind of reaction when they see a human infant, which explains the evolutionary origins of the reaction.

Harp seal pups epitomize the infant schema at its most extreme. Anyone who can bring himself to club a harp seal pup while its large, trusting eyes gaze upward probably has a family to support and strong cultural encouragement for doing the job. Perhaps it is unfortunate that harp seals are harvested. But more critical is a situation in which limited resources are being invested in protecting harp seals and other emotionally attractive animals while less cute species move closer to extinction.

Harp seal numbers are thought to total between two and three million. They are hunted along their migration route from the high Arctic to the whelping grounds in the Gulf of St. Lawrence. In recent years, the harvest of harp seal pups has been a subject of emotional controversy. There is some historical precedent for opposition to the hunt. On several occasions, the seals have been seriously overhunted, but government protection has allowed the harp seal to recover to levels healthy enough to pose occasional competition for the fishing industry. In response, some governments have moved to limit their numbers. Each harp seal eats about 1½ tons of food every year, so three million harp seals must eat close to nine billion

HARP SEAL
Pagophilus groenlandicus

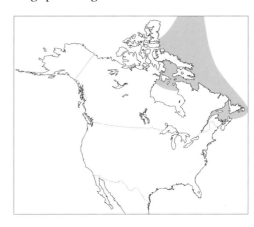

Mammal: *Pagophilus groenlandicus*, harp seal
Meaning of Name: *Pagophilus* (lover of ice and frost); *groenlandicus* (of Greenland)
Description: resembles harbor seal in head and body form but is proportionately stockier in the thoracic region; color varies considerably and depends on the sex and on a sequence of immature coats from newborns' to adults'; males have a silvery background color; head is dark gray or black to just behind the eyes; small, dark, irregular splotches develop into a dark saddle along the flanks and over the back as the seal grows older; female is similar, but face and saddle are lighter (grayish brown); pups are born with a white coat that begins to shed after about 1 week and, in 3 to 4 weeks, is completely replaced by a silvery coat with small, dark, irregular splotches
Total Length: male, 4.5 to 6.5 feet; female, 4.6 to 6 feet
Weight: up to 401 pounds
Gestation: 11.5 months (including a 4.5-month period of delayed implantation)
Offspring: 1
Age of Maturity: male, 3 to 8 years (perhaps 1 or 2 years later); female, 3 to 7 years (usually 4.5 years)
Longevity: approximately 30 years
Diet: mainly fish (especially capelin and polar cod); to a lesser degree, crustacean macroplankton; young pups begin with euphausiid shrimp and amphipods
Habitat: pelagic species; inhabits the edge of the Arctic pack ice and the sub-Arctic waters of the North Atlantic
Predators: man, sharks, killer whale and polar bear
Dental Formula:
3/2, 1/1, 4/4, 1/1 = 34 teeth

Cute and controversial, the harp seal pup and other emotionally attractive animals have been able to secure scarce conservation resources while more threatened animals are ignored.

ment—that have caused serious depletions of the harp seal population.

Most of the current protest over the harvest of harp seals focuses on the killing of the appealing snow-white pups. From a biological standpoint, though, this is the appropriate stage to harvest the animal. Natural mortality would kill many of the pups. In a way, the hunt maximizes the overall productivity of the population. However strong the emotional reaction to killing pups may be, a controlled harvest at current levels does not threaten the harp seal.

Several biological management issues are involved here. Is there enough information about the species to manage it? What level of harvest will ensure a healthy harp seal population? What level of harvest will alter ecological relationships in the harp seal's habitat? What impact will more extensive fishing have?

Whether or not harp seal killing should continue, even in a rational and humane way, is a philosophical and emotional issue and not a biological one. Can it be argued that a mammal deserves to be safe from harvesting in a sustainable fashion simply because it is more appealing than a chicken or more intelligent than a lettuce? The danger of an argument based on emotive reaction to the killing of a cute pup is that it diverts attention from the problem of acquiring data needed to solve existing management problems.

Management problems, the intensity of the harvest and ecological pressures on the harp seal will inevitably increase. Human population growth and human competition for fish, increasing oil-spill pollution, industrial residues and pesticides will exert greater pressure on the harp seal. As the human population inexorably increases, exploitation of animals such as the harp seal will intensify rather than abate. In the face of this virtual certainty, perhaps the best we can do for the harp seal is to manage its harvest properly and establish the methodologies needed to prevent the severe depletions that have been inflicted on their populations in the past.

pounds of fish and krill annually.

To the nation as a whole, the economic value of harp seals is not particularly great. Canadians earn about $5.5 million from the annual harvest, making it a small contributor to total revenues from the luxury-fur industry. However, the global and national perspective does not alter the fact that for many of the people who live near the harp seal's migratory routes, the harvest is an important material and cultural practice. Suggested employment alternatives such as aquaculture and the expansion of the conventional fishery could prove to be more environmentally destructive, although more socially acceptable. In most cases, the people who have traditionally depended on seal hunting have had little impact on harp seal populations. It is large corporations and government management—or mismanage-

BEARDED SEAL
Erignathus barbatus

The bearded seal has a thick set of whiskers it uses when browsing on the seabed for food, and the large claws on its front flippers are probably good for digging through mud and silt. Crab, shrimp, various fish and probably most other species it encounters in the bottom sediments make up its diet; on occasion, its stomach has even been found to contain mud and pebbles as well. Because of its method of feeding, the bearded seal's range is restricted to areas of the Arctic Ocean where the water is less than 650 feet deep. Winter populations must move to the Bering Sea or south toward the Gulf of St. Lawrence to avoid heavy pack ice.

The bearded seal is unsociable. Neither sex seems to tolerate others of the same species near its onshore site. Males are probably less polygynous than other pinnipeds because of the females' territoriality.

The bearded seal's reproductive biology is unusual. Females have two pairs of teats and give birth to twins. The pups are relatively helpless (altricial) and stay with their mother for longer than is common among the pinnipeds. Females breed only in alternate years because of the long period before weaning. Thus despite their fecundity, their long-term reproductive rate is the same as that of most seals. Producing twins may be an adaptation that capitalizes on particularly productive feeding years, when females have accumulated large stores of fat.

Males and females both reach 660 pounds or more. The meat, blubber and hide of the bearded seal has been an important resource for both the Inuit and polar bears.

Its thick whiskers allow the bearded seal to browse the seabed for food, while the large claws on its front flippers may be used to dig into the mud and silt.

BEARDED SEAL
Erignathus barbatus

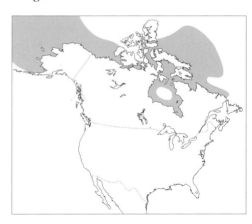

Mammal: *Erignathus barbatus*, bearded seal
Meaning of Name: *Erignathus* (very + jaw) refers to the rather deep jaw; *barbatus* (bearded) refers to the seal's abundant whiskers
Description: characteristic long white whiskers resemble a prominent bushy mustache; external opening of ear is large, pigmented and easily seen; square, spadelike foreflippers due to the middle digit being the longest; 4 mammae (which are not found in other Arctic phocids); pelage composed of stiff, smoky gray hairs with a darker brown cap and dorsum
Total Length: 6.9 to 9.5 feet
Weight: 551 to 716 pounds (maximum 875 pounds)
Gestation: 10.5 to 11.5 months (including a 2.5-month period of delayed implantation)
Offspring: 1 or 2 every second year
Age of Maturity: male, 7 years; female, 6 years
Longevity: up to 31 years
Diet: mollusks (whelks and cockles) form much of the diet along with other bottom-living animals (shrimp, crab, holothurians, octopus) and fish such as sculpin, polar cod and flounder
Habitat: found along coasts and on ice floes in the Arctic Ocean and adjoining seas; prefers shallow coastal waters that are ice-free in the winter along with gravel beaches and ice floes that are not too far out to sea
Predators: killer whale and polar bear
Dental Formula:
3/2, 1/1, 4/4, 1/1 = 34 teeth

DEVICES FOR DIVING

Seals are capable of some amazing underwater achievements. Although they do not dive as deeply or for as long a time as whales, they may reach depths of 2,000 feet and remain submerged for an hour. Because seals are easier to study than whales, their special adaptations are better understood.

Seals perform their diving feats with a lung capacity little greater than that of humans. When a dive starts, the seal's circulatory system slows down and reorganizes. The objectives while the animal is underwater are to maintain an oxygen supply to vital organs such as the brain and to direct carbon dioxide and other waste products to less essential areas of the body.

The seal's face has nerves that trigger a diving reflex when it submerges. When the signal is received, the heartbeat drops immediately from 150 beats per minute to 8 to 12 and veins are constricted, reducing the blood supply to many muscles, organs and noncritical parts of the body. The kidneys stop filtering blood, but the brain remains well supplied.

Seals have a larger volume of blood in their bodies than most land mammals do, and it is rich in oxygen-carrying red cells. In addition, the seal's muscles contain large quantities of myoglobin, a molecule that carries oxygen, which enables the muscles to coast along on stored oxygen when they are cut off from the circulatory system. The seal is insensitive to the breathing response triggered in humans by the buildup of carbon dioxide in the blood.

When the seal finally surfaces, its heartbeat shoots as high as 250 beats per minute. It more fully clears its lungs as it exhales and inhales than a land-based mammal does.

During the dive, the oxygen-burning activity in much of the muscle and tissue mass is reduced, which means that less body heat will be generated. Veins running through brown fat tissue (a special set of cells that generates heat) maintain the temperature of the blood which feeds the heart, brain and other vital organs while the seal is submerged in cold water.

The seal must also contend with high pressure underwater and the risk of the bends when surfacing. Because water pressure could cause body cavities and sinuses to collapse, the seal has few sinus cavities in its skull. Its ribs are attached flexibly, and the lung cavity is not attached to the body wall, so water pressure can flatten the chest and lungs of the seal without tearing tissue or breaking bones.

Seals can also avoid the bends, a potentially fatal affliction. Nitrogen gas in the lungs is absorbed by tissues under pressure and then boils out like a carbonated soft drink as the animal shoots to the surface. Seals have a number of devices that eliminate the risk: They exhale before they dive; the walls of the breathing channels are lined with cartilage, which absorbs little gas; and pockets of fat in the sinuses and along the lung walls can absorb and release nitrogen without causing trouble.

The high pressure of the dive could also create problems for the seal's heart and circulatory system. To avoid pressure becoming too intense, a large bulb in the aorta—the main exit channel from the heart—balloons during the dive as a sort of safety valve that eases the pressure on the rest of the system.

The seal's ear has a dual protective system. Membrane and muscle close it off when required, and blood sinuses engorge to reduce the volume of gas in the ear canal and increase sound transmission from the water through the sinus to the inner ear.

The seal's adaptations for diving are very like those of whales. This is another case where two unrelated organisms have evolved similar adaptive designs to deal with the same kind of environmental problems.

Pinnipeds such as the harp seal, below, have evolved respiratory and circulatory systems that enable them to dive to great depths. Some species can go as deep as 2,000 feet.

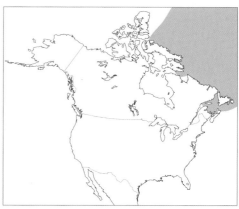

Mammal: *Cystophora cristata*, hooded seal
Meaning of Name: *Cystophora* (bladder-carrying); *cristata* (crested) refers to the male's peculiar pouch that forms a crest on the nose and can be inflated like a bladder
Description: the nasal apparatus is the most remarkable feature: part of the elastic nasal cavity can be inflated to form a distensible hood that runs from the crown to the upper lip, which it overhangs, proboscislike, in older animals; an inflatable nasal membrane can be extruded to form a bubble-gumlike balloon when the hood deflates; general background color is steel-gray with irregular black patches that become smaller on the neck and belly; face is black to just behind the eyes; young are born with a distinctive slate-blue coat dorsally, shading abruptly to light silver-gray on the sides and belly (therefore called bluebacks); an earlier whitish foetal coat is shed before birth
Total Length: male, 6.5 to 9 feet; female, 5.8 to 7 feet
Weight: male, 904 pounds; female, 595 pounds
Gestation: 11 months
Offspring: 1
Age of Maturity: 4 to 6 years
Longevity: 20 to 32 years
Diet: octopus, squid, shrimp, mussels, starfish, herring, capelin, cod, redfish, Greenland turbot
Habitat: pelagic species; inhabits the edge of the drifting Arctic pack ice; rarely found on firm ice
Predators: man, polar bear, sharks and killer whale
Dental Formula:
2/1, 1/1, 4/4, 1/1 = 30 teeth

The male hooded seal is considerably larger than the female and has evolved eye-catching displays. A male threatens other males by inflating a large inner nasal sac through its nostril.

HAIR SEALS *Phocidae*

HOODED SEAL *Cystophora cristata*

Among the true seals, females and males are usually of much the same size and appearance. But with hooded seals and their close relatives the elephant seals, males have evolved comparatively large bodies and some flamboyant displays. The male hooded seal has the unusual and, some would say, gruesome habit of blowing the inner nasal sac out through his nostril so that it emerges looking like a bright red bladder. He can also pump up the nasal bladder when it is drawn into the head, creating a large bulge on his face that looks less like a hood (this is the basis of the seal's name) than a massive, swollen black blister.

These bizarre traits are examples of what can result when mate selection is based on male displays. Males blow their nasal bubble when they are hauled out on the breeding grounds and guarding a female and often her pup. The bladder is some kind of threat and may indicate the size of the male. Older males are more likely than younger ones to blow out the blood-red bladder, and immature males lack the ability.

Female aggression toward other females may prevent polygyny, even though haul-outs are densely aggregated, a pattern of behavior that is often associated with harem-style breeding. Males are very aggressive at breeding time and will threaten human intruders. At 900 pounds, a large male must be taken seriously.

Hooded seals follow the same migratory pattern as harp seals, since they both breed on pack-ice edges. The hooded seal is larger than the harp seal, however. It also dives more deeply and feeds on larger fish and organisms such as starfish and octopus.

The hooded seal population is thought to be roughly half a million.

NORTHERN ELEPHANT SEAL *Mirounga angustirostris*

When feeding, northern elephant seals range as far north as Alaska, although their breeding activity is limited to the coasts of California and Mexico. Elephant seals dive deeply, going as far down as 650 feet, feeding on rays, sharks and other organisms they encounter in the inshore waters.

Elephant seals are the largest of all the pinnipeds. Males are three times larger than females, reaching a length of nearly 20 feet and a weight of 8,000 pounds or more, far longer and heavier than the average loaded pickup truck. The "elephant" part of the name refers to the male's huge size, great snout and loud bellowing roars.

During the winter breeding season, elephant seals congregate on sandy beaches—a spectacle that ranks as one of the most bizarre and extreme expressions of sexual selection and male-male combat in the animal kingdom. The elephant seal's long proboscis can be inflated. When the tip of its snout extends into the mouth and the nostrils point toward the voice box, the whole affair acts as an echo chamber, magnifying the seal's bellowing. Its roars can be heard a

By inflating its proboscis and inverting its nostrils so that they point into the mouth and toward the voice box, a male elephant seal can emit a roar audible a mile away.

mile away and signify the ferocity of a mature bull. Males fight fiercely for control of a harem, pounding their massive chests into each other and gashing their rival's face and proboscis. The neck of the mature male has a thick, rough hide as a defense against bites from rivals. Though only a tiny fraction of male elephant seals gain harems, the rewards for successful combat are great, as 5 percent of the males enjoy roughly 90 percent of all the matings. A male may in-

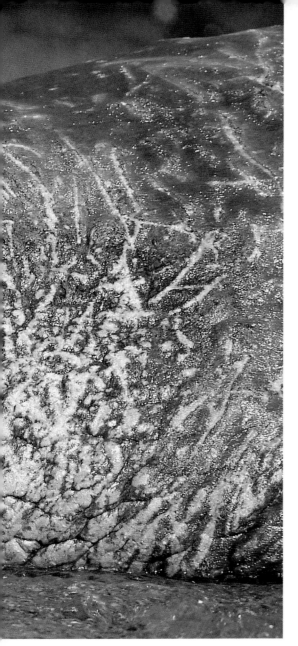

seminate 100 different females in a single mating season.

The intensity of physical combat is such that while elephant seals may be sexually mature after five years, they are generally unable to acquire a harem until age 10. Even then, the effort of warding off rivals means that the harem masters are soon exhausted. Males rarely survive more than four years of harem ownership. During the breeding season, which may extend for two months or more, males do not leave the harem to feed. They must fight and breed, depending on stored body fat as their sole energy source.

During the time female elephant seals are receptive to mating, they are accompanied by young pups that are ready to be weaned. The furious charges of fighting males crush 10 percent of the pups and may also injure many females. Males are also heedless of the wishes of females. They try to copulate with any and every female that comes within reach. Sexually immature females, pregnant females, females with newborn pups and receptive females all receive equal treatment. The elephant seal male grabs the female by the neck with his jaws, then throws himself down and mates with her. Females that resist are slapped and bitten into submission. When a female wishes to leave the harem and enter the ocean to feed, subdominant males hovering at the edge of the breeding harem waylay them and try to copulate. Subdominant males are so intent that they may inadvertently kill females that attempt to bypass them.

Female elephant seals give a characteristic scream when mating. This may simply be the consequence of being set upon by 8,000 pounds of male elephant seal; however, it has also been interpreted as an adaptation. The female is best served by mating with a proven male, the harem keeper that has survived many years of feeding and fighting and that is obviously free of serious genetic defects or diseases. By screaming, the female may prevent a subdominant and less-proven male from copulating with her. Her scream alerts the harem master, who rushes over and attempts to throttle the intruder. After breeding season, males and females disperse to feed. They tend to return to the same breeding grounds each year.

During the 19th century, hunters slaughtered virtually all elephant seal populations. By the time they were given complete protection, only 50 animals remained. Since then, populations have grown to roughly 45,000, but the colonization of their former range has been slow. Now that they are protected from humans, only sharks and killer whales prey on them. Fortunately, populations continue to rebound rapidly.

NORTHERN ELEPHANT SEAL *Mirounga angustirostris*

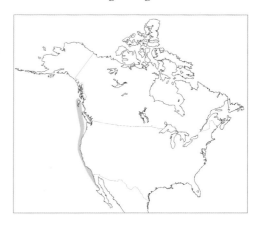

Mammal: *Mirounga angustirostris*, northern elephant seal; the largest pinniped
Meaning of Name: *Mirounga*, derived from *miouroung*, an Australian native name for the seal; *angustirostris* (narrow snout)
Description: a rather obese seal; large head, long snout and thick, creased neck; short, thickened foreflippers and bilobed hind flippers; males have a remarkable proboscis that hangs over the mouth but can be inflated, at which point it curves downward into the mouth; nostrils are located at the tip of the proboscis; proboscis is actually an extension of the nasal cavity and is divided by the nasal septum; short, dense pelage is dull brown to yellowish gray, lighter on belly
Total Length: male, 18 to 19.7 feet; female, 10.2 to 12.1 feet
Weight: male, 8,157 pounds; female, 1,984 pounds
Gestation: 11.3 months (including a 3-month period of delayed implantation)
Offspring: 1
Age of Maturity: male, 4 to 5 years (becomes territorial breeding bull at 9 or 10 years); female, 3 to 5 years
Longevity: 15 years in captivity
Diet: deep-water bottom-dwelling marine life (ratfish, sharks, dogfish, eel, rockfish and squid)
Habitat: pelagic species found in warm, temperate seas except during breeding, which takes place on deserted beaches off the coasts of subtropical continental and oceanic islands
Predators: large sharks (especially white shark) and killer whale
Dental Formula:
2/1, 1/1, 4/4, 1/1 = 30 teeth

RACCOON *Procyonidae*

The procyonids are not northern animals, and the raccoon is the only member of the group that is familiar to most temperate-zone North Americans. The others are limited to more southern climates: coatimundis and ringtails in the dry American southwest and kinkajous in the forests of Central and South America. Procyonids are small-to-medium-sized animals, not much larger than a small dog. Many climb trees or forage in forest habitats, and most are nocturnal.

The Procyonidae split off from the canids roughly 20 million years ago. Their bodies reflect adaptations to a forest environment: They have long tails that are prehensile in some species and used for gripping tree limbs, their claws are long and sharp, and their forepaws are well coordinated and capable of sophisticated manipulations. Many species have faces reminiscent of smaller canids such as foxes, but in keeping with their omnivorous diet, procyonids lack specialized carnassial and canine teeth. Their claws are nonretractile, and they walk on the soles of their feet.

Some taxonomists consider pandas to be members of this family despite their bearlike appearance. Others consider them a separate family, since the two panda species are obligate herbivores of Asia, while the other 15 procyonids are omnivorous and found only in the Americas.

COMMON RACCOON *Procyon lotor*

The masked bandit hardly needs any introduction. The common raccoon has profited from human contact and become a familiar animal to most humans, even those living in large cities. It is one of the few medium-sized wild mammals that has done well in urban areas, and the only limit to its success has been its inability to tolerate the cold winters of the boreal forest in tundra regions.

The recent success of the raccoon results from the fact that it is omnivorous and adaptable. The raccoon readily incorporates novel foods into its diet and, because of its manual dexterity, can handle items as diverse as crayfish, watermelon, snakes and the contents of well-closed garbage cans. The list of foods that have been eaten by raccoons would run into the thousands. In nature, they eat almost every edible fruit, berry and nut within their range as well as insects, worms, slugs, snails, mussels, oysters, seafood of all kinds, small mammals, birds as large as geese, bird eggs, rabbits, turtles, lizards, frogs, many kinds of fish and carrion and have even been known to kill sheep.

Not surprisingly, handling this array of food items requires a brain capable of problem solving and learning. Many food items are handled not through instinct but after watching the mother, which indicates that foraging techniques may be culturally transmitted from one generation to the next. For instance, the offspring of the first raccoon to discover how to eat watermelon may have learned the technique from their mother without having to evolve or discover the behavior by themselves. Intelligence tests show that raccoons are smarter than cats but not smarter than rhesus monkeys. Raccoons often wet their food before eating it so that they can feel for inedible matter which needs to be discarded.

Although some procyonids form social groups,

Until they effected their successful move into human urban and suburban neighborhoods, raccoons were almost always found close to water, where they traditionally hunt and bring their food.

Intelligent and omnivorous, raccoons eat almost any kind of animal as well as hundreds of plants. Their manual dexterity allows them to handle a wide variety of foods.

raccoons are not social—the only extended social contact is between a mother and her offspring. Females mate in spring and give birth in summer to a litter of one to seven young. They stay with the mother, den with her during the winter and disperse the following summer. Under good conditions, they may reproduce the same year that they disperse. The male provides no parental care, and the female aggressively excludes males from the den area.

Normally, raccoons den and forage in areas that have water. Dens are located in hollow trees, rock crevices, abandoned animal burrows or any reasonably well-protected cavity. Winter den sites may be occupied for as long as four months, but raccoons are not deep hibernators. They put on large stores of fat and may lose 50 percent of it over the winter. They sleep during most of the cold season, but their temperature and metabolic rate do not drop to the extent that those of deep hibernators do. Sometimes groups of raccoons will den together in an attempt to reduce

winter heat losses. Depending on the productivity of the habitat, their home ranges may run for a few miles. Their ranges overlap extensively, and they exhibit little territoriality, although they may fight over food when it is concentrated in one area.

Raccoons are eaten by raptors and large mammals such as pumas, wolves and coyotes. On the East Coast, these predators have been largely exterminated, so there are few checks on raccoon populations other than hunting, road deaths, starvation and disease. In some areas, raccoons are so common that they destroy almost all the nests of waterfowl.

NORTH MEETS SOUTH

We tend to think of the jaguar and the ocelot as cats of the Amazon and South America; porcupines and raccoons, on the other hand, are usually understood to be northern mammals. The fact is, however, that each had its

origin in the opposite hemisphere.

Long ago, North and South America were separated by a sea channel that was some 250 miles in width, and the mammals of north and south evolved in isolation. Then, some three to five million years ago, the Panamanian land bridge rose out of the ocean, and the fauna and flora of the two continents began to mix. Among the northern mammals that went south were peccaries, skunks and a number of canids, including wolves and foxes. Cats, bears, deer, shrews, squirrels, kangaroo rats and rabbits also traveled south, as did the mastodon, which is now extinct on both continents. Horses, which also later became extinct on both continents, went with them, and so did tapirs, which died out in the north but thrived in the south. Camels, which originated in North America, are now extinct here, but they still survive as llamas in the Andes.

Southern mammals also made inroads into the north, with armadillos, opossums and porcupines moving into North America, but monkeys, anteaters and various rodents penetrating only as far as Central America. The exchange was symmetrical: 14 of today's 35 South American families came from North America, while 12 families from South America were added to the 35 North American families. As a result of the exchange and the symmetrical extinction that followed, the two continents came to share 22 families. Once totally dissimilar, they have now become more alike than different.

The number of families remained roughly the same after the exchange, which suggests to biogeographers that the migrations were responsible for the extinction. The saber-toothed cats that went south, for example, are thought to be responsible for the sudden demise of the saber-toothed marsupials.

An interesting result of the exchange is that many formerly North American groups, such as dogs and mice, suddenly flowered in South America and split into many species. It may have been the great diversity of tropical plants and the richer and more distinct habitats that encouraged more specialization and speciation. Certainly, the few South American groups that penetrated deep into the north have not diversified. Instead, a few species, such as the porcupine, have become extraordinarily successful and have taken up wide geographic ranges.

Although this young raccoon is perfectly at home in the trees of a northern forest, its ancestors evolved in South America and migrated north some three to five million years ago.

COMMON RACCOON
Procyon lotor

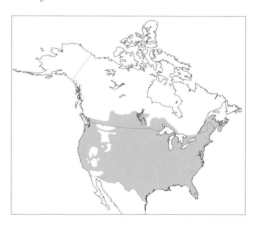

Mammal: *Procyon lotor*, common raccoon

Meaning of Name: *Procyon* (before + dog) refers to the fact that the raccoon was believed to have arisen from the same ancestral stock as dogs; *lotor* (washer) alludes to the raccoon's habit of wetting its food prior to eating; the name raccoon is from Algonkian *arathcone*, which can mean either "he scratches with his hands" or "least like a fox"

Description: about the size of a fat cat; short, bushy tail with four to six prominent rings; long, fine coat, grizzled gray, giving a salt-and-pepper effect; the sides are grayer than the back, and the underparts are brownish with a whitish wash; a black mask extends across the cheeks, eyes and nose; pale gray bars above and below the large eyes

Total Length: 2.5 to 3.1 feet

Tail: 8.5 to 10.2 inches

Weight: 12 to 30 pounds (up to 55 pounds)

Gestation: 60 to 73 days (average 63)

Offspring: 1 to 7 (usually 3 or 4); 1 litter per year

Age of Maturity: male, 2 years or older; female, 40 percent breed as yearlings

Longevity: often live more than 4 years in the wild; 13 to 16 years in captivity

Diet: omnivore; fruits, berries, acorns, sweet corn, crayfish, crabs, other arthropods, June beetles, grubs, grasshoppers, crickets, frogs, fish, small mammals and birds (including poultry and pheasants) as well as eggs

Habitat: wooded areas along waterways, river valleys, timbered and brush areas; successful in cities and suburbs as well as rural areas

Predators: bobcat, red fox, coyote, wolf, fisher and great horned owl; ravens prey on young

Dental Formula:
3/3, 1/1, 4/4, 2/2 = 40 teeth

WEASELS, BADGERS & OTTERS
Mustelidae

The weasel family is a highly carnivorous group of some 56 species found on every continent but Australia and Antarctica. The group has penetrated every terrestrial habitat and many aquatic ones: Martens hunt in the trees of northern, temperate and tropical regions; weasels frequent the cracks, crevices and tunnels of terrestrial habitats; otters have invaded oceans and freshwater ecosystems; and wolverines are powerful scavengers of the boreal forest.

Most mustelid family members have evolved a mouth with fewer but more specialized teeth, many having large, sharp slicing canines, cutting carnassials (incisors capable of fatal bites) or, in the case of omnivorous badgers, heavy crushing molars. Mustelids usually kill their prey with an instinctive bite to the base of the skull, their incisors slipping between the neck's vertebrae to sever the spinal column. Their elongated and triangular face is like a cat's, with a shortened muzzle that enables them to breathe as they apply their tenacious neck bite.

Mustelids have long, streamlined bodies relative to their short limbs, and their long tails further enhance movement, acting as balancing devices for running and making sharp right-angled turns.

They have well-developed anal glands that figure prominently in communication and defense. They use the glands to mark territories or express discontent and hostility. Normally, the mustelids are solitary animals, predators that hunt alone, and most species exhibit little social behavior. Many species are pugnacious and will hiss and threaten when intruders approach. Being intelligent, mustelids are quite curious and, in some cases, highly playful animals.

FUR APPEAL

Sable, ermine, mink, otter, beaver—the best furs come from animals that nature has had to protect from the cold. The quality of fur comes from its value as insulation to the animal that produced it, and the long, thin weasels and other mammals that spend their lives in cold water have the finest, thickest fur coats. The sea otter is one example: It spends its life in the cold northern seas, and at one time, it provided the most expensive fur in the world. A single sea otter pelt sold for $1,000 at the turn of the century, a time when well-paid workmen earned a dollar a day.

Of course, there is some fur-trapping in the southern hemisphere. It is no accident, however, that most of the tropical animals whose furs command a high price are river otters or high-altitude rodents. The trade in spotted-cat furs is an exception, but it has more to do with fashion novelty than fur quality. These beautiful, decorative furs were developed by the animals more for the sake of camouflage than for insulation.

Mammal fur is usually made up of two distinct kinds of hair: long, coarse guard hairs in the outer coat and short, fine hairs in the undercoat. Often, the hair has been further modified, guard hairs

The powerfully built wolverine is strong enough to pull down and kill animals as large as caribou, and it uses its keen nose to locate newborn calves. Yet this member of the weasel family is more scavenger than hunter, and it will trek for miles in its search for carrion.

becoming spines (as in porcupine quills or pig bristles) or awns (which are the common guard hairs in most mammal fur). These are coarse hairs, usually with a flattened tip and a narrow base. The underhairs may be velus (extremely fine, downy hairs), fur (short, dense and fine) or wool (long and curly).

The guard hairs of aquatic mammals such as beavers and otters are broad and flat and lie, overlapping closely, on the densely curled underfur. Caught between the two kinds of fur is an insulating layer of air bubbles that prevents heat loss to the highly conductive water. Aquatic mammals spend a great deal of time grooming and oiling their coats, and beavers even have a special split toenail for that purpose. If the fur were not cleaned and oiled, it could not do its insulating work.

Some guard hairs are particularly prized for a special texture. The fur of the wolverine, for example, is widely used in the north for lining parka hoods and cuffs because the hairs are designed to shed frost and snow.

Northern mammals usually have different winter and summer coats, the summer coats being much thinner. In fact, some large mammals such as sheep show no sign of underwool development until September.

In some animals, there has had to be a trade-off between insulation and mobility. The insulation value of the coat is a function of its length and density, and some small mammals such as lemmings have very long fur relative to their body size. However, a thick coat would limit the ability of animals such as weasels to forage in narrow crevices. Similarly, many aquatic animals cannot afford to sacrifice mobility for warmth. Most seals, for example, have lost their underfur completely and rely on blubber for insulation. Streamlining also takes precedence over other functions for aquatic animals, and both seals and sea otters have lost the erector muscles that "raise the hackles" of cats and dogs and make them look large and ferocious when threatened.

In winter, some increase in fur density is also gained when the skin shrinks as the animal loses weight. The difference in fur density between a fat summer shrew and its thin winter self may be as much as 31 percent.

Like the rhinoceros, humans evolved in tropical Africa and lost most of their fur in the process. In our journey northward, however, we have had to borrow the furs of other mammals to keep us warm. In fact, the fur trade provided the impetus behind much of the explo-

ration of the northern part of the continent. Only recently in human history have we come to rely on plant fibers and synthetic textiles made from petrochemicals; at the same time, ironically, the demand for fur as a luxury item has resulted in the extinction of some animals and the threatened extinction of others.

The problem is one of poor management; the wise culling of overextended populations—the lynx, for example, when it has expanded beyond the resources of the snowshoe hare—would serve a useful purpose by preventing disease and starvation. Fur is a natural renewable resource, and its harvest is potentially less destructive than the conversion of nonrenewable petrochemicals into clothing. Even the production of natural textiles such as cotton has meant the wholesale destruction of valuable forests and grasslands. Unfortunately, there are many times more humans than there are most species of wild mammals. It is unlikely that fur can ever be worn by more than a tiny fraction of the world's population.

Adapted for a life in the water, the river otter has a streamlined body and a short, oily pelage with dense underfur and guard hairs that helps to insulate it from the water.

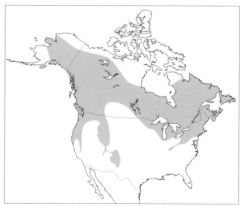

AMERICAN MARTEN
Martes americana

Mammal: *Martes americana*, American marten, pine marten

Meaning of Name: *Martes* (marten); *americana* (of America)

Description: long, lustrous pelage; varies in color from pale buff to reddish and dark browns; ears are pale and edged with white; head is lighter than the rest of the body; underparts are pale brown with irregular creamy or orange breast spots; unlike most other mustelids, it has semiretractable claws

Total Length: male, 21.7 to 25.4 inches; female, 19.3 to 23.7 inches

Tail: male, 6 to 8.5 inches; female, 5.5 to 7.8 inches

Weight: male, 1.5 to 2.9 pounds; female, 1.3 to 1.7 pounds

Gestation: 220 to 275 days (including a period of delayed implantation)

Offspring: 1 to 5 (usually 3 or 4)

Age of Maturity: 15 to 24 months

Longevity: 5 or 6 years in the wild; 18 years in captivity

Diet: mostly rodents and other small mammals, particularly voles; also birds, fruits, insects, carrion, amphibians, reptiles, fish and shellfish

Habitat: found in climax coniferous forests; in the west, it occurs in stands of spruce and fir (mostly mature trees), and in the east, it occurs in cedar swamps and mixed stands of both conifers and hardwoods; since humans have disturbed its natural habitat, it is also found in cutovers, around logging camps, picnic sites and dumps

Predators: loggers and trappers are major predators; also fisher, bobcat, wolf, lynx, coyote and, to a limited extent, the great horned owl

Dental Formula:
3/3, 1/1, 4/4, 1/2 = 38 teeth

One of the few weasels possessing semiretractable claws, the American marten uses them to climb among the treetops and run along narrow branches in pursuit of squirrels and birds.

AMERICAN MARTEN
Martes americana

The American marten is a weasel of the northern coniferous forest. Unlike most other weasels, it has semiretractable claws that can be extended for better tree climbing. It feeds on small prey, preferring small rodents to rabbits and hares. Its ability to run through the trees along limbs proves useful when birds are nesting, squirrels are abundant or competition from fishers is heavy. In winter, the marten acts more like other weasels, following tunnels in the snow in pursuit of rodents such as voles and mice. The meat diet is supplemented in summer with fruits, berries and insects, but even then, 80 percent of its food is animal prey. It will eat yellowjacket hornets in autumn.

The marten is much smaller than the fisher and has a more delicate and pointed face. Males are larger than females and, unhindered by parental duties, range farther than females. Both exclude members of the same sex from their territories. They are more abundant than fishers, and given the smaller size of their territories, a forest can support a fairly large marten population. Pine martens do not follow a boom-and-bust population cycle as fishers do, and as the many species of small rodents they prey on may have independent population cycles, the marten food supply is steady.

As in the fisher, marten females produce a litter of roughly three kits in spring, using a tree hollow as a den. The young reach maturity in their second year.

FISHER *Martes pennanti*

The fisher is a large, powerful mustelid found in the northern coniferous forest, a habitat shared with the marten. The fisher is larger than the marten, about the size of a fox, with a relatively massive skull, and thus tends to be most effective hunting on the ground. It is, however, well equipped for tree climbing, having semiretractable claws that will extend from the paw, a long bushy tail for balance and a special muscle that attaches to the shoulder blade for additional climbing power. The wrist and foot joints are flexible, and the hind foot can swivel 180 degrees, allowing the fisher to ascend and descend trees headfirst, an ability it shares with the marten.

Fishers are voracious hunters. Rabbits and rodents form the bulk of their diet, but they will climb trees to pursue squirrels and search out bird nests.

They swim well and often forage along streams and ponds to feed on muskrat and even mink. Fishers have a reputation for eating mainly porcupine, but their diet is actually more diverse than that of martens: They will eat any mammal or bird they can kill, scavenge carrion and, in summer, feed to a limited extent on berries.

The most famous item in their diet is the porcupine, an animal that few other predators besides pumas eat. To kill such prickly prey, the fisher circles the porcupine continuously for up to half an hour, biting it in the head until it is immobilized, then flipping it over and attacking its unprotected belly. The porcupine's tendency to retreat to a tree limb is a hindrance, but a fisher can scale trees quickly and attack from above because of its ability to descend headfirst. On the ground, the low-slung fisher is able to deliver its bite to the head without stooping, which enables

The well-built fisher is among the very few North American mammals able to kill and eat porcupines. When plentiful, they constitute up to a quarter of the fisher's diet.

it to avoid the flailing tail of quills. The quills are dangerous weapons, and some fishers are reported to have died of quill wounds. Large porcupines and those in dens are able to fend off fisher attacks.

The fisher's circling attack seems instinctive—captive fishers that have not had the benefit of parental guidance or previous experience can kill porcupines. Fishers are reported to use a special technique for hunting porcupines. When they go after rabbits, fishers zigzag back and forth through the underbrush until they flush a victim and then run it down. For porcupines, however, they travel long distances in a straight line until they find a trail or den. Anecdotal evidence from areas where fishers have been restocked suggests that they are able to reduce large porcupine populations (as well as the tree damage they inflict), but this has not yet been proven conclusively.

The fisher's territory is a regular hunting circuit of up to 18 miles in diameter, which it covers every 4 to 12 days, moving approximately one to three miles a day, depending on the abundance of food. Males travel over larger areas than females, but the lighter females tend to forage more in the trees and avoid open areas.

Like most weasels, fishers stay active all winter. They may remain in their dens in severe weather, especially after eating a large meal, but for no longer than a few days. They are most active at night but will sometimes venture out during the day.

Fishers are sexually dimorphic, males being twice as large as females. Males provide no parental care and are believed to be polygynous, using their large size to exclude other males from their range. They use a secretion from their anal glands to scent-mark posts around their territories, especially at breeding time, but it is not the same secretion as the foul, potent anal musk they release when they are threatened or while they are fighting.

In keeping with the pattern of sexual dimorphism, males do not breed until the age of 2, while females may breed at 1 year. Breeding takes place in early spring, but the embryos do not implant and begin to grow until the next winter. Pregnant fishers den high up in hollow trees and give birth to litters of usually three altricial (helpless) kits. The kits stay with the mother for three to four months and then disperse.

Fishers show a tendency to follow a 10-year population cycle, lagging a year or two behind the cycle of the snowshoe hare, especially in areas where hares are the main prey. Because they are such wide-ranging and actively curious animals, fishers can easily become victims of traps set for other furbearers in regions where trapping is heavy and have been extinguished in the southern end of their range.

Although the large-skulled fisher is built for hunting on the ground, it is an accomplished climber and uses tree holes for dens in which to rear its young.

FISHER *Martes pennanti*

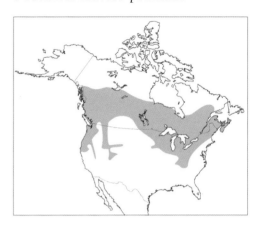

Mammal: *Martes pennanti*, fisher
Meaning of Name: *Martes* (marten); *pennanti* (named after T. Pennant, an English zoologist)
Description: thick, glossy coat; grizzled gray mantle because of tricolored guard hairs; rump, tail, feet and belly are glossy brown to black; irregular white or cream patches on the chest, in underarm region and around the genitals; in winter, the color ranges from deep brown to black, with light-colored hairs around the face and shoulders
Total Length: male, 2.8 to 3.5 feet; female, 2.5 to 3.1 feet
Tail: male, 13 to 15.5 inches; female, 10 to 14.5 inches
Weight: male, 5.5 to 12 pounds; female, 3 to 7 pounds
Gestation: 338 to 358 days (including a period of delayed implantation)
Offspring: 1 to 6 (average 2 or 3)
Age of Maturity: male, 2 years; female, 1 year
Longevity: 7 years is average lifespan in the wild (maximum 10 years); may live longer than 10 years in captivity
Diet: generalized carnivore; will eat any animal that it can overpower; also birds, fish, snakes, toads, insects and carrion; some plant material (fruits, seeds, berries and fern tips); one of the few animals that feeds on porcupine
Habitat: prefers continuous forest in the vicinity of watercourses; always in areas of extensive overhead canopy; avoids open areas
Predators: man is the major predator; possibly wolf, but a fisher would probably be too agile
Dental Formula:
3/3, 1/1, 4/4, 1/2 = 38 teeth

ERMINE *Mustela erminea*

Ermine is the luxuriant white fur that once lined the cloaks and sleeves of medieval European aristocracy. It starts out, however, as the winter coat of a small weasel that ranges widely throughout the northern hemisphere. The ermine is found in most kinds of northern forest, in mountain meadows and all across the tundra, everywhere except in shortgrass prairie and marshland.

Ermines thrive on the small rodents whose burrows they usurp for residences. Their size limits them to small prey, however, and unlike long-tailed weasels, they are not usually able to kill rabbits or hares.

Like all weasels, the ermine has three vocalizations—a trill, a screech and a squeal. The trill is used for communication among weasels, especially between mother and offspring or between siblings. The screech is used to startle prey and predators and may be followed by a lunging bite. Squealing, as in other mammals, expresses pain or distress.

The breeding behavior of the ermine resembles that of long-tailed weasels. They have delayed implantation and produce one litter in spring.

LONG & SKINNY

There are advantages to being long and skinny. Weasels can slip down crevices and crannies in the rocks in pursuit of small prey and follow shrews and pikas into their burrows. When it is their turn to be pursued, they can retreat to those same cracks and holes to

Perhaps best recognized for its stunning white winter coat, the ermine, or short-tailed weasel, makes its living largely on a diet of the northern forest's small rodent residents as well as fish, bird eggs and carrion.

escape the larger, fatter carnivores that prey on them.

There is, of course, a catch: The long, skinny shape of a weasel may enable it to catch more food, but it also allows it to lose more heat than the rounder and more compact animals do. The weasel, therefore, needs to consume a great deal more food to keep the fires burning.

Weasels, like many small mustelids, have a resting metabolic rate 10 percent higher than is usual for mammals of their weight. The least weasel in its Arctic range is an even more extreme example, with a resting metabolic rate 400 percent above average. That is the cost of staying active all year in the north if one happens to be long and skinny. These animals have to be able to generate a lot of heat to make up for the heat they lose. Not all mustelids demonstrate this pattern. Burrowing mustelids such as badgers, for example, have compact bodies and metabolic rates that are actually lower than normal for their body mass. It is long, skinny carnivores in general and not mustelids in particular that have evolved such high metabolic rates.

Weasels can exploit their high metabolic rate by being busy when prey is abundant. The proverbial and supposedly improvident weasel that kills every last chicken in the henhouse is not engaging in a wasteful, murderous spree. It is gathering food for its stockpile. Caches of more than a hundred rats and mice have been found, supplies that allow the weasel to stay in the insulated warmth of its grass-lined, snow-covered burrow in the very cold weather and keep itself warm by slow, steady feeding. And when it sleeps, it curls up into a ball to cut down on radiated heat loss, in effect changing its shape from long and skinny to round and compact.

The problem of the weasel's skinniness is compounded by the small size of its stomach. Studies have shown that a weasel is restricted to eating less than an ounce or so of meat at a time and can do it only once every few hours. On the other hand, it *has* to eat every few hours in order to survive, which makes food caching an absolute necessity. It is ironic: The long, slender shape of the weasel makes it an effective hunter but an ineffective eater, yet because it loses heat at a very high rate, it must eat more, and more often, than other mammals do just to stay warm.

ERMINE *Mustela erminea*

Mammal: *Mustela erminea,* ermine, stoat, short-tailed weasel
Meaning of Name: *Mustela* (weasel); *erminea,* from ermine, the Old French word for the white winter color phase (in the brown summer pelage, it is referred to as stoat)
Description: in summer, this animal is rich brown dorsally; creamy white on the outer sides of the legs, flanks and the ventral surface, including lips and underside of legs and toes; the tail is tipped with long, stiff black hairs; a white line runs down the hind legs, connecting the white of the underparts with that of the toes; in winter, the coat is pure white except for the black tip on the tail
Total Length: male, 9.9 to 13 inches; female, 8.5 to 10.2 inches
Tail: male, 2.5 to 3.5 inches; female, 1.5 to 2.8 inches
Weight: male, 2.4 to 5 ounces; female, 1.5 to 2.5 ounces
Gestation: 10 months (including a period of delayed implantation)
Offspring: 4 to 9 (average 6); 1 litter per year
Age of Maturity: male, about 10 months (February or March following birth); female, 60 to 70 days
Longevity: up to 7 years in the wild
Diet: eats mainly small rodents; also earthworms, reptiles, amphibians, fish, birds, eggs, insects and carrion
Habitat: wide range from open tundra to deep forest; prefers areas with vegetative or rocky cover; also found in coniferous or mixed forests, tundra, shrub borders, lakeshores and meadow boundaries
Predators: coyote, badger, fox, marten, wolverine, fisher, black snake, domestic cat, hawks and owls
Dental Formula:
3/3, 1/1, 3/3, 1/2 = 34 teeth

LONG-TAILED WEASEL
Mustela frenata

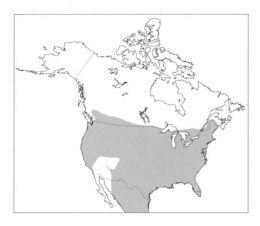

Mammal: *Mustela frenata*, long-tailed weasel
Meaning of Name: *Mustela* (weasel); *frenata* (bridle) refers to the bridlelike mask characteristic of this species in the more southern parts of its range
Description: in summer, the coat is cinnamon-brown above and buff-colored ventrally; tail has a black tip; in winter, it is pure white (including the whiskers) except for the black terminal quarter of the tail
Total Length: male, 13.8 to 18 inches; female, 11 to 14.3 inches
Tail: male, 4.1 to 6 inches; female, 3.3 to 4.7 inches
Weight: male, 6 to 9.5 ounces; female, 2.5 to 4.5 ounces
Gestation: 205 to 337 days (including a 7-month period of delayed implantation)
Offspring: 3 to 9 (usually 6)
Age of Maturity: male, late spring following birth; female, 3 to 4 months
Longevity: probably up to 3 years
Diet: primarily rodents and other small mammals; also eats some birds, insects and occasionally snakes, fruits and berries
Habitat: prefers open brushy or grassy areas near water; land-use practices have not affected it, and it occurs in croplands, fallow fields, fencerows, small woodlots and even suburban residential areas
Predators: gray fox, red fox, coyote, gray wolf, bobcat, lynx, hawks, owls and man
Dental Formula:
3/3, 1/1, 3/3, 1/2 = 34 teeth

The skinny body and short legs of the long-tailed weasel enable it to follow rodents and other small mammals into their burrows and pursue them along narrow connecting runways.

LONG-TAILED WEASEL
Mustela frenata

The long-tailed weasel is the largest of the true weasels. Despite its size, its diet is no different from that of the other weasels, consisting mainly of rodents. Like the larger weasels, this species consistently kills cottontails, waterfowl, muskrats and ground squirrels as well as some birds.

The geographic range of the long-tailed weasel extends farther south than those of the closely related least weasel and ermine. It ranges from southern Canada all the way down into northern South America, preferring the open habitats of grasslands and semidesert.

Mating occurs in spring and summer, with implantation and birth delayed until spring. The litter usually consists of half a dozen kits that are blind and helpless at birth. Males offer no parental care, and the young remain with their mothers only until autumn. Females, which are smaller than males, mature in their first spring, but males may take another year to reach sexual maturity.

The long-tailed weasel shares the ermine's characteristic black tail tip, which is most conspicuous when its coat has turned white for the winter. The southern populations of the long-tailed weasel stay brown all winter, but in the north, this species, like the ermine, turns snow-white. Possibly the tail tip remains black to deter predators. Experiments using hawks trained to attack forms resembling weasels showed that the black tail tip caused confusion—the birds often directed their strikes to the tail tip, as if it were the head, and not to the hind end of the body. Hawks missed in their attacks on models with black-tipped tails more often than they missed models with a black mark in the middle or without any black mark at all. This raises the question as to why the least weasel does not also retain a black tail tip. One possibility is that its small size and northerly location might preclude keeping a long tipped tail from freezing.

BLACK-FOOTED FERRET
Mustela nigripes

The black-footed ferret, a large weasel that had the misfortune to develop a specialized taste for prairie dogs, is now the rarest mammal in North America. Massive poisoning campaigns organized by ranchers and farmers to wipe out the prairie dog have almost eliminated its even more vulnerable predator. The tide may have turned, however. As a result of recent efforts to protect the prairie dog, its populations are growing, and there is hope that black-footed ferret numbers will increase as well. However, ferret populations—numbering only a few individuals in most known localities—have yet to show any signs of increase.

Ferrets are confined to the shortgrass prairie, where prairie dogs thrive. Like badgers, after they kill and dispose of a prairie dog, they modify the chambers of their victim's burrow and move in. Again like badgers, they eat a generalized diet of small mammals, birds, snakes and even young antelope. Almost nothing is known of other aspects of their behavior, however.

The black-footed ferret is the rarest North American mammal because its principal prey, the prairie dog, has been almost eradicated in poisoning campaigns by ranchers and farmers.

BLACK-FOOTED FERRET
Mustela nigripes

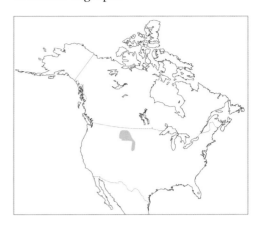

Mammal: *Mustela nigripes*, black-footed ferret
Meaning of Name: *Mustela* (weasel); *nigripes* (black foot)
Description: creamy white to buffy or yellowish brown; has a dark brown mask across the eyes; also has dark brown cheeks, feet, legs and end of tail
Total Length: male, 1.7 to 1.9 feet; female, 1.6 feet
Tail: male, 4.5 to 5.5 inches; female, 5 inches
Weight: 2.1 to 2.5 pounds
Gestation: 42 to 45 days
Offspring: 1 to 5 (usually 4)
Age of Maturity: 1 year
Longevity: 12 years in captivity
Diet: probably eats mainly prairie dogs; also other small mammals, ground-nesting birds and snakes
Habitat: mainly arid short mixed-grass prairies closely associated with prairie dog towns
Predators: hawks and owls
Dental Formula:
3/3, 1/1, 3/3, 1/2 = 34 teeth

MINK *Mustela vison*

Adaptations for life in the water, such as partially webbed feet and oily, thick insulating fur, allow the mink to catch fish and other aquatic organisms that are unavailable to most weasels.

Mink are wetland weasels most commonly found in marshes and near the shores of lakes and streams, where they hunt both along the shore and underwater. With short, stubby legs and a sturdy, pointed face, minks tend to resemble most other weasels, except that they are semiaquatic and have partially webbed feet. Their fine, lustrous fur is thick and oily and was designed by nature to insulate them for a life in cold northern waters.

In their foraging strategy, they are also like other weasels, patrolling a circuit,

investigating likely spots and rushing in to scare up small animals. On land, mink hunt mainly small rodents, but they will also take frogs, snakes, shrews, rabbits and birds. Underwater, they eat mostly fish and some crayfish and salamanders. Male mink, which are larger than females, can kill muskrats and rab-

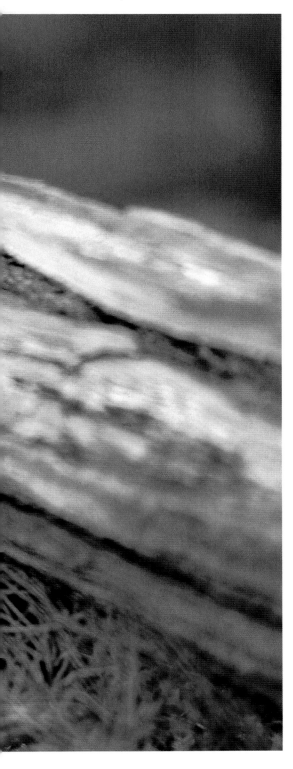

bits, which may be major food items in some areas. Females often take over muskrat dens for their own use.

The foraging circuit usually encompasses one-half to two miles of shoreline. Much smaller circuits are reported for West Coast mink, however, because they forage in the intertidal zone, where every tide brings in plentiful food. The male, as in other mustelids, ranges over a wider area than the female. Both sexes seem to be territorial and mark their boundaries with strong-smelling excretions from scent glands.

Adult mink are solitary for most of the year, but when the breeding season arrives, males begin to roam in search of receptive females. Courtship ends with a prolonged and violent mating during which the male may savagely bite the female's neck. Copulation, which induces ovulation, is repeated several times daily for a few days.

A gestation period of approximately one month ends with the birth of anywhere from two to ten kits, although the average is about five. The kits stay with the mother for the summer and disperse in autumn. The male provides no parental care.

Pollution is becoming a major problem for wild mink. Because they feed so heavily on fish that absorb and concentrate pesticides, mercury and PCBs, they are exposed to high levels of waterborne pollutants. Wild mink populations have been shown to suffer from mercury poisoning and PCB levels that either kill them or prevent them from reproducing. Most of the fur for mink coats now comes from mink ranches. Unpolluted areas still yield several hundred thousand mink each year, however, and trapping is the only major control of mink populations.

At one time, another species, the sea mink, *Mustela macrodon*, was commonly found along the Atlantic coast. It was exterminated by trapping, however, before scientists had the opportunity to describe it. The last sea mink was trapped at Campobello Island in New Brunswick in 1894.

MINK *Mustela vison*

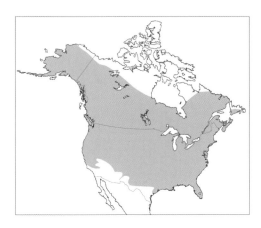

Mammal: *Mustela vison*, mink
Meaning of Name: *Mustela* (weasel); *vison* is of obscure origin, either from the Icelandic or Swedish word *vison* (weasel) or possibly from the Latin word *visor* (scout)
Description: thick, soft, lustrous pelage; the guard hairs are glossy and somewhat oily; the color varies from rich brown to black; it is paler ventrally, with white splashes on lower lip, chest and lower abdomen; has a white chin patch
Total Length: male, 19.3 to 24.4 inches; female, 16.5 to 23.5 inches
Tail: male, 6.2 to 8.3 inches; female, 5 to 8 inches
Weight: male, 1.5 to 5 pounds; female, 1.7 to 2.6 pounds
Gestation: 39 to 78 days (including varying period of delayed implantation)
Offspring: 2 to 10 (usually 5); 1 litter per year
Age of Maturity: male, 18 months; female, 12 months
Longevity: 3 (possibly 4) years in the wild; 10 years in captivity
Diet: primarily a carnivore; small mammals, fish, frogs, crayfish, insects, worms and birds; eats some plant material
Habitat: along streams and lakes in swamps and marshes; if it occurs away from the water, it prefers second-growth cover of mixed shrubs, weeds and grasses and the edges of cultivated fields and pastures
Predators: hunters and trappers are their main enemies; also great horned owl, bobcat, red fox, coyote, wolf, black bear and domestic dog
Dental Formula:
3/3, 1/1, 3/3, 1/2 = 34 teeth

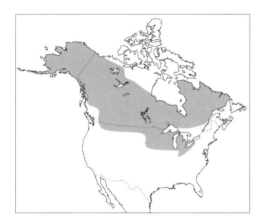

Mammal: *Mustela nivalis*, least weasel
Meaning of Name: *Mustela* (weasel); *nivalis* (snowy) refers to its color in winter
Description: resembles a long, slender mouse; in summer, the coat is brown dorsally and white ventrally, sometimes splotched with brown spots; the feet are whitish with furred soles; in winter, it is completely white except for a few black hairs at the tip of the tail
Total Length: male, 7.2 to 8.5 inches; female, 6.5 to 7.1 inches
Tail: male, 1 to 1.5 inches; female, 0.87 to 1.1 inches
Weight: male, 1.2 to 2.2 ounces; female, 0.88 to 2 ounces
Gestation: 35 to 37 days
Offspring: 3 to 10 (usually 4 or 5); 2 or more litters per year
Age of Maturity: male, 8 months; female, 4 months
Longevity: approximately 1 year
Diet: almost entirely small rodents; also amphibians and insects
Habitat: open woodlots, cultivated fields, meadows, brush areas, mixed forests, fencerows, marsh edges and streamside vegetation
Predators: long-tailed weasel, gray fox, red fox, domestic cat, snakes, hawks and owls
Dental Formula:
3/3, 1/1, 3/3, 1/2 = 34 teeth

The smallest of the true carnivores, the least weasel exploits its diminutive stature by pursuing voles, lemmings and other rodents into their retreats.

LEAST WEASEL *Mustela nivalis*

The least weasel is the smallest of the true carnivores. It specializes in small rodents such as mice, voles and lemmings as well as insectivorous shrews and moles. Often, it will take over the burrow system of one of its victims and use it as a home base. The tiny weasel will drag its victims home to cache and then pluck their fur to line and insulate its central burrow.

Insulation is very important, for with its small but long, skinny body, the least weasel has a metabolic rate equivalent to that of some shrews. In their Arctic range, they may elevate their metabolic rate by as much as 400 per-cent to stay warm, burning food equal to half their body weight every day.

The least weasel's range is less than 2 acres. It feeds on small mammals that do not hibernate and are available all winter, which may account in part for its unusual life history. It has a continuous breeding system—females become mature within a few months of birth and may breed several times in a year. Unlike other weasels, which have delayed implantation, the least weasel's pregnancy starts after mating and lasts roughly 35 days. A litter of three to ten kits is born and weaned after four weeks. The male offers no parental care, and when food is scarce, it may drive the female out of its territory.

WOLVERINE *Gulo gulo*

The wolverine is an animal of superlatives. It is the most powerfully built of all the weasels, with a massive, bony skull, a wolflike jaw and a bone-crushing bite very like that of the African hyena. Though it can bring down an adult caribou, it is better known as a robber and a scavenger. Any creature that tries to cache food in the north—including grizzlies, foxes, wolves and humans—has to reckon with the sensitive nose and strong paws of this animal. Its huge claws and powerful forearms enable it to dig into soil, flip large rocks and tear through logs.

For all its fierce appearance, the wolverine is more of a scavenger than a hunter. Trackers have found that it will travel great distances in search of carrion or a food cache rather than hunt. Most hunting weasels tend to zigzag back and forth in their search for food, but the wolverine follows a characteristically straight trail. In areas where big game is common, it lives mostly on the carrion from large mammal carcasses and patrols an extensive home range that varies from 115 to 770 square miles, depending on the habitat. Males typically range farther than females.

The wolverine seems to prefer to live in snowy regions, and its large, flat, heavily furred feet, designed rather like snowshoes, carry it over deep snow. Thus it remains active at times of the year when bears are hibernating and wolves move only with difficulty. In winter, when deer and caribou flounder in the deep snow, they are vulnerable to the attack of the more mobile wolverine. Wolverines habitually cache the meat from their kills, either by burying it or pulling it up into a tree. The wolverine also pounces on small game and digs out burrow-dwelling animals, and arctic foxes, ptarmigan and ground-dwelling squirrels form an important part of its diet. In summer, however, when competition from other predators is much more fierce and the prey is fleeter, the wolverine may be forced to feed on wasp nests and berries.

The wolverine can be a tireless traveler, moving as far as 20 miles in the course of one night's foraging. A hunted wolverine, moving without a rest, has been trailed for 40 miles. It is feats of stamina and endurance like these that have given rise to legends about the powerful wolverine.

The wolverine needs to control an extensive territory in order to find enough large game to support itself, and in the course of regular hunting patrols, it marks its range intensively. Wolverines not only scent-mark with their large glands, wiping the foul secretions on boulders and branches, but like bears, they also rake and scar trees in passing. One wolverine was found to have marked 26 trees in one night. Both sexes are territorial in that they occupy well-defined areas. Although there is considerable overlap in some territories, conflict is avoided by the carefully timed patrols of different animals, and they do not usually run into each other. It may be that territorial marking is intended to prevent individuals from using the same area at the same time rather than to establish exclusive access to a piece of land. The sensitive nose of the wolverine can detect the territorial musk over long distances. Thus direct physical contact is minimized, and wolverines have not been seen fighting to establish territories. Wolverines have been heavily trapped in the areas where they have been studied, however, and it is possible that in the absence of predation and trapping, adults would resort to aggression to prevent juveniles from establishing conflicting territories.

Males tolerate and mate with females during the spring and summer. Implantation is delayed, however, and the females do not give birth to their two to five kits until the next spring. The den is usually dug into snow or established in a rocky crevice. The mother feeds the young by herself, takes them on foraging excursions and allows them to den with her over their first winter. When spring comes, they disperse.

WOLVERINE *Gulo gulo*

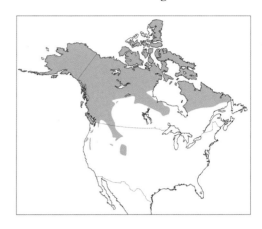

Mammal: *Gulo gulo*, wolverine
Meaning of Name: *Gulo* (glutton); probably eats no more than other carnivores but has a reputation for greed
Description: low, robust body shape; large compared with weasels; dark yellow-brown to almost black, darkest on the mid-dorsal saddle, feet and tail; paler on the cheeks and forehead; two pale buff or yellowish to light brown stripes run along the flanks and meet at the base of the tail; underparts are dark brown with some irregular creamy white spots on the chest and throat
Total Length: male, 3.1 to 3.5 feet; female, 2.5 to 3.1 feet
Tail: male, 7.8 to 10.2 inches; female, 6.5 to 9.8 inches
Weight: male, 25 to 36 pounds; female, 14.5 to 33 pounds
Gestation: 215 to 273 days (including a period of delayed implantation)
Offspring: 2 to 5 (usually 2 or 3); 1 litter every second or third year
Age of Maturity: second or third year
Longevity: probably several years in the wild; up to 17 years in captivity
Diet: omnivore, but primarily a scavenger; small game and, in winter, some larger game animals (white-tailed deer, caribou, moose), carrion, eggs of ground-nesting birds, edible roots and berries
Habitat: tundra and taiga zones; in mountains near tree line; among rocky outcrops and on steep canyon sides or open plains
Predators: man is a major enemy; also wolf packs and large bears
Dental Formula:
3/3, 1/1, 4/4, 1/2 = 38 teeth

It has been suggested that female wolverines may allow their daughters to take up a territory within or adjacent to their own, but information about this is still sparse. Studying the social behavior of such wide-ranging animals would require a heroic long-term effort. In the future, however, it may be possible to follow radio-collared animals via satellite to gain information not only on the movement of individuals but also on their interactions with other members of their own species.

It is likely that many juvenile wolverines die at the time of dispersal, but few animals will tackle an adult. There is a record, however, of a wolverine being attacked and killed by wolves, and another was apparently wounded by a puma. The puma's long reach and agility make it much more capable than most animals of dealing efficiently with a wolverine. There seems to be no animal that eats wolverines.

Many people fear wolverines for their reputation as fierce predators, and trappers hate them because they sniff out and destroy meat set out along traplines. As a result, they have been shot, trapped and poisoned and have consequently disappeared from much of their southern and eastern ranges.

WALKING SOFTLY

The foot of the northern mammal is caught in a bind. The problem is that it has to perform a whole range of conflicting functions. In summer, it must carry the animal swiftly over hard surfaces. It may have to help it climb trees or scramble over rocks. Then winter comes, and the foot must deal with an unstable mix of snowy powder, slush and ice.

While the wolverine's large, furry feet may slow it down in summer, they are strong and have large claws, enabling it to dig, flip large rocks and tear up logs in search of food. In winter, they act as snowshoes, allowing easy movement over the snow.

Since winter is a time of high heating costs—and that means extra rations of food for mammals that are active in the cold—an animal's means of dealing with snow is crucial to its survival. Many northern carnivores such as the lynx and the wolverine are actually very efficient at moving through the deep powdery snow, and winter is the time of their prosperity. They have feet that act as snowshoes, with a large surface area relative to body weight. In summer, however, their large, furry feet tend to slow them down. Other species such as the wolf have feet that are adapted for running over hard ground but will leave the animal floundering through deep snowdrifts when winter comes.

The hoofed animals—deer, antelope and elk—have feet primarily designed to absorb the stress of heavy bodies pounding over solid ground. The snows of winter can both help and hinder these animals, for although food is much harder to find, predators are easier to avoid. Caribou, in particular, because they have a larger dewclaw than most artiodactyls, are buoyed up on the snow by very wide hooves. In winter, they travel mostly on hard-packed caribou trails. When they see a wolf pack, however, they jump off the trail and into the deep snow. Even if the wolves choose to follow them, and usually they do not, the predators soon bog down in the snow, and the caribou leave them behind without difficulty.

Moose are not so fortunate. They have about the same ratio of body weight to surface area of foot as their predators, and they sink just as deeply into the snow. Probably for that reason, moose will often stand and fight in winter instead of running.

The less powerful deer cannot fight wolves, so they try to stay in shallow or hard-packed snow, where their superior speed can defeat the predator. This is probably why deer gather in winter in what are known as deeryards. They create a dense maze of hard-packed trails that crisscross the area around the yard,

escape routes prepared in advance for when wolves approach. In soft snow, a wolf sinks in less than a deer, which is forced to bound high over the drifts to avoid bogging down. Often, however, when the snow reaches chest height, the deer becomes exhausted. In conditions like these, the wolverine, which has the lightest tread of all the predators, can kill deer and even caribou.

It is probably the deep snows that limit the northern range of the deer. In periods of warming, such as the present one, deer tend to move farther north; correspondingly, in colder periods—for example, in the so-called "little ice age," between 1350 and 1800—caribou have moved south to take over the abandoned range of the deer.

Species such as bison and antelope have relatively small feet in relation to their weight and are restricted primarily to open prairie, where the wind blows areas clear of snow. In Wood Buffalo National Park in northern Alberta and the southern Northwest Territories, where snow is deep, wolves can kill even the biggest buffalo in winter, when the large bulls are unable to maneuver. In many species of deer and bovid, there is a selection for heavy male body size, which increases the prowess of males in fighting for control of the harem. Ironically, the increase in weight that contributes to breeding success probably means more winter mortality. Among artiodactyls, it may be the need to walk softly in winter that limits the tendency toward ever greater size.

AMERICAN BADGER
Taxidea taxus

....

Badgers are diggers. They have taken the mustelid tendency to pursue rodents into their burrows one step further by evolving the bones and muscles necessary to dig them out. The badger has a heavy-boned body that is flattened to enable it to slip into small burrows. The forelimbs are armed with long, stout claws for digging, while the claws on the hind legs are short and shovel-like for scooping away the dirt the fore-claws have loosened. The eyes are small and have a special membrane that protects them from dirt.

Badgers dig for many kinds of rodents, some of them larger than the usual rodent prey—ground squirrels, pocket gophers, marmots and prairie dogs. Their techniques are often quite sophisticated. When they go after ground squirrels, for example, they

The badger's formidable claws and jaws protect it from all but the largest predators. It can burrow amazingly quickly, both to protect itself and to excavate rodents.

may plug all the doors but one before they proceed to dig the squirrel out. Alternatively, they may dig a connecting tunnel into the one remaining entrance-way and simply wait for the ground squirrel to leave.

To protect themselves from coyotes

and grizzlies, badgers tend to dig very large burrows for themselves, often up to 10 feet deep and 30 feet wide. To save on the cost of construction, they may take over and renovate a prairie dog burrow after, of course, they have eaten the occupants.

The badger is a great fighter and is not easily killed, even when taken by surprise. Its compact body and powerful claws and teeth mean that any predator smaller than a grizzly must take care when attacking. The badger uses any hesitation on the part of the attacker to dig itself into the soil. It can disappear into the earth almost miraculously in a very few minutes.

The morphology and feeding habits of the badger suggest that it evolved on the grasslands, where the soil is deep and ground-dwelling rodents are abundant. Normally, badgers are restricted to a dry, open habitat such as the prairies; however, they have been able to colonize some farmland in southern Ontario, where their large burrows tend to interfere with agriculture. In much of their range, badgers are hunted or poisoned. They also suffer because of the extermination of the ground squirrels and prairie dogs on which they live.

PLAYING TO WIN

Most mammals play. But why? The concept of play is difficult to define; it is almost impossible to study. Of course, pleasure is implicit in the notion of play, and animals at play seem to perform certain actions simply for the pleasure of it. Often, however, these actions are actually a light-hearted imitation of more serious behavior, and most biologists have come to believe that play is functional. The animal at play is rehearsing the behavior on which its success will one day depend. The pleasure of playing is simply nature's way of encouraging the animal to practice and develop its skills.

Behaviorists distinguish between play and exploration, which is the investigation of an object in an attempt to understand what it is and what it does. They also distinguish between play and problem solving, in which the animal has a specific goal. Play is more complex: Through it, the animal learns how to interact with its environment. It also learns how to experiment and to adjust its tactics in the face of new situations. In play, there is no fixed goal but merely a toying with optional actions and outcomes. In the real world, play—a shadow of the life-and-death contests of later life—translates into much cavorting and romping.

Play is much more highly developed in mammals that are large, long-lived, intelligent and social. Shrews, for example, do not seem to play much; otters, on the other hand, play frequently and with great gusto. In fact, most aquatic mammals seem especially playful, probably because of their intelligence and long lives rather than because of their environment.

In some mammals, the forms of play behavior are relatively predictable. Foxes play by racing around and knocking each other down as they will later do in earnest when they are hunting. Squirrels also play by running in circles, making sharp turns, leaping and going through the motions of courtship. When people dangle a string or drag it across the floor or make scratching noises with their fingers to entertain a kitten, they are mimicking the sounds and movements of small mammals and the kitten is learning to hunt.

In more sophisticated animals, play is more complex, flexible and wide-ranging. Monkeys, for example, use play to discover new behaviors, new foods to eat and new ways to handle it. It has been found that when a strange food is introduced to a troop of monkeys, it is the youngest monkeys that learn to incorporate it into their diet. Play tends to promote this flexibility, and once mature animals have put playful learning behind them, they are less apt to learn. Hence the expression "You can't teach an old dog new tricks."

AMERICAN BADGER
Taxidea taxus

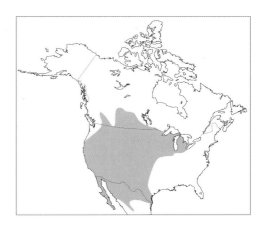

Mammal: *Taxidea taxus*, American badger
Meaning of Name: *Taxidea* (badgerlike) because of its general resemblance to the common badger of Eurasia; *taxus* (badger)
Description: has a shaggy pelage, longer dorsally, especially on the flanks, where a fringe is formed (may be as long as 3.5 inches); back has a grizzled appearance; underparts are creamy, legs are brown, and feet are blackish; tail is covered in stiff, light brown hairs; head has a distinct pattern—the muzzle, crown and nape of neck are dark blackish brown with a white mid-dorsal stripe running from the muzzle to the shoulders; white cheeks; ears are white trimmed with black; behind the eyes on each cheek is a black crescentic spot
Total Length: 2.4 to 2.8 feet
Tail: 4.7 to 6.2 inches
Weight: 7.9 to 26.5 pounds
Gestation: 6 to 9 months (including a period of delayed implantation)
Offspring: 2 to 5 (usually 4)
Age of Maturity: male, second breeding season following birth; female, first breeding season following birth
Longevity: 4 or 5 years in the wild (maximum 14); in captivity, one lived 23 years, 8 months
Diet: ground squirrels are a major component of its diet; also other small mammals, birds, bird eggs, reptiles, arthropods and carrion
Habitat: dry, open prairies, grasslands, farmlands and parklands; clay and sandy soils are suitable for its burrow
Predators: coyote, golden eagle, grizzly bear and man
Dental Formula:
3/3, 1/1, 3/3, 1/2 = 34 teeth

NORTHERN RIVER OTTER
Lutra canadensis

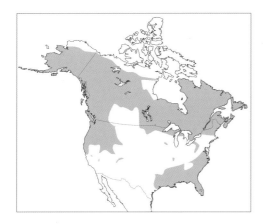

Mammal: *Lutra canadensis*, northern river otter

Meaning of Name: *Lutra* (otter); *canadensis* (of Canada) because this species was first described from Canada

Description: muscular, streamlined body with broad, flattened head; legs short and powerful; feet with fully webbed toes and furred soles; short, oily pelage has a dense underfur and rich brown guard hairs; throat has a silvery sheen

Total Length: male, 3.1 to 4.5 feet; female, 2.9 to 3.8 feet

Tail: male, 13.5 to 20.1 inches; female, 12.5 to 17.5 inches

Weight: male, 15 to 30 pounds; female, 10 to 25 pounds

Gestation: 245 to 380 days (including a period of delayed implantation)

Offspring: 1 to 6 (usually 2 or 3)

Age of Maturity: male, mature at 2 years but doesn't breed successfully until 5th year (young males are often rejected by females); female, 2 years (has been known to breed at 1 year)

Longevity: 13 years in the wild; 14 to 20 years in captivity (maximum 23 years)

Diet: fish constitute bulk of diet; also aquatic invertebrates, amphibians, mammals and birds

Habitat: extensive water is the principal component; marshes, points of land extending into water and wooded streambanks are preferred; found in all types of inland waterways as well as estuaries and marine covers

Predators: bobcat, lynx and coyote; wolf may catch otters migrating overland; bald eagle, great horned owl and large game fish may take young

Dental Formula:
3/3, 1/1, 4/3, 1/1 = 36 teeth

The streamlined form of the northern river otter makes it a fast and agile underwater predator able to catch almost any kind of freshwater fish.

NORTHERN RIVER OTTER
Lutra canadensis

The northern river otter is a freshwater mustelid. This almost completely aquatic animal is found in rivers and lakes in virtually all parts of North America, from the edge of the tundra to the Gulf of Mexico. It has adapted to its watery environment in much the same way as the sea otter, and it has developed the same dense fur, large lungs, webbed feet, short legs and heavy crushing molars. Unlike its seagoing cousin, however, the northern river otter dens on land and forages along the shore; it has been known to travel over large expanses of land. It uses scent glands to mark the banks of its river territory, another trait not shared with the sea otter.

Otters breed in late winter or early spring. Implantation is delayed, and after a pregnancy that probably lasts only two months, the female gives birth to one to six kits in the spring. Otters are not equipped for digging, and the female usually seeks out an abandoned beaver lodge or the burrow of some other animal on the banks of a stream or lake. Failing that, she may settle into a hollow tree.

Like other den nesters, the otter has altricial kits—that is, born blind and helpless. Sea otter kits have opened their eyes and are swimming at the age of 2 weeks, but the young river otters remain blind until they are 3 weeks old and do not swim until 6 to 9 weeks. It takes two years for the kits to mature sexually and disperse. They continue to grow for several years after that, however, the males eventually reaching a larger size than females.

Otters, both male and female, tend to establish separate territories, although competition among the males prevents many of them from holding a breeding territory until they are at least 5 and perhaps as old as 7 years.

Although the mother initially cares for the kits without assistance from the

The northern river otter usually comes ashore to eat the wide range of prey—including fish, frogs and salamanders—that it pursues underwater with its eyes open.

male, he may rejoin her later to assist in raising the young. The otter family spends a lot of time at play, their games a means of teaching skills to the young and helping them develop the coordination they will need for an independent life. The playful, social nature of young otters makes them easy to train in captivity. They have even been used to catch fish for human consumption.

Otters, like all successful pursuit predators, are intelligent enough to catch and handle a wide variety of prey. Indeed, their ingenuity is sometimes remarkable. They have been known to punch holes in beaver dams, and then as the water in the beaver pond recedes, they wade in to feast on the trapped fish and frogs. They are also fast and versa-

tile: They dash after fish; they dig into the mud of the river bottom in search of crayfish, frogs and salamanders; they launch submarine attacks on floating waterbirds; and they plunder bird nests. The otter is also a fighter. It will follow a muskrat into its burrow and kill it, and it is one of the few animals that may be able to kill a beaver in its lodge. In winter, otters have been seen fishing for bluegills under the lake ice. When they seize one, they bring it to a hole and flip it out onto the ice, where they can consume it at leisure.

Few animals have the opportunity to prey on the swift, agile otter as it darts through the water, but wolves and coyotes may sometimes surprise them and kill them on land.

SEA OTTER *Enhydra lutris*

S ea otters are the largest and most completely aquatic of all mustelids— of most carnivores, in fact. Only seals and whales have adapted more completely to life in the watery world.

Sea otters are now found mostly in the richly productive inshore waters of the Pacific coast of North America, but they formerly ranged all around the northern Pacific rim, from Japan northward to the Bering Sea and Alaska all the way south to Baja California. Before the turn of the century, by which time overhunting had reduced them to a few tiny, isolated populations, the northern distribution was probably limited only by the pack ice and the southern distribution by the low productivity of tropical waters. In recent years, sea otter populations have begun to recover, however, and there are now several thousand of these animals along the Pacific coast.

The sea otter has adapted very precisely to its environment, distinguishing itself in a number of ways from terrestrial mustelids. For example, since chemical communication is of limited value in the ocean, the sea otter has lost the anal scent gland of other otters. Retractile claws in the forepaws are used for grabbing fish and shellfish, which require extensive manipulation. Webbed hind feet with elongated toes that act as flippers enable the otter to scull efficiently even when floating on its back but make for very slow, awkward running on land. The sea otter does not have an insulating layer of blubber to keep it warm but depends on its thick fur coat, made up of as many as 800 million tightly packed hairs to keep the water from touching its skin. The sea otter is also adapted for swimming underwater. It has small ears with valvelike flaps that keep the water out and a stout, muscular tail that acts as a rudder.

Sea otters tend to live in fairly shallow water, around 200 feet in depth, although they have been known to dive as deep as 300 feet. They feed mostly

Composed of 800 million tightly packed hairs, the sea otter's thick coat keeps water from touching its skin, one of the many adaptations to its watery environment that make it the most aquatic of all mustelids. Even its pups appear to be born in the water.

on bottom-dwelling mollusks and sea urchins, and their massive jaws and teeth are adapted for crunching shells. When the shell is very hard, however, the otter resorts to tools. As it floats on its back in the water, it places a shellfish on its chest and pounds it with a rock until it breaks.

Abalone is one of the otter's favorite foods. It is also partial to crabs, squid,

rockfish and clams, but it is the animal's taste for abalone that has resulted in conflict with humans. After the sea otter was made extinct along the California coast, the abalone population expanded and a lucrative new fishery came into being. The otters are back now, however, and they are competing with humans for the abalone.

Most of the sea otter's life is lived in

the water. They mate in the water, and the single pup that results is probably born in the water. In the southern part of the range, at least, pups can be born at any time of year. The newborn pup is somewhat more precocious than the young of other mustelids, but it is still unable to swim or dive before it reaches the age of 2 weeks. The mother provides all the parental care and carries the pup around on her chest or back. The pup remains with the mother for roughly a year and depends on her for food for most of that time.

Sea otters are eaten by killer whales, sharks and possibly bald eagles, but none of these predators is thought to exert a major effect on populations. In fact, even though hunting has ceased, humans are still the greatest threat to the sea otter. The danger now comes in the shape of major oil spills. Oil reduces the insulation value of the fur, and an oiled sea otter will die of cold within a day or two.

COMMUNITY CONTROL

Not many good things can be said about the extermination of an animal population. Often, however, one benefit arises from the carnage, and that benefit is knowledge. In a few cases, extermination by overhunting and trapping has been like a giant experiment that helps ecologists see and understand the role played by one species in its relationships with others. The sea otters have given scientists just this kind of opportunity.

Off the West Coast of North America are two island chains—the Rat Islands and the Near Islands. The islands are similar in topography—both have the same rocky coast, are set in the same sea and have the same climate. The Rat Islands have sheltered an abundant colony of sea otters for the last 30 years, but otters were hunted out in the Near Islands, and only very recently have a few animals reappeared there.

There is one other difference between the island chains. The Rat Islands are surrounded by thick beds of kelp, while the Near Islands are not. Great underwater forests of the giant algae grow in the intertidal area of the Rat Islands out to a depth of some 250 feet, and they support a rich array of marine organisms. These stands of kelp are so thick, they also reduce wave action and water turbulence along the shore. The Near Islands, on the other hand, have virtually no kelp to protect them or nourish life-forms in the surrounding sea.

Sea urchins, which graze on kelp, make up much of the otter's diet. In places where sea urchins are free from sea otter predation, as they are on the Near Islands, the ocean floor is carpeted with them. In fact, they have become so abundant that they have grazed the kelp forest to destruction. On the Rat Islands, however, the sea otters eat all the biggest sea urchins, leaving only the smaller shellfish thinly scattered throughout the kelp.

Of course, there are disadvantages to kelp. The reduced turbulence allows sediment to settle, and bottom dwellers such as mussels are buried and smothered. Thus in the Near Islands, thick mussel beds and stands of barnacles have grown up, in the order of 1,000 for every square yard, compared with only five in the same area off the Rat Islands. Nevertheless, on the whole, kelp forests are considered to be among the most biologically productive environments on Earth. Fish thrive there, for example, so islands that have sea otters and kelp are also rich in fish-eating seals and bald eagles. Needless to say, few seals and eagles frequent the Near Islands.

This is an example of a simple community: Otters eat sea urchins, and in turn, sea urchins eat kelp, kelp supports invertebrates, and seals and eagles eat invertebrates. In more complex communities, the web of ecological interaction is less straightforward. No one can know in advance with any certainty what impact the elimination of one species will have on the others.

SEA OTTER *Enhydra lutris*

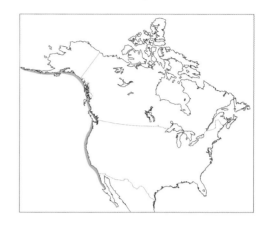

Mammal: *Enhydra lutris*, sea otter
Meaning of Name: *Enhydra* (otter), derived from *enhudro*, which means living in the water; *lutris* (otter)
Description: extremely well adapted to an aquatic environment, so much so that it resembles the pinnipeds—short, weak limbs with completely webbed feet and long, webbed toes forming long flippers; short, fleshy, naked ear pinnae; brownish black with white-tipped guard hairs on the head and neck, giving it a grizzled appearance; paler on the throat, chest and head
Total Length: male, 4.2 to 5.5 feet; female, 3.5 to 4.2 feet
Tail: male, 14.2 inches; female, 10.2 to 11 inches
Weight: male, 48.5 to 99.2 pounds; female, 33.1 to 70.5 pounds
Gestation: 6.5 to 9 months (probably a period of delayed implantation)
Offspring: 1 (can have young every year but probably do so at greater intervals)
Age of Maturity: male, 5 to 6 years; female, 4 years
Longevity: 10 to 11 years on average
Diet: slow-moving fish, marine invertebrates such as sea urchin, abalone, crab, starfish, octopus and mollusks; also some seaweed
Habitat: in seas off rocky reefs, inlets, rocky coasts and soft-sediment communities; rarely more than half a mile from shore; rests on kelp beds and rocky shores
Predators: killer whale, sharks, bald eagle and man
Dental Formula:
3/2, 1/1, 3/3, 1/2 = 32 teeth

SKUNKS *Mephitidae*

Until recent DNA work, skunks were classified as a subfamily within the family Mustelidae, but they are now considered their own family, Mephitidae. The family includes nine species, three of which occur in temperate North America. Their bold patterns and coloration, slow movements and well-developed pair of scent glands are all part of their defensive strategy and serve as a warning to would-be predators.

STRIPED SKUNK *Mephitis mephitis*

All members of both Mephitidae and Mustelidae have anal musk glands that they use to express aggression and displeasure, a characteristic skunks have developed to the extreme. The musk glands of the striped skunk, which are about the size of grapes, are surrounded by powerful sphincter muscles. When the skunk is annoyed or frightened, those muscles force the fluid musk down a duct and out through a kind of nipple that can be protruded from the anus. The skunk has considerable muscular control over the spray and can produce a fine cloud of mist or direct a concentrated stream on objects as far away as 16 feet. At distances of 6 to 10 feet, the skunk's aim is accurate enough to score a hit on most large mammals.

The musk gland contains about a tablespoonful of an oily solution of sulfur alcohol called butylmercaptan, enough to produce half a dozen sprays. If eaten, the musk will poison the nervous system and can cause death; as an external spray, however, its effects are only temporary, although intensely nauseating and irritating. Skunks are not immune to their own spray and try to avoid spraying if they are likely to be soiled themselves. Probably the high physiological cost of manufacturing the musk also makes them hesitant to spray. The skunk has evolved a very conspicuous black-and-white coloring to deter its enemies.

A skunk also uses a wide range of behavioral threats to frighten predators away before it resorts to the spray. It arches its back and walks toward the intruder. It hisses, clicks its teeth, stamps its front feet and does headstands with the tail raised in a very clear warning. Some skunks can spray from the headstand position, but the striped skunk bends its body into a U-shape with head and anus pointed in the same direction.

Predation is probably less of a problem for skunks than for mustelids. However, its defensive system does not render it completely immune to attack. Great horned owls kill and eat skunks, as does a range of large mammals—no doubt very hungry ones—including pumas, coyotes and fishers.

Skunks, unlike the mustelids, are omnivorous and will eat virtually anything they can catch or find, including a wide variety of berries and fruits, small mammals, bird eggs and nestlings, young rabbits and frogs. Insects, however, are the most important part of their diet, and skunks grub extensively in the upper soil layers and under rocks and logs. They are especially significant predators of social insects such as hornets and bumblebees. The skunk digs into the nest, and as the insects emerge to defend the colony, the skunk grabs and kills them by rolling them between its tough palms. Their taste for bees makes skunks a minor

Although they are omnivorous and eat almost anything, from fruits and bird eggs to frogs and young rabbits, striped skunks spend most of their time rooting and grubbing through the upper soil layers in search of insects, an essential part of their diet. This young skunk will learn to forage from its mother.

STRIPED SKUNK
Mephitis mephitis

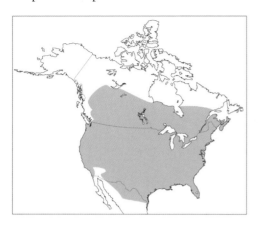

Mammal: *Mephitis mephitis*, striped skunk
Meaning of Name: *Mephitis* (noxious smell)
Description: shiny black pelage with a narrow frontal white stripe between the eyes and two broad white dorsal stripes running from the nape of the neck to the base of the tail; the underside, legs and feet are blackish; there may be white blotches on the chest; the tail may or may not have a white tip; each foot has five slightly webbed toes with claws
Total Length: male, 20.6 to 26.8 inches; female, 20.2 to 25.6 inches
Tail: male, 7 to 11 inches; female, 6.9 to 10.5 inches
Weight: male, 2.8 to 9.9 pounds; female, 2.1 to 8.5 pounds
Gestation: 59 to 77 days (probably some delay in implantation)
Offspring: 1 to 10 (usually 4 to 6); rarely may be a second litter
Age of Maturity: female has first litter at 9 months to 1 year
Longevity: one lived 42 months in the wild; approximately 6 years on average in captivity (up to 13 years)
Diet: omnivore; rodents and other small mammals and vertebrates; insects, grasses, leaves, buds, grains, nuts and carrion; may eat bird eggs and nestlings; also mollusks
Habitat: prefers areas of mixed woods, grasslands and open prairie, usually close to water; also found in mixed agricultural and tree-cleared land; thrives in suburban areas
Predators: birds of prey, bobcat, fox, fisher, badger, lynx, golden eagle, coyote and puma
Dental Formula:
3/3, 1/1, 3/3, 1/2 = 34 teeth

The skunk is normally a night-active animal that searches for food using its keen sense of smell. Its secret weapons are its warning coloration and the grape-sized musk glands that contain an oily solution which when sprayed has sickening and irritating effects on the victim.

pest of the honeybee yard. They scratch at hives, and as the bees emerge, they kill them and stuff them into their mouths. The rolling technique is also used to process hairy caterpillars.

Skunks, since they like a mixture of open space interspersed with pockets of cover, have profited from human settlement. They also eat many of the fruits, insects and small mammals associated with disturbed habitats. In some areas, they have become so common that they are the major predator of waterfowl eggs and nestlings, young rabbits and ground-nesting game birds.

When foraging, skunks tend to stick close to their dens, which may be hollow trees, rock cavities or abandoned animal burrows. They stay in dens

above the ground in summer, but when winter comes or when females are pregnant or newly delivered of a litter, they prefer to hide away below ground. They line the winter burrow with vegetation and spend several months there in a dormant state, although they do not hibernate. Sometimes, several skunks den together for the winter.

Northern skunks breed in spring. Females begin to breed at the age of 9 months and give birth to a single litter of one to ten kits every year. The males provide no parental care and are probably polygynous. The young remain with the mother all summer, foraging with her until autumn, when some disperse. Others may den with the mother the first winter and leave her in spring.

WESTERN SPOTTED SKUNK
Spilogale gracilis

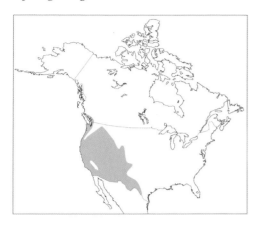

Mammal: *Spilogale gracilis,* western spotted skunk
Meaning of Name: *Spilogale* (stain or spot + marten-cat or weasel); *gracilis* (slender)
Description: slimmer and smaller than other skunks; silky black fur with six horizontal white stripes on neck and shoulders; irregular white stripes and spots on sides; white spots between the eyes; tail tipped with white plume
Total Length: 13.6 to 18.8 inches
Tail: 4.3 to 7 inches
Weight: 1 to 1.5 pounds
Gestation: about 120 days (including a period of delayed implantation)
Offspring: 4 or 5
Age of Maturity: male, 5 months; female, 4 to 5 months
Longevity: approximately 10 years
Diet: in winter and spring, primarily mammals such as cottontails, voles and mice; in summer and fall, insects and plants are the main food items, including beetles, larvae, fruits and corn; also bird eggs and occasionally lizards, snakes and frogs
Habitat: scrub and farmlands, open areas
Predators: owls, domestic dog and domestic cat
Dental Formula:
3/3, 1/1, 3/3, 1/2 = 34 teeth

The black-and-white coloring of the spotted skunk is a warning to would-be predators.

EASTERN SPOTTED SKUNK
Spilogale putorius

A slimmer version of its striped relation, the eastern spotted skunk has the same powerful spray and black-and-white warning pattern. Unlike the striped skunk, however, this species can spray while performing the threatening headstand display. It walks on its forelegs toward its target and sprays by arching its back.

The eastern spotted skunk prefers a drier habitat such as the western scrubland and canyons, where the striped skunk is less common. It is more agile and athletic than the striped skunk and is able to climb trees. It is also more social than other skunks and will share dens in winter. Although it is highly omnivorous and adapted for digging and grubbing for invertebrates, this skunk is more carnivorous than its insect-loving cousin is. In other respects, however, it seems to share much of the life history and breeding behavior of the striped skunk.

The **western spotted skunk, *Spilogale gracilis***, is closely related to its eastern counterpart. The two were considered to be a single species at one time. Since their ranges do not overlap much, the best way to distinguish them is according to range.

EASTERN SPOTTED SKUNK
Spilogale putorius

Mammal: *Spilogale putorius,* eastern spotted skunk
Meaning of Name: *Spilogale* (stain or spot + marten-cat or weasel); *putorius* (bad smell)
Description: black with six white stripes running down the back, flanks and rump; stripes may be broken into spots for part of their length; a white spot on forehead and more white spots in front of the ears; the long tail has a black tip and a white plume
Total Length: male, 13.9 to 18.1 inches; female, 12.7 to 17.3 inches
Tail: male, 4 to 6.2 inches; female, 3.5 to 5.5 inches
Weight: male, 1.5 to 1.9 pounds
Gestation: 50 to 60 days
Offspring: 4 to 7
Age of Maturity: male, 5 months; female, year of birth
Longevity: approximately 10 years
Diet: omnivore; in summer, mainly vegetable matter and insects; in winter, rodents and other small mammals; also birds and their eggs, carcasses, lizards, snakes and frogs
Habitat: brushy, rocky and wooded habitats, scrubland, farmland, along streams and among boulders; avoids heavy forests and wetlands
Predators: great horned owl, domestic dog and domestic cat
Dental Formula:
3/3, 1/1, 3/3, 1/2 = 34 teeth

CATS *Felidae*

Cats are the most specialized of all carnivores, and their tooth and claw adaptations for capturing and devouring meat are taken to the extreme. Large canine teeth and reduced molars allow the cat, after it has stalked and seized its prey, to finish it off with a single lethal bite.

The most extreme and ferocious examples of feline killers were the saber-, scimitar- and dirk-toothed cats, which have been extinct since the last ice age. The saber-toothed tiger was as large as the lions that roamed the plains of Canada and the United States until some 10,000 years ago and are now found only in Africa. These cats preyed on slow-moving herbivores, using their long, flattened canines like daggers. The knifelike blades were more than 8 inches long in some species and had serrated edges for severing tendons, muscles and arteries in the neck of their prey. Most of the ancient cats had long necks to facilitate striking and long forelimbs to reach up and grapple with the animals they attacked.

The large herbivores—mammoths, mastodons, camels and horses—became extinct in North America at the end of the last ice age, although some of them survived in altered form in Africa and Asia. Their disappearance from the western hemisphere meant the end of the large cats on this continent. The largest surviving cat worldwide is the Siberian tiger, which can weigh as much as 850 pounds. Its teeth are not as specialized as those of the extinct species, so it was able to vary its diet and survive the disappearance of giant game.

Similarly, in North America, the cats that survived—the mountain lion, the bobcat and the lynx—were the least specialized and able to eat smaller prey. Unlike the mustelids or the canids, the felines show little diversity of form, and all of the surviving cats have a catlike appearance. This reflects a uniformity in the way they move and hunt and what they eat. Cat species differ primarily in body size, habitat and range of prey.

Cats are not long-distance runners like the canids. Some of them are extremely fast sprinters, however—the cheetah, over distances of less than a mile, is the fastest land mammal on Earth. The paws and claws of a cat are specifically designed for climbing trees and attacking prey, not for running. Three-quarters of the world's cats live in forests, and most species—even those that hunt in the savanna—can climb trees. Thus they have retractable claws that they can extend to grip bark or claw prey. When cats are on the move, the claws are withdrawn into the paw, so a cat print looks very different from a dog's. Only in the cheetah, a species specialized for running over grasslands, have the claws become incompletely retractable and somewhat doglike.

Cats also have relatively short muzzles compared with canids and a reduced nasal cavity. This allows a cat to breathe as it bites and buries its teeth into the neck and throat of its prey.

Cats are distinguished by a remarkable sense of balance that allows them to climb trees and leap and twist through the air. A cat, as the saying goes, always lands on its feet. It is not just the supple body and fine coordination that allow this graceful orientation but a kind of gyroscope in the inner ear. As the cat twists through the air, the sensitive inner ear directs the brain and neck muscles to pull the head into a horizontal position,

Cats such as the mountain lion kill smaller prey by slipping their sharp canine teeth between the victim's vertebrae and severing its spinal cord with a single surgical bite. The mountain lion often waits motionless for hours in a tree above a game trail and then drops down on the the back of a passing deer, elk or moose.

and the rest of the body follows suit.

Most cats hunt at night and have large eyes and acute vision. In bright daylight, cats see just as well as humans; in the dark, however, their eyes are six times as sensitive as ours. The bright shine of a cat's eyes caught in the beam of car headlights is caused by reflection from a membrane at the back of the eyeball, the tapetum lucidum, that catches any light not absorbed by the retina and bounces it back into the eye so that it can be read again. Cats have huge irises, which open at night to let in the maximum amount of light; during the day, the irises close to cat's-eye slits to protect the sensitive retina. The cat's whiskers are also adapted for night hunting, and they serve as sense organs to guide the animal around obstructions. The cat's hearing is as sensitive as our own, but smaller cats—like dogs—can hear a range of high-pitched sounds to which we are deaf. Their ears help them locate the rodents and insectivores that use ultrasound for hunting communication.

Cats rely on a combination of vision, hearing and smell to find their prey. When a cat has identified and located its prey by sound or scent and has stalked it or set up an ambush, it is the eyes that guide the final attack.

Except for lions and male cheetahs, most cats are solitary hunters, eating only those animals they can subdue alone. This limits the size of their prey to animals of roughly their own size or slightly larger. The large cats are an exception, and they use specialized killing techniques to take grazers much heavier than themselves. They are the only carnivores able to do so.

Most cat attacks follow the same pattern. The cat slink-runs quickly toward its prey, holding its body close to the ground, then it freezes to watch its victim and assess its vulnerability. Its tail twitching back and forth and its paws

The bobcat's adaptability in terms of prey and habitat has allowed its populations to expand when most other cat populations are on the decline.

perhaps kneading the ground, the cat is otherwise motionless. It may slink-run again, or it may step forward slowly in a low crouch to further close the gap. Finally, it rushes forward, still crouched, to launch its final attack.

Anchoring itself firmly to the ground with its hind legs, the cat seizes the prey by the forequarters and delivers a killing bite to the animal's neck, just behind the head. The sharp canine teeth slip between the spinal vertebrae to sever the spinal cord, and the hunt is over. On larger prey, especially those with horns, the bite may be delivered to the throat so as to sever the windpipe, and the animal suffocates. Cats that eat smaller prey such as birds use their forepaws to bat and scoop the prey toward them before they kill it.

Of the 35 species of cat found throughout the world, 28 are small tropical cats, and they have the most diverse feeding habits of all. Besides small mammals and birds, they will eat frogs, insects, snails, turtles and fish.

Even the smallest cats are formidable predators, able to kill species larger than themselves. They feed high in the food chain, and like all top-level carnivores, they demand a lot of room for their hunting activities and tend to have a dispersed distribution. They also defend their territories tooth and claw. Few species of cat—except for lions and cheetahs—belong to complex societies. As every cat owner knows, a cat likes to go its own way.

WHY EAT MEAT?

At first glance, vegetarians seem to have it all over carnivores. To begin with, their food grows all around them, and it does not run away, kick or claw in self-defense; an obligate carnivore spends its whole waking life trying to find enough meat to live. And when it does find its prey, a demanding chase ensues, often followed by a battle during which the hunter may be kicked, clawed, bitten or otherwise injured.

The obvious question is, Why bother?

The answer is that plants are not as defenseless as they look: Many contain toxins that most mammals cannot digest and are, in effect, biochemical weaponry. For example, the caffeine in coffee and various other plants and the nicotine in tobacco are natural insecticides that upset the metabolism of most mammals. People use modest amounts of sage in cooking because they like the aromatic essential oils, but in nature, these oils poison the vital gut bacteria of grazers.

Literally thousands of these defensive plant compounds exist. Herbivores deal with them to some extent by grazing selectively, but their bodies have also had to evolve sophisticated enzymes to break down and excrete toxins. Caribou and squirrels, for example, can eat the *Amanita* mushroom that will poison a human being, but they pay a high physiological price to manufacture the enzymes that allow them to do it.

Meat acts as a filter, so carnivores do not need to produce costly protective enzymes. They eat meat that is free of poison, and because it is almost identical to their own body in composition, it is easy for them to digest and convert into useful compounds.

The nutrient content of plants is low, and most of their energy is bound up in hard-to-digest cellulose and lignin molecules. Herbivores must enlist the services of bacteria to break down much of the woody material of plants, and they typically have huge stomach sacs where these processes are carried out. The carnivore's stomach and gut are small and compact by comparison.

The lack of mineral salts in vegetation is another problem that confronts herbivores, and they have to search long and hard for plants with a high salt content. That is why flocks of wild sheep and herds of cattle are often seen congregating at rare salt licks. Carnivores are much more fortunate in being able to get trace elements of minerals directly from meat.

Meat may be relatively scarce and hard to catch, but many species have found that the pursuit pays off.

MOUNTAIN LION *Puma concolor*

While the mountain lion is also known as cougar, puma and panther, it is most commonly called the mountain lion, an undeserved name and one that reflects only the very recent and greatly reduced range of this great cat. The mountain lion, still found in remote mountainous terrain from Tierra del Fuego to the Yukon, used to range from east to west in North America, in every kind of habitat, wherever deer and elk were found. The eastern populations have long since been hunted and poisoned out of existence, and only a few small, isolated populations in Florida and the prairies testify to the cougar's onetime range.

Only a careful, deliberate reintroduction would establish mountain lion populations in the east, but no public outcry to encourage this has so far been heard, and the government has taken no action. Perhaps an element of fear is a part of the reluctance to promote this feline, for mountain lions grow to a great size. The heaviest on record is the 220-pound cat shot by Teddy Roosevelt, but it is believed that many individuals grow much larger.

Although mountain lions are shy, secretive animals, they can be very dangerous to humankind. Starving cats have been known to maul people, and they will often prey on livestock within their range. Ordinarily, however, they tend to prey on deer—and here, they come into direct competition with humans. The deer-hunting lobby strongly resists programs that could result in fewer deer for them to shoot or less space for them to shoot in. The puma's needs are great: A single cat requires a range of 40 to 200 square miles, so a huge hunting reserve would have to be set aside if a viable, self-sustaining population of mountain lions were to be reintroduced in the east. Public education would be basic to the success of such a program.

Western populations are still subject to hunting pressure, although every state and province regulates it in some way. However, the biggest threat to the mountain lion comes not from the hunter's gun but from the habitat destruction that follows in the wake of

The specialized hunting techniques of the mountain lion enable it to bring down deer and other big game, resulting in direct competition with human sport hunters.

The act of copulation for cougars lasts less than a minute, but male and female may mate many times over.

agriculture, forestry, mining and virtually any other form of human development.

The mountain lion's diet, principally deer, elk and moose, is very selective, and it can survive only in areas that support these large herbivores. The puma will turn to porcupines, beaver and other small mammals, however, when big game is scarce. In fact, the porcupine is a fairly common prey of the mountain lion. It probably flips the porcupine with its paw, stunning it, and then bites into the unprotected underside. It cannot be an easy skill to learn, and young pumas are known to have died from quill wounds.

The home range of the mountain lion shifts with the season and the availability of food. In summer, its range is larger and tends to expand as the elk and deer migrate to higher summer grazing lands. In winter, its range contracts as the deer move down into sheltered valleys. Males have larger ranges that tend to overlap those of several females.

The larger size of the male and its greater range are tied to polygynous breeding biology, since males will fight each other for breeding rights. Like all cats, resident breeding males mark their territories. The mountain lion does this with urine and excrement and by scraping the soil where debris is piled and marking it with scent from a gland in the foot pad. Males also rake the trees vigorously with their forepaws, just as the domestic cat does.

Female mountain lions do not come into heat at a particular time, and estrus appears to be controlled by the abundance of food. This means that the males, if they are to mate, must be consistently vigilant. In cats, ovulation is induced by copulation, and the first male that copulates with a female is the father of her offspring. Although copulation lasts less than a minute, it may take place many times during the period of female estrus.

The female bears her kittens in a simple den, perhaps in a rocky cave or under a fallen tree in the dense brush. The one to six kittens are weaned at 4 to 5 weeks of age, but they may stay with their mother for as long as two years—the length of time necessary for them to learn the complicated hunting techniques they will need for survival. They have to learn how to deliver a fast, efficient killing bite while they avoid being kicked, gored or dragged and smacked into tree limbs by their fleeing prey. It is not uncommon for mountain lions to be killed by their prey. Young, inexperienced mountain lions and old adults that are too weak to pursue their natural prey will kill livestock. The young animals disperse after two years but do not breed until they are 3 years old.

Females often have to defend their kittens from male mountain lions, particularly when a new male takes over the range of another. If the new resident kills the kittens fathered by the previous male, the female will come into estrus and he can mate with her sooner.

MOUNTAIN LION
Puma concolor

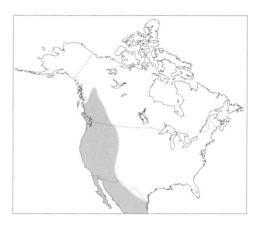

Mammal: *Puma concolor*, mountain lion, puma, cougar, panther
Meaning of Name: *Puma* (puma); *concolor* (of the same color)
Description: distinctive long tail; adult color varies from tawny red to tawny gray to chocolate-brown; darker on the mid-dorsal line; belly is pale buff; chest and throat are white; backs of ears, tip of tail and stripes on muzzle are black; pink nose pad is bordered by black, which extends to the lips; a vertical black stripe over each eye disappears with age
Total Length: male 5.5 to 9 feet; female, 5 to 5.7 feet
Tail: male, 26 to 35.4 inches; female, 20.9 to 32.3 inches
Weight: male, 147.7 to 227.1 pounds; female, 79.4 to 132.3 pounds
Gestation: 90 to 96 days
Offspring: 1 to 6 (usually 3 or 4)
Age of Maturity: male, 3 years; female, 2 to 3 years (does not breed successfully until situated in a home area)
Longevity: 8 years or more in the wild; 19 years in captivity
Diet: carnivore; deer is most consistently important food; eats other large cervids and bovids, porcupine, beaver, snowshoe hare, mice, squirrels, muskrat and raccoon; occasionally preys on domestic stock and even eats fish and snails
Habitat: highly adaptive; a variety of habitats from swamps and wooded river valleys and lowlands to dense coniferous forests and high mountains; requires some woody cover and abundant prey animals, especially cervids
Predators: man is major predator; young may be attacked by larger carnivores, eagles and large hawks; males will eat kittens
Dental Formula:
3/3, 1/1, 3/2, 1/1 = 30 teeth

The wide, furry paws of the lynx act like snowshoes, making it an efficient predator in deep snow. Although its preferred prey is the snowshoe hare, it can kill animals as large as deer.

LYNX *Lynx canadensis*

The lynx has adapted very precisely to a particular environment: namely, the boreal forest. More accurately, it has adapted to the snowshoe hare that lives there. The lynx is an active, mobile predator that hunts most successfully throughout the long, dark winters of the north. Indeed, studies show that its hunting efficiency actually increases in winter. This it owes to a number of very special adaptations.

The lynx has wide, furry paws that act like snowshoes to distribute its weight over the snow and long legs to carry it unimpeded through the deep white powder. The fine, thick fur of its coat has a soft gray-brown color that blends into the gloomy forest shades. Sounds are muffled in the snow-choked forests, and it is thought that the lynx's long ear tufts amplify sound. The tail is short so that it does not drag in the snow.

Although the lynx can kill animals as large as deer and will also eat smaller mammals and birds, it prefers to prey on the snowshoe hare whenever it is available. In fact, the lynx's prosperity is so intimately linked with the snowshoe hare's that they share 10-year cycles of boom and bust. The increase in the number of hares is closely followed by an increase in the number of lynx; then, as the hares deplete their food resources and their populations begin to dwindle, the lynx also decline.

At the low point of the hare's population cycle, the number of lynx pregnancies drops and the survival rate of kittens plummets, a pattern that is as old as the lynx itself and not inherently dangerous to either species. At least that was true until humans entered the picture. Now, trapping and loss of habitat mean that high mortality rates among lynx during the low part of the cycle may prevent them from rebounding during the subsequent abundance of hares. Thus lynx populations are newly vulnerable and have declined in the last century, each 10-year peak being lower than the one before.

Fur-trading records of the Hudson's Bay Company dating back some 200 years show that in peak years, lynx were once 70 times as abundant as in low years; now, the rebound brings them to a level only six times higher than the low point. Wildlife biologists are now seeking a trapping moratorium during the low part of the lynx cycle, but high fur prices at times of low abundance provide a strong economic argument to the contrary, so the lynx, like many spotted cats of the tropics, is threatened by the luxury-fur trade.

Another problem confronting the lynx is loss of habitat through human settlement and the clearing of forests. The lynx, if it is to find enough food to sustain itself, must have a large home range. In fact, recent studies of the lynx in Manitoba have established that one animal ranges through 60 to 85 square miles. Researchers were forced to conclude that even Riding Mountain National Park in southern Manitoba—all 1,136 square miles of it—was "not large enough to sustain a viable lynx population over time."

Some lynx move considerable distances—one, for example, moved 300 miles before being trapped. Although it is possible that some will migrate from overcrowded areas to places where there is more room and better food, they will not cross large areas of cleared land, so it would be difficult for them to recolonize many of the areas where they have been eliminated.

Lynx are shy, solitary animals. Except for females with kittens, they do not hunt together. They breed once a year, in spring, and the female produces a litter of one to five kittens, which she raises without assistance from the male. The den site is primitive, often a simple crevice hidden in the brush or in a hollow log. The kittens stay with the mother until she is ready to mate again the following year. The young may also breed that year, especially if snowshoe hares are abundant.

The social relationships of lynx are not clear. Some researchers report that males exclude other males from their territory but tolerate females; other scientists report the opposite pattern. It may be that the territoriality of the lynx varies with the abundance of prey and that several home ranges overlap in times of plenty.

The lynx has few natural enemies, although wolves may kill a lynx if they catch it in the open and a wolverine may be able to drive it away from a kill. Some lynx have even been injured by deer that succeed in lacerating them with sharp hooves.

Lynx kittens depend on their mother to teach them hunting techniques that will ensure their success in the wild once they leave her, about a year after their birth.

LYNX *Lynx canadensis*

Mammal: *Lynx canadensis*, lynx
Meaning of Name: *Lynx* (lamp, to see) refers to the animal's bright eyes and keen sight; *canadensis* (of Canada)
Description: prominent ruff around face; pointed ears are tipped with long pencils of black hairs, and ear tufts are more prominent than the bobcat's; coloring can be fawn, yellow-orange or blue; guard hairs give the coat a frosted appearance; underparts are buffy; short tail with black tip; black stripes on forehead and around facial ruff that resembles a double-pointed beard at throat; large feet have dense growth of coarse hairs in winter
Total Length: male, 2.5 to 3.5 feet; female, 2.5 to 3.2 feet
Tail: male, 2 to 5.5 inches; female, 3 to 4.8 inches
Weight: male, 14.8 to 37.9 pounds; female, 11.2 to 25. 6 pounds
Gestation: 60 to 65 days
Offspring: 1 to 5 (usually 2 or 3)
Age of Maturity: male, 33 months; female, 21 months
Longevity: up to 24 years in captivity
Diet: rabbits and hares form major part of diet, especially snowshoe hare; also rodents, birds, fish, deer and other ungulates; carrion is an important winter food
Habitat: primarily dense climax forests with heavy undergrowth; may range into mountains, rocky areas, tundra and the edge of the Arctic prairie
Predators: coyote, wolf and man; large owls and eagles will prey on kittens
Dental Formula:
3/3, 1/1, 2/2, 1/1 = 28 teeth

A bobcat kitten, left, is curious about almost everything. A somewhat older member of the clan, above, enjoys a catnap in the shade of a cliff in the American Southwest.

BOBCAT *Lynx rufus*

The bobcat is the slightly smaller southern counterpart of the lynx. The long legs, very wide feet and long ear tufts that make the lynx such an admirable winter hunter are lacking in the bobcat, as it adapted to a less snowy habitat. Its fur has a distinctively mottled pattern that provides camouflage in the brushy scrubland where it is commonly found.

Lynx and bobcats do not share the same territory. Where bobcats have been introduced into the range of the lynx—as on Cape Breton Island—they have tended to segregate, bobcats gravitating to low coastal areas, where winter snow is light, and lynx moving up into the snowy highlands.

What snowshoe hare is to lynx, cottontail rabbit is to bobcat—that is, the most important element of its diet and the basis of its prosperity. However, the bobcat is much less specialized than the lynx, in terms of both food and habitat. Bobcats are found everywhere from the dry deserts of the southwestern United States to well into the cold boreal forests, wet bogs and mountain meadows of the north, although they do not thrive in deep snow. Their only requirement is woody cover. They prefer rough terrain with rocky caves and ledges for their dens, but where these are lacking, they are flexible enough to set up housekeeping in protective clumps of brush.

Bobcats eat mostly rabbits and hares, but they supplement their diet with large numbers of birds and small mammals, and occasionally, they prey on young white-tailed deer and pronghorn antelope. Rabbits are commonly ambushed by bobcats as they pass along well-traveled game runs, while deer are usually attacked when they have bedded down. There are records, however, of the bobcat leaping down on its prey from tree limbs. It is the flexibility of the bobcat, in terms of both food and habitat, that has allowed it to increase its range at a time when most other cat populations are declining.

The social behavior of the bobcat is similar to that of the lynx, especially when it comes to territoriality. There is one record of a female bobcat killing and eating a juvenile, apparently a trespasser on her home range.

The breeding behavior of bobcats tends to follow the same pattern as that of other solitary cats. Males are polygynous, offering no parental care, and they drive other males away from the estrous female. Sometimes several males will contest for one female, and many bobcats wear battle scars from the breeding season.

Mammal: *Lynx rufus*, bobcat
Meaning of Name: *Lynx* (lamp, to see) refers to the animal's bright eyes and keen sight; *rufus* (reddish) refers to the general coloration of the body
Description: shorter legs and smaller feet than lynx; coat is tawny brown above with numerous black spots, especially along the midline from the head to the base of the tail; tip of the tail is blackish above and white below, with subterminal black bars; underparts are white with black spots; tawny limbs have black horizontal bars; a prominent streaked ruff on each cheek extends down the side to below the lower jaw; short blackish ear tufts
Total Length: male, 2.5 to 4.1 feet; female, 2.5 to 3.1 feet
Tail: male, 5.2 to 6.7 inches; female, 5 to 6.5 inches
Weight: male, 14.1 to 40.3 pounds; female, 9 to 33.7 pounds
Gestation: 50 to 70 days
Offspring: 2 to 5 (usually 3); in southern part of range, 2 litters per year
Age of Maturity: female, 1 year, but does not mate until second year
Longevity: 12 to 14 years in the wild; maximum 32 years, 4 months in captivity
Diet: primarily a small-game predator (rabbits, rodents and birds); larger prey such as deer are occasionally taken; also reptiles, insects and snails; will eat untainted carrion
Habitat: hardwood forests, mountainous areas, semideserts, brushland, rocky hillsides and swamps; occupies agricultural lands and the outskirts of cities; only requirement is woody cover
Predators: puma, coyote, wolf and man
Dental Formula:
3/3, 1/1, 2/2, 1/1 = 28 teeth

WHALES, DOLPHINS & PORPOISES *Cetacea*

Whales' ancestors once plodded around on land. They had fur, legs and, presumably, all the features of land mammals. The ancestral whale probably came from the same stock that gave rise to ungulate mammals such as deer, cow, hippopotamus and elephant. It may have been a resident of marshy areas. One scenario for the evolution of whales begins 60 million years ago in an area now filled by the Mediterranean and Arabian seas. The large semiaquatic reptiles such as the plesiosaurs and ichthyosaurs were dying out, and the habitats they occupied—marshes, shallow-water estuaries and swamps—became available to ancestral whales.

The first recognizable cetaceans, the Archaeoceti, or archaic whales, appeared 50 million years ago. They were highly elongated, with long snouts and tiny hind legs, adaptive trends that modern whales continued to develop. This ancient group of whales became extinct some seven million years ago. Two other suborders of cetaceans came to dominate: the Odontoceti, the toothed whales, and the Mysticeti, the baleen (or whalebone) whales. These whales continued the trends of body streamlining—heads elongating, nostrils becoming blowholes and hind limbs disappearing. In the 60 million years since whales' ancestors entered the sea, they have lost all but the smallest traces of the features typical of terrestrial mammals. And in their redesign, we see some of the most complete and elegant examples of adaptation to a life in water.

Water is an unforgiving element and demands great modification of the basic mammalian body plan. It is viscous, hundreds of times denser than air. To move through water is costly for all but the smooth and streamlined. Water has a tremendous capacity to absorb calories, and warm-blooded animals must deal with the perpetual and high energy drain imposed by cold oceans.

Some of the redesign that has taken place in whales is obvious from a glance at any photograph or accurate drawing. Hind limbs have been lost, except in rare individuals that have a few protruding bones. The forelimbs have been reduced, and their skin and muscle have become flippers used for steering. Only a few bristles of hair remain, and the skin has lost its sweat glands. Whales' eyes have been reduced in size and fixed in position. The ear opening is just big enough to admit a matchstick. Larger whales swim with such power that water resistance could snap flexible neck vertebrae. Although small cetaceans such as dolphins have retained unfused neck vertebrae and some flexibility of the neck and head, most whales' neck bones are fused. No neck or shoulder structure is obvious. Instead, the body is molded into a smooth, streamlined fusiform shape. The skull has been "telescoped," the jawbones drawn far out in front of the nostrils. The position of the blowholes at the top of the head enables the whales to breathe while swimming largely submerged. Genital organs have been moved inside a slit along the body and are exposed only during mating. The breasts have evolved a special set of muscles that pump the milk outward, which means that a large external nipple is unnecessary for feeding. All of these are

Only its dark eyes betray a hint of color on the otherwise all-white beluga, or white whale. Even its mouth and tongue are white. The beluga is sometimes able to elude the predatory orca by pausing motionless and camouflaged among broken chunks of Arctic ice.

The bowhead whale's huge head, for which it is named, makes up one-third of its body length, and its jaws accommodate baleen plates that can be 14 feet long.

adaptations for movement through water.

Less obvious but just as critical to life in an aquatic environment are some of the changes in the whales' physiological and sensory capabilities. So that whales can spend great stretches of time submerged between breaths (some species can stay down for more than an hour), their muscles contain huge amounts of myoglobin, a protein similar to hemo-globin that absorbs oxygen. Whale muscle can absorb twice as much oxygen as terrestrial-mammal muscle. Whale blood contains twice as many red blood cells as that of terrestrial mammals, increasing the whale's ability to transport oxygen through its body. Whales can go longer without exhaling than land mammals because of their high tolerance for carbon dioxide and

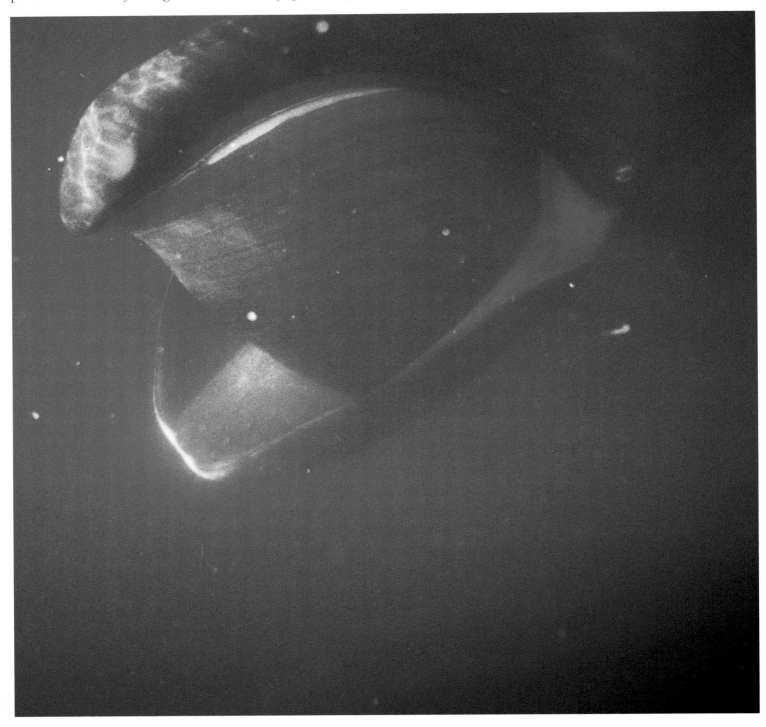

lactic acid in the blood, waste products that they must eventually dispose of through exhalation. When a land mammal breathes, it uses only 4 percent of the oxygen in the air. Because of the greater efficiency of a whale's lungs and blood, it uses 12 percent.

Anyone who has felt the eardrum-piercing pain of even a shallow dive in a backyard pool knows that water exerts a great pressure. At a depth of 33 feet, a body is subjected to twice the pressure it is on the surface, yet some whales—sperm whales, for example—can dive as deep as 9,000 feet and experience 300 times the surface pressure with no ill effects. When humans go scuba diving, they breathe compressed air, which keeps the lungs inflated in spite of the crushing pressure of the water. The disadvantage of this system is that it can cause caisson disease, or the bends. Under pressure, the nitrogen gas that makes up about three-quarters of the air dissolves and enters the blood and tissues. If the pressure is suddenly released during a fast ascent, the nitrogen comes boiling out like soda from a bottle that has been shaken and opened. It can seriously damage the tissues and organs of the body.

To prevent this, whales have a single collapsible lung that compresses, forcing the air up into the nasal passages and windpipe. There, thick linings prevent the transfer of nitrogen into the blood and tissues. For whales, large, permeable lungs would be a liability, not an asset, which explains the observation that the deepest-diving whales actually have small lungs compared with those of shallow-water whales.

Another major adaptation to the water is the development of sonar, or echolocation. The toothed whales emit sounds and listen to the echoes that return, which enables them to navigate and locate objects in the murkiest of water. In fact, one species of river dolphin is entirely blind. Harbor porpoises can use echolocation to detect a wire as thin as 0.02 inch. Dolphins can spot a sphere the size of a large marble 10 feet

away, a baseball at 20 to 30 feet and a school of mackerel at 100 to 350 yards.

Researchers still disagree about which actual structure whales use to perceive sounds. Some cetaceans have a strange oil-filled sinus (called a melon) in the forehead. The melon could act as a kind of acoustic lens to focus sound waves, in much the same way as the lens of the human eye focuses light. Other researchers argue that the melon is actually a hydrodynamic and orientation device that enables the animal to assess depth and direction. The same function is thought to be served by the huge sinus cavities and sinus hairs of whalebone whales. There is also disagreement about how whales generate the sounds they make. Cetaceans lack true vocal cords and use other structures such as the blowholes, air sacs and larynx for sound production. Their sounds may vary from high-frequency clicks to low rumbles. These have different transmission and reflection properties; the high-frequency sounds are used for object location and lower-frequency sounds are used for orientation.

All whales have a limited sense of smell; they have a reduced olfactory lobe in the brain and no olfactory surface. Thus there is probably no chemical communication among cetaceans. They have taste buds, however, and can taste what they eat.

Although the small eyes of cetaceans are of little use underwater, there is evidence that they are useful above water. They may act like pinhole cameras. In bright light, the pupil shuts down to a tiny slit, which would give a very sharp image of distant objects and may enable whales to recognize landmarks such as coastlines. Dolphins may scan the horizon looking for flocks of feeding seabirds as a clue to the whereabouts of schools of fish. Migratory whales, in particular, may use their eyes to plot direction from the positions of the sun and moon. Many whales take advantage of their ability to see great distances above water by raising their heads out of the water and looking

around, a behavior called spy hopping.

The adaptations to aquatic life among the various whales, dolphins and porpoises are diverse. The skull, for example, varies substantially from one family to another and reflects the degree of divergence from the skull design of the ancestors of whales.

The two living suborders of whales are easily distinguished by their feeding apparatus and blowholes. The baleen whales have two external blowholes but no teeth. The toothed whales have one blowhole and peglike teeth. There are now 11 species of baleen whales in four families and about 66 species of toothed whales in six families.

Baleen is a series of plates that grow in the mouth. They are not teeth. Made of a protein somewhat like that in human fingernails, the baleen has a smooth outer surface and an inner surface that is rough and coated with bristly, hairlike structures. The plates are arranged like the teeth of a comb, one row running along each side of the mouth. The bristles on the inside of the comb turn in toward those from the opposite side, making a sievelike structure that filters fine particles of food.

Baleen whales filter-feed on a variety of organisms ranging from plankton no bigger than a grain of sand to shrimplike krill and medium-sized fish. They use the baleen in a variety of ways. Some whales swim, letting water flow past the bristles and plates, which strain continuously; others gulp a huge load of water containing prey, then force the water out through the plates; still others suck up a mixture of food and water. Baleen whales do not seem to use echolocation to find food, which is appropriate since their food is often a cloudy soup of tiny zooplankton. By feeding low on the food chain, baleen whales have access to the huge food resources of the open ocean, an ecological niche that has enabled them to become the largest creatures on Earth.

The toothed whales are generally smaller and use echolocation to hunt prey such as fish and squid.

GRAY WHALE *Eschrichtiidae*

GRAY WHALE *Eschrichtius robustus*

With no fossil record and only one living species, Eschrichtiidae is distinct from all other baleen whale families. The gray whale has only two to four throat grooves, and its baleen plates are the shortest of all baleen whales, only a foot long, while some other species have plates as long as 12 feet. Grays have more hair than other whales and rows of bristles around their lips. These differences are probably adaptations for bottom feeding. Gray whales are also the only baleen whales with distinctly gray mottled skin and no dorsal fins.

Unlike other baleen whales, the gray feeds on the bottom of the ocean and has poorly developed throat grooves. These are expandable pleats that, in other species, make it possible to swallow and sieve a huge mass of plankton or fish. The gray has a different feeding strategy. It dives to the bottom, rolls sideways and plows its head through the mud, sucking up sediment. The mass of mud and bottom-dwelling animals is then filtered through its short baleen plates. Feeding whales often surface with muck and water streaming out of their mouths and are attended by seabirds that pick out scraps the whales have missed or rejected. The gouges the whales leave in the mud are selectively depleted of small amphipod crustaceans; it is thought that their foraging has an important role in regulating the bottom-dwelling invertebrate communities of the shallow northern seas. The huge population of barnacles and whale lice carried by the gray whale is responsible for its unique mottled pattern.

Gray whales hug the West Coast, which brings them within easy range of whale watchers and researchers, and as a result of their proximity, they are well understood. Grays are best known for their long migration, said to be the longest journey of any mammal. Some may travel from the high Arctic seas to tropical Mexican lagoons, an annual circuit of 12,500 miles.

A conflict between their feeding and calving needs prompts grays to migrate. Cold Arctic waters, particularly in the Bering and Chuckchi seas, are highly productive in summer and ideal for feeding, but they are poor for calving. Relatively small when born, young gray whales lack the insulating blubber necessary to withstand constant submersion in Arctic seas. Tropical waters produce less food, but they are mild and do not stress the young calves.

Grays migrate south in pods, segregated according to sex and size. Late-term pregnant females start south in the autumn, adult males follow later, and immature animals leave last. Pods of up to 16 whales move along at top speeds of 4 to 5 miles per hour and cover roughly 60 miles in a day. The whales seem to travel 24 hours a day and apparently do not sleep during the entire journey, which takes from 2½ to 3 months. Gray whales winter for two or three months in shallow lagoons off California and Mexico. The lagoons are so shallow that the whales are occasionally stranded at low tide, but they remain calm and simply wait for high tide to float them again.

Females give birth from January through March in warm, sheltered lagoons and stay segregated from the males. Females with calves leave the

A conservation success story, the gray whale has virtually recovered its prewhaling population in North America. Juvenile grays have been known to exhibit "friendly" behavior to whale watchers, appearing alongside boats to be scratched and petted.

GRAY WHALE
Eschrichtius robustus

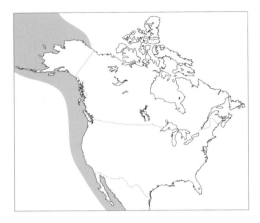

Mammal: *Eschrichtius robustus,* gray whale
Meaning of Name: *Eschrichtius* (named after D.F. Eschricht, a Dutch zoologist); *robustus* (oaken or strong)
Description: fusiform body that looks tapered at both ends when viewed from above; relatively small, triangular-shaped head slopes down at a sharp angle from a pair of blowholes; large mouth curves slightly upward; in place of the dorsal fin, there is a low hump beginning two-thirds of the distance along the back, followed by a serrated ridge; irregular rows of hair on upper and lower jaws, especially on lips; 138 to 174 yellow baleen plates on each side of mouth
Color: mottled gray; heavily flecked with white scars caused by whale lice and barnacles embedded in the hide
Total Length: male, 40 to 50 feet; female, 46 to 50 feet
Weight: 44,000 to 81,400 pounds
Gestation: 11 to 13 months
Offspring: 1
Age of Maturity: 5 to 11 years (average 8 years)
Longevity: 70 years
Diet: mainly benthic organisms (amphipods are a staple of the diet), crustaceans, mollusks, worms and small fish
Habitat: coastal temperate waters along shallow continental shelves and closer to shore than any other large cetacean
Predators: killer whale and large sharks
Dental Formula: 0

southern waters in the spring, somewhat later than the males. The mothers and young whales also travel more slowly than males. Mothers defend calves strongly and continue to nurse until the calves are as old as 9 months.

Courtship takes place in the winter lagoons, and because roughly half the females are pregnant or lactating, there are several males for every receptive female. Although females have been seen rolling and splashing in the company of three or four males, male-male combat is not overt.

Migrating grays are thought to feed little, but this is uncertain. They do, however, remain close to the coast, which once made them vulnerable to all manner of coast-based fisheries. However, it was only when 19th-century whalers began killing pregnant and nursing females in their calving lagoons that the population began to crash. Gray whales were hunted almost to extinction along the west coast of North America and are currently on the verge of extinction in Korean waters. They once existed along the coast of Europe but became extinct, presumably because of overhunting by Basque whalers. Fortunately, in North America, they are now thought to be approaching their previous population densities.

Some conservation measures have worked successfully for the gray, and in turn, it has proved a good ambassador, entertaining thousands of whale watchers and thus increasing public awareness of and concern for the problems confronting other whales. Gray whales are even reported to exhibit "friendly" behavior to whale watchers, some individuals appearing regularly alongside boats to be scratched and petted. The gray whales' amicability may be because they are itchy from their heavy infestations of barnacles and whale lice, but it may mean something more.

Found close to shore along the West Coast during the summer months, gray whales migrate up to 12,500 miles each autumn to calve in shallow Mexican waters.

RORQUALS *Balaenopteridae*

The Balaenopteridae family contains six species distributed throughout the oceans. Rorquals are streamlined compared with right whales. They also have distinctive ribbed skin folds along their throats. They have a bowed jawline and feed using baleen sieving, but prey size varies among the different species. The skin folds act as expanding pleats, allowing the whales to gulp massive loads of seawater, krill and fish. They then force the seawater out, straining the food with their baleen. All species except the tropical Bryde's whales follow a north-south migration, giving birth in warm areas and moving to the high latitudes to feed during summer. These are large, long-lived whales; some species live 100 years. They tend to have long pregnancies of about a year and nurse their calves for six to seven months. Many rorquals have yet to recover from near extinction caused by whaling, and they remain threatened.

MIGRATION

Researchers have found surprising parallels between the migrations of the giant whales and those of birds. Whales and birds might seem as different from each other as any two animal groups could be, but they do have important energetic similarities that make long-distance migration economically attractive.

Long-distance migrants, be they whales, birds, bats or fish, normally store food before migration and feed relatively little en route. Whales can travel huge distances because they store and move cheaply a massive amount of energy-rich fat. Birds can migrate so far because the most efficient flying velocity is very fast. A bird burns energy at a high rate, but it also covers distance at a high speed. A 2-ounce bird can carry enough fat to fly 600 miles without feeding. A larger bird with a higher optimum flight speed and a lower transport cost can fly even farther. Whales must travel at slower speeds, since the most efficient swimming velocity is much lower than that of flying. However, whales burn their fuel at a very slow rate. So a whale can migrate as far as a bird simply by accumulating a huge store of fat and taking longer.

Birds and whales seem to migrate for the same reasons. Winter mortality rates are lower in warmer areas, and so is the cost of maintaining body temperature. Food, however, is less plentiful. Migratory birds rear their young in the Arctic because of the tremendous explosion of insect and other food sources in the summer months, and 24 hours of daylight allow foraging to continue for much longer periods than in the tropics. For whales, extensive sunlight and the upwelling of nutrients in the cold oceans cause massive blooms of planktonic plants that in turn produce population explosions in the animals and fish that feed on the plants. Plankton densities in the Arctic summer may exceed those in the tropical wintering grounds by a hundred times. Migratory whales generally calve in the warmer wintering grounds, but calving is not the time of the highest energy costs for the female. Breast-feeding is usually more costly than pregnancy, and the young calves continue to breast-feed and grow at great rates in the Arctic summers.

The expandable throat pleats of rorquals such as this humpback allow the whale to gulp in massive amounts of water containing krill and fish that it then strains out for food.

Climatic history has played a key role in whale migration. Whales probably evolved in warm-water regions when much of the world had a similar climate. As the Earth became more polarized, with greater temperature extremes, and the continents continued to drift apart, whales began to move and breed seasonally, extending their range until journeys such as the 12,500-mile migrations of the gray whale had evolved.

The cues that whales use to migrate are even less well understood than those used by migratory birds. It is thought that whale migration is stimulated by changes in day length that cause hormonal changes. Some observers believe that gray whales follow bottom topography along the coast. Radio-tracking studies of dolphins off the coast of California indicate that they also follow undersea floor features. When gray whales encounter an unfamiliar region such as a deep canyon on the ocean floor, they may "spy hop," that is, raise their heads entirely out of the water vertically and look around, possibly for landmarks. How deep-water whales such as blue and sei find their way is not known. Like birds, they may use the sun and the stars to plot directions. In any case, it is likely that young whales depend on following older whales to learn migration routes. By selectively taking the largest, oldest and most knowledgeable whales, human whalers have probably depleted a valuable information pool. The loss of information about where and when to travel may be one reason why some of the migratory whales have been so slow to recover.

ON BEING BIG

A single blue whale is as massive and burns as much energy as the entire human population of a 2,000-resident North American town. A mature blue whale is longer than three railroad boxcars, weighs between 150 and 200 tons (as much as 40 bull elephants) and can eat 4 tons of food and burn 1.5 million calories a day. The blue whale is the largest, longest and heaviest animal that has ever lived on Earth. Its large size is made possible by the freedom and buoyancy provided by seawater.

For land animals, gravity makes large size a liability and a constraint. The cost of falling, for example, goes up sharply as the weight of an animal increases. The great evolutionary biologist J.B.S. Haldane expressed it graphically: "You can drop a mouse down a 1,000-yard mine shaft, and on arriving at the bottom, it gets a slight shock and walks away, provided that the ground is fairly soft. A rat is killed, a man is broken, a horse splashes."

The laws of physics dictate that large, heavy animals hit the ground with a greater speed and force than small animals. Because small animals have a large surface area relative to volume and weight, the forces of friction and turbulence in the air when they fall come close to canceling out the force of gravity.

Larger animals have other problems associated with their relatively small surface area. They may have trouble radiating enough of the heat that their body chemistry generates. By living in cold ocean waters, whales can dissipate large amounts of heat because of water's efficiency as a conductor and heat absorber. And by floating in seawater, which provides support against gravity, whales can become long and thin and have relatively delicate bones. Only creatures as small as worms and snakes, whose bodies usually rest on the ground, can be long and skinny on land. For larger animals, the strain of gravity is too great.

Mammal: *Balaenoptera acutorostrata*, minke whale; smallest baleen whale in North America

Meaning of Name: *Balaenoptera* (whale with a strong dorsal fin); *acutorostrata* (sharp or pointed beak) refers to the fact that this whale has a more pointed snout than other whales

Description: streamlined body tapering posteriorly; medially ridged and pointed rostrum and small mouth; 40 to 70 throat pleats terminate halfway between the tip of the flippers and the navel; tall, falcate dorsal fin; 270 to 348 yellowish white baleen plates

Color: dark gray to black with white underparts from the lower lip to flukes; a major diagnostic feature is a diagonal white band on the upper surface of the pectoral flippers

Total Length: 20 to 30 feet (maximum 35 feet)

Weight: maximum 22,000 pounds

Gestation: 10 to 11 months

Offspring: 1 every 1 or 2 years

Age of Maturity: 7 to 8 years

Longevity: 50 years

Diet: small fish, some squid, krill and copepods

Habitat: open polar and temperate seas over the continental shelf; seldom found farther than 100 miles from land; often enters bays and estuaries; moves farther into polar ice fields than any other rorquals

Predators: killer whale

Dental Formula: 0

The minke whale is the smallest of all rorquals and North America's smallest baleen whale, and until recently, it was ignored by commercial whalers. Typically a shallow diver that stays down for only a few minutes, the minke will go deeper for krill or fish when necessary.

MINKE WHALE
Balaenoptera acutorostrata

Measuring 26 feet when full-grown, the minke whale is the smallest rorqual. Smallness made minkes unattractive to whalers when larger whales were available, so relatively little is known about the species. Some populations are highly migratory in the typical baleen whale fashion. Others seem to stay in one area for most of the year. Migrant minkes can travel far into the breaking pack ice and are occasionally trapped there. They are usually solitary or in groups of only a few individuals, except in rich feeding grounds, where several hundred may concentrate to feed. They eat small fish and krill and often engage in lunge-feeding and breaching. Like humpbacks, their pursuit of schools of fish brings them into conflict with fishermen. They are often killed in fish traps and nets and are now the target of commercial whalers. Unlike other rorquals, minkes will approach ships, and they are reported to be relatively acrobatic, breaching and rolling belly-up. They have a distinctive V-shaped head, and in northern regions, they often have a white band running diagonally across their flippers.

SEI WHALE
Balaenoptera borealis

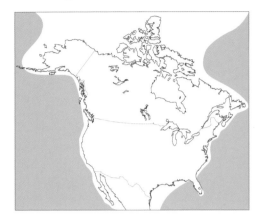

Mammal: *Balaenoptera borealis*, sei whale
Meaning of Name: *Balaenoptera* (whale with a strong dorsal fin); *borealis* (of the north)
Description: heavier body form than the other rorquals; relatively short pectoral flippers; large dorsal fin situated relatively forward; 40 to 62 pinkish throat grooves that extend to only midway between the base of the flippers and the navel
Color: bluish gray dorsally; bands of gray on sides extend from lower jaw backward and meet on the abdomen; belly is grayish white near the ventral grooves; irregular white splotches on throat and chest
Total Length: male, 26 to 60 feet; female, 36 to 57 feet (maximum 69 feet)
Weight: 60,000 pounds
Gestation: 10 to 12 months
Offspring: 1 every 2 or 3 years
Age of Maturity: 6 to 12 years
Longevity: up to 74 years
Diet: small planktonic crustaceans such as copepods (*Calanus* spp) and several species of krill as well as fish
Habitat: pelagic species, primarily temperate open seas far from shore; migrates to subtropical waters for winter
Predators: killer whale and man
Dental Formula: 0

An open-ocean specialist, the swift-swimming sei whale skims the water's surface for food. Its delicate baleen plates are capable of sieving out the tiniest plankton.

SEI WHALE *Balaenoptera borealis*

Sei whales are unpredictable. They migrate, but with an irregular rhythm, so their movements cannot be accurately predicted the way those of gray whales can. The word sei comes from the Norwegian term for the pollack fish that arrive off the coast of Norway at the same time as the whales. It is possible that both pollack and whales feed on the same plankton. When sei whales swim, they veer erratically and travel at speeds of up to 30 miles per hour, faster than any other member of their family. They feed at or near the surface. Seis have the most finely fringed baleen of all whales, with bristles only 0.004 inch in diameter, and are capable of taking tiny planktonic organisms. But true to their unpredictable character, they will also gulp fish. Seis are strictly pelagic and rarely come close to shore to feed.

The seis' broad diet, irregular occurrence and lack of a heavy blubber layer meant that whalers ignored them until the other large rorquals had been decimated. Sei populations were then heavily hunted even though almost nothing was (or is) known about them. Commercial whaling of seis has now ceased, and they seem to be recovering.

In the water, the sei can be distinguished from blue and fin whales by its more forward and erect dorsal fin and by its heavier body form. Its social behavior is still largely unknown, except that it usually tends to travel in small groups of two to five companions.

BLUE WHALE
Balaenoptera musculus

The blue whale is the largest creature ever to live on this planet. Almost every statistic on this animal is remarkable. The calf is almost 23 feet long at birth and weighs 3 tons. It grows at the rate of 8.8 pounds an hour. The largest recorded blue was a 100-foot-long female weighing an estimated 150 tons. Blues are migratory and largely solitary whales, sometimes found in pairs. They feed in shallow areas, gulping as much as 8 tons of krill per day.

The only small number associated with the blue whale is its population. Blue whales were brought to the point of extinction and today number only about 11,000. The destruction of their populations deprived humans of another valuable resource. George Small, who has documented the history of the blue whales' slaughter, writes: "The failure of the International Whaling Commission to protect the blue whale destroyed a large and perpetual source of food. At an optimum population level—about 60,000, according to the population experts hired by the Whaling Commission—the blue whale could have supplied man in perpetuity with a sustainable yield of some 6,000 whales an-

nually. Six thousand blue whales with an average length of 80 feet could produce some 580,000 long tons of raw material. From that, man could produce 105,300 tons of oil, enough to supply 2.5 ounces of margarine or edible oil a day every day for a year to 4,138,000 adult human beings. In addition, 189,000 long tons of meat could be produced, enough for a 6-ounce steak every day for a year for 3,090,000 adult human beings. That food supply has been destroyed."

But the significance of the near extinction of the blue whale is more than shortsighted exploitation. It is a lesson and a warning: When a limited international resource is exploited by nations competing selfishly against others for a larger share, the resource will be squandered. Harvesting of the large baleen whales ceased only after they became so rare that they were of minor economic importance. In every instance, the countries with the largest stake in the industry continued to exploit the resource the longest. Whale populations are on the increase in many cases, but as the world's human population grows and nations are forced into more intense competition for food, we may expect whales to be once again subject to self-serving nationalistic policies.

Weighing up to 150 tons, the blue whale is the largest animal that has ever lived, and it has an appetite to match—a single whale gulps down as much as 8 tons of krill a day.

BLUE WHALE
Balaenoptera musculus

Mammal: *Balaenoptera musculus*, blue whale; the largest living animal
Meaning of Name: *Balaenoptera* (whale with a strong dorsal fin); *musculus* (little mouse) could be a tongue-in-cheek description
Description: torpedo-shaped body with an extremely small dorsal fin; 70 to 118 ventral grooves; scattered rows of short hairs on lips, rostrum and around the nares and a beard at the tip of the lower jaw; 250 to 400 short, coarse baleen plates
Color: bluish gray above, mottled with gray or grayish white oval spots on flanks, back and belly; undersurfaces of flukes and flippers are pale; may be yellowish blotches on throat and navel
Total Length: 70 to 85 feet (maximum 100 feet)
Weight: up to 300,000 pounds
Gestation: 10 to 12 months
Offspring: 1 (rarely twins) every 2 or 3 years
Age of Maturity: approximately 10 years; male, when reaches 74 feet; female, when reaches 79 feet
Longevity: possibly up to 110 years
Diet: krill (planktonic crustaceans), usually of the genus *Euphausia*, is their exclusive food
Habitat: open water of polar and temperate seas; sometimes found in shallow inshore waters; occurs in places where deep water, rich in nutrients, upwells to the surface and nourishes phytoplankton
Predators: occasionally a pod of killer whales
Dental Formula: 0

FIN WHALE
Balaenoptera physalus

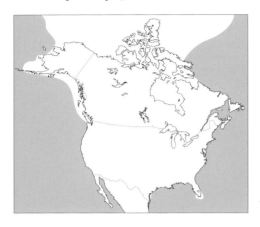

Second in size only to the blue whale and similar in appearance, the fin whale is also a speedy swimmer and has been known to travel as far as 180 miles per day.

Mammal: *Balaenoptera physalus*, fin whale, fin-backed whale

Meaning of Name: *Balaenoptera* (whale with a strong dorsal fin); *physalus* (pipe or wind instrument) refers to the blowhole through which the whale breathes and makes whistling sounds

Description: long, sleek body tapering posteriorly; V-shaped snout with single median dorsal ridge; 60 throat grooves extend from tip of lower jaw to navel; dorsal fin is high and strongly hooked behind; back is distinctly ridged posterior to dorsal fin

Color: slate-blue above and white below; right side of face is paler than left side; right front baleen plates are pale gray, and the rest are alternating yellowish white and blue-gray stripes; the left plate of the baleen is blue-gray behind; there is a grayish white chevron behind the head

Total Length: 60 to 70 feet (maximum 88 feet)

Weight: up to 99,000 pounds

Gestation: 11 to 12 months

Offspring: 1 every 3 years

Age of Maturity: 4 to 12 years

Longevity: some are estimated to have lived up to 114 years

Diet: various kinds of small fish, krill and other pelagic crustaceans and squid

Habitat: pelagic; seldom found in water less than 700 feet deep; occurs in both inshore and offshore waters

Predators: killer whale and man

Dental Formula: 0

FIN WHALE
Balaenoptera physalus

The second-largest of the baleen whales and the most abundant, fin whales are known for their inexplicable head coloration, white on the right side and dark gray on the left. One theory holds that they use the white side to scare and herd fish and the dark side as camouflage. Fin whales eat a variety of plankton as well as fish, which they may locate with low-frequency echolocation. Like many fish eaters, fins are capable of spurts of speeds of up to 20 miles per hour, and they are among the deeper-diving baleen whales, descending to 750 feet. A fin whale tagged with a radio transmitter has been recorded traveling 180 miles in a day. They migrate north to south alone or in groups of two to seven. Little is known about their social behavior.

UNDERCROWDING: THE ALLEE EFFECT

Undercrowding may be as great a threat to survival as overcrowding. The ecologist W.C. Allee demonstrated that some organisms may actually have reduced survival rates if they become too rare. He showed that fish, for example, are less able to survive stress as individuals than as members of a group. Whales are probably particularly vulnerable to the Allee effect. Many species rely on cooperative hunting to gather much of their food; others rely on the learning and experience of older group members to migrate successfully; and whales that exist dispersed over the high seas must expend more time and effort to find a mate when they are rare.

Many populations typically go through phases of population growth: a fast growth rate at intermediate densities; a slow, stable birth-and-death rate at high densities; and a lag phase at low densities when both birth and death rates are low. A species could get stuck in a lag phase, especially if predation is constantly cropping the population. This may be one reason for the slow increase of some of the larger baleen whales even though they are no longer hunted. The bowhead population of Hudson Bay, an immense area of water, has declined to a few hundred. The right whale population is limited to a few hundred in the northern Atlantic and Pacific. This may result in low pregnancy rates or possibly decreased calf survival to the point that the birth rate is canceled out by the death rate.

HUMPBACK WHALE
Megaptera novaeangliae

Humpbacks are known as both singing whales and gentle giants. Only the former description is accurate. Humpbacks do sing one of nature's most complex songs. It is now known that singing is a form of male-male competition. Humpbacks also use more direct forms of combat. Docile around divers and whale watchers, male humpbacks smash and slash each other with their tails, frequently drawing blood.

Observation and interpretation of humpbacks' elaborate songs became possible only through great efforts made to photograph and sex the species. The variegated black-and-white markings, particularly on the tail flukes, can be used to identify each individual humpback. Studies have revealed that singers are males courting females and that fights often occur between lone males and those escorting females.

Like other baleen whales, humpbacks migrate to high-latitude waters in summer for feeding and return to tropical areas in winter to mate and calve. Their preferred habitats are shallow shelf and bank areas, rather than deep ocean, and they are readily seen along both the east and west coasts of North America. They may congregate in groups of several hundred while feeding on dense fish and krill schools. Within these large congregations, several whales may forage cooperatively. On the breeding grounds, usually only two or three individuals occur together, groups that often consist of males escorting females due to come into estrus.

Humpbacks are stout, stocky whales compared with other members of their family. Although slow swimmers, they are by far the most acrobatic rorquals. Their spectacular breaches, "spy hopping" and fluke slapping make them one of the mainstays of the whale-watching industry. Their acrobatic abilities are put to use during feeding. Humpbacks are known to eat larger-sized prey items, inch-long krill and schools of small fish such as capelin, herring, anchovy, sardine and arctic cod. They take the cod by rushing dramatically into schools. One humpback was found with six cormorants in its stom-

Mammal: *Megaptera novaeangliae*, humpback whale

Meaning of Name: *Megaptera* (big fin) refers to the unusually large flippers; *novaeangliae* (of New England)—the first specimen described scientifically was obtained along the Maine coast in New England

Description: the long, scimitar-shaped flippers are unique, as they carry a string of fleshy knobs and indentations on the forward edge; these knobs are randomly distributed on the top of the head and lower jaw; distinctive rounded projection on tip of lower jaw; ventral pleats are spaced relatively far apart and extend from the rim of the lower jaw to the navel; blow is wide and balloon-shaped; 320 to 360 black baleen plates on each side with pale gray bristles

Color: usually black above and white below; forward edges and undersurfaces of flippers and flukes are white

Total Length: male, 36 to 47 feet; female, 38 to 48 feet (maximum 59 feet)

Weight: 66,000 pounds

Gestation: 11 to 13 months

Offspring: 1 every 1 to 3 years

Age of Maturity: 6 to 12 years

Longevity: up to 77 years

Diet: krill and other planktonic crustaceans and small schooling fish

Habitat: usually along the coast, on the continental shelf, along island banks or in bays and estuaries; sometimes found in open seas

Predators: killer whale

Dental Formula: 0

Telltale knobs and bumps on its head, bulging eyes, a tail that is unique to each whale and a stout, stocky body shape are some of the identifying features of the humpback.

ach; the birds were probably engulfed accidentally during a lunge for cod.

The feeding behavior of humpbacks has led to conflict with humans in shallow coastal waters where both fish. Humpbacks often become entangled in nets, to the detriment of both whales and fishermen. Entanglements may be the result of the overfishing of capelin. Large European fleets have fished the Grand Banks capelin heavily for human food as well as for livestock feed and dog food. As the capelin have declined on the Grand Banks, humpbacks may have been forced inshore to feed on shallow-water capelin, and it is here, in the shallows, that the whales run into gill- and seine-net operations.

Humpbacks have several distinctive features besides their stocky body form. Their 16-foot flippers are longer than those of other whales. They also exhibit a series of curious lumps on their upper and lower jaws. These protuberances each contain a coarse hair and probably act as tactile sensory organs with such functions as measuring water currents. Humpbacks also have crusty white and pinkish growths on the face, throat and fins. Called callosities, these blotches can be used to identify individual humpbacks. Callosities are parasitic infestations of barnacles and whale lice. They may be unpleasant for the whales, which could explain why humpbacks enter river mouths to bask in fresh or brackish water. The change in salinity may kill the parasites.

In addition to the whale lice and barnacle encrustations, humpbacks' skin is often marked with oval scoop-shaped scars, possibly the marks of a 2-foot-long shark, *Issistius brasiliensis*, the cookie-cutter shark, which bites neat oval chunks of blubber out of various whales and dolphins.

AQUATIC SONGSTERS

It makes sense to use sound as a means of underwater communication. Light travels only a few hundred yards underwater at best, and chemicals are easily dispersed in the ocean. Sound travels at a high speed in water—five times as fast as in air—and it travels far. The explosion of a depth charge in Australian waters was registered in Bermuda, 12,000 miles away. Whale songs can be detected at least 115 miles away from the singer.

Every cetacean studied produces sounds. Whales and dolphins use the larynx, or voice box, and possibly their lips, blowholes and air sacs in the head to produce chirps, clicks, grunts, barks, squeaks, moans and whistles as well as extremely complicated singing. While the songs of animals such as crickets, frogs and birds are specifically for mating, whales use their songs for a number of purposes. Dolphins, for example, use pure-tone whistles for a variety of messages unrelated to courtship. These whistles can act as signatures, allowing dolphins to recognize one another. They may communicate moods such as excitement, distress or aggression, and they also give information on the location of the individual sending the signal. But singing is usually considered a courtship device used by mammals and birds to advertise their territorial status and to court mates and repel rivals.

In whales such as the humpback, this sort of behavior has evolved into an extremely sophisticated performance, possibly the most complicated serenade in the animal kingdom. The song of the humpback whale is an intricate sequence of sounds that may take over half an hour to sing. It has a beginning and an ending, and the sequence of chirps, bleeps, moans and other strange noises that make up the song follows a definite order repeated in the same manner time after time. The song consists of syllables that are organized into recurring groups, and these groups, known as motifs, are used to produce six basic themes. Each whale sings its own distinctive variation, but at any one time, the whales in a given area sing a song that is recognizably the same. If a whale is interrupted in its singing, it will later pick up the melody where it left off.

Only male humpbacks sing and only on the breeding grounds. Their songs appear to be primarily a courtship device. One possible explanation for their songs' complexity is that they provide useful information to the female and to rivals about the experience and learning ability of the singer. This notion is reinforced by the observation that the songs are not static. Over a period of years, the songs in an area change, sometimes radically. When the whales sing, they do not sing together. Several whales may be singing at the same time, but each individual is singing his own song at his own pace. Since humpbacks are social and live to an old age and since males engage in combat, recognition of individual males by their songs is probably valuable to both the singer and the audience. Poorly matched rivals will avoid fighting each other, losers may avoid whales that have beaten them, victors may advertise their prowess and identity, and females and young males may listen and act accordingly.

FOOD WEBS

Ecologists use the term food web for the interconnections, indirect and direct, that exist among a great diversity of organisms. One of the main tasks of ecology is to determine what organisms are part of a food web and how changes in the abundance of one species will affect other members of the web. Even the simplest of food webs is highly complex. The Arctic has far fewer species than do temperate or tropical regions, and ecologists wrongly assumed that Arctic food webs would be easy to understand. In some ecological systems, it is possible to determine what effect the abundance of one animal has on another, but usually only in hindsight, after the change has taken place.

Baleen whales were a conspicuous part of the oceanic food web, and their destruction, especially in the Antarctic,

Humpback whales are renowned among whale researchers for the complexity of their long courtship songs.

has provided biologists with an unpleasant but interesting large-scale experiment. The presence or absence of a baleen whale obviously affects hundreds of species, ranging from whale lice and barnacles that live on the whale to seabirds and dolphins that join it during feeding to orcas and humans that feed upon the whale. However, the most obvious impact the loss of these whales had was on the population of krill and other plankton. When the whales were devastated, large quantities of krill were left unharvested and were thus available to other predators. Baleen whales in the Antarctic probably harvested 180,000 tons of krill annually, but their decline

meant that only one-sixth as much was being consumed. In the Antarctic, this seems to be having unexpected effects. Fur seals had been virtually destroyed in the Antarctic by the turn of the century—only a tiny remnant stock survived, clinging to existence for several decades. These seals eat krill, and when the whales were destroyed, fur seal populations exploded, doubling every four to five years. There are now close to 1,000,000 Antarctic fur seals.

That might sound like unqualified good news. But the seals' increase has hurt other species. Breeding female seals, for instance, erode the grassy shoreline nesting areas of seabirds such as the albatross. Nest sites are reduced in number, and the lack of grassy cover means that predatory birds such as skuas, which eat nestlings and eggs, are

better able to hunt. Crab-eating seals—which, despite their name, feed heavily on krill—are also experiencing population increases, and so are the leopard seals, which prey on crab eaters. Penguins may be on the rise because some of the fish they prey on eat krill. All of these changes may prevent the recovery of the krill-eating whales.

Who could have predicted that the invention of oil lamps and the Victorian taste for thread-waisted women squeezed by corsets of baleen would have affected the fortunes of the Antarctic albatross in the late 20th century? One of the most basic principles of ecology is illustrated in these transformations: All the world is ultimately joined in one large food web, and altering parts of it will have consequences that are impossible to anticipate.

RIGHT WHALES *Balaenidae*

All four species of right whales reside in temperate and northern waters, but three are absent from tropical and Antarctic regions (southern right whales have been seen in small numbers in Patagonia, the South Pacific and Indian oceans and Antarctic waters). They almost became absent from all regions; their common name, the right whale, was given to them by whalers looking for the best species to harpoon.

The pygmy right whale is found only in southern temperate oceans, the northern right whale is found in the North Atlantic, and the bowhead is a resident of the Arctic. None of these species migrates far. All of them are chunky, heavy whales, and all share certain anatomical features that separate them from other baleen whales. Right whales have no throat grooves. They have a deeply curved jawline, and their baleen plates are long and thin. (Baleen is a horny substance that grows in rows of plates that are attached along the upper jaws of baleen whales and used to filter food from the water.) The baleen of right whales was used to make corsets, umbrellas and anything else that required a flexible, springy rod. A single whale yielded up to a ton of baleen. Right whale baleen plates are adapted for sieving tiny copepods and krill in the surface waters, which is slow, steady work. These whales rarely dive. This and their 2-foot layer of valuable blubber made them the "right" whales to hunt. They are so blubbery, they even float after being harpooned, a further attraction for whalers.

IT'S LONELY AT THE TOP

Every ecosystem is made up of three components: primary producers, usually plants; consumers such as herbivorous animals, which eat the plants; and secondary consumers, which eat the herbivorous animals. Primary producers use the energy in sunlight to build large, complex organic molecules from commonplace raw materials such as carbon dioxide and simple nitrogen compounds. All other levels in a food chain consume either primary producers, other consumers or the organic detritus resulting from the death and decay of primary producers and consumers.

The image of a food chain is used by ecologists to explain the passage of food energy from the sun into plant biomass and then through various types of animal consumers. Each time a given amount of food is eaten, digested and turned into a new form of plant or animal, a large proportion of the

A resident of the Arctic, the bowhead—one of the four species of right whale—makes its living by filter-feeding copepods, krill and amphipods in the Arctic seas. The bowhead's jaw accommodates its 360 baleen plates, which skim out the small planktonic animals as the bowhead swims, mouth open, on the water's surface.

chemical energy stored in the food source is given off as heat. Transformation of one species into another via digestion and molecular synthesis involves breaking and re-forming chemical bonds, which requires energy.

Little of the energy from one trophic level is turned into biomass at a higher level, because much of the energy involved in biomass conversion is lost as heat. Insects may convert as much as 60 percent of their food into making more insects, whereas a warm-blooded predator turns only 3 percent of food energy into duplicating its kind. A ballpark figure for energy conversion is around 10 to 20 percent. In other words, each time biomass passes along the food chain to a higher level, 80 to 90 percent of the energy is lost as waste heat. So 1,000 pounds of phytoplankton will support 100 pounds of plankton-eating fish, which will support only 10 pounds of a fish-eating predator such as a seal. The seal, in turn, will support only 1 pound of a higher-level predator.

This inefficient conversion limits the length of food chains and explains the size and population limits on large predators. Killer whales, for example, are not very abundant, certainly not as abundant as the filter-feeding whales that eat lower in the food chain. A baleen whale eating phytoplankton and krill has hundreds of times more food energy available to it than a killer whale.

Conversion inefficiency also explains why there are no "super" killer whales as large as blue whales. Killer whales are large compared to other dolphins, but they only weigh one-tenth as much as the baleen whales. In addition, a sizable predator must bear the cost of building and maintaining its bulky, warm-blooded body. The bigger the animal gets, the greater the cost, which means there is even less energy available for reproduction. This is why killer whales are rare and why they have not evolved to a larger size. They are already big enough to eat anything that swims in the ocean. Becoming larger would simply increase their maintenance costs.

NORTHERN RIGHT WHALE
Balaena glacialis

Northern right whales are similar in many respects to bowheads. They, too, have large heads with long baleen plates and chunky bodies, and they tend to occur alone or in small groups and swim near the surface, where they skim copepods and krill. But northern right whales differ in many respects from bowheads. Northern rights' baleen is only half as long, they prefer temperate waters, and they have been brought even closer to extinction.

A distinctive feature of right whales is their callosities—warty, rough encrustations in specific spots near the eyes, jaws and other parts of the head, throat and belly. These are infested with whale lice (cyamid amphipod crustaceans), barnacles and worms. The callosities may be pure white or various shades of yellow, orange and pink. Their function is not known. They are not simply a result of parasitism, because evidence of incipient but uninfested callosity patches are seen in embryos. It is almost as though the whales' skin is designed to be colonized by parasites. Callosities could act as splash deflectors. Males, which have larger callosities than females, might use them to scrape each other. Regardless of their function, they serve the purpose of allowing whale identification, since each right whale has a slightly different pattern.

Another unique aspect of right whale

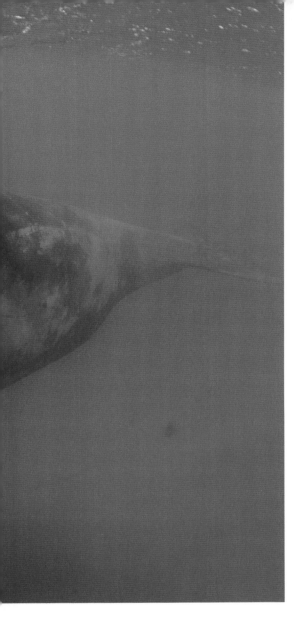

The head and belly of the northern right whale—a species found in southern seas as well as northern—are marked by distinctive patches called callosities.

anatomy is the huge size of the male testes. One testicle weighed 1,157 pounds, five times the weight of the testicles of the larger blue and gray whales. This suggests that the mating strategy of male right whales may involve considerable sperm competition. Instead of sequestering females by fighting and mate guarding, males may compete by inseminating females more often and with more sperm. Mating is indeed reported to be promiscuous for this species. A female may be surrounded by two to six males attempting

to copulate with her. The female remains on the surface, and the male mates from below, belly to belly, holding on with his front flippers.

Females probably reproduce only every three years, so there may be a low availability of mates for males. Unbred females become much sought after, and unreceptive females go to great lengths to dissuade males. They may lie on their backs, keeping their genital region up in the air and inaccessible to the males, who will attempt to roll them over anyway. This may also explain why a right whale can sometimes be observed in a headstand with its tail emerging straight out of the water. An alternative suggestion is that the whale is "sailing," using the flukes to catch and travel with the wind while resting.

Females with calves segregate themselves from males when they are in the winter breeding grounds, probably because of male harassment. Right whale aggregations appear to be loose and based on food availability.

Right whales are highly acrobatic for their size and are capable of bending their head to their tail. Since they feed by placid filter skimming, swim slowly and usually dive for only a few minutes at a time, it is unlikely that feeding requires this much flexibility. Again, it may be related to their mating system. Right whales frequently breach and tail slap. They utter deep belchlike groans. They are reportedly playful and have been seen cavorting with navigation buoys, sea lions and dolphins. Unfortunately, their docile, approachable nature made hunting them easy for whalers. Only a few hundred northern right whales remain, and many of those depend on areas such as the Bay of Fundy, which is perpetually at risk from the development of oil terminals, hydroelectric dams and other disruptions.

Even though right whale whaling ceased half a century ago, these whales have not recovered. There may simply be too few spread too thinly and exposed to too many environmental problems for them ever to rebound.

NORTHERN RIGHT WHALE
Balaena glacialis

Mammal: *Balaena glacialis*, northern right whale, right whale, black right whale
Meaning of Name: *Balaena* (whale); *glacialis* (of the ice) is inappropriate, as they are not confined to Arctic seas but are also found in southern oceans
Description: rotund whale with large, paddle-shaped pectoral flippers; no dorsal fin or throat grooves; large head is approximately one-quarter of the body length; jaw is highly arched and curves upward along the side of the head; large, yellowish oval rugose callosity known as the bonnet at tip of snout; other smaller warty protuberances on snout and lower lip and above the eyes; 228 to 259 dark brown to dark gray baleen plates on each side
Color: brown to black, mottled overall with irregular white splashes on chin and belly
Total Length: male, 36 to 48 feet; female, 31 to 60 feet
Weight: male, 49,000 pounds; female, 51,000 pounds
Gestation: 11 to 12 months
Offspring: 1 every 2 to 4 years
Age of Maturity: 10 years
Longevity: not known
Diet: primarily planktonic crustaceans (especially the copepod *Calanus* spp), krill and some small fish
Habitat: temperate seas along coasts in shallow water; prefers the continental shelf and sometimes occurs in large bays
Predators: killer whale and man
Dental Formula: 0

BOWHEAD WHALE
Balaena mysticetus

The bowhead is named for its huge head—up to one-third of its body length—and for the great curve of its lower jaw. The jaw accommodates the bowhead's 360 thin, bristle-covered baleen plates, which measure up to 14 feet long. The whale uses them to skim small planktonic animals out of the water, usually as it swims at the surface with its mouth open. Bowheads also stir up sediments in shallow regions, and recent observations suggest that they feed extensively in the water column. Still, as a rule,

they do not dive deeply, and they usually resurface within 20 minutes. Bowheads sometimes feed cooperatively, with as many as 14 individuals moving along in formation like a series of combines.

Like other Arctic whales, bowheads migrate with the ice pack, to open southern waters in winter and back to the north along the melting ice when summer comes. Usually, they travel alone or in small groups segregated by sex. Little is known about bowheads' social interactions, but they are probably much like those of the northern right whale. As with most baleen whales, females grow larger and mature later than

The slow-moving bowhead rests on the surface before submerging; the spread of its powerful tail flukes can measure 18 feet.

males, usually at around 4 years of age.

Bowheads were hunted to the brink of extinction by the turn of the 19th century. They probably owe their survival to the advent of spring steel, which replaced baleen. Today, 4,000 survive, at most, and despite a commercial whaling ban, the populations are not increasing adequately. With the pace of Arctic oil development accelerating, concern for the bowhead has increased. There is also concern about the contin-

ued hunting of bowheads by the Alaskan Inuit. The hunt, a traditional part of Inuit culture and economy, is now being conducted with modern technology, including grenade-tipped harpoons, making its justification on traditional cultural grounds questionable.

SPERM COMPETITION

Male mating strategies take many forms. Some males increase their offspring by attempting to acquire harems; others may use a mating plug or intense monogamy to gain exclusive ac-cess to a single female. Males may also court females with elaborate displays, or they may succeed in the breeding game primarily through sperm competition.

Researchers have observed a correlation between the size of the testes and the amount of sperm competition and promiscuity in a species' mating system. This relationship was first described for primates: monkeys, gorillas and humans. The ratio of testicle weight to body weight is very high for chimpanzees. Chimps have a promiscuous mating system in which males and females may copulate several times an hour for several days every month. By contrast, gorillas have a harem mating system in which one huge male excludes all others and gains exclusive access to a harem. Males in this sort of mating system typically invest heavily in weaponry to repel other males but put little effort into sperm production. Gorillas' copulation rates are very low compared with those of chimpanzees, and accordingly, the gorilla has a low testes-to-body-weight ratio. (Humans are intermediate.) The same correlation has been found in animals ranging from mountain sheep to sandpipers. Promiscuous species have high testis weights; in monogamous species or those in which a female has several mates (polyandry), the male invests little in testis development.

The same sort of differences appear to exist in whales. Male harem defenders such as dolphins and other odontocetes tend to be much larger than females. Gray and other baleen whales show the reverse trend, females being the larger sex. This suggests that male-male combat is not particularly important in their mating strategy. Males in a promiscuous system such as that of the northern right whale typically attempt to copulate with as many females as they can and as often as possible. In such a system, there is probably a good correlation between the amount of sperm produced and the number of offspring a male will sire. This may account for the huge size of the northern right whale's testicles, each of which is a half-ton sperm factory.

BOWHEAD WHALE
Balaena mysticetus

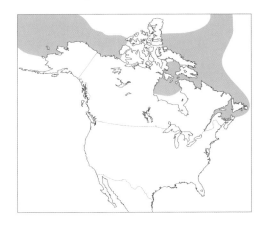

Mammal: *Balaena mysticetus*, bowhead whale

Meaning of Name: *Balaena* (whale); *mysticetus* (whale with a mustache) refers to the sheets of whalebone or baleen plates that hang down from the upper jaw

Description: resembles a huge tadpole with an enormous head (one-third of the body length); seen from the front, the mouth forms a trough cradling the narrow, depressed snout inside the arched lower lip; lips and snout have rows of short white bristles; very long, narrow baleen plates; approximately 360 plates on each side, the longest being in the middle—they are dark gray or black, sometimes with whitish front edges

Color: mainly black; chin is unevenly white, sometimes with a series of grayish to black spots; also some white flashes on belly and a pale gray area on tail stock

Total Length: average 57 feet (maximum 66 feet)

Weight: maximum 152,000 pounds

Gestation: 10 to 13 months

Offspring: 1 every 2 or 3 years

Age of Maturity: 4 years

Longevity: possibly 40 years

Diet: mainly zooplankton (copepods, amphipods, euphausiids and pteropods)

Habitat: primarily an Arctic species found in association with ice floes and in shallow waters; frequents bays, straits and estuaries in summer

Predators: killer whale

Dental Formula: 0

WHITE WHALE & NARWHAL
Monodontidae

This family has only two members, both distinctive: the narwhal, with its spiraling tusk, and the beluga, unmistakable because of its brilliant white color. Though they appear different at first glance, belugas and narwhals have much in common: Both are high-Arctic specialists and have thick layers of blubber; both travel in spectacular herds and aggregations.

BELUGA *Delphinapterus leucas*

Belugas are highly social, producing sounds variously described as screams, moos and trills in a range that humans can hear. Whalers called them "sea canaries." The Russians, who gave them their common name, meaning whitish, also have an expression, "screaming like a beluga," for noisy people. Unlike most whales, the beluga has a fairly flexible neck and mouth, and its face is capable of a wide range of expressions.

The beluga is a shallow-water specialist, using its mobile neck and face for bottom feeding on a wide variety of invertebrates and fish. It may even use its flexible lips to suck prey off the seafloor. This whale has a thick skin and a thick layer of blubber. Up to 40 percent of its body may be blubber, as opposed to 15 percent for warm-water dolphins. Both adaptations are useful for a life close to Arctic pack ice.

In winter, pack ice forces belugas to deeper, open water, where they may be seen with narwhals, but in summer, belugas head toward shallow estuaries for feeding and breeding. Sometimes this involves migrations of several hundred miles through pack-ice areas to the mouths of large rivers in the Arctic. There are also some relatively stationary populations such as the one in the mouth of Quebec's Saguenay River. Belugas sometimes swim up large rivers for great distances, traveling 600 miles into the Yukon and even up the Rhine into Germany, possibly to feed on runs of fish such as young salmon in some areas. This habit, combined with their eye-catching white color and gregariousness, makes belugas one of whale watching's most spectacular sights.

Belugas normally travel in large herds that are densely aggregated during the breeding season. In some areas, such as the Mackenzie River estuary, thousands of belugas may come together to breed. The complete social structure within these large herds is unknown, but there is segregation by sex and age. Pods consist of either males or mothers and calves. Males grow larger than females and have multiple mates, so some harem activity is possible. Females are ready to breed when they are 4 to 7 years old and calve every two to three years, which they do segregated from the herd in quiet bays. Calves are dark, not white, and remain with their mothers for two years.

Belugas are thought to have the richest vocal repertoire of all whales, in keeping with their intensely social nature. Their gregariousness, coupled with their preference for shallow estuaries, makes belugas vulnerable to pack-hunting killer whales, polar bears and humans, who have been particularly hard on belugas. The Quebec government bombed belugas in the St. Lawrence River in the 1930s to protect the cod fishery, and the Manitoba government allowed the promotion of

The white beluga is among the few whales with a face flexible enough to allow it to produce a wide range of expressions and also to forage for food in the bottom sediments of rivers and coastal waters.

BELUGA
Delphinapterus leucas

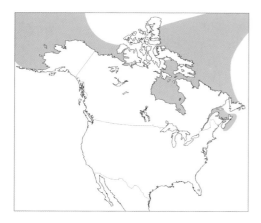

Mammal: *Delphinapterus leucas*, beluga, white whale

Meaning of Name: *Delphinapterus* (finless dolphin); *leucas* (white); beluga is derived from *belyi*, Russian for white

Description: fusiform body tapers to a distinct "neck"; small head and short beak; upper jaw protrudes slightly ahead of the melon; back has a narrow ridge of small bumps behind the middle; no dorsal fin; blowhole is crescentic

Color: the smooth, thin skin is creamy white in adults, brown in young calves and various grays in juveniles; adults have brown eyes

Total Length: male, up to 16 feet; female, up to 13 feet; size depends on particular stock

Weight: male, 3,300 pounds; female, 3,000 pounds

Gestation: 13 to 14 months

Offspring: 1 every 2 or 3 years

Age of Maturity: male, 8 or 9 years; female, 4 to 7 years

Longevity: 25 to 30 years

Diet: an opportunistic feeder, it eats many species of fish, including cod, herring and capelin, as well as octopus, squid, crab, shrimp, clams and worms

Habitat: cold seas of Arctic zone along coasts in shallow bays and estuaries and in mouths of rivers; also occurs in deep offshore waters and can survive and feed in warmer waters

Predators: killer whale, polar bear and man

Dental Formula: 32 to 40 teeth

beluga sport hunting during the late 1960s and early 1970s. Various commercial fisheries have also concentrated on beluga harvesting. A major fishery operated at Churchill, Manitoba, producing meat for prairie fur farms. In the Northwest Territories, another fishery produced canned *muktak*, the blubbery skins sought by the Inuit as food. These fisheries shut down when it was learned that belugas contained dangerously high concentrations of mercury.

At present, only native hunting of belugas is permitted, although netting for aquariums is also allowed. Belugas are not endangered, but some of their populations are threatened by overhunting, and others are vulnerable to oil spills and developments such as river damming and oil terminals.

SWIMMING ISN'T EASY

Swimming involves a difficult feat of engineering. An animal or boat that produces turbulence—swirling and eddying of the water—will expend a great deal of energy. Dolphins, for example, can swim at the rate of 15 knots for long periods. If they produced turbulence at that speed, the effort required would be comparable to that of a human being climbing 17,680 feet in an hour, a level of exertion beyond possibility. How is it, then, that dolphins can produce bursts of speed calculated at 24 miles per hour, blue whales are able to cruise at 23 miles per hour and killer whales can reach 36 miles per hour, faster than most oceangoing ships?

When a body moves through water, a boundary layer of water forms around it. The thickness and turbulence of this layer determine the amount of drag there will be. If the water around the body slows down because of friction, the boundary layer is disrupted, and a large, swirling wake forms, creating drag behind the animal or ship. When the boundary layer flows smoothly, there is little wake and little drag. A streamlined shape minimizes the break-

up of the boundary layer, but that alone is not enough to allow high-speed swimming. For real speed, the surface of the shape must allow the water to move in a laminar fashion—in smooth sheets instead of in turbulent eddies.

Researchers once thought dolphins had a special skin that rippled under pressure and reduced turbulence, but attempts to demonstrate this have

A coat of blubber constitutes up to 40 percent of the beluga's body weight, adapting it for the chilly life near Arctic pack ice. The gregarious whale travels in large herds.

failed. Dolphins may, however, use a special muscular shiver that sheds turbulence and reduces drag when they are moving at high speed.

Dolphins are not especially fast swim-mers—they just seem fast. Actually, large whales such as the 60-to-90-foot fin or blue whales can swim as fast as any dolphin. There is a peculiar paradox involved in the speed of these largest whales. For a wide range of sizes, there is a good correlation between how large a fish or whale is and the speed at which it can swim: the larger it is, the faster it can go. There are also two types of speed: that of active swimming and that reached during brief bursts of full power. A dolphin swimming at full power reaches 33 feet per second, a speed that is merely the active cruising speed for a blue whale. In theory, blue whales could reach a speed of 270 miles per hour, but they never do, probably because such high speeds are of no use to them.

NARWHAL *Monodon monoceros*

Possessor of the world's largest tooth, the narwhal is credited with being the inspiration for the legend of the unicorn. The spiral tusk is one of the male narwhal's two teeth. It begins to erupt from the male's upper lip when it reaches about 1 year of age and grows as long as 10 feet. In the past, it has been wrongly suggested that the tusk is an adaptation for hunting food, attacking predators and making breathing holes in the ice. The tusk's true function is suggested by sexual dimorphism. Except for rare individuals, females lack this tusk. Male narwhals have been observed crossing tusks, so it is likely that they are used in the same way as the horns and antlers of other male mammals. They enable both males and females to assess the owner's age and territorial status and are perhaps used in male-male combat. Males often have scars on their heads, and broken tusks are not uncommon.

In winter, narwhals, like belugas, move through pack ice to deep-water regions of the high Arctic, but unlike belugas, they remain offshore or in deeper inlets in summer and do not bottom-feed extensively. They can dive several hundred yards and are faster swimmers than belugas. They eat fish such as flounder, halibut and cod, along with squid, octopus and other invertebrates. They are also highly gregarious and vocal. Males grow larger than females do and take twice as long to mature. The male narwhal's size and the presence of the tusk suggest intense male-male competition. Large groups of this whale do occur, but smaller groups of 20 or so individuals segregated by age, size and sex are more common.

Pack ice dictates the range and movement of narwhals. Fast-forming ice may occasionally trap and kill them, and whales in pack ice may be easier prey for polar bears and even walrus. The human desire for ivory is a potential threat to narwhals, although the Canadian government regulates the Inuit trade in narwhal tusks.

The 10-foot-long tusk of the male narwhal, which pierces its upper lip, is a specialized tooth probably used in battles over mates.

BIOCONCENTRATION

A beluga calf shot by hunters in the St. Lawrence River in 1973 had 800 parts per million of PCBs and 827 parts per million of DDT in its blubber. In mammals such as beef cows, concentrations above a few parts per million would be cause for alarm. DDT is an agricultural chemical that was banned long ago in North America, and PCBs, used in the chemical industry, are also strictly controlled. How did they show up in a marine mammal in such concentrated amounts?

Compounds such as DDT, which are chemically synthesized, are highly stable. Few organisms have the enzymes needed to break them down and detoxify them because they have never existed in nature. These factors account for both DDT's persistence and its effectiveness as a poison. What is less obvious is why it should become concentrated in animals such as belugas. It is, however, an inevitable result of the way food chains work and the tendency of many pesticides and pollutants to dissolve in or adhere to organic material rather than dispersing evenly through water. DDT, for example, sticks to organic detritus such as decaying plant and animal remains that are found on the bottoms of ponds and other bodies of water. When this detritus is eaten by insects or fish, the DDT dissolves in the animal's fat.

It takes 10 pounds of insects to make 1 pound of fish muscle, so the concentration of chemicals increases dramatically with each step in the food chain. A typical pattern has been worked out for a freshwater food chain in which the water itself contained only 0.00005 parts per million of DDT. In plankton, the concentration rose to 0.04 parts per million; in minnows, it had increased to 0.94 parts per million; predatory fish also had 0.94 parts per million; and the fish-eating cormorants had 26.4 parts per million, a million times higher than the water's initial level of DDT.

Pesticides and pollutants that bioconcentrate and are slow to break down may be under control in developed countries such as Canada and the United States, but large amounts continue to be used in the Third World. Pesticide pollution of the oceans is increasing, and these pollutants are being carried to the farthest reaches of the Arctic. Now that commercial whaling is controlled, pollution of the ocean stands as one of the greatest long-term threats to the whales that sit at the top of the food chain.

NARWHAL
Monodon monoceros

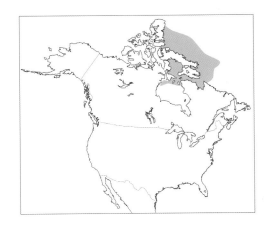

Mammal: *Monodon monoceros*, narwhal
Meaning of Name: *Monodon* (single tooth); *monoceros* (single horn) refers to the fact that the canine in the male develops into an enormous horn; narwhal, meaning corpse whale, comes from Old Norse—the whale's pallid color is said to resemble that of a floating corpse
Description: short, blunt, rounded head; no dorsal fin; the striking feature is a long, spirally twisted horn that projects through the upper lip of the male (its maxillary tooth); series of 2-inch-high bumps visible along the dorsal midline from the middle of the back to the tail
Color: adults are dark bluish gray or brownish with slate-gray blotches on the back and sides; newborns are slate-gray and become lighter with age
Total Length: male, 20 feet; female, 14 feet
Weight: male, 3,500 pounds; female, 2,000 pounds
Gestation: 14.5 months
Offspring: 1 (rarely twins) every 2 or 3 years
Age of Maturity: male, 8 or 9 years; female, 4 to 7 years
Longevity: 40 years
Diet: squid, fish (arctic cod, halibut, flounder and skate), cephalopods and crustaceans
Habitat: deep waters of the high Arctic along the edge of land-fast ice and ice floes; avoids shallow seas and bays
Predators: Inuit hunters, killer whale and the occasional rogue bull walrus
Dental Formula: 1 or 2 teeth

DOLPHINS *Delphinidae*

With 32 species found in all oceans and many tropical rivers, Delphinidae—the dolphins and their relatives—is the dominant cetacean family. The group originated recently, during the last 10 million years. The youth of Delphinidae and the high rate of speciation among its members are reflected in the incomplete genetic isolation of dolphin species. Hybrids between the supposedly distinct species are sometimes found in nature, and in captivity, crosses between members of different species and even members of what are considered to be different genera and families have occurred.

In size, dolphins range from the yard-long tropical river dolphin to the massive 7-yard-long killer whale. All members of this group, however, have a highly streamlined shape, with a central sickle-shaped dorsal fin and well-developed teeth in both jaws. Many species also have a prominent forehead and a beaklike mouth. As a group, Delphinidae exhibit striking color patterns that differ greatly from one species to another. Dolphins may use the color patterns as social signals and for identification of different species, since they often occur in mixed schools and are more gregarious and vision-oriented than other cetaceans. Dolphins' teeth are peglike, which distinguishes them from porpoises, which have flattened teeth.

Much of what is known about dolphin behavior and physiology is based on studies of the bottlenose dolphin, a species of warmer temperate and tropical waters. It is the best-known dolphin, the species most often used as a performer in aquariums and films. The bottlenose, which comes with a built-in smile, is capable of spectacular leaps. It is highly social, a superb imitator and one of the few cetaceans that can survive and breed in captivity. Some—but not all—of what is known about the bottlenose is typical of the entire dolphin family.

Bottlenoses, like many of the other dolphin species, are opportunistic hunters, and the prey that they select appears to influence their social groupings. Dense fish schools may attract herds of hundreds and even thousands of dolphins. Herman Melville, author of *Moby-Dick*, called the aggregations "hilarious shoals, which upon the seas keep tossing themselves to heaven like caps in a Fourth of July crowd."

Subgroups of several to a few dozen individuals appear frequently within large herds. There is some segregation by sex and size. Large adult males, for example, rarely occur with subadult males; young males may form bachelor groups or join adult females. And females with calves may group together. In general, though, the herd composition and structure is loose, and there may be little long-term association among family members except between mothers and offspring. Although calves are weaned after 18 months, they continue to associate with their mothers for as long as six years. Dolphin groups that stay together can coordinate their hunting activities and work together to repel sharks, chasing them away aggressively. Observations of those in captivity have also revealed that bottlenoses are prodigiously sexual, much to the embarrassment of some aquarium audiences. While many cetaceans mate only at specific times, dolphins mate throughout the year. Males begin making sexual advances when they are only a few months old, attempting to copulate with everything from sea

The jet-black upper body of the Pacific white-sided dolphin is a startling contrast to the whiteness of its lower surface, making this highly sociable dolphin one of the most striking members of its family.

turtles to other dolphins of either sex. The penis is rich in nerve endings and capable of coordinated movements, which seems to allow it to act as a tactile organ for feeling and exploring objects.

During courtship, dolphins bite and nip each other, often gently, but adults may escalate their activity to violent play that involves leaping from the water, rushing at each other and smashing heads and bodies together. This kind of activity between a male and a female usually ends in copulation.

Similar smashing contact often occurs between males, with older, larger males attempting to damage smaller ones. Males often have many scars in their genital region, presumably from attacks by other males. Aquarium operators acknowledge male-male aggression as one of the problems of keeping dolphins together. In the battle to establish dominance, one male may rape another. According to one account, when two large male Atlantic bottlenoses were first put together, they began with the usual open-mouthed threats and ended with sexual pursuit, two successful intromissions by the victor and somewhat reluctant submission by the loser. The entire episode lasted one hour and was not seen again. The loser, who had been the dominant animal in the community until then, never reestablished himself, nor was he seen to try. Whether this kind of tactile aggression also occurs in wild dolphins is not known.

The bottlenose and other dolphins have sophisticated sound-production and echolocation abilities. Bottlenoses send out clicking sounds, then read the echoes to determine the size, range, shape and even substance of underwater objects. Listening only to echoes, they can interpret with enough subtlety to distinguish between objects differing by only 0.004 inch in thickness, between shapes such as cubes and cylinders and between cylinders made of different metals. To process sound so precisely requires much neural circuitry, and that, no doubt, accounts for the huge size of the dolphin's brain.

COOPERATIVE HUNTING

Cetaceans have developed sophisticated forms of cooperative hunting. Bottlenose dolphins use their intelligence to coordinate the herding and trapping of fish, one extreme example of which was observed in a salt marsh in Georgia: Pairs of dolphins herded fish into the shallows until waves stranded the fish onshore. The dolphins then swam onto the land to eat and returned to the water with the next wave.

Humpback whales often form groups of three to seven to concentrate fish such as herring. Herring are minuscule compared with the whales. To group them into enough of a concentration to make them a profitable prey item, humpbacks use a technique known as bubble-netting. One or two whales dive beneath a herring school and swim around and around in a great closing spiral, releasing air bubbles as they go. The rising bubbles frighten the herring, they draw toward the center, then the humpbacks lunge in together, swallowing herring by the thousands. They probably use some auditory communication to coordinate the lunge.

The most skillful of all coordinated hunters are probably killer whales. Unlike humpbacks and most other dolphins, killer whales live in stable social groups in which individuals are closely related, and they stay together and communicate among themselves for many years. Thus, like lion prides and packs of wolves and African wild dogs, a pod of killer whales has all the ingredients needed to develop into a highly skilled unit capable of harvesting prey items far too hefty or swift for an individual to manage. The fastest fish, dolphins, large whales, sharks, sea turtles and sea lions all fall prey to packs of killer whales.

Author Erich Hoyt witnessed a remarkable salmon hunt by a killer whale pod off British Columbia, a hunt so well coordinated that it is imitated and used by commercial fishing boats in finding and catching salmon. The pod of 16 individuals, 60 to 100 feet apart, moved slowly up the coast in a line, herding salmon by shooting out of the water and whacking their heads down or smacking their flukes. The noises spooked the salmon and forced them to move. Gradually, the orcas moved into a circular formation, a living seine net, around the fish and began to close in. Soon, the salmon school was tightly packed, jumping and boiling, and the killer whales began to feed one at a time, each rushing in to gulp fish while the others maintained the circle.

Cooperative food gathering in cetaceans, as in other mammals, may be one of the driving forces of sociality. It enables those who forage cooperatively to harvest a greater range of food, and in the case of killer whales, it is a way for younger and smaller family members to receive the benefit of an increased food supply.

HOW SMART ARE THEY?

The brain of the bottlenose dolphin is as large as a human's, and a sperm whale's brain, at 11 pounds, is four to five times as large. Brain size and dolphins' ability to imitate and learn complicated tricks in captivity lead some to suggest that they possess an intellect comparable to our own. But it is difficult to get scientists to agree on a definition of human intelligence; defining and measuring intelligence in another species is all but impossible.

Intelligence is often defined as the ability to solve problems and use reason. This raises two questions, however: What are the problems to be solved, and how do we measure success? Problems that involve visual memory would prove that dolphins are dumb indeed. In nature, dolphins have less use for visual information than for other kinds of signals. Their streamlined, rigid facial structure means that they use facial expressions relatively little, and although they see well, sound is a much better medium for detecting and sending signals. The same animals tested in prob-

Highly intelligent, social and cooperative, the killer whale is also a fierce and relentless hunter that uses, among other weaponry, its powerful flukes as a club to stun its prey.

lem solving with sounds would seem much more intelligent.

Researchers cannot study intelligence independently of the environment in which a species lives. It may be difficult to conceive of the kinds of tests that would reflect dolphin intelligence, simply because we know so little about what they do in the wild and how they perceive their world. Problems involving variables such as the size of a fish school, the species in the school and the rate at which it is moving are what the large dolphin brain is adapted for solving. Dolphin brains are not designed for communicating with humans.

Many researchers have assumed that intelligence depends on language and that language is necessary for ordered thought and reasoning. Because dolphins use a variety of complicated sounds, people have often assumed or attempted to show that dolphins use language in the same way humans do. Some have even said that dolphins can

learn to speak to humans. Again, there is no ecological reason to expect dolphins to use a human-style system to solve their radically different aquatic communication problems. There is also no evidence that dolphins have evolved a language system with syntax and structure like that of humans.

A more objective way to define intelligence may be to compare the capacity of different brains for processing information. The volume of the brain is correlated with the amount of information it is able to store and decipher. On this scale, dolphins do rank as intelligent, although not as intelligent as humans. This still leaves unanswered the question of what dolphins use their large brains for. One possibility is that processing the echolocation signals for distances, speed, textures and other measures from a barrage of echoes uses a large amount of the brain. Bats, however, do not have such large brains even though they are faced with a similar task of processing echolocation information. A more likely explanation is that dolphins use a great deal of brain circuitry to communicate with one another and solve prey-capture problems.

Most dolphins are long-lived generalized feeders, encountering hundreds of different prey items in almost infinite permutations and combinations. They depend on group coordination for capturing this prey, probably using techniques they have learned from older, more experienced dolphins.

One of the features of captive dolphins that has impressed humans is their superb ability to mimic. Bottlenose dolphins in captivity have picked up pieces of tile and used them to scrape algae off the tank window after watching human tank cleaners doing the same. A 6-month-old aquarium dolphin that saw someone puff cigarette smoke against the glass observation window swam off to her mother, collected a mouthful of milk, swam back to the observation window and puffed out her own cloud of milk. It is safe to say that these actions are never performed in the wild. However, when animals live a long time, are social and must handle a great variety of prey, the ability to copy what others are doing must be highly adaptive. Dolphins are like primates in this respect, and possibly both groups have developed large brains for just that reason.

ATLANTIC
WHITE-SIDED DOLPHIN
Lagenorhynchus acutus

PACIFIC
WHITE-SIDED DOLPHIN
Lagenorhynchus obliquidens

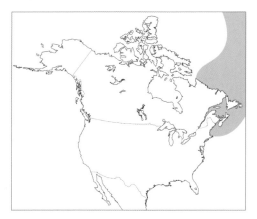

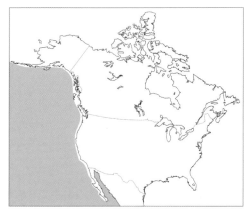

Mammal: *Lagenorhynchus acutus*, Atlantic white-sided dolphin, the "jumper"

Meaning of Name: *Lagenorhynchus* (bottlenose); *acutus* (sharp, pointed) may refer either to the dorsal fin or to the short, distinct beak

Description: stout, robust body; short but distinct black beak; tall, hooked dorsal fin

Color: black above and white below; sides are variable with zones of gray, tan and white; long white band on the sides runs below dorsal fin to above anus; black stripe from corner of mouth to junction of pectoral fin

Total Length: 6 to 9 feet

Weight: 400 to 515 pounds

Gestation: 10 to 12 months

Offspring: 1 every 2 or 3 years

Age of Maturity: male, older than 4 to 6 years; female, older than 5 to 8 years

Longevity: male, 22 years; female, 27 years

Diet: fish (herring, hake, mackerel, smelt, anchovies), small squid, crustaceans, whelks

Habitat: pelagic species occurring in cool offshore waters

Predators: killer whale and sharks

Dental Formula: 120 to 132 teeth

Mammal: *Lagenorhynchus obliquidens*, Pacific white-sided dolphin

Meaning of Name: *Lagenorhynchus* (bottlenose); *obliquidens* (slanted) may refer to sharply hooked dorsal fin

Description: cylindrical fusiform body; small beak; slender hooked dorsal fin; keeled slender tail stock

Color: black back fading to gray on the flanks, fins and flukes; white underparts; tip of lower jaw is black; two pale gray or white stripes on each flank and another pair on the tail stock; a narrow dark stripe between corner of mouth and flipper is continuous with dark lips

Total Length: maximum 7.5 feet

Weight: 180 to 300 pounds

Gestation: 10 to 12 months

Offspring: 1

Age of Maturity: when attains length of 6 feet

Longevity: 20 to 30 years

Diet: wide variety of small fish and squid

Habitat: cool offshore temperate to sub-Arctic waters; also the outer edge of the continental shelf or close to shore near deep canyons

Predators: none recorded (probably killer whale and sharks)

Dental Formula: 116 to 128 teeth

The Pacific white-sided dolphin, like its Atlantic cousin, is small, social and athletic. Not only does it bow ride with boats, but it seems to seek out the company of larger whales and small companions such as Dall's porpoises and even sea lions.

WHITE-BEAKED DOLPHIN
Lagenorhynchus albirostris

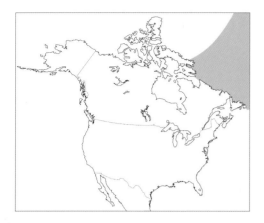

Mammal: *Lagenorhynchus albirostris*, white-beaked dolphin

Meaning of Name: *Lagenorhynchus* (bottlenose); *albirostris* (white snout)

Description: robust, streamlined body with very small beak; high, slender dorsal fin

Color: dark gray to black above and white or light gray below; flanks have two grayish areas in front of, behind and below dorsal fin; pale band across beak, but lips outlined in black

Total Length: maximum 10 feet

Weight: male, 440 pounds; female, 400 pounds

Gestation: 1 year

Offspring: may give birth to 2 or more, but usually only 1 survives

Age of Maturity: unknown

Longevity: unknown

Diet: squid, fish (cod, herring, mackerel, capelin, anchovies), crustaceans, whelks, octopus

Habitat: pelagic in cold offshore Arctic waters

Predators: no known predators except man

Dental Formula: 88 to 100 teeth

Insulated from the frigid waters of the colder regions of the Atlantic by a layer of blubber, the white-beaked dolphin hunts for squid, hermit crabs and snails in the ocean depths.

WHITE-BEAKED DOLPHIN
Lagenorhynchus albirostris

A northern specialist, the white-beaked dolphin is distinguished by a thick layer of blubber and a willingness to venture farther north in the Atlantic than other dolphins. Its insulation allows it to dive deep in search of food, but it is also an athletic leaper. Groups range from 10 to 500 or more animals. Even though white-beaked dolphins have fewer teeth than many other dolphins, they eat a wide variety of food, ranging from hermit crabs and snails to fish. The preferred fare, however, appears to be soft-fleshed squid, which may account for their shortage of teeth.

LONG-FINNED PILOT WHALE *Globicephala melas*

Long-finned pilot whales are larger than all other dolphin family members except the killer whale. Males may reach a length of 23 feet and females 17 feet, and the largest individuals can weigh 2 to 3 tons. Males mature at age 12 and females at age 6. Pregnancy lasts 15 to 16 months, and females nurse their calves for as long as 20 months, which means they have a low reproductive rate. Strong bonds exist between mothers and offspring and possibly among other relatives. When one pilot whale is wounded, it is usually attended by other members of the school.

The long-finned pilot whale can be distinguished by its dark black-brown color and its protruding forehead that gives it the common name "pothead." It may use this forehead melon to echolocate schools of squid. Potheads eat fish and rummage along the bottom, but their main food is squid, and its behavior and ecology seem to influence those of the pilot whales. Rather than following a rigid or pronounced migration system of their own, they aggregate and follow the activity of the squid.

A large population of pilot whales once existed around Newfoundland, and the heavy whaling there has supplied much information on the species. In Newfoundland, potheads reach inshore waters in June and July and remain there to feed until October and November, when they head offshore to areas washed by warm Gulf Stream currents.

Their movement duplicates that of the squid *Illex illecebrosus*, which moves inshore for its summer feed on capelin, herring and mackerel. *Illex illecebrosus* has an explosive growth pattern. Young squid are spawned offshore at the edge of the continental shelf in late autumn, and their parents die after spawning. The young squid feed mainly on krill and other plankton over the winter. At the start of summer, when they weigh a few ounces, they move inshore and begin eating capelin, mackerel, herring

and other fish and grow at a phenomenal rate, until by the end of the summer, they weigh almost a pound. They are not only bait for the line-fishing of cod but also a major food for seals, seabirds (such as fulmars and shearwaters) and pilot whales, which can each eat as much as 10 tons of squid in a year.

Some pilot whales live year-round at the edge of the continental shelf, where squid are constantly available. It is their ability to track the squid that earned them the name "pilot whale." Not only fishermen but also seabirds and other dolphin species rely on sightings of pilot whales to guide them to fishing or squid-jigging grounds.

Pilot whales are highly gregarious, which may be a result of feeding on concentrated schools of squid. Aggregations of pilot whales in the hundreds and thousands have been reported. When not feeding, they often lie floating together, almost touching, like log rafts. The herding behavior may have evolved in response to shark and killer whale attacks. Pilot whales seem to respond to threats in a coordinated manner, following leaders and emitting individual distinctive distress calls. Unfortunately, herding has made the species vulnerable to stranding and mass slaughter. Frequently, hundreds of pilot whales become stranded along beaches and usually die. The cause is unknown, and none of the explanations suggested so far—disorientation due to storms, parasites disrupting the sonar navigation, frenzied feeding or stress-induced suicide—are plausible.

Regardless of the cause, mass stranding appears to be related to the intense cohesiveness of pilot whale schools. At one time, Newfoundland pilot whalers took advantage of the behavior to herd large schools into bays and then run them aground to be butchered. In 1956 alone, 10,000 pilot whales were killed in Newfoundland, and the meat was sold for pennies a pound to mink farms. This led to a serious depletion of pilot whale stocks in the area until whaling was banned in 1972.

LONG-FINNED PILOT WHALE
Globicephala melas

Mammal: *Globicephala melas*, long-finned pilot whale, Atlantic pilot whale, pilot whale, pothead

Meaning of Name: *Globicephala* (bulbous head) refers to large, rounded melon; *melas* (black) refers to main body color

Description: slender, robust body with thick, bulbous head that is sometimes squarish in front; very long, sicklelike pectoral fins

Color: black with an indistinct dark gray saddle behind the dorsal fin and small dark gray spot behind each eye; pearl-gray anchor-shaped patch running from throat to anus

Total Length: male, 13 to 23 feet; female, 11 to 17 feet

Weight: 1,800 pounds (maximum 6,000 pounds)

Gestation: 15 to 16 months

Offspring: 1; female bears 5 or 6 in lifetime (possibly every 3 years)

Age of Maturity: male, 12 to 13 years; female, 6 years

Longevity: estimated maximum 40 to 50 years

Diet: squid; fish (especially cod) are eaten only if squid are not available

Habitat: generally pelagic but may occur in inshore waters in summer; often found on the edge of the continental shelf, where depths quickly drop from 600 feet to the ocean floor, where there are plenty of squid

Predators: no known predators except man

Dental Formula: 36 to 48 teeth

ORCA *Orcinus orca*

Killer whales are the biggest and most formidable of all dolphins. With adult males reaching lengths of up to 32 feet and weighing as much as 9 tons (the equivalent of two elephants), orcas are the largest predators in the world, perched at the pinnacle of the oceanic food chain. As adept in the water as they are sizable, killer whales can reach speeds of 30 miles per hour

and leap high enough that their mouth is 40 feet above the surface. They can, and do, eat the largest animals of the oceans, including other whales, seals, sharks, sea lions, sea turtles and a great variety of fish.

Many researchers compare orcas to wolves. Like wolves, orcas are not only top-level carnivores but also highly social, intelligent and cooperative. Orcas and wolves have both been vilified and maligned because they are carnivores

The orca, or killer whale, is the ocean's top-level carnivore, able to capture and eat whales and other large marine mammals.

and were once thought of as a threat to human life and the human economy. The public has now discovered that orcas are not to be feared and persecuted but admired. Numerous observers have reported that orcas are strangely loath to attack humans in either water or boats. In captivity, orcas have proved to be gentle subjects, and in the wild, they live in an orderly manner, usually displaying little of the ferocity attributed to them by earlier writers. In the words of biologist Richard Ellis, "The killer whale is not a murderer, neither is it a jolly circus clown to be made to jump through hoops for our entertainment. The real orca lies somewhere between these extremes."

Orcas are no more deserving of the name "killer" than is a baleen whale that kills and eats billions of krill. Orcas, however, are capable of attacks that provoke negative visceral reactions in humans, and it is easy to understand why witnesses to some incidents of predation have found them overpowering and shocking. A film crew once photographed orcas ripping apart a young blue whale in a coordinated manner. A few orcas herded the blue whale on either side, while others prevented it from diving too deeply, and some forced it down just far enough below the surface to interfere with its breathing. At the same time, other orcas shredded the blue's tail flukes and tore away the dorsal fins. Large bull orcas ripped chunks of blubber and flesh away and dug a 6-square-foot cavity in the whale's side. The event was surrounded by much blood and gore. But the hunt of the killer whale, like that of wolves, wild dogs or chimpanzees, is simply an adaptation that allows the animals to harvest prey far larger than themselves. It is an adaptation that humans have employed in a similar fashion throughout evolutionary history, and it is one of the driving forces favoring the evolution of social behavior.

The social system of orcas is based on groups known as pods, extended family groupings with amazing stability in membership. It appears that a killer whale stays in its pod for life. Perhaps when a pod grows too large—with more than 50 individuals—it becomes inefficient, and a mature female may leave to start her own pod. In smaller pods, sons and daughters may remain together with their mothers and dominant males for

many years. Calves associate with their mothers for as long as 10 years, possibly much longer. Some researchers describe the orca social system as a matriarchy that grows until smaller matriarchal groups split off from it.

Members of a pod communicate with sound, and each pod appears to have its own dialect. It is likely that different pods compete with each other, at least indirectly. Larger pods appear to maintain better foraging areas in regions of high salmon density, for example. Smaller pods are forced into the role of transients that range farther and take less profitable food items. Some researchers believe that these transient herds perpetrate most of the attacks on large whales and that these whales are not preferred prey. From time to time, several orca pods join together temporarily in large aggregations, the significance of which is unclear. The gatherings may simply be the result of prey concentration. Even in the company of outsiders, pods maintain their integrity, which is probably facilitated by their distinctive dialects.

Male orcas may live for 50 years and females for as long as 100. Because they are long-lived and remain together, they have the opportunity as well as the genetic incentive to develop highly cooperative behaviors, especially those requiring learning and teamwork among group members.

Killer whales are sexually dimorphic. Males grow larger than females and mature at a later age—16 years as opposed to 8 to 10 for females. The dorsal fin of the male is almost twice the size of the female's, reaching a height of 6½ feet; it may be used to signal size and age. During the breeding season, large bulls may be pugnacious, and it is likely that a harem system operates in the pod, with each large bull having access to three or four females. Normally, there are far fewer females than males available for mating because of the long birth interval. In theory, females can give birth every third year, but in nature, one calf in 10 years is more typical.

ORCA *Orcinus orca*

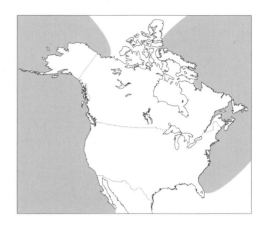

Mammal: *Orcinus orca*, orca, killer whale
Meaning of Name: *Orcinus* (whalelike); *orca* (whale)
Description: powerful streamlined body without much of a neck; large, blunt head with very small beak on upper jaw
Color: shiny black above and white below; white ventral band extends from the lower jaw and widens at the base of the pectoral fins, then narrows to form a trident-shaped mark, with the central prong running midventrally to the base of the flukes; the other two prongs reach around to the posterior flanks; oval white patch just above and behind the eye and an indistinct gray saddle behind the dorsal fin
Total Length: male, about 25 feet (maximum 32 feet); female, maximum 26 feet
Weight: male, 19,800 pounds; female, 12,000 pounds
Gestation: 12 to 16 months
Offspring: 1 every 10 years (some reproduce at 3-year intervals)
Age of Maturity: male, 16 years; female, 8 to 10 years
Longevity: male, 50 years; female, 100 years
Diet: opportunistic feeder; consumes fish (salmon, cod, herring), squid, baleen whales and other smaller cetaceans, pinnipeds, sea turtles, penguins and other aquatic birds
Habitat: upper layers of cooler seas; prefers coastal to pelagic waters; often enters shallow bays, estuaries and mouths of rivers
Predators: man
Dental Formula: 40 to 56 teeth

PORPOISES *Phocoenidae*

Of the world's six porpoise species, two occur in North America. Their fusiform body plan includes a reduced dorsal fin, small jaws, a blunt snout and the flat teeth that distinguish them from dolphins. All porpoises seem to be fish- and squid-feeders that pursue their prey at high speed.

HARBOR PORPOISE *Phocoena phocoena*

Measuring only 5 feet long when fully grown, harbor porpoises are the smallest cetaceans in northern North American waters. These shy animals are often seen but difficult to study. Perhaps their size makes them vulnerable to and wary of predatory sharks and killer whales.

Harbor porpoises are shallow-water specialists and feed on a wide variety of prey. Their group sizes and movements are closely linked to the movements of the fish they eat. Sometimes harbor porpoises are seen alone or in groups of a few individuals, but on the East Coast, large groups of up to 50 form. Little is known about their social life, except that it seems unstructured, possibly to allow them to adjust to changing fish dispersions. Sex-segregated groups occur, with mature males in some bands and females with calves and juveniles in others.

The harbor porpoise has a low reproductive rate for its small size. It takes three to six years to mature, and females probably give birth only every other year, since gestation takes 10 or 11 months and weaning another half-year or more.

Because they feed in shallow bays, harbor porpoises are sensitive to pollution. In the Bay of Fundy, they suffer from high levels of DDT, PCBs, mercury and other chemical pollutants. In large areas of Europe, harbor porpoise populations have been decimated, possibly because of pollution. In some locations in North America, the native practice of hunting them for food continues, although this is less harmful to their populations than the mortality caused by the monofilament gill nets set for fish. No reliable population estimates exist, making it impossible to determine whether they are seriously threatened, but they are declining.

Among the smallest of cetaceans, the harbor porpoise is usually less than 6 feet long. Its proximity to human populations is causing its numbers to decline, as pollution, fishing and ship traffic take their toll.

HARBOR PORPOISE
Phocoena phocoena

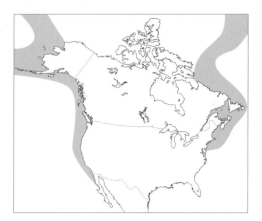

DALL'S PORPOISE
Phocoenoides dalli

Mammal: *Phocoena phocoena*, harbor porpoise

Meaning of Name: *Phocoena* (porpoise)

Description: features that distinguish them from dolphins include blunt, short beak and spade-shaped teeth (rather than conical, as in dolphins); stout body and blunt head; triangular dorsal fin with six small tubercles on its leading edge

Color: dark gray or black above, fading to light grayish brown on sides (may be speckled in overlap zone); white belly; black stripes run from flippers to corners of mouth and lower lip

Total Length: about 5 feet, maximum 6 feet

Weight: up to 140 pounds

Gestation: 10 to 11 months

Offspring: 1 every 1 or 2 years

Longevity: 6 to 10 years; rarely exceeds 13

Diet: schooling fish (herring, hake, pollack, capelin, whiting), bottom-living fish, squid, octopus and crustaceans

Habitat: sub-Arctic and cold temperate waters; generally inshore in shallow waters along the continental shelf and often in bays, harbors, estuaries and the mouths of large rivers

Predators: killer whale, large sharks and man

Dental Formula: 44 to 52 teeth

Mammal: *Phocoenoides dalli*, Dall's porpoise

Meaning of Name: *Phocoenoides* (porpoise); *dalli* (named after William H. Dall, an American naturalist)

Description: extremely robust with small head and flukes; short, straight mouth with poorly defined beak

Color: slate-gray to shiny black overall; white blaze on belly extends onto the sides as large oval white patch, sometimes with faint dark spots below and behind the dorsal fin; flippers, posterior margin of tail stock and tip of the dorsal fin may be pale gray or blotched

Total Length: male, 6 to 7 feet; female, 5 to 7 feet

Weight: male, 210 to 290 pounds; female, 150 to 330 pounds (maximum 480 pounds)

Gestation: 11.4 months

Offspring: 1 every 3 years

Age of Maturity: male, 8 years; female, 7 years

Longevity: a few have lived more than 16 years

Diet: deep-sea fish, squid and crustaceans

Habitat: in cool waters usually well offshore and beyond the outer edge of the continental shelf; occasionally in deep inshore waters

Predators: killer whale, sharks and man

Dental Formula: 44 to 52 teeth

DALL'S PORPOISE
Phocoenoides dalli

The Dall's porpoise speeds through the deep waters along the west coast of North America. With a huge heart and a powerful body capable of driving the animal along at 30 knots, it is a pursuit predator of many kinds of fish. Whale watchers delight in seeing

these brightly marked black-and-white-splotched animals throwing up shearing wakes with their sharp turns. Dall's porpoises rarely breach but frequently ride bow waves. Most of their feeding is thought to take place in medium-depth water of less than 650 feet, making them creatures of neither deep, open ocean nor shallow bays; they most often occur near the edge of deep water and probably dive to feed on bottom fish.

Dall's porpoises travel in small groups, and little is known of their social behavior. With adult males reaching 7 feet, they are among the largest porpoises and have a long breeding and weaning interval, calving every three years and weaning after two years. Even though abundant, the Dall's porpoise is at risk where deep drifting gill nets are in use.

The squat, thick body form of the Dall's porpoise makes it a powerful swimmer that sends up "rooster-tail" sprays of water as it zigzags in pursuit of fish.

BEAKED WHALES *Ziphiidae*

Beaked whales range from 9 to 36 feet long and swim in all oceans, but they are the least known of the whales. Indeed, they have been called the least known of all mammalian families. Beaked whales do not normally occur within sight of land or even on the continental shelf, and there are few observations of living specimens. They seem to be deep-ocean specialists capable of diving for bottom organisms and squid. Eighteen species have been described, and there are likely others.

Most species of beaked whales are difficult to identify. As a group, they can be recognized by their small heads, slim bodies tapered at both ends and elongated jaws that form a beak. Tail flukes lack a distinct notch to separate the right from the left. The dorsal fin is small and set far back toward the tail. Beaked whales' flippers are short and rounded.

The elongated jaws from which the beaked whale derives its name appear to be designed for catching squid, an adaptation that may explain the diversity of the group. Squid are abundant, they exhibit great species diversity, and their ecological distribution is wide. The richness in beaked whale species may reflect the variation in squid ecology, with different beaked whale species feeding on different squid populations. The beak itself is an unlikely apparatus, being virtually toothless, but the whales are apparently able to use it to clamp down on slippery squid. A rough palate keeps the squid in place.

Some beaked whale species are still hunted for food and oil, but fortunately for the whales, the meat and oil appear to have laxative properties.

The natives of the Kamchatka Peninsula in Soviet Asia used it "as a treat for undesirable guests."

Most of what is known about beaked whales is based on the hunted species. They can stay submerged for two hours and descend 1,500 feet in a minute. Some species may have unusually long gestation periods of up to 17 months, which are the longest of any whale.

NORTHERN BOTTLENOSE WHALE
Hyperoodon ampullatus

The northern bottlenose is the best known of all beaked whales, a distinction it unfortunately owes to commercial whaling. This is the largest bottlenose species, with males reaching a length of more than 27 feet. Robust and heavy-bodied for beaked whales, males may have a girth of 20 feet and weigh 3 to 4 tons. The Norwegian whaling industry, in particular, has sought out bottlenoses. Unlike most members of the family, they are not elusive or shy but will often approach ships, apparently out of curiosity. Bottlenoses are also among the more social of beaked whales, occurring in pods of 4 to 10 animals, which may be family groups. When one member of the pod is harpooned, the others remain with it until it is dead, becoming easy targets themselves.

The northern bottlenose has a distinct sexual dimorphism. Not only are males usually one-third larger than females, but they also have a massive, bulging forehead. This forehead melon is filled with oil, like the sperm whale's, and may be either an adaptation for deep diving or a sexual trait.

The northern bottlenose whale was named for the prominent melonlike shape of its forehead. The bulge may be an adaptation for deep diving, enabling the bottlenose to deflect sound and thus find its way about in the depths of the dark ocean.

NORTHERN BOTTLENOSE WHALE
Hyperoodon ampullatus

Mammal: *Hyperoodon ampullatus*, northern bottlenose whale

Meaning of Name: *Hyperoodon* (palate + tooth)—the first specimen described supposedly had tiny teeth in the palate (this is misleading, as they have two teeth in the lower jaw); *ampullatus* (provided with a flask or bottle) refers to the long snout in front of the bulging forehead

Description: robust, narrow, cylindrical body with a short beak; adult male has bulbous forehead, or melon, rising abruptly from the beak; blowhole is an indented area behind the forehead; usually two throat grooves

Color: young whales are blackish brown and lighter below, and older ones are light brown with light blotches on the back and sides that increase in size with age; very old whales are yellowish brown with whitish beaks and heads

Total Length: male, up to 32 feet; female, up to 26 feet

Weight: male, 8,000 pounds; female, 7,000 pounds

Gestation: 1 year

Offspring: 1 every 2 or 3 years

Age of Maturity: male, 7 to 11 years; female, 8 to 12 years

Longevity: at least 37 years

Diet: arctic squid (*Gonatus fabricii*); bottom-dwelling echinoderms such as sea stars and sea cucumbers; fish

Habitat: pelagic; frequents cold, deep (usually more than 3,300 feet) Arctic waters of the North Atlantic; generally well offshore; may approach polar ice packs in summer

Predators: killer whale

Dental Formula: 2+ teeth

SPERM WHALES *Physeteridae*

GREAT SPERM WHALE
Physeter macrocephalus

Moby Dick, the "great white" whale created by Herman Melville in his classic 19th-century novel, was actually a great sperm whale. Nomenclature aside, it was an apt choice of adversary—huge, fierce and heavily hunted by whalers.

In fact, it is because great sperm whales have been harvested for so long that they are probably the best known of all the whales. Unfortunately, most of what has been discovered is based on the study of their corpses.

The great sperm is the largest of all toothed whales. It is easily identified by its huge, squarish head, which makes up a third of its length. Its S-shaped blowhole produces a distinctive spout that shoots forward at a 45-degree angle and to the left of the animal. This species has rippled, wrinkled-looking skin. The blocky shape of the head accommodates the spermaceti organ, an oil-filled cavity bound with ligaments, veins, arteries and nerves and connected to one of the nasal passages. The high-quality spermaceti oil in this structure, which was once used as fuel for lamps, is the source of the sperm whale's common name.

The exact function of the spermaceti organ remains unknown. It may act as an acoustic lens for focusing incoming and outgoing sounds used in echolocation, and it could even enable the whale to produce enough sound to stun prey at close range. Other theories hold that the organ absorbs nitrogen during a dive or is involved in lung evacuation. Some researchers say that it controls buoyancy: Cold ocean water flooding the head cavities would solidify the oil into a dense wax that would pull the whale down like a weight during a dive. To ascend, the whale would pump hot blood around the cavity, liquefying the oil, which would then act like a float. Unfortunately, none of these ideas has been proven.

What is known is that sperm whales are formidable divers. They stay down for at least 80 minutes and eat bottom-dwelling sharks in areas where the ocean is more than 2 miles deep. Most of their hunting probably involves echolocation; they vocalize with clicks when diving.

Their long, deep dives make them difficult to observe, and except for what relates to whaling, relatively little is known about their behavior. True to Herman Melville's whaling epic, large, lone bull males do attack whaling boats, which they may mistake for other male sperm whales. Mature males attack and tooth-rake each other, producing long slashes in the skin.

Sperm whales are the most sexually dimorphic of all whales, males being more than three times as heavy as females at maturity. Females are sexually mature at 7 to 12 years, but in males, maturity is delayed until age 9 to 19, and status as a dominant male with access to a female group may not occur until age 27.

Males probably compete for access to the basic social unit of sperm whales, the nursery school, a social unit that seems to consist of 10 to 40 adult females, their calves and juveniles of both sexes. Mature males associate with a nursery school during breeding season but are solitary most of the rest of the year, although they do sometimes join together in schools. Males tend to migrate farther

The large, blocky head of the adult sperm whale creates an instantly recognizable silhouette against a backdrop of sunlight streaming through the ocean water.

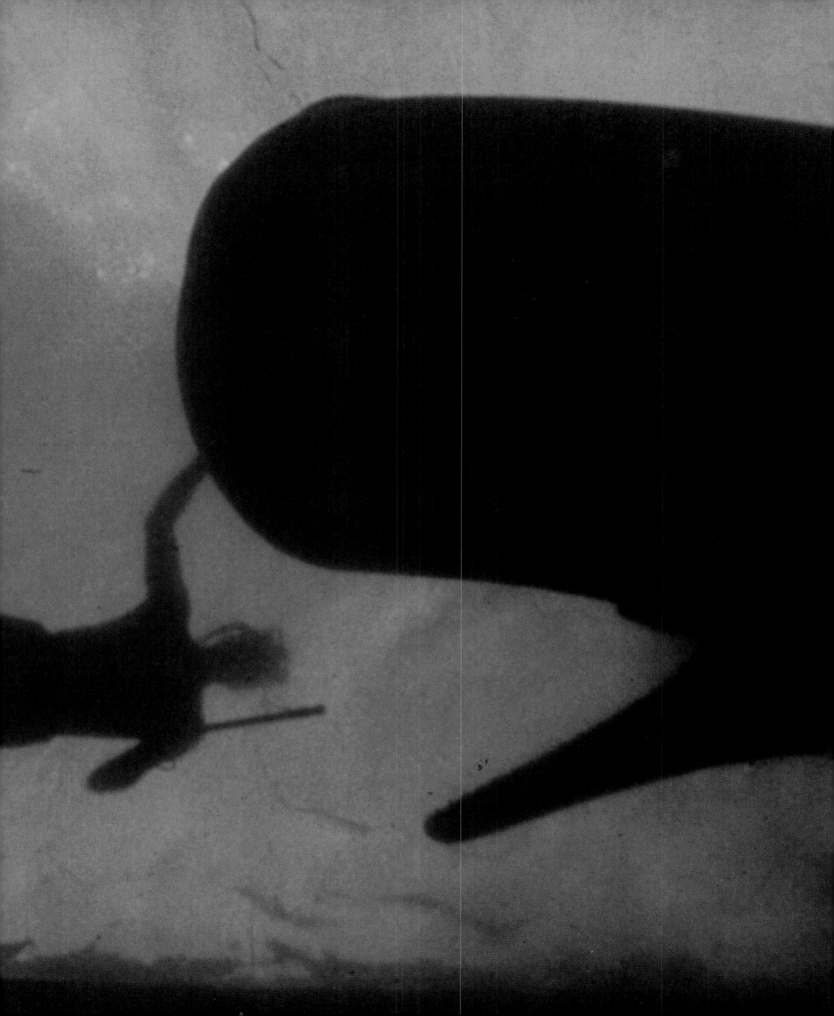

GREAT SPERM WHALE
Physeter macrocephalus

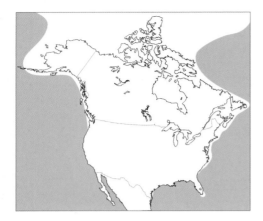

Mammal: *Physeter macrocephalus*, sperm whale; the largest toothed mammal in the world and the most sexually dimorphic of all cetaceans

Meaning of Name: *Physeter* (blowpipe or bellows) refers to the blowhole on the top of the head; *macrocephalus* (long head)

Description: enormous squarish head, one-quarter to one-third of body length; the huge spermaceti organ is filled with up to 500 gallons of waxy oil; blunt, squarish snout projects far beyond the lower jaw tip; only one blowhole, situated on the left side near the tip of the snout; small spout projects forward at a sharp angle; the usual dorsal fin is replaced with a hump followed by a series of bumps; ventral keel

Color: back is brownish gray and appears shriveled; ventrally, it is lighter with white splashes at the navel and on the lower jaw; older animals often have a pale gray whorl on the snout

Total Length: male, 36 to 61 feet (usually 50); female, 26 to 40 feet

Weight: male, 77,000 to 110,000 pounds; female, 25,500 to 36,500 pounds

Gestation: 14 to 17 months

Offspring: 1 (rarely twins) every 4 years

Age of Maturity: male, reaches puberty at 9 years, is sexually mature at 19 but has no opportunity to breed until 25 to 27 years; female, 7 to 12 years

Longevity: up to 77 years

Diet: primarily squid, including giant species, but also several species of sharks and other deep-sea fish

Habitat: pelagic; in temperate and tropical oceans along the edge of the continental shelf or near oceanic islands, usually at depths of 3,000 to 6,000 feet, or farther out to sea

Predators: man

Dental Formula: functional teeth on lower jaw only, 18 to 25 on each side

than females, moving as far north as 70 degrees latitude, while females normally stay within 40 degrees of the equator. At the higher latitudes, the males are usually solitary.

Sperm whale groups exhibit cooperative behavior. When one is wounded, the others form a circle around it, a trait exploited by whalers who then proceed to harpoon the defenders.

Although sperm whales eat a wide variety of deep-sea fish, they prefer squid and will battle even giant squid, the world's largest invertebrate at about 60 feet long. The giant squid's suction-cupped tentacles leave scars the size of dinner plates on the whales' skin. Perhaps this explains why sperm whales more often eat smaller squid, consuming up to 28,000 at a time.

But even small squid have horny, indigestible beaks that the whales must eliminate. They coat masses of them with a waxy substance and excrete them as a lump called ambergris, which is sometimes found floating on the ocean or washed ashore. Ambergris is used as a fixative by the perfume industry. For centuries, perfume wearers have been anointing themselves with a potion based on sperm whale dung.

Sperm whales also accumulate large quantities of fat that accounts for up to a third of their body weight. The store of blubber may be important in their migrations—they winter in warmer tropical regions and move to the high latitudes to feed in summer. Ironically, it was the life-sustaining fat rendered into whale oil that made these whales so attractive to the whaling industry. They have been hunted heavily for centuries and continue to be hunted by onshore whaling operations, but they are not considered endangered. Nonetheless, the great, battle-scarred bulls that inspired the legend of Moby Dick have all been killed.

A deep diver, the great sperm whale is able to swim thousands of feet beneath the ocean surface to prey on giant squid that grow as long as 60 feet.

CLOVEN-HOOFED MAMMALS *Artiodactyla*

From a human perspective, artiodactyls are the world's most important wild mammals. As humans evolved from hunters to farmers, they chose a number of artiodactyls for domestication—goats, camels, pigs, oxen, cattle, buffalo and sheep—that have, over time, provided important sources of food and muscle power. The history of humanity has been shaped by these animals more than by any others, and their value has been assured by their ability to harvest and digest great volumes of vegetation that is unpalatable to and indigestible by humans.

The artiodactyls first appeared some 54 million years ago. Then, they were small animals with relatively short legs and generalized teeth. Most species weighed less than 11 pounds and were omnivorous, eating various fruits and vegetation and probably scavenging the occasional bit of meat or small animal, a tendency still shown by the pigs and their close relatives, the hippopotamus and the peccary. This line of artiodactyls has retained short legs and a squat body. Their teeth still include large canines, and pigs, at least, are still highly omnivorous. The main artiodactyl group, however, evolved long legs and a foot-and-body plan designed for efficient running as well as teeth and a specialized stomach for handling a purely vegetarian diet.

These ruminant artiodactyls have lost or reduced their upper canines and have evolved a long set of broad molars with complicated crescent-shaped ridges along their surfaces. This is an adaptation for cutting and grinding vegetation. Their stomach has developed into a multichambered fermentation device that uses microorganisms to break down hard-to-digest molecules and convert them into useful forms. The pigs, hippos and peccaries, however, retained their single stomach.

The shift from omnivory to browsing and grazing resulted in the evolution of a different body form. The limbs of a vegetarian are of little use in catching or manipulating food; artiodactyls accomplish this with a flexible neck and lips. The rough tongue pushes vegetation against the lips and the roof of the mouth, while the lower teeth shear it off. Meanwhile, the limbs evolved into superb instruments of locomotion. As their legs became specialized solely for walking and running, their feet took on a new shape. All species walk on their third and fourth toes, the tips of which have become sheathed in a strong hoof material; their side toes have been reduced. Numerous other adaptations that lengthened the stride and increased the ability to run also evolved.

Artiodactyls are often active in exposed places, and they have well-developed senses of sight and smell to deal with predators. Many of them are gregarious and rely on herding to reduce the risk of being eaten by predators. They tend to have single large, precocial offspring that are ready to run soon after birth. The young of open-habitat animals, such as bison and caribou, can walk within a few hours and join their mother as she moves around. This is the "follower" strategy. Woodland deer, by contrast, have well-camouflaged, altricial young that are relatively helpless for several weeks and must pursue the "hider" strategy for survival.

Wild and rocky terrain is the typical habitat of bighorn sheep, but they will range farther into the open grasslands and tundra than will mountain goats.

DEER *Cervidae*

Deer are woodland browsers. Although they have the typical long-legged, long-necked grace of open-plains grazers, most deer are associated with wooded areas and limited open habitat. They will graze in meadows and grasslands, especially in summer, when herbaceous vegetation is plentiful, but when danger threatens, they retreat to cover. In winter, they are browsers, and much of their food consists of twigs and leaves clipped from trees and shrubs rather than grasses. Most of the world's deer species are found in subtropical forests or forest-edge habitats. A few, such as the caribou, spend much of their lives beyond the trees; some—the tiny Asian water deer, for example—live in reedy marshland; and others such as the mule deer range well into open grasslands or other open habitats. Species vary widely in size—Asian musk deer are the size of an average dog, while moose are larger than a horse.

Deer evolved in Eurasia, probably in heavy north-temperate and subtropical forests, eventually coming to North America and then moving into South America. Some species such as caribou are found only in the northern hemisphere; others such as elk are recent immigrants. Deer have never reached Australia, nor have they penetrated Africa, either because of the barrier posed by the Sahara or because of competition from other grazing mammals. In the New World, deer replaced a wide variety of deerlike browsers and grazers that had arisen in other now extinct groups. Although deer are among the most sought-after game animals, as yet there is not even agreement on exactly how many species exist. Recent estimates range from 19 to 45.

Deer are distinguished by their antlers, bony growths on the skull that all species have except one, a small Asian deer. Antlers are important in mating and courtship: Most deer tend to be polygynous, form harems and engage in male-male combat using antlers. The only species in which the females have antlers is caribou.

The herd size of deer varies greatly from one species to another. White-tailed deer and moose, which live in dense forests, are far less gregarious than open-habitat species such as caribou and elk. Being part of a herd has distinct advantages in open areas, where highly visual predators such as wolves and coyotes are a threat. In this sense, herding behavior is much like the schooling behavior of minnows and other fish that are food for larger predators. Being part of a group is a way for individuals to reduce the chance of a predator singling them out for attack. Individuals that are vulnerable because of injury, illness or age may conceal themselves in the crowd. A group also has more eyes for detecting the approach of predators, so each individual can devote more time to feeding and less to watching.

Large herds of grazing mammals may actually encourage the growth of preferred species of food plants by heavily cropping an area, something that occurs in African savannas, where large herds of grazers are found. Their heavy cropping maintains grassland communities and prevents less palatable shrubs from taking over. Herds of North American caribou may also have this effect, although the idea has yet to be tested.

By contrast, it is known that more solitary species such as deer which depend on shrubby browse are unable to control the growth of the

The size of a male's antlers is a clear indicator of his age and strength, although the horns of the white-tailed deer, right, are not nearly as impressive as those found in cervids that frequent more open terrain.

forest when they are at naturally low densities. Under natural conditions, they depend on fires and severe storms to open up new stands of brush habitat.

Deer-family herds are often segregated by sex, females and immature offspring in one group and males in bachelor herds usually composed of animals of a similar age. Segregation may serve several purposes. Wolves single out and attack individuals that appear to be abnormal, so it would pay an individual to join a group as similar to itself as possible.

Antlered males exhausted after the fall rut, for example, would be conspicuous and vulnerable among a group of antlerless females. Bachelor males in a group of peers likely benefit from the opportunity to develop the sparring skills they will need in combat for mating territories later in life. Females may benefit from joining other females because older females will know the whereabouts of good feeding areas and locations that offer defense from predators.

The herding instinct of some deer

species suits them to domestication. It would be very difficult to farm a solitary species such as moose, but red deer and reindeer are farmed in Europe, where they provide meat, milk products and velvet from their antlers, which is sold to the Orient as an aphrodisiac.

Born helpless, the speckled white-tail fawns are nursed by their mothers for as long as three months, which represents the only example of prolonged social contact in the lives of these otherwise solitary deer.

ELK *Cervus elaphus*

The elk, or wapiti, is one of the most vocal of all mammals, and for many people, the sound of its bugling epitomizes the autumn wilderness. The elk is larger than other *Cervus* species. Its bugle is higher-pitched, a difference that reflects the variations in habitat among the different species and subspecies. Forest animals such as the red deer of Europe need a call that will travel through vegetation—a deep, low-frequency bugle that thick greenery does not muffle. Elk, which frequent forest-edge and open habitats, use a higher-frequency sound that travels well across unobstructed open space.

Elk are harem breeders, and the male bugles to broadcast his size and strength with the intent of luring females into a harem. Studies have shown that bugling and roaring are honest advertisements of male strength, as they demand a great deal of energy. Because bugling is a valid test of male vigor, females are attracted to the males who bugle the loudest and the most often. A bugling male may be of higher genetic quality than a noncaller; at the very least, he is unlikely to be weakened by contagious or hereditary diseases. Subdominant males may try to bluff by bugling but are immediately challenged by a dominant territorial male and attacked if necessary. Thus the bugle is a reliable clue that females can use to choose a mate, and the most vocal males do have the highest reproductive success.

There is considerable anecdotal evidence that in this species, it is the female that chooses the male and not vice versa. A male may try to herd females and keep them in the harem with threat displays and even antler attacks, although these are more likely demonstrations of his prowess than effective tactics, as females can easily leave when he is preoccupied with male rivals or courting females.

It is to the female's advantage to examine as many males as possible and to use as many criteria as possible to assess their qualities as mates. Antlers are used to impress females, and regardless of their size, males deprived of their antlers are unable to attract and hold mates. Antlers can reach a weight of nearly 30 pounds and a span of 5 feet, and they require special strengthening of the neck muscles. Males advertise their reproductive state and territorial position with scents in their urine and with secretions from a facial gland. Reproductive hormones are excreted in the urine, so it is a reliable signal of reproductive condition. Males spray their belly, mane and face with urine, often spreading it farther by urinating on the ground and wallowing in it until mud and urine are caked on their fur and face. This is mainly an activity of large bulls, and the smell of their wallows excites cows and young male elk.

The cost of all this male advertising is high, and it dictates important changes in the feeding and movement strategies of bulls. In summer, they must eat more than females and move greater distances in search of browse if they are to accumulate the fat and muscle needed to withstand the fall rutting season. Bulls in summer are less sociable than females, but when they are in open habitats, they may band together for protection from predators.

After the rut, bulls are depleted of energy, and their antlers make them conspicuous to predators such as wolves, which are adept at cutting out the most vulnerable animals. In forest habitats, males may lose their antlers and forage alone, but in open areas, they tend to retain their antlers for a longer time because they are used in dominance contests for access to food.

Females tend to be highly social. They depend on herd living to reduce predation on themselves and their calves. A group of females, for example, will attack and kick coyotes, and they will run as a unit from more serious predators, the older, more experienced animals acting as leaders. Females do not entrust the welfare of newborn calves to group defense, however.

ELK *Cervus elaphus*

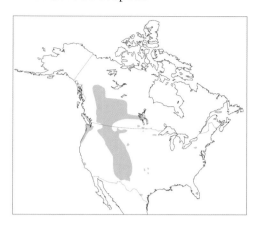

Mammal: *Cervus elaphus*, elk, wapiti; the second-largest member of the deer family
Meaning of Name: *Cervus* (stag, deer); *elaphus* (stag, deer); wapiti is from a Shawnee word meaning white rump
Description: majestic, widely branching antlers arise from large burrs high on the head; each antler consists of one heavy beam with several tines that sweeps up and back from the head and over the shoulder; tawny brown in summer; darker on face, belly, neck and legs; prominent pale-colored patch on rump and buttocks; in winter, darker brown head, neck, belly and legs contrast with paler brown on back and sides; males have long, dense mane
Total Length: male, 7.5 to 8.9 feet; female, 5.9 to 7.9 feet
Tail: male, 4 to 7 inches; female, 4.5 to 7 inches
Weight: male, 584 to 1,100 pounds; female, 414 to 660 pounds
Gestation: 249 to 262 days
Offspring: 1 (sometimes 2)
Age of Maturity: male, 2 years but cannot challenge other stags until 4 or 5 years; female, 2.5 years
Longevity: 14 to 26 years
Diet: largely grasses and herbs but also a variety of woody plants; will strip bark from trees if grasses and shoots are scarce
Habitat: woodlands and open lands, mountain meadows, foothills and plains; frequents swamps, coniferous forests and newly cut areas
Predators: mountain lion, wolf, lynx and coyote; wolverine, bobcat, black bear and golden eagle will kill unprotected young
Dental Formula:
0/3, 1/1, 3/3, 3/3 = 34 teeth

Calves are born away from the herd by lone females who have sought out some protected area of cover. This is a clear demonstration of the elk's origins as a forest animal that has only recently become a herding animal in the semiopen areas of North America. At birth, calves have a speckled coat that serves as camouflage in the dappled light of the forest, and unlike plains-adapted animals such as bison and pronghorns, they are relatively helpless when born and slow to become mobile.

The hider strategy of the mother elk entails elaborate precautions. She meticulously eats the afterbirth and even the soil and leaf litter in the area of the newborn to minimize scents that predators might pick up. She may even eat the feces and urine of her offspring

as an additional safety measure. The mother visits her calf only half a dozen times a day to nurse it, staying apart from it the rest of the time but close enough to hear it bleat. She will attack smaller predators such as coyotes and may decoy larger predators away. At a distinctive female alarm bark, the calf will crouch and remain still. The calf may stay in seclusion for as long as three weeks before it joins a nursery herd of mothers, calves and yearlings.

The mothers, calves and juveniles herd together, separate from the bulls, until the autumn rut. Both groups shift with the snowmelt, moving to higher and cooler ground as the summer progresses. Generalized grazers and browsers, they feed on a wide variety of grasses, shrubbery and other vegetation.

The harem-breeding system of elk has favored males evolving huge antlers and the powerful neck and chest muscles necessary to defeat rival males.

Elk have been eliminated from most of their southern and eastern range, but in the western-mountain and plains areas, they are still abundant, their herds totaling some 400,000 or more. In the west, hundreds of thousands of sportsmen hunt elk each autumn; the number of hunters has increased by several hundred percent since the 1950s. Naturalists also search out elk. Both groups exert pressure on elk populations. It has been shown, for example, that cross-country skiers may influence winter elk movements in a season when movement is a potentially large drain on energy reserves. As elk users increase, management plans that have traditionally met the needs of humans will have to deal with the elk's reduced range. Recreational development, urban expansion, mining, logging and housing diminish the wilderness further every year.

WHAT'S IN A NAME?

The use of Latin binomials, such as *Odocoileus virginianus* to name the white-tailed deer, does not sit well with many people. Latin is a dead language, and few people ever study it—not even biologists. Scientific names and the system of nomenclature stand as a barrier between nature and those who would contemplate it. Rare is the nature lover who will go to the trouble of learning what the difference between an order and genus is or what the artiodactyls are. Such pleasures are usually reserved for university students training to become professional biologists. Nevertheless, anyone who enjoys observing and thinking about nature will find the Latin names worth the small amount of effort they take to learn. Few things help more in understanding and appreciating the diversity of living creatures.

People have always classified living organisms. The essence of the system has been a lumping of like with like: Chairs look like chairs, and tables look like tables. Biologists approached animal classification with the same method for many centuries. With the discovery of the principle of evolution, however, biological classifiers known as taxonomists, or systematists, became obsessed with developing a classification system which reflected the evolutionary process and the different evolutionary relationships that exist between different kinds of organisms.

Splitting things into categories is the simplest way to handle a great deal of complex information, and that is how biological identification proceeds. When we look at an organism, we subject it to a series of questions that are designed to sort it into ever finer categories.

The most fundamental category—the kingdom—is easily understood. Does an organism belong in the plant kingdom or the animal kingdom? Even this general classification is a bit more complicated than it used to be, since there are now five recognized kingdoms—bacteria, protozoans and fungi as well as animals and plants.

Groupings such as kingdoms are based on shared characteristics, and biologists look for similarities and differences between and within groups. The differences between plants and animals are obvious, and the similarities within each group are also clear. But as we proceed through the classification system looking for finer groupings, the characteristics are less obvious and require careful study.

The animals are next divided into groups called phyla. Mammals are members of the phylum Chordata, which means they have an internal skeleton and a large nerve cord in the back. Thus birds, reptiles, amphibians, bony fish and several other groups besides mammals are chordates. To the evolutionary biologist, the significance of such shared features as a nerve cord or an internal skeleton is that all the members of a phylum had a common ancestor from which they diverged.

The next major division is the class. Mammals form the class Mammalia. All the members have fur, mammary glands and some other less obvious shared features. They are a neat grouping, clearly separated from other classes such as reptiles. The class Mammalia can then be divided further. For example, all the mammals that have shearing carnassial teeth are placed in the order Carnivora. The order is then divided into families such as cats, dogs and bears. All the members of the dog family share certain features which indicate that dogs, wolves and foxes had a common ancestor and that they are different from bears and cats.

A distinct organism such as the wolf has two Latin names, *Canis* and *lupus*, that refer to the next two divisions, genus and species. The genus is a grouping of closely related species (coyotes, dingoes, domestic dogs and jackals are all members of the genus *Canis*), while the second part of the binomial, the species name, distinguishes the individual within the genus. Thus the wolf is *Canis lupus* and the coyote *Canis latrans*.

All living things can be traced through this hierarchical structure from the species we see today back through groups that reflect a long and diverging evolutionary history. The wolf provides an apt example of the classification process: kingdom, Animalia; phylum, Chordata; class, Mammalia; order, Carnivora; family, Canidae; genus, *Canis*; species, *lupus*.

This is certainly not an easy system to absorb quickly, and some species do not fit neatly into it. Biologists still disagree, for example, on whether pandas are members of the bear or raccoon family, and many fossil records are incomplete, providing only bits and pieces of evidence that could fit an animal equally well into different categories. Categories are often hard to assess, and there is constant debate on the merits of classifying a group as a separate family. Is the pronghorn different enough from other artiodactyls that it should be placed in its own family, or is it better placed in Bovidae along with bison and cattle? These kinds of questions will always be there, awaiting refinement of our knowledge. But the system is worth learning now.

The organization of diversity is the first step toward understanding and enjoying the animal kingdom fully. Things are certainly clearer if one uses Latin binomials when deciding whether the brush wolf is a gray wolf, a timber wolf or a coyote. It is definitely *Canis latrans*, a close relative of *Canis lupus*, the gray wolf. And from the evolutionary perspective, we can appreciate the graceful beauty of a pronghorn a little better when we know that it shares a common artiodactyl ancestor with the pig.

WHITE-TAILED DEER
Odocoileus virginianus

The bright upright tail of a fleeing white-tailed deer may be a signal designed to discourage predator pursuit by indicating that the deer is alert to the predator's presence.

White-tailed deer are far more solitary than other northern cervids such as elk and caribou. They are creatures of the thickets whose lives are based on concealment to avoid the attention of predators. In many respects, this species' life history resembles that of the cottontail rabbit. The white-tailed deer occupies a small section of forest and is far less migratory than the other cervids, often having a home range of only 40 to 200 acres. This enables the individual to become familiar with the terrain and all the escape routes.

Females do not band together either at birthing time or when their calves are maturing, pursuing a hiding strategy to the extreme. They give birth to one or two fawns over a wider seasonal range than most large herbivores, anytime from early spring to late summer. Occasionally, in protected spots, three or four fawns may be born. A mother with more than one fawn will keep them in separate places to reduce the chances of a predator finding them all. She returns to nurse them only a few times a day to avoid drawing attention to them.

The fawns are born in a relatively helpless state, unable to travel for several days after birth. They rely on their stillness, reduced odor and speckled coat for concealment, and only after three weeks do they begin to travel with their mother. The early association of the fawns with their mother seems to be the only prolonged social contact in white-tailed deer. They nurse for as long as three months and stay with the mother even after weaning. Males may leave their mother at the fall rutting season to join up with a few other yearling males, or they may defer this until the spring. Female fawns stay with their mother over the winter and may remain with her for as long as four seasons, although the mother may leave for a while at the time of the rut. Whether the extended female association results in the inheritance of territory or is merely a way of passing on maternal experience is not known.

Like all cervids, male white-tailed deer grow antlers in preparation for the attempt to acquire a harem of breeding females. In autumn, they rub trees with their scent glands and thrash the vegetation with their antlers to mark out territories that they defend from other bucks. There is little vocalization except for a baa-ing as a male follows a female, and the rut seems less intense than that of the elk. Similarly, the antlers of this species are generally smaller than those of cervids from more open habitats. Males may also stay with a single female for several days to several weeks, and mate guarding may be an alternative to trying to establish large harems. Intensity of predation and lack of visibility in the forest may have constrained the white-tailed male's polygynous tendencies.

Once the rutting season has passed, white-tails are hard to hear or see in the forest. When surprised, they sail over logs and brush in bounding leaps and can outdistance most pursuit predators. The larger cats such as puma and lynx rely on surprise to catch adults, and wolves normally depend on favorable snow conditions and pack hunting to run them down.

The white-tail is a relatively southerly deer whose range extends into South America, but recently, it has been expanding northward. A generalized browser, it favors shrubbery of all sorts, so the cutting, clearing and subsequent regrowth of northeastern forests have been favorable to it, as has the extermination of populations of many large carnivores. What seems to limit northern deer populations is a combination of snow conditions and food sufficiency. In northern areas, deer yard up in thick stands of conifers for protection from the wind, often preferring shelter to venturing out to forage, as their coats are not very thick and their small hooves not designed to handle soft or lightly crusted deep snow. To escape from wolves, for example, they rely on a series of crisscrossing, hard-packed trails that radiate from the deeryard. Without these, they would flounder and tire in chest-deep snow, and wolves could easily run them down.

The restriction of activity and feeding range that results from relying on these winter trails leads to dominance patterns. Older females establish priority and are first to reach the food and snip off favored browse.

The weapons of the female and the male without horns are the forefeet. Capable of inflicting hard blows, female white-tails have broken bones and otherwise severely injured lone wolves.

Hunting is the major control on white-tailed deer populations. Two million are shot every year in North America, and in urban areas, car-deer collisions account for as many kills as hunters do. Feral and unleashed domestic dogs are another important mortality agent, accounting for up to 10 percent of the winter kill. Nevertheless, their multiple offspring and early age of reproduction allow white-tails to remain one of the most abundant of all large game animals.

WHY WAVE A FLAG?

Surprise a white-tailed deer, and its usual response is to snort, turn tail and run. As it does, it lifts its tail, flashing the white underside conspicuously as it bounds away. This seems an unlikely behavior for a forest animal that is cryptically colored and secretive in its other movements. Why should it wave a flag at predators?

A multitude of possible explanations exists. It might act as a startle display at close range, the sudden flare of white causing the predator to hesitate, allowing the deer a crucial split-second head start. This sort of startle display is well developed in various insects and frogs, so it is at least a potentially plausible idea. But most mammalian predators such as pumas and wolves should be undeterred by such a display, especially after they have seen it a few times.

Another possibility is that the flag warns other deer about an approaching predator. This could be valuable in several ways. It might cause other deer to startle and reveal themselves to the predator, reducing the probability that the signaler would be attacked. This

sort of selfish manipulation may be likely in groups of unrelated animals, but if the deer is surrounded by its own offspring or other kin, it might simply be a mutually beneficial warning. Related to this is the idea that the raised white tail might enable offspring to follow their mother as she bounds through the forest. But the signal is not used so selectively. Lone deer wave their flags just as social animals do.

The third possibility is that the signal is a direct communication between the deer and the predator, the deer signaling "I have seen you. I know you are a predator." This could be beneficial to the deer in two ways. It may help resolve any uncertainty the deer has about whether the predator is hunting—the deer can settle any confusion by exposing itself to test the intentions of the predator. Alternatively, it may be an attempt to discourage the predator by indicating that the deer is aware of its enemy and can probably outrun it. Most predators must rely on ambush or surprise attack to capture a deer.

This last idea has received the most support. The flag is useful to the predator, since the predator can save itself the unprofitable stalk and chase if the deer knows it is there. The deer, of course, is not signaling to save the predator from exertion; it merely seeks to prevent an attack.

A test of these ideas revealed that deer flag when they are alone, not just when they are in groups, and that the flag is directed toward the threat, not other deer. This suggests that the warning hypothesis is not a strong possibility. Interestingly, not all deer flag. Those that are surprised at close range or see a predator making a second approach to resume a chase do not flag but simply get going, suggesting that the deer realizes the tail has failed to discourage the predator. In the test, the deer most likely to flag were those that saw the predator approach from afar and had time to make their exit. Discouraging pursuit is likely why it sometimes pays to wave a flag.

WHITE-TAILED DEER
Odocoileus virginianus

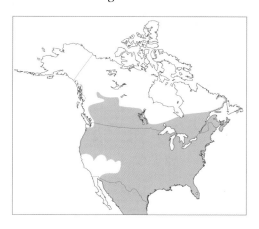

Mammal: *Odocoileus virginianus*, white-tailed deer

Meaning of Name: *Odocoileus* (hollow tooth) refers to well-hollowed teeth; *virginianus* (of Virginia)

Description: male antlers spread back, out and then forward, curving inward on an almost horizontal plane, with sharp unbranched tines; in summer, reddish tan on back; in winter, grizzled gray on the upper parts; in both seasons, white on belly, throat, eye ring and inside ears; black nose, tawny fringed ears and black spot on each side of white chin; on the inside of the hocks are preorbital glands and pear-shaped tarsal glands surrounded by stiff white hairs

Total Length: male, 6 to 7 feet; female, 5.2 to 6.5 feet

Tail: 5.9 to 11 inches

Weight: male, 151 to 311 pounds; female, 90 to 210 pounds

Gestation: 195 to 212 days

Offspring: 1 to 3

Age of Maturity: male, 1 year but does not get a chance to mate until older and stronger; female, most at 1 year (a few at 7 months)

Longevity: up to 16.5 years in the wild but seldom past 10; 20 years in captivity

Diet: browsers; in winter, buds and twigs of shrubs and saplings as well as needles and leaves of evergreens; in summer, grasses, fruits, forbs and green foliage of shrubs and saplings, needles of evergreens, mushrooms

Habitat: forests and forest edges, cedar swamps and swamp edges, open brushy areas, mixed farmland; on the prairies, found in wooded coulees during the day and forage on open prairie in the evening

Predators: carnivores (coyote, wolf, lynx, bobcat and feral dogs)

Dental Formula:
0/3, 0/1, 3/3, 3/3 = 32 teeth

MOOSE *Alces alces*

Reaching a weight of 1,800 pounds, the moose is the largest cervid and, next to the bison, the largest land animal in North America.

The moose is a boreal-forest specialist. Not common in mature coniferous forests, which are dark and support little shrubbery in the undergrowth, the moose favors mixed forest with open areas and the edges of watercourses. Its common name is an Algonkian word meaning twig eater or bark stripper, and it is indeed a browser, clipping a wide variety of trees and shrubbery. In winter, however, when snow is heavy, the moose will forage in thick mature coniferous forest in which the understory is relatively clear of snow and offers protection from the wind.

The moose's long legs seem to be an adaptation for snowy winters. Moose can high-step their way through deep snow, and their broad hooves provide good support in wet, boggy areas. The boreal forest is crisscrossed with lakes and rivers, and moose are excellent swimmers. They will take to the water to escape predators such as wolves, and they feed heavily on water plants in summer. Moose have even been seen diving and swimming underwater in search of water plants.

Like other creatures of the boreal forest, the moose is solitary, more of a loner than any other North American cervid. Although a few moose may yard together in winter, they travel alone most of the year. In spring, females give birth to a single calf, which they defend with great vigor. The calf is weaned by autumn and stays with the mother through the winter and spring until she gives birth again. Females may tolerate the presence of the calf for as long as a year, but otherwise, they solicit company only during the autumn rut. Unlike other cervids, the female takes the most vocal role in the rut. She bawls out a long, loud moan that summons any bulls in the area. The call is effective and has long been imitated by hunters.

Since moose are generally widely dispersed, males do not attract and defend a harem of females as do open-habitat cervids such as elk. Instead, the bull patrols the area, advertising his presence with urine and other scent marks, thrashing the vegetation with his antlers and creating wallows. If he encounters a male, he attempts to chase him out of the area. If he encounters a female, he mates with her if she is receptive, and if she is not, he stays with her and waits up to several weeks for her to come into estrus. The dispersion of the females limits a male's opportunity for polygyny. Nevertheless, successful mating seems to depend heavily on the male's ability to defend a mating territory. In some areas, small groups of males and females may congregate for mating, but this has not been well documented.

Moose antlers are among the most massive of all animal antlers; some may stretch 6 feet and weigh more than 70 pounds. They represent a tremendous investment of nutrients, even though they are cast off every season. To support and wield their antlers, bulls de-

A thick network of blood vessels is needed to grow the massive antlers seen on the adult bull moose. The animal must also build huge neck muscles to support their weight.

velop huge neck muscles. Their weight may increase by almost a third before the rut and drop to 10 percent lower than normal afterward. During the rut, males can be extremely belligerent and will charge humans and even cars.

The expanding range of white-tailed deer has brought them into a dangerously increased contact with moose. White-tails are host to the parasitic meningeal worm, *Parelaphostrongylus tenuis*. Although of little consequence to deer, it attacks the moose's nervous system and will cause paralysis and eventual death. Contact between white-tails and moose can fuel infections and lead to a serious moose-population decline.

A TASTE FOR SALT

It's a good bet that moose would like the taste of junk food, especially potato chips, as most herbivores in the north have a difficult time getting enough salt. The mammalian body uses the sodium molecules of salt in all sorts of jobs: transmitting electrical impulses along nerves, maintaining pressure within cells and effecting the movement of compounds through membranes. Meat eaters get plenty of salt in their diet, but northern herbivores usually have to feed on terminal twigs and branches of conifers and deciduous wood plants all winter long. These are low in sodium, so by the time spring arrives, the animals' salt reserves are greatly reduced.

This accounts for some strange behavior in browsers. It explains why porcupines love to eat canoe seats, outhouses and virtually anything that has come in contact with sweat or urine. It is why sheep and deer will travel many miles to salt licks, even though they are exposed to predators along the way. And it explains why moose go swimming and diving in the summer. Moose have been seen diving to a depth of 15 feet in search of underwater plants that contain salt.

Aquatic plants concentrate salt and other minerals. Some species, such as milfoil and the *Potamogeton* pond weeds, have sodium concentrations 10 to 400 times higher than in the woody plants moose browse on in winter. Moose have definite preferences for these over other kinds of water plants, and they have favorite lakes that they visit to the exclusion of others. The ideal lake for a salt-hungry moose is a shallow one with a high mineral content and a good flow of water in and out of it. The degree to which it has these features and the density of the water plants in it determine how much salt a moose can acquire over the summer. There is some suggestion that moose may build up a sufficient reserve of sodium to get them through the winter. They seem to store sodium in their large rumen, whose fluids make up 15 percent of their total body weight. Over the winter, they deplete this reserve.

It has also been suggested that the need for sodium and the intense use of aquatic plants may cause population cycles in moose. In years of moose abundance, they eat, trample and otherwise destroy aquatic-plant populations. They also strip the bark from the trees and eventually kill them. As their sodium sources decline, so does the moose population, which will rebound once the plant populations recover.

Not all the moose's foraging ecology revolves around sodium. They must meet other nutrient demands for protein, vitamins and carbohydrates. When aquatic plants are available, moose pursue a foraging strategy that maximizes energy intake rather than minimizing feeding time. An energy-maximizing strategy might be expected in large adult moose that are faced with building up fat reserves.

Compared with smaller mammals, moose have few predators to fear aside from wolves, and a healthy adult can usually fend off wolves in the summer. Mothers with calves, however, must compromise. They often swim to islands where plants are less rich in energy and sodium but where there are no wolves, apparently taking the risk of predation into account in their foraging tactics.

MOOSE *Alces alces*

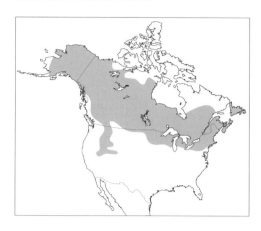

Mammal: *Alces alces*, moose; the largest living member of the deer family

Meaning of Name: *Alces* (elk); moose is derived from the Algonkian word moos ("eater of twigs" or "he strips off bark")

Description: prominent drooping snout and a dewlap, or "bell," hanging from throat; males have large, flat, palmate (shovel-shaped) antlers with small prongs projecting from the borders; brittle, stiff pelage; reddish brown to black, with gray legs; lower belly and underside of legs are whitish; males have brownish foreheads, females more gray; first year, animals are reddish

Total Length: male, 7.5 to 9.2 feet; female, 6.5 to 8.5 feet

Tail: 2 to 4.7 inches

Weight: male, 849 to 1,800 pounds; female, 727 to 873 pounds

Gestation: 226 to 264 days

Offspring: 1 (sometimes 2, rarely 3)

Age of Maturity: male, 2 to 3 years but rarely has the opportunity to breed until 5 or 6 years old; female, 2 to 3 years

Longevity: up to 27 years

Diet: primarily a browser; in winter, twigs and shrubs, bark of saplings; in summer, leaves from upland plants, large quantities of water plants, forbs, grasses and foliage

Habitat: wooded areas and early successional stages of evergreen forests; swamps, lakeshores adjacent to forests, muskegs and streams of great boreal forests; also tundra; in winter, found in mosaics of mature and young coniferous, deciduous and mixed stands

Predators: wolf is major predator; grizzly bear, black bear, wolverine and mountain lion prey on calves

Dental Formula:
0/3, 0/1, 3/3, 3/3 = 32 teeth

CARIBOU *Rangifer tarandus*

Caribou are the dominant grazers of the tundra and far northern forest. In Lapland and Russia, they have been domesticated as reindeer, making them the most northerly of all domesticated animals. Of all cervids, they show the greatest adaptation to a life spent in the cold, walking on snow and boggy tundra. Their feet are the widest of all the deer; usually defunct toelike dewclaws are well developed to help carry the animal over deep snow. The hooves show distinct seasonal differences: In summer, the hoof pads are soft and spread wide for walking on the tundra, while in winter, they harden and dense hair grows between the toes to protect the toe pads from abrasion by ice and crusted snow and to prevent skidding and slipping on icy surfaces.

One of the most unusual features of caribou is that the females have well-developed antlers. They are not as large as the males' but are still impressive. Moreover, females retain their antlers until calving time in spring, while males shed theirs just after the autumn rut. The females may signal social/sexual status with their antlers, and there is some evidence that they use them as a mineral bank from which they reabsorb nutrients as their pregnancies progress. It is likely that they recoup only a small amount of the total nutrient diversion, however, for growing antlers is a severe drain on the deer's mineral resources.

There are clearly dominance relationships among members of a caribou band, but exactly what benefits females achieve with their antlers is not clear. Possibly, they increase a female's winter access to food, as caribou may use them to dig deep craters in the snow in their search for food, which is particularly important to pregnant females.

Caribou are gregarious animals that typically herd together and travel as seasonal nomads over long distances. Most herds have summer and winter ranges that they move between, often traveling 600 miles or more. Generally, they move south to better cover in the northern taiga forests in winter and into more open habitats in summer. When selecting their summer grounds, the caribou tend toward windswept areas to avoid the biting flies that may otherwise torment them and their newborn calves.

Some caribou herds undertake spectacular migrations, with tens of thousands of animals following traditional routes across hundreds of miles of northern wilderness.

There are several nonmigratory populations, such as the herds on Peary Island in the high Arctic and in the Shickshock Mountains in the Gaspé Peninsula. The woodland caribou of the boreal forest are migratory but do not move as far as some populations do. In keeping with their forest habitat, they live in smaller groups. In open areas such as the barren grounds, bands coalesce into herds of 10,000 animals streaming across the countryside. They wear huge trails in the landscape, usually following traditional routes, fording and swimming great rivers on their journey.

The spring movement to calving grounds is led by the older pregnant females. Hostile to others, pregnant females separate from the group to calve alone, possibly in an attempt to reduce the chances of attracting predators. A single well-developed, precocial calf is born, able to run within hours of birth.

In summer, caribou are grazers rather than browsers, feeding on grasses, sedges, mosses and lichens, a favorite food. Even in the more southerly woodlands, where plant life is diverse, caribou eat lichens gleaned from trees. The reindeer gut has special bacteria for digesting the complex chemicals in lichens.

Unfortunately, lichens collect radioactive fallout from atomic testing, so the body of an adult reindeer contains concentrations of it from tons of lichens. The Inuit who eat caribou have been found to have absorbed radioactive compounds at concentrations that are several hundred times the level in urban North Americans.

In winter, the caribou's diet also includes browse from shrubs such as willow and birch. Caribou will also eat lemmings when they are plentiful as well as cast-off antlers that litter the tundra.

While much of the summer's nutrient intake goes into fat stores for the winter, a lot of it is devoted to the growth of antlers. In males, antler development starts in early spring and continues until late summer, when large males will have produced racks 4 feet wide. As the animals move south and toward treed areas, the antlers harden and the caribou thrash the velvet coating off against the shrubbery. Females begin developing antlers in summer and do not rub the velvet off until late autumn. Some females do not develop antlers, and it may be that they either have too few nutrients for the task or are following a different nutrient-investment strategy.

Male caribou do not maintain a harem in the way that elk do, being closer to moose in their reproductive strategy. A bull will follow one female as she approaches estrus, and prime bulls may interrupt one another to fight over a female. After the rut, the large, weakened males are prime targets for wolves. Perhaps one reason females retain their antlers is to distinguish themselves from the vulnerable males.

Wolves are the main predators of both calves and adult caribou, and many biologists feel that wolves regulate caribou populations effectively. When human hunters become involved as well, however, certain caribou populations cannot withstand the onslaught. Caribou have been eliminated in the southern areas of their range, while in parts of the north, hunting pressure is progressively weakening the stock. A number of wolf-control programs have been established in an effort to preserve caribou populations and to allow traditional hunting to continue.

The success of highly migratory herds may depend on the existence of well-traveled routes. Oil pipelines and related developments are threats to herds with set migration patterns, and hydroelectric dams in Quebec have recently been cited as the cause of large kills of tens of thousands of migrants. Despite these problems, caribou remain one of the most important animals for northern peoples, and there is scope for further sustainable use in the Arctic.

....

ANTLERS AS STATUS SYMBOLS

Humans have a reverence for horns and antlers. The traditional ceremony used in many cultures to crown royalty is a recognition of the power and status that a full set of horns or antlers brings to its bearer.

In the deer family, antlers are a clear indicator of a male's reproductive status. The size of the antlers provides both females and other males with a reliable clue to the bearer's quality and vigor. The same is true of the horns of bovids (cows and sheep). Both horns and antlers are bony outgrowths from the skull, the chief difference being that antlers are shed yearly, while horns stay on the animal and grow bigger every year. Antlers are covered with a velvety skin that grows as the antlers grow and contains blood vessels that provide nourishment for the bone growing beneath. Horns, unlike antlers, are covered with a hard keratin fiber. Castrated males of both families will either lose the horns or antlers they have or fail to grow them. Pronghorns are similar to

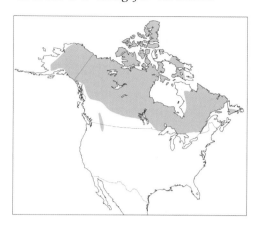

CARIBOU *Rangifer tarandus*

Mammal: *Rangifer tarandus*, caribou, reindeer; the only genus of the deer family in which both sexes are antlered

Meaning of Name: *Rangifer* (reindeer) from the Old French *rangifère*; *tarandus* (reindeer or animal of northern countries)

Description: compact, heavyset; large hooves; large, blunt, well-furred muzzle and short, broad, heavily furred ears; long ventral mane; variable antlers; slender, palmate mahogany-colored antlers (not all does have them) with one prominent tine down over nose; color varies with subspecies and season but is basically chocolate-brown, darker on the face, chest and dorsal tail surface; creamy white neck and mane; white belly, rump and ventral tail surface; brown legs with white "socks" above hooves

Total Length: male, 5.2 to 7.5 feet; female, 4.5 to 6.7 feet

Tail: male, 4.5 to 6 inches; female, 3.9 to 5.5 inches

Weight: male, 134 to 400 pounds; female, 138 to 260 pounds

Gestation: 215 to 240 days

Offspring: usually 1 (sometimes 2)

Age of Maturity: male may be excluded from mating by older males until the third year; female, 16 months

Longevity: average in the wild is 4.5 years (maximum 13 years); in captivity, maximum 20 years, 2 months

Diet: browser and grazer; lichens are a mainstay of diet, especially in winter

Habitat: prefers mature coniferous upland habitats surrounding the Arctic tundra and taiga zones; also found in remote alpine meadows; uses semiopen and open bog more in winter

Predators: man is chief predator; also wolf, grizzly bear, wolverine and lynx; golden eagle may prey on young

Dental Formula:
0/3, 1/1, 3/3, 3/3 = 34 teeth

horns, but they are branched and the keratin fiber covering is shed each year.

Antlers are dependable clues to the health and vigor of their bearer because they are expensive to produce in terms of the calcium and other minerals that would otherwise go to the skeletal system. In fact, antlers and large horns cost males more than pregnancy or lactation costs females. The size of the antlers reflects a male's ability to forage more and range farther, ample proof of his health and abilities. Antlers and horns are not signals that can be easily faked.

In theory, an individual could build large, impressive but hollow and weakly reinforced antlers or horns, but such duplicity would not go undetected. Male bighorn sheep and other horned and antlered mammals often aggregate in groups that appear to be arenas for displaying and comparing antlers and body size. To assess status and dominance, males engage in direct tests of one another's vigor, often in the form of sparring matches such as the antler wrestling of elk and caribou. In rather formalized encounters, males wave and lower their antlers in a display that emphasizes their size. If either rival is unconvinced, they lock antlers in a pushing, twisting sparring match in which the weaker male, having assessed his opponent, can withdraw before the fight escalates. If one party is not subdued by the other's performance, he may decide to charge and fight seriously, an action that usually leads to severe injuries and sometimes death.

Mating success is closely tied to success in male-male dominance contests, so antlers and horns have been designed for just that rather than for repelling predators. In fact, much evidence suggests that huge horns or antlers are more of a hindrance than a help. Female deer do not usually have antlers, and the males shed theirs after the rut is over. In sheep and goats, the males' horns are usually much larger than those of the females, which again suggests that the horns' main function is for male-male competition and not defense against predators.

The size of the antlers of a given species of deer is a reliable indicator of how polygynous the species is. Harem-breeding species such as elk have huge antlers; the acquisition of a harem is a high-yield, high-cost system. Males that can pay the price of large antlers get to father a large number of offspring. On the other hand, in some deer species, the females are so dispersed that there is little opportunity for assembling a harem and consequently little value in a large rack of antlers. Males may get more mates by searching widely or simply by following a single female until she is ready to mate. This is the pattern shown by small forest species of deer that live where antlers are more of a liability than they are to open-habitat species. In any case, the less polygynous forest deer have smaller antlers.

Caribou are the only kind of deer in which both males and females have antlers. The females' smaller antlers are retained till calving season; the males' are shed after the fall rut.

The male mule deer's reproductive strategy has led to the evolution of large antlers. Both male and female display widespread mulelike ears, an adaptation for detecting predators.

MULE DEER *Odocoileus hemionus*

The mule deer is a western version of the white-tailed deer, although it is larger and adapted to more open, arid habitats. The mule deer does not have the raised white tail flag of the white-tail, and its run is a stiff-legged gait that contrasts with the more graceful bounds of the white-tail. Males have antlers that branch into four prongs on either side when they reach full size.

In keeping with its habitat—open areas, where sound travels over long distances—mule deer have larger ears than white-tailed deer, hence their name. They are also more gregarious and seek safety in herds to increase their ability to detect predators. In winter, when bucks have lost their antlers, they join females and juveniles, forming large bands of several dozen individuals. Like other western cervids, these bands move with changing snow conditions and follow an altitudinal migration in mountainous areas. Their distribution and movement may be most influenced by the availability of water or lush grazing that would fulfill their water needs.

Mule deer have a typical autumn rut in which large males attempt to attract a harem of females. The females give birth in spring, usually to twins. It is not clear

MULE DEER
Odocoileus hemionus

Mammal: *Odocoileus hemionus*, mule deer
Meaning of Name: *Odocoileus* (hollow tooth) refers to well-hollowed teeth; *hemionus* (a half-ass, a mule) refers to the fact that it has very large ears like a mule's
Description: body is larger and stockier than white-tailed deer's; large metatarsal gland (2 to 6 inches) is surrounded by stiff brown hairs; dichotomously branched antlers on males are not prongs from a main beam; in summer, pelage varies from reddish to tawny brown above with a dark brown forehead; white face with black muzzle; rump patch, thighs, belly, throat and inside of ears are white; tail is either black-tipped or black on top; winter coat is dark or grizzled brown
Total Length: male, 4.7 to 6.2 feet; female, 4.5 to 5 feet
Tail: male, 5.9 to 7.9 inches; female, 4.5 to 7.9 inches
Weight: male, 110 to 473 pounds; female, 69 to 159 pounds
Gestation: 195 to 212 days
Offspring: 1 to 3 (usually 2)
Age of Maturity: 1.5 years
Longevity: seldom more than 10 years in the wild; 25 years in captivity
Diet: browser; feeds mostly on evergreen twigs, saplings and shrubs; also grasses, forbs, herbs, mushrooms, nuts and lichens
Habitat: open coniferous forests, subclimax brush and shrubs, chaparral, shrubby grasslands, steep, broken terrain and river valleys
Predators: mountain lion, wolf, coyote, lynx, bobcat and bear; golden eagle may prey on fawns
Dental Formula:
0/3, 0/1, 3/3, 3/3 = 32 teeth

whether mule deer fawns are more precocial at birth than white-tails, but their use of open habitats would predict it.

SEXUAL SELECTION

Darwin's most famous book is *On the Origin of Species by Means of Natural Selection*, the massive tome in which he carefully laid out his theory of evolution and natural selection. Most of an animal's traits, such as the spotted coat of a fawn or the strong jaws of a wolverine, seem obviously beneficial to the individual that bears them. Darwin had no difficulty explaining how these adaptations could be developed and refined through the process of natural selection. But many features troubled him, such as the gross red bladder the hooded seal blows out of its nose or the massive antlers on the head of the male elk.

How could natural selection have favored these bizarre traits? They look like vulnerabilities that would increase the risk of being noticed by predators, increase the effort of locomotion and decrease the animals' abilities to forage efficiently. To answer the question, Darwin wrote another massive book, *The Descent of Man and Selection in Relation to Sex*, in which he developed the theory of sexual selection. Its main intent was to explain the evolution of the strange traits and behaviors that would seem to decrease rather than increase an animal's ability to survive.

Darwin noted that the most elaborate and bizarre traits were associated with courtship and tended to be more highly developed in males than in females. For example, once past the breeding season, male artiodactyls tend to throw off their antlers, tone down their roaring and scent-marking and begin acting and looking like females. Darwin suggested that certain traits could evolve if they increased an individual's success at courtship, mating and producing offspring, even if the individual's likelihood of survival was reduced. What really mattered was whether they raised or lowered the individual's total number of descendants. Thus, even though a male's antlers and rutting behavior might make it more vulnerable to wolves, they would help the male father more offspring, and that would favor the same features in the evolutionary process.

Darwin recognized two ways in which males could increase their reproductive success through sexual selection. They could evolve characteristics that would improve their ability to conquer other males in combat over access to females, or they could increase their attractiveness to females.

Females tend to produce offspring at a high physical cost. They have large eggs, long pregnancies and major child-rearing responsibilities, so the total number of offspring they can expect to produce in a lifetime is low compared with the number a male could father. This means that males, with their billions of sperm, must compete for a limited number of female eggs. In addition, females tend to be selective about which males father their few offspring. These conditions set the stage for the evolution of displays that indicate the male's health and freedom from defects and the development of male weaponry for use against male competitors rather than predators.

Until opposed by a stronger selective pressure such as predation, sexually selected traits will continue to evolve if they give an individual an advantage in mating. Thus it is a mix of selective pressures that determines the appearance of an animal. Judging by male rutting and displays, sexual selection is a potent evolutionary force. For male artiodactyls, antlers and horns must have more advantages than disadvantages.

As a result of sexual selection, we see vast differences between male and female approaches to courtship, the males often aggressive, singing and performing elaborate rites, and the females standing aloof and selective, repelling the advances of young, untested males. These patterns are the result of sexual selection, a process set in motion not long after the beginning of life itself.

Dozens of pounds of minerals and large amounts of energy go into the construction of a male caribou's antlers. Their coating of velvet is thrashed off against shrubbery prior to the autumn rut.

PRONGHORN *Antilocapridae*

Although similar in design to the African antelope, pronghorns are found only in North America. Once considered members of Bovidae, pronghorns have now been classified as a separate family, Antilocapridae, because every year after the rut, they shed the outer layer of keratin fiber that covers their horns, while bovids retains theirs. North America was once home to more than a dozen different species of pronghorn, a family that dates back 20 million years, but all except the one we know today have become extinct.

PRONGHORN *Antilocapra americana*

Pronghorns, or antelopes, are among the fastest animals in the world. They have been clocked at 61 miles per hour, slightly slower than a cheetah, but a cheetah gives out after less than a mile, while a pronghorn can run at least 4 miles at a steady 45 miles per hour. The pronghorn is probably the world's fastest middle-distance mammal.

The speed of the pronghorn is an adaptation to the open plains. A large male weighs less than 150 pounds, and like many small animals, its only defense against most large carnivores is to outrun them. Its skill at doing so has made the pronghorn relatively incautious, more likely to investigate a strange intrusion than to retreat immediately. The first settlers of the grasslands found that by waving flags, they could attract pronghorns within easy rifle range, and North American herds of some 20 to 40 million were reduced to fewer than 30,000 animals. Populations have recovered somewhat since that time, and there are now about half a million animals.

Pronghorns resemble the bison in their migratory habits. As the seasons progress, they are constantly on the move, adjusting their position along a circuit according to the snow and the availability of food. Their range may cover a couple of hundred miles, as they are selective grazers that seek out high-energy food—forbs and shrubby browse rather than coarse grasses.

Pronghorns have a polygynous breeding system. Larger males may scent-mark a territory and try to attract a group of females to it, although there have been reports that in some areas, males try to join and guard a harem instead. This difference appears to depend on the quality of the forage. If the forage is lush and worth defending, a male will set up a territory, but if it is not, he will opt to join a harem. After the rut, males join up with mixed-sex herds for the winter, which is also when various bands may coalesce to form large herds of several thousand individuals.

In spring, females that are about to give birth pursue the hider strategy, which is rather out of keeping with their open-plains habitat. They leave the group and search out a protected spot, where they usually give birth to twins. The kids stay hidden for as long as three weeks, even though they can stand up within hours of birth. Because pronghorns offer no group defense to predators, relying on their speed to escape, kids that join the group too early could be cut out from the herd and attacked by coyotes. Mothers and young kids herd together for the summer. The young males disperse the following spring and travel in all-male bands until they achieve territorial status.

Pronghorns are the fastest middle-distance runners on Earth, capable of reaching speeds of 61 miles per hour. With large males weighing only 150 pounds, the pronghorn's sole defense against predators is running.

SPREADING THE RISK

When it comes to hunting, most mammalian carnivores are creatures of habit. Once they have discovered a prey item and a means of finding it, they will specialize in it until it becomes scarce. Artiodactyl fawns are an ideal prey for many carnivores—they are tender and easy to carry, and they put up little resistance. Wolves, coyotes, bobcats and grizzlies all eat fawns and calves of grazing animals during the birthing season.

The tendency of intelligent carnivores to specialize on particular prey in certain seasons is said to be responsible for the phenomenon of birth synchrony—females giving birth around the same time. Eighty percent of bison calves are born within a three-week period. The same is true for elk and some deer, and the periods for pronghorn, caribou and mountain sheep are even shorter.

The young born later in the season suffer higher predation, because they attract the attention of predators that have learned how to find infants. Young that are born early, before predators develop their taste and skills, are much more likely to survive. If the mothers force the birthing season back too early in spring, however, bad weather becomes a greater risk than predation.

The synchronous birthing of large herding animals has the potential to swamp predators. During much of the year, no vulnerable fawns or calves are available to predators, which exist in relatively low numbers and are dispersed over a wide area. Thus when calving season arrives, there are more calves than they can harvest, and the young born at the height of the season will suffer the least from predation. Unfortunately for this idea, nonherders and those in small bands such as white-tails and sheep show the same amount of synchrony as herders such as buffalo do.

There is a difficulty with the idea that birth synchrony in these species is an antipredator adaptation. Wolves and grizzlies live a long time, and they have good memories; naïve individuals represent a small segment of the population. Predators learn at an early age when calving season occurs and will exploit it annually for the rest of their lives. It seems more likely that females give birth synchronously according to climatic conditions and use other measures to reduce the risk to their young as well as the returns to predators so that they will search for alternative prey.

The most crucial period for an artiodactyl is between its birth and the time it can run with its mother and the herd. Mothers have several tactics for protecting their young during this period. Deer with more than one fawn hide them in different locations. Caribou have been known to deal with wolves and bears by moving into mountain areas to increase the effort the predators must make, to the point where it is more economical for them to search out other prey items.

Such a hiding strategy has been studied in pronghorn antelope. Coyotes seem to be the main predators of young pronghorns. Mothers will stand guard within sight of their fawns' hiding places, occasionally attacking predators and running down patrolling coyotes and kicking them. The pronghorn mother using the hider strategy must make a complex tactical decision, however. She must remain close enough to her young to be aware of danger to them yet not so close as to reveal their location to intelligent predators such as the coyote. Females try to stand about 70 yards away from their young, just far enough to make it unprofitable for coyotes to search the surrounding area. A coyote would have to search a large area around the mother, which would bring it a lower average return on its efforts than hunting ground squirrels would.

Females have a second defense. In theory, a coyote could simply follow a mother as she heads off to feed her calves, but mothers stay away from their young for so long that, once more, coyotes have more to gain by hunting ground squirrels.

Mother pronghorns are not in com-

Built for speed, the pronghorn has adaptations befitting the long-distance runner—a smaller stomach than slower grazers, so it won't have to run with a full belly, and proportionately larger lungs and heart.

plete control of the situation, however. In order to keep track of their young, they have to look at them at the risk of revealing the hiding place to predators. A patient coyote could narrow the search by observing the direction of the mother's most frequent gaze and potentially get twice the energy it would from a ground squirrel, which would make the effort worthwhile.

BORN TO RUN

One of the best ways to deal with a problem is to run away from it. That discovery has been made by many successful lineages but especially by the artiodactyls, which count in their membership some of the world's fastest land animals. The ancestors of the speedster antelopes, or pronghorns, were slow, squat, piglike animals. The evolution of today's animal runners was a response to the new demands and opportunities offered by the open plains. To become fleet-footed, artiodactyls had to evolve from a body suited for a life close to the ground, rooting and grubbing much as hogs do now.

The most obvious design simplification came in the feet. The number of toes was reduced to produce a compact hoof so that only the tips of the toes make contact with the ground. This has several advantages. On uneven ground, a wider foot is more likely to be injured. A small foot also means that the body weight will be more evenly distributed on the bearing surface, and more important, a small, light foot takes less energy to move back and forth. Moving a heavy foot at the end of a long limb is analogous to lifting a heavy weight with one's arm extended.

The energetic cost of the long artiodactyl limbs is reduced by a lean, economical shin. The lower legs of antelopes, like those of racehorses, look almost absurdly thin, as though they have no strength at all. In fact, they are tightly bound with ligaments and tendons which run to the large upper-leg muscles that provide most of the leg power. These muscles are close to the body, which keeps the center of gravity high so that the runner can leap and maneuver around obstacles and still retain its balance.

The length of the stride is one of the two basic determinants of a runner's speed. Artiodactyls have no clavicle, or collarbone, and this allows the shoulder blade to shift forward, lengthening the stride by as much as 20 percent. The backbone is also used to increase the stride. Fast runners such as pronghorns and cheetahs have a very flexible spine. When the animal runs, the spine curves in on itself in a concave shape, allowing the hind legs to reach forward until the hind feet are actually ahead of the forelimbs. Then the back legs push, the forelegs lift up and reach ahead, and the backbone and spinal muscles unleash, propelling the animal's entire forequarters forward. The coiling and unleashing of the backbone, hind legs swinging ahead of the forelegs, is the hallmark of the fastest mammals.

Speed comes only partly from length

of stride, though. The second basic adaptation is the rate of the stride. The bones have been reduced in number to allow more rapid movement, but the number of flexible joints has increased. An animal cannot move faster than its feet, and the rate at which the foot moves ahead is determined by the number of joints involved. Adding another movable joint with muscles to pull the limb ahead increases the speed at which the end of the limb moves.

The mobile spine and shoulder blades act as extra joints, but the artiodactyl's foot has another moving joint within the toes; the heel is raised off the ground, which frees the toes to act as units of propulsion. A special ligament called the springing ligament runs from the toes to behind the shinbone. When the animal puts weight on its foot, the toes stretch into a horizontal position, extending the ligament like an elastic band. Then when the weight is released, the ligament flicks the foot back, as anyone who has watched trotting horses has seen. This flexible strip of ligament gives the foot a final bit of thrust as it leaves the ground, without the expense and weight of a muscular unit pushing and pulling.

Artiodactyls also have a ligament that lightens the neck. Grazers with long, striding legs need a long neck. Coupled with the weight of antlers and horns, this would normally require a huge, heavy set of neck muscles. Instead, artiodactyls have a long neck ligament, the nuchal ligament, that runs along the back of the neck to the vertebrae between the shoulder blades and makes it easy to maintain various head postures without heavy neck muscles.

Finally, as every human runner knows, it is impossible to sprint with a full belly. The fastest North American mammal, the pronghorn, has a very small stomach—half the size of those of slower grazers—and proportionately larger lungs and heart. The smaller stomach means that the pronghorn, like other specialized athletes, has a more selective diet which includes the most nutritious plants on the range.

PRONGHORN
Antilocapra americana

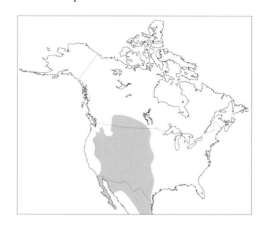

Mammal: *Antilocapra americana*, pronghorn, antelope

Meaning of Name: *Antilocapra* (horned animal—probably an antelope—and she-goat); perhaps a corruption of antholops, which seems to refer to the beautiful eyes of the animal; *americana* (of America)

Description: very large eyes; males and females have black horns with an anterior prong and curved tips; horns are covered by a layer of skin with specialized hairs; tan back with a creamy white rosette on the rump; bucks have a black face that extends as far as the base of the horns; does have black on muzzle only, with the rest of the rostrum brown, fading to pale gray about the horns; two white throat bars

Total Length: 4.1 to 4.8 feet

Tail: 2.3 to 7 inches

Weight: male, 100 to 150 pounds; female, 71 to 104 pounds

Gestation: 230 to 252 days

Offspring: 1 to 3 (usually 2)

Age of Maturity: 1.5 years (however, males cannot mate successfully until they are 3 years old)

Longevity: usually 4.5 years in the wild (maximum 14 years)

Diet: both browser and grazer; wide variety of weeds, shrubs, forbs, grasses, cacti and other plants; likes sagebrush

Habitat: gently to strongly rolling plains, prairies and foothills; prefers areas with water and an abundance of low-growing vegetation

Predators: coyote is main predator; also bobcat and grizzly bear; bobcat, golden eagle and raven prey upon newborns

Dental Formula:
0/3, 0/1, 3/3, 3/3 = 32 teeth

OXEN, GOATS & SHEEP *Bovidae*

Bovids are grassland animals that originated in Europe and later invaded Africa, Asia and North America. A few species have become creatures of the high mountains and tundra. Yaks, muskox and mountain goats dominate the top of both the Old and New Worlds.

Another group, the antelope, radiated to the tropical savannas. During the ice ages, when the boreal forest progressed southward, most bovids moved with it into dry parts of Africa and India. This geographical area remains the center of diversity today—antelope, kudu, eland, wildebeest and buffalo dominate the natural landscape. Few species have penetrated into North America, because the Bering land bridge filtered out groups that were not adapted to the cold conditions of the north. Many of the species that once existed in North America, such as giant bison and many kinds of antelope, became extinct in the Pleistocene epoch a million years ago.

Bovids differ from cervids in several distinct ways. Instead of antlers, they have horns that are never shed and are usually found on both sexes. They are more grazers than browsers, although goats are excellent browsers of shrubs.

The world supports 111 different bovid species. The northern part of North America is home to several species that represent distinct radiations within the family. The mountain goat, or mountain antelope, follows the typical goat pattern of being restricted to cliff areas with limited amounts of meadow grazing. The sheep graze in meadows and grasslands, retreating to rocky areas when danger threatens. United by their fear of predators, sheep are more social than goats, which tend to be territorially defensive about food and less concerned with predators.

The muskox is a type of goat antelope that has adapted to the tundra of the far north. Bison are allied with a recently evolved and advanced grassland lineage that has given rise to cattle, yaks and African buffalo. North America used to host many other kinds of bovids, but they became extinct during the last ice age.

A northerly species that lives among the highest mountains of North America, the Dall's sheep has a herding instinct that is activated when it passes through open areas of tundra in search of food and becomes more vulnerable to attacks by predators such as wolves.

BISON *Bos bison*

In the last century, bison numbered between 40 and 60 million in North America. The first white explorers to reach the western grasslands reported great herds blackening the plains as far as the eye could see.

The bison, also called the buffalo, was the mainstay of the Plains Indians, but neither they nor wolves nor silver-tipped grizzly bears constrained its numbers. A full-grown bull, the largest land animal in North America, weighs a ton and stands 6 feet high at the shoulder. A pack of wolves or a grizzly no doubt found the bull too formidable a foe to bother with and probably took only calves, the old and the injured. Winter blizzards were likely the main sources of mortality.

The Plains Indians made use of the bison's stampeding behavior. When they hunted, they would run the bison over cliffs or into box canyons for easy dispatch. Themselves subject to the population limiters of disease, starvation and warfare, they never threatened the abundance of the buffalo.

It was the arrival of settlers from Europe, along with railroads and professional buffalo hunters, that quickly reduced the buffalo to bleached bones on the prairies. Eventually, even the bones were picked by the destitute Plains Indians, who sold them by the trainload to be ground into fertilizer. In less than a century, the millions had been reduced to fewer than 1,000. It was only the persistence of a few isolated populations that kept the buffalo from going the way of the passenger pigeon.

Ironically, much of the shortgrass prairie where the buffalo once thrived turned out to be suitable only for

With males weighing in at almost a ton and standing 6 feet high at the shoulder, the bison is North America's largest terrestrial mammal. Its impressive size makes it virtually invulnerable to most predators.

livestock grazing. The irony persists. Buffalo grow better on a natural range and digest native vegetation more efficiently than cattle do. Cattle are more efficient only under feedlot conditions or when given high-quality hay. A bison is also better able to deal with predators and withstand winter in the plains.

Bison are compact and covered with thick, shaggy fur that once enabled them to range as far as the Northwest Territories. It is unlikely that their fine adaptation to the grasslands will ever be exploited on a scale comparable to what existed in the past, however. Bison are migratory, moving hundreds of miles with the seasons. Their routes were often traditional, involving hundreds of thousands of animals that wore deep paths across the landscape. Some of the traditional buffalo routes are still visible from the air.

Bison had a tremendous effect on local conditions in the grasslands. Their wallows became temporary ponds in spring, home to salamanders and other aquatic organisms. They often frequented prairie dog towns, browsing on the plants that prairie dogs avoided, their hoofprints and dung then favoring the growth of grasses eaten by prairie dogs. The system of grasses extracting soil nutrients and then being continuously cropped and turned into dung by bison is thought to have been a major factor in building the deep, rich soils of the prairies. Bison grazing is thought to have encouraged many shortgrass species that tend to become extinct locally when other vegetation is not kept short and open. Cowbirds followed the herds, eating the insects that were disturbed by the bison.

If populations were stable at about 50 million and the average female reproduced every two years, it can be calculated that at least a billion pounds of buffalo were recycled every year by predators, parasites, scavengers and decomposers.

Bison are sexually dimorphic, the males being much larger than the females. Bulls attempt to mate with as many females as possible in late summer and autumn. The rut is extremely loud, and the roars of the bulls can be heard five miles away. They use foot stamping, urination and a variety of snorts and other threats to intimidate rivals and attract females. Bulls do not form harems. Their strategy is to follow and defend one female, repelling the advances of other bulls, until she is ready to mate. Contesting males stand side by side, comparing sizes. If the contestants are evenly matched and the roaring and threatening escalate into a fight, the males will charge and ram each other with their heads, a behavior that accounts for the bull's massive front end. They use their relatively short horns to try to gore their opponent in the belly or flanks if he should falter.

Females usually give birth to a single calf in spring or summer. Able to stand within half an hour and run after three or four hours, the calf is well adapted for life on the open plains. It stays with its mother in a nursery herd and trails close by for a period of three weeks. It may then mix with other young calves in the herd, but it continues to recognize its mother and may not be weaned for almost a year. A mother, and sometimes the entire herd, will defend a calf against intruders, but large herds usually respond to danger by stampeding away. Individual bison can be dangerously aggressive, even outside the rutting season, and have been known to kill humans who fail to respect their wildness and power.

RUMINATION

People who become strict vegetarians soon learn that they have to devote a lot of effort to food selection. They must devise schemes to obtain adequate protein and B vitamins from food or else rely on commercial preparations. The reasons for this are simple. Humans are omnivores with a physiology designed for a diverse diet that includes some an-

BISON *Bos bison*

Mammal: *Bos bison*, bison, buffalo; North America's largest terrestrial mammal
Meaning of Name: *Bos* (ox, cow); *bison* (wild ox, buffalo)
Description: massive head and forequarters that appear out of proportion to its slim hindquarters; massive hump on shoulders; tail has terminal hair tassel; short black horns on the sides of the head; large nostrils; slate-blue tongue; matted, woolly undercoat; head, shoulders and forelegs are covered with a shaggy, dark brown mane; hindquarters are coppery brown; head and beard are almost black
Total Length: male, 9.9 to 12.5 feet; female, 6.5 to 7.5 feet
Tail: male, 17 to 32 inches; female, 18 to 21 inches
Weight: male, 1,014 to 2,000 pounds; female, 794 to 1,100 pounds
Gestation: 270 to 300 days
Offspring: 1 every 1 or 2 years
Age of Maturity: male, 2 to 3 years; female, some as yearlings but usually 2 to 4 years
Longevity: 20 years in the wild; potential may be 40 years
Diet: grazer; mainly grasses, forbs, sedges and other ground forage
Habitat: wide range of habitats; open, arid plains, open forests, grasslands and meadows, river valleys and mountainous areas
Predators: grizzly bear, gray wolf and puma; predators usually prey on young or old animals, as even a pack of wolves cannot easily overcome a lone bison
Dental Formula:
0/3, 0/1, 3/3, 3/3 = 32 teeth

imal protein and vitamins. A diet that consists only of plants is low in nutrients. Much of a plant is composed of structural support molecules, tough items that make up the bulk of plant biomass and act as its skeleton. The generalized mammalian stomach is inefficient at breaking down and processing these molecules and liberating what nutrients they do contain.

Artiodactyl grazers have devised an effective solution to the problem posed by such a bulky, low-nutrient and hard-to-digest diet; they have evolved a large multichambered gut. Their stomach has enlarged and divided into several chambers, one of which is known as the rumen.

The rumen is part of a system of mechanical and chemical breakdown in which the grazing ruminant swallows, without chewing, fresh and relatively tough vegetation. The saliva that follows the food down helps control its moisture content and the acidity of the gut. The fresh, coarse material passes into the rumen, where digestive enzymes mix with it, producing a great soup of fluids, saliva, plant material and fermentation microorganisms. A sievelike structure skims off coarse particles, now softened by the enzymes in the gut, and the mass of material is regurgitated back into the mouth several hours later. The animal then chews its cud, as it is called. This system allows the animal to adjust its feeding time so that it can harvest food when the weather and visibility for predator detection are good. The time-consuming job of shredding and finely grinding the plant material is left for when the animal is resting in a safe and comfortable spot.

The rumen is a fermentation chamber, home to distinct and specialized microorganisms. They do the difficult chemical work of digesting molecules of plant materials such as cellulose and lignin, substances from which lumber and paper are made. Once the nutrients are extracted from the plant material, they can pass through the sieve and continue along to the other chambers of the stomach and then into the intestines for further digestion and finally absorption into the bloodstream. Where the small intestine becomes the large intestine, there is a final large fermentation chamber, the cecum, that finishes the extraction process. In this system, ruminants not only break down plant material efficiently but also obtain many vitamins that are synthesized by the fermentation bacteria.

The heat given off by fermentation may be of some use in cold climates. Cold- and dry-climate artiodactyls enjoy another digestive advantage over grazers with different systems: They can recycle nitrogen wastes. The mammalian body is continually breaking down proteins that produce urea in the blood—a chemical filtered out by the kidneys and excreted as urine. Ruminants can recycle the urea from the blood into the rumen, however, where microorganisms feed on it in a process similar to fertilizing compost to get the microorganisms working more effectively.

The implications are broad. In winter, in order to reduce their body-heat requirements, northern mammals minimize the amount of snow and ice they eat, which reduces the amount of hot urine they must excrete. Their ability to conserve both water and heat by recycling urea has allowed ruminant grazers to dominate the high Arctic and the driest deserts, both of which have climates that place a premium on water conservation.

The other large mammalian grazers belong to the order Perissodactyla, which includes horses, tapirs and rhinoceroses. While they lack a rumen, they use a hind-gut digestive chamber. There are advantages and disadvantages to both artiodactyl and perissodactyl systems. A ruminator such as a cow can extract two-thirds of the nutrients from its food, but a horse extracts less than half. A cow may take almost four days to pass a meal through its system, while a horse can do it in as little as two days, leaving room for more food. This is why horses are known as hay burners. They have evolved a less efficient but faster extraction system.

The dissimilarities of the two systems probably account for the different body sizes and degrees of species diversity in the two families. Ruminants can specialize on certain plants that hind-gut digesters cannot. Being more efficient, ruminants need a smaller volume of food, so they can select rarer but more nutritious species. They can afford to be small-bodied, like the pronghorn antelope, since they exist on relatively less food. This is why they are ecologically more diverse than hind-gut fermenters. If a ruminant and a hind-gut fermenter are forced to exist on the same amount of vegetation, however, the ruminator could grow larger, since it gets more out of its food.

The largest grazers, such as elephants, are hind-gut fermenters that can process huge volumes of coarse woody material quickly. They follow a quantity-not-quality strategy and must therefore be large and range widely. Hind-gut fermenters also have more control over their rate of gut clearance—the more they eat, the faster it passes through, so they can adjust behaviorally to the quality of the forage. Ruminators ruminate at a slow, steady rate and cannot change their rate of digestion.

Since body size affects many other traits, such as predator resistance and tolerance to cold, the development of the rumen has had profound implications for humans. It is the ruminators that humans have specialized in domesticating, and it is the ruminating gut that is the model for the way we produce foods such as bread, cheese, beer and yogurt. Much modern biotechnology is based on the fermentation process that artiodactyls have been using for millions of years.

European settlement, the railroad and professional buffalo hunting in the past century reduced the total population of the bison, which once blackened the western plains "as far as the eye could see," from close to 60 million to as low as 1,000.

MOUNTAIN GOAT
Oreamnos americanus

The mountain goat is the most skilled rock climber of all North American mammals. It moves with confidence along ledges barely wide enough to accommodate it. Mountain goats will leap from ledge to ledge across deep chasms without hesitation and have a repertoire of maneuvers that would excite the most skilled mountain climbers. Goats have been seen in virtual free falls when descending steep, two-sided rock chutes by bouncing from wall to wall to break their speed as they go. One goat that walked far out along a thin ledge above a 400-foot drop found the ledge petering out and executed a cartwheel to turn around, planting its front feet on the ledge and walking its back legs up along the cliff face until it was turned and could retreat.

A mountain goat's legs are short and muscular, with hooves designed to take the impact and wear of rock but still provide spring and traction. The two-toed hoof has a stiff outer rim with a flexible pebbled pad on the central surface. The dewclaws (thumbs) provide a grip when moving down against a steep surface.

Goats are at home where predators are unable to reach them, but they pay a price for the security—there is very little grazing on the cliffs they inhabit. This makes them more solitary and far less social than mountain sheep, which travel in bands for protection. Unlike sheep, mountain goats will defend feeding areas vigorously in times of food shortage.

The horns of the female mountain goat are almost the same size as the male's, and both sexes use them to defend feeding areas. Males do not bother with a drawn-out ritual of horn comparison like that of the more social

A calm disposition and fearless agility make mountain goats skilled rock climbers. Nearly vertical cliffs offer these animals a safe haven where no predators dare to follow.

sheep but put interlopers to flight as quickly as possible, attempting to drive their sharp, lancelike horns into their opponents' flanks and bellies. Sometimes they will try to butt each other over cliffs. Males are not dominant over large females that hold their own feeding territories.

Horns are also useful against predators. They tend to be better weapons than antlers, which may be one reason why bovid females have horns. A mother goat will stay with her kid for up to a year and will defend it aggressively against lynx, wolverines and other predators. Predation seems to be a relatively minor pressure on mountain goat populations, and only when adults venture into meadows to feed do they become vulnerable to predators such as grizzlies. Golden eagles have been seen trying to knock adults from their ledges, and they do take the occasional kid, but they are not an important mortality factor. By far, the major causes of death are winter avalanches and falls. Starvation in severe blizzards is also a danger.

Males are polygynous, as are the other artiodactyls, defending rutting territories in autumn and engaging in vicious fights. Although they are not true goats in the narrow sense of the word, actually belonging to a group known as mountain antelopes, the males do carry the typical goat odor. They produce copious glandular secretions behind their horns that they wipe off around their territory. They also urinate and ejaculate frequently on their beards, wearing the smell as testimony of their maleness.

The musky taint is in their meat, making them virtually inedible for humans, so they have been little hunted except by those who wish to mount their heads as trophies. The biggest threat to their populations is the development of roads that bring increased human activity to their habitats, although their remote terrain makes them less vulnerable than many other North American mammals.

MOUNTAIN GOAT
Oreamnos americanus

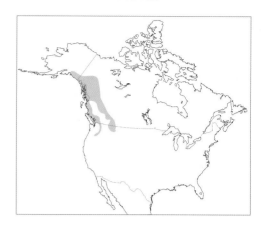

Mammal: *Oreamnos americanus,* mountain goat

Meaning of Name: *Oreamnos* (mountain lamb); *americanus* (of America)

Description: short, black recurved horns with basal annulations and smooth shiny tips; pair of black glands at base of horns; creamy white; sometimes brownish dorsal line or yellow wash; black lips, nostrils, horns and hooves

Total Length: male, 5.1 to 6.7 feet; female, 3.9 to 5.2 feet

Tail: male, 3.7 to 5.5 inches; female, 3.5 to 4.7 inches

Weight: male, 143 to 249 pounds; female, 100 to 212 pounds

Gestation: 147 to 178 days

Offspring: 1 or 2 (occasionally 3)

Age of Maturity: male, 39 months; female, 27 months

Longevity: 12 years in the wild (maximum 14 years for males, 18 years for females)

Diet: part grazer, part browser; feeds on various high-mountain vegetation such as grasses, mosses, lichens, woody plants and herbs; salt licks are important

Habitat: rugged mountains with steep slopes; prefers steep, grassy talus slopes at the base of cliffs in alpine tundra or subalpine areas; associated with low temperatures and heavy snowfall

Predators: mountain lion, eagle, grizzly bear, wolverine, wolf and coyote; eagles prey on the young

Dental Formula:
0/3, 0/1, 3/3, 3/3 = 32 teeth

MUSKOX *Ovibos moschatus*

The muskox may look like a great, shaggy ox, but its closest relative is a goatlike species found in the Himalayas. The muskox evolved its characteristic ox form when it invaded the cold Asian grasslands and spread north into Siberia and later across the Bering land bridge into North America.

The muskox is not as big as it looks. Under its shaggy coat, it is a relatively small animal compared with the bison. Bulls usually reach a weight of about 750 pounds, 1,450 pounds being the maximum recorded for an animal fed and raised in captivity.

The massive fur coat is composed mainly of long threads of very fine-quality wool, considered to be the highest-quality wool in the world. The outer coat is overlaid with long, coarse guard hairs that can be up to 2 feet long. Heat-losing extremities such as the tail and ears are buried in the coat,

In an example of their best-known defensive strategy, these three muskox protect their young from wolves by forming part of an outward-facing circle around the herd's calves.

an adaptation that allows the muskox to survive at the very limit of the tundra, where snow lies on the ground 10 months of the year.

Muskox can weather temperatures of minus 40 degrees F without increasing their metabolism. They are slow-moving in the depth of winter and probably conserve energy by being relatively inactive and reducing their intake of water to avoid the energy drain of converting cold snow to warm urine and excreting it.

The muskox is not a migratory animal but limits itself to local areas of well-vegetated tundra where wind, drainage and an optimal snow accumulation provide reasonable growing conditions. Muskox browse and graze most of the Arctic shrubs, sedges, grasses and forbs, but they do not eat the quantities of lichens that caribou do. The depth of snow is a primary constraint on the variety of their diet, as some plants—the taller ones such as willows—are easier to dig out in winter.

The basic social unit of the muskox is a band of females, their juvenile offspring and a single bull that treats the band as a harem, staying with it for most of the year. The dominant bull provides leadership in repelling predators, setting routes and fording rivers. There is also a dominance hierarchy among the cows, and when the bull is absent, certain females assume the leadership role. In spring, bulls leave their herd and either forage alone or join bands of younger animals. At the approach of rutting season in late summer and autumn, they become aggressive and fight one another to assume leadership of a group of females. The bulls' horns are larger than those of the females, and they grow together across the forehead in a heavy band that is used for head butting.

A female bears a calf every spring or two, depending on her physical condition. The calf is precocious, up and following its mother around on the first day. Females form stable groups that include the young of the year as well as immature males and older females. It is likely that many of the female offspring remain in the mother's group, and this may account for their methods of group defense.

A band of females and offspring, with or without a bull, is an integrated unit that cooperates in defense against predators. Their most famous protective strategy is an outward-facing ring of adults around the calves. Their cooperative nature extends to preserving energy by lying together for warmth when resting and breaking trails for one another as they move through the snow.

The only serious predators of muskox are wolves, which may dash into a herd to pull down a calf or occasionally try to kill a lone adult. An adult in good condition, though, is difficult prey, for muskox have a goatlike agility. Their broad hooves have a sharp outer rim and a soft inner area that enables them to grip, turn and scramble about on ice and rocky substrates. The skull is massively reinforced, and the horns are lethal weapons. They are strong swimmers, and a lone muskox may, if harassed, wade into water, where it is virtually invulnerable.

The greatest source of mortality is the stress of overwintering. On Bathurst Island in 1973, a winter storm that left a layer of frozen snow and ice over the vegetation killed half the area's muskox population.

Muskox are now protected, but their preserves remain open to mining and oil development, which may prove disastrous for such sedentary and easily disturbed animals. Muskox in a defense ring are easily shot, and many regional populations have been extinguished, although efforts have been made to reintroduce them. Southern sport hunters pay thousands of dollars for the chance to shoot a muskox, providing an occasional source of income for northern peoples. One alternative—increasing the size of muskox herds and using them for wool production—is under study. Approximately 10,000 muskox currently inhabit the continent.

MUSKOX *Ovibos moschatus*

Mammal: *Ovibos moschatus*, muskox
Meaning of Name: *Ovibos* (sheep + cow); *moschatus* (musky) refers to strong, musky odor of urine
Description: bulls have massive keratinous horns with only a narrow groove separating their cores (females' horns are not as large); horns sweep downward close to the skull, then tips turn upward and outward; an overcoat of long guard hairs hangs about the body; dark brown to blackish; creamy yellow saddle and stockings; females and juveniles have lighter foreheads; fur is short and grayish on muzzle and legs
Total Length: male, 6.5 to 8.1 feet; female, 6.5 feet
Tail: male, 4.5 to 6.5 inches; female, 2.5 to 6 inches
Weight: male, 580 to 1,450 pounds; female, 617 to 650 pounds
Gestation: 8 to 9 months
Offspring: 1 (rarely 2) every 1 or 2 years
Age of Maturity: 3 to 5 years (as early as 18 months in captivity)
Longevity: 20 to 25 years
Diet: browser and grazer; willow, tundra grasses, forbs and sedges
Habitat: Arctic tundra with sufficient forage; in summer, moist habitats such as river valleys, lakeshores and seepage meadows; in winter, hilltops, slopes and plateaus
Predators: wolf is main natural predator and usually preys on lone animals; also grizzly bear
Dental Formula:
0/3, 0/1, 3/3, 3/3 = 32 teeth

BIGHORN SHEEP
Ovis canadensis

The mountains of the west are a safe haven for agile climbers like the bighorn sheep, whose life is a compromise between the security offered by rocky ledges and rugged terrain and the feeding grounds in flatter but more exposed ground. While goats have specialized in cliff life and make occasional excursions into meadows, sheep tend to gravitate to open meadows and head for rocky areas when they need protection.

Bighorn sheep live in bands that travel and forage together for additional protection from predators. The composition of the band centers on the ewes, usually several older females that provide leadership to younger ewes, immature males and lambs. Rams nearing sexual maturity, around the age of 3, band together in all-male groups led by older males. The older males separate from the females in spring to begin their summer feeding in preparation for the autumn rut.

In summer, the bands are on the move constantly, grazing and clipping along traditional routes with well-marked trails. They follow a typical altitudinal migration from the valleys in winter, where large groups of up to a hundred individuals may herd together. In spring, the males set off for higher ground, followed by the female bands. Their movement may follow as many as six different ranges and seasonal phases, as determined by the snow, lambing season, rutting and the need to visit mineral licks.

Female bands may consist of more than 15 individuals, many of which are closely related, while male bands are smaller, usually about half a dozen individuals of varying ages and sizes. The males sort themselves into a dominance hierarchy, a situation that inevitably requires compromise. While an animal might raise its status by joining a smaller group where it will have a greater opportunity for leadership, it will feed less efficiently, as sheep in small groups spend much more time scanning for predators than they do grazing.

Predator pressure comes in many forms. Mountain lions, wolves, coyotes, lynx, bobcats, bears and golden eagles all prey on sheep. The response of the sheep is usually to flee to rocky terrain, but larger rams may turn to fight lone coyotes. The spring lambing time is a period of major mortality. Even though lambs are born on rocky ledges that are inaccessible to most predators and are hidden until they are a week old and able to walk, golden eagles still take a heavy toll.

The aggregation of females into bands creates conditions favorable to harem-guarding males. In the autumn rut, males attempt to control access to and mate with all the receptive members of a female band. This produces spectacular head-cracking duels between the largest bighorn males. The force of two rams charging full speed into each other creates a loud crack like the sound of a gunshot and may break the horns and skull of smaller males. There is also a great deal of subtle interaction between males. They seem to gather in groups to compare horns and body size. They also use homosexual mountings to express dominance, a subdominant male

The substantial curling horns of male bighorn sheep are used in ritualized displays and violent head-smacking duels that determine dominance and access to females.

BIGHORN SHEEP
Ovis canadensis

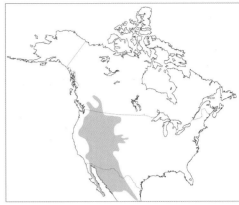

Mammal: *Ovis canadensis*, bighorn sheep, mountain sheep

Meaning of Name: *Ovis* (sheep); *canadensis* (of Canada), although not confined to Canada

Description: massive brown spiraled horns have many annulations; horns grow from the skin over a concealed bony core and are not shed; ewes' horns are shorter; pelage has a thick gray fleece underneath and is composed of an outer coat of long, brittle, bone-white guard hairs with brown tips; brown back, darker on chest, face and legs; brown tail; belly, backs of legs, muzzle and large rump patch are ivory-white

Total Length: male, 5.2 to 6.1 feet; female, 4.6 feet

Tail: male, 4 to 6 inches; female, 4 inches

Weight: male, 287 to 344 pounds; one female weighed 139 pounds

Gestation: 171 to 178 days

Offspring: 1 (occasionally 2)

Age of Maturity: male, 3 years but does not breed until 7 years because of social factors; female, 2 to 3 years

Longevity: 15 years in the wild

Diet: grazer and browser; grasses and sedges are the staple food; also forbs and browse plants; mineral licks containing salts are sought primarily in spring and summer

Habitat: mountain slopes with sparse tree growth; rugged terrain and alpine meadows; requires dry slopes with less than 60 inches of snowfall, since it cannot paw through deep snow to feed

Predators: bobcat, mountain lion and eagle can attack on rocky slopes; wolf, puma, coyote, bear and lynx may take newborns or diseased sheep

Dental Formula:
0/3, 0/1, 3/3, 3/3 = 32 teeth

Mountain sheep band together for extra protection from predators and to defend the newest members of the herd. Nevertheless, spring lambing is a time of high mortality for the young.

being forced to submit to mounting by a more dominant male or risk an escalated attack.

The male physiological investment in big horns and fighting seems to be ultimately limited by a higher rate of mortality. A survey of sheep skulls has shown that the rate of horn development is correlated with a higher death rate. Males that spend more time and effort than average in rutting may have a greater mating success, but eventually, they face exhaustion and increase their susceptibility to starvation and predation in the winter.

Females take an active role in the courtship proceedings, fending off the attempts of young, subordinate males and seeking out large males. Some younger males are able to sequester females and force them to mate, however. In these cases, a female may copulate simply to reduce the amount of time she has to spend with a subordinate male. Once she is free of him, she can seek out a preferred male. A female will generally mate with several different rams during the same rutting season, and there are always surplus males ready to replace a tired older male.

DALL'S SHEEP *Ovis dalli*

The Dall's sheep is a more northerly and graceful species than the bighorn sheep. It lives among the highest mountains of North America and ranges into the tundra. Its habitat, especially in winter, when it moves down the mountain slopes, is more open than that of the bighorn. When Dall's sheep pass through large expanses of tundra without protective rocky areas, they are vulnerable to wolves, which encourages social herding. As winter sets in, snow forces them into open areas, where food is more accessible; their winter range, then, becomes a compromise between the need for foraging grounds and the risk of predation.

The rut of Dall's sheep is similar to the bighorn's. Males use a stand-up display, rising high on their hind legs before they charge, a forceful signal designed to warn the opposing male of its attacker's size.

THE OVERKILL

Magnificent as it may appear, the mammal world of modern-day Canada and the northern United States would look pathetic to humans of an earlier time. Just 10,000 or 11,000 years ago, North American humans had a much richer array of species to contemplate—giant beavers the size of bears, woolly mammoths, elephantlike mastodons, saber-toothed tigers, lions, yaks, camels, horses, giant ground sloths, llamas, antelopes, tapirs, peccaries and giant hyenalike dogs. All in all, several dozen genera, entire families and many hundreds of species became extinct in the last ice age.

The vision conjured up by the list of extinct mammals is reminiscent of the large fauna of present-day Africa—elephants, hyenas, jackals and large, predatory cats all feeding on a rich array of grazers.

Why so many North American fauna disappeared is an intriguing question, especially as Africa lost so few species by comparison. There are two schools of thought: One blames the loss on climatic changes; the other blames it on human hunters.

The first idea is difficult to test, because the extinct animals are not available for study. The second idea is more open to consideration, since an answer would depend on the time at which human hunters came into contact with New World fauna, and that can be determined by archeological digs. The essence of the "overkill hypothesis," as it is known, is that when humans first crossed the Bering Strait from Siberia and spread down through the Americas, they hunted the large game animals to extinction.

This may seem farfetched, as it is hard to imagine how hunters with a technology no more sophisticated than spears and bows and arrows could have dispatched mammoths, lions and saber-toothed tigers. Nevertheless, some compelling patterns fit the hypothesis and are not readily explained by the notion of climatic change.

Many small mammals have become extinct over the last three million years, but they did so gradually, without any sharp upsurge in the decline rates. By contrast, the larger mammals disappeared suddenly, many in the last 10,000 years, soon after the arrival of the hunters. In that period, 65 to 75 percent of large North American animal species died out, while in Africa, there was only a 10 percent decline. The basis of the theory is that in Africa, humans and large game animals had a history of contact over millions of years. The human hunting rules and territories that evolved over this period limited the hunt, even after the advent of more sophisticated hunting technologies, and prevented overkill. Interestingly, Australia has an even greater extinction rate than North America, as does New Zealand. The extinctions there also peaked just after the arrival of humans.

This raises the question of how early hunters could achieve such a devastat-

Slender curving horns and graceful movements make the Dall's sheep one of the most handsome artiodactyls. Also known as the thinhorn sheep, it is slightly smaller than the bighorn, or mountain, sheep.

ing overkill. Evidence indicates that 11,000 years ago, the Clovis people used buffalo drives to send animals by the hundreds to their death over cliffs and that mammoths were also killed by efficient methods. Many grazers such as the giant ground sloth were defenseless, as were other larger mammals such as horses, camels and yaks. Once

DALL'S SHEEP *Ovis dalli*

Mammal: *Ovis dalli*, Dall's sheep, thinhorn sheep
Meaning of Name: *Ovis* (sheep); *dalli* (named after W.H. Dall, an American zoologist)
Description: slender horns (compared with other sheep) that have a more corrugated keel on the outer curl than those of bighorn sheep; northern race is creamy white with a few dark hairs along the spine and tail; southern race is slate-brown except for a white rump patch and muzzle and white on inside of hind legs and forehead; between these two races are populations with integrated color such as the saddle-backed sheep of the eastern Yukon Territory
Total Length: southern race male, 4.3 to 5.8 feet; northern race male, 4.5 to 5 feet; female, 4.5 feet
Tail: southern race male, 3 to 4.3 inches; female, 3 inches; northern race male, 3.5 to 4.5 inches; female, 3.9 inches
Weight: southern race male, 200 pounds; northern race male, 165 to 198 pounds; female, 126 pounds
Gestation: slightly less than 6 months
Offspring: 1 (sometimes 2)
Age of Maturity: male, probably 18 to 36 months; female, probably 18 to 30 months
Longevity: 14 years
Diet: primarily grasses and sedges
Habitat: in summer, rough terrain, alpine tundra slopes; in winter, lower, drier south-facing slopes
Predators: lynx, wolverine, coyote, grizzly bear, wolf and golden eagle; wolves prey on them primarily during migration when they cross flat stretches of tundra
Dental Formula:
0/3, 0/1, 3/3, 3/3 = 32 teeth

weakened, the remnants of those populations could have been eradicated by large carnivorous cats that then starved for lack of prey.

But why did some animals, such as bison, survive the overkill? Proponents of the overkill hypothesis suggest that the surviving animals, such as moose, muskox, caribou and grizzlies, were virtually all recent immigrants from Siberia—animals that had already had a long evolutionary interaction with hunters in Asia.

And what ended the killing? The establishment of tribal territories with hunting taboos and the development of agriculture are possibilities; in any case, no large mammals are known to have become extinct in the 8,000 years before the European conquest of North America.

The cycle began again with the European colonists, a new race with new technologies and a lack of experience with North American fauna. Only rising human populations with diverging interests prevented the colonists from hunting to extinction large mammals such as bison, pronghorn, elk and even the white-tailed deer.

BIBLIOGRAPHY

ANIMAL BEHAVIOR, ECOLOGY & EVOLUTION

Alcock, J. *Animal Behavior: An Evolutionary Approach*. 3rd edition. Sinauer Associates Inc. Publishers, Sunderland, Massachusetts, 1993.

Darwin, C. *The Descent of Man and Selection in Relation to Sex*. Appleton, New York, 1871.

————. *On the Origin of Species by Means of Natural Selection*. John Murray, London, 1859.

Dawkins, R. *The Extended Phenotype: The Gene as the Unit of Selection*. W.H. Freeman and Company, Oxford, 1982.

————. *The Selfish Gene*. Oxford University Press, New York, 1978.

Eisenberg, J.F. *The Mammalian Radiations: An Analysis of Trends in Evolution, Adaptation and Behavior*. University of Chicago Press, Chicago, 1981.

Fagen, R. *Animal Play Behavior*. Oxford University Press, New York, 1981.

Gould, J.L. *Ethology: The Mechanisms and Evolution of Behavior*. W.W. Norton & Company, New York, 1982.

Gould, S.J. *Ever Since Darwin*. W.W. Norton & Company, New York, 1977.

————. *Hen's Teeth and Horse's Toes*. W.W. Norton & Company, New York, 1983.

————. *The Panda's Thumb*. W.W. Norton & Company, New York, 1980.

Krebs, J.R. and N.B. Davies, eds. *Behavioural Ecology: An Evolutionary Approach*. Blackwell Science, Cambridge, Massachusetts, 1997.

Lehner, P.N. *Handbook of Ethological Methods*. Garland STPM Press, New York, 1979.

McFarland, D., ed. *The Oxford Companion to Animal Behavior*. Oxford University Press, New York, 1981.

Sebeok, T.A., ed. *How Animals Communicate*. Indiana University Press, Bloomington, 1977.

Sparks, J. *The Discovery of Animal Behaviour*. Little, Brown and Company, Boston, 1982.

Wilson, E.O. *Sociobiology*. The Belknap Press of Harvard University Press, Cambridge, Massachusetts, 1980.

GENERAL MAMMALOGY REFERENCE BOOKS

Chapman, J.A. and G.A. Feldhamer. *Wild Mammals of North America: Biology, Management and Economics*. The Johns Hopkins University Press, Baltimore, Maryland, 1982.

Jones, C. et al. *Revised Checklist of North American Mammals North of Mexico, 1997*. Occasional Paper no. 173, Museum of Texas Tech University, 1997.

Macdonald, D., ed. *The Encyclopedia of Mammals*. Facts on File, New York, 1984.

Nowak, R.M. and J.L. Paradiso, eds. *Walker's Mammals of the World*, volumes 1 & 2. 5th edition. Johns Hopkins University Press, Baltimore, Maryland, 1991.

Savage, A. and C. Savage. *Wild Mammals of Western Canada*. Western Producer Prairie Books, Saskatoon, Saskatchewan, 1981.

Seton, E.T. *Life-Histories of Northern Animals*. Charles Scribner's Sons, New York, 1909.

Stoddart, D.M., ed. *Ecology of Small Mammals*. John Wiley & Sons, Inc., New York, 1979.

SPECIFIC TOPICS

Albone, E.S. *Mammalian Semiochemistry: The Investigation of Chemical Signals Between Mammals*. John Wiley & Sons Limited, Chichester, West Sussex, 1984.

Finerty, J.P. *The Population Ecology of Cycles in Small Mammals: Mathematical Theory and Biological Fact*. Yale University Press, New Haven, Connecticut, 1980.

Kurten, B. and E. Anderson. *Pleistocene Mammals of North America*. Columbia University Press, New York, 1980.

Lyman, C.P. et al. *Hibernation and Torpor in Mammals and Birds*. Academic Press, Inc., New York, 1982.

Peters, R.H. *The Ecological Implications of Body Size*. Cambridge University Press, Cambridge, Massachusetts, 1983.

Purves, P.E. and G.E. Pilleri. *Echolocation in Whales and Dolphins*. Academic Press, Inc., New York, 1983.

Schmidt-Nielsen, K. *How Animals Work*. Cambridge University Press, Cambridge, Massachusetts, 1972.

RECOMMENDED GENERAL ACCOUNTS OF MAMMALS

Chiroptera

Barbour, R.W. and W.H. Davis. *Bats of America*. University of Kentucky Press, Lexington, 1969.

Fenton, M.B. *The Bat: Wings in the Night Sky*. Key Porter Books, Toronto, 1998.

————. *Bats*. Facts on File, New York, 1992.

————. *Just Bats*. University of Toronto Press, Toronto, 1983.

Hill, J.E. and J.P. Smith. *Bats: A Natural History*. University of Texas Press, Austin, 1984.

Kunz, T.H., ed. *Ecology of Bats*. Plenum Press, New York, 1982.

———— and P.A. Racey. *Bat Biology and Conservation*. Smithsonian Institution Press, Washington, D.C., 1998.

Lagomorpha

Chapman, J.F. and J.E.C. Flux. *Rabbits, Hares and Pikas: Status Survey and Conservation Action Plan*. Gland, Switzerland, International Union for Conservation of Nature and Natural Resources, 1990.

Rodentia

Roze, U. *The North American Porcupine*. Smithsonian Institution Press, Washington, D.C., 1989.

Woods, S.E., Jr. *The Squirrels of Canada*. National Museums of Canada, Ottawa, 1980.

Carnivora

Busch, R.H. *The Wolf Almanac*. Fitzhenry & Whiteside, Toronto, 1995.

Craighead, F.C., Jr. *Track of the Grizzly*. Sierra Club Books, San Francisco, 1979.

Gittleman, J.L., ed. *Carnivore Behavior, Ecology and Evolution*, volume 2. Cornell University Press, Ithaca, New York, 1989.

Harrington, F.H. and P.C. Paquet, eds. *Wolves of the World: Perspectives of Behavior, Ecology and Conservation*. Noyes Publications, Park Ridge, New Jersey, 1982.

King, J.E. *Seals of the World*. 2nd edition. British Museum (Natural History), London, 1983.

Klinghammer, E. *The Behavior and Ecology of Wolves*. Garland, New York, 1978.

Koch, T.J. *The Year of the Polar Bear*. Bobbs-Merrill, New York, 1975.

Lawrence, R.D. *The Ghost Walker*. McClelland & Stewart, Toronto, 1983.

Lynch, W. *Bears: Monarchs of the Northern Wilderness*. Greystone Books, Douglas & McIntyre, Vancouver/Toronto, 1993.

Mech, L.D. *The Arctic Wolf: 10 Years With the Pack*. Raincoast Books, Vancouver, 1997.

————. *The Wolf: The Ecology and Behavior of an Endangered Species*. University of Minnesota Press, Minneapolis, 1970.

Powell, R.A. *The Fisher: Life History, Ecology and Behavior*. University of Minnesota Press, Minneapolis, 1982.

Ridgway, D.H. and R.J. Harrison, eds. *Handbook of Marine Mammals*. Volume 1: *The Walrus, Sea Lions, Fur Seals and Sea Otter* (1981); Volume 2: *Seals* (1981); Volume 3: *The Sirenia and Baleen Whales* (1985); Volume 4: *River Dolphins and Larger Toothed Whales* (1989); Volume 5: *Dolphins* (1994). Academic Press, London.

Wayre, P. *The Private Life of the Otter*. B.T. Batsford Ltd., London, 1979.

Cetacea

Evans, P.G.H. *The Natural History of Whales and Dolphins*. Facts on File, New York, 1987.

Ford, J.K.B., G.M. Ellis and K.C. Balcomb. *Killer Whales*. UBC Press, Vancouver, 1994.

Gaskin, D.E. *The Ecology of Whales and Dolphins*. Heinemann Educational Books Ltd., London, 1982.

Herman, L.M., ed. *Cetacean Behavior: Mechanisms and Functions*. John Wiley & Sons, Inc., New York, 1980.

Hoyt, E. *Orca: The Whale Called Killer*. Camden House Publishing Ltd., Camden East, Ontario, 1981.

Artiodactyla

Calef, G. *Caribou and the Barren-Lands*. Canadian Arctic Resources Committee, Ottawa, 1981.

Chadwick, D.H. *A Beast the Color of Winter: The Mountain Goat Observed*. Sierra Club Books, San Francisco, 1983.

Clutton-Brock, T.H., F.E. Guinness and S.D. Albon. *Red Deer: Behavior and Ecology of Two Sexes*. University of Chicago Press, Chicago, 1982.

Geist, V. *Mountain Sheep: A Study in Behavior and Evolution*. University of Chicago Press, Chicago, 1971.

Peterson, R.L. *North American Moose.*. University of Toronto Press, Toronto, 1955.

Russell, H.J. *The Nature of Caribou: Spirit of the North*. Greystone Books, Vancouver, 1998.

Wemmer, C., ed. *Biology and Management of the Cervidae*. Smithsonian Institution Press, Washington, D.C., 1987.

IDENTIFICATION & LIFE-HISTORY GUIDES

Alden, P. *Peterson First Guide to Mammals of North America*. Houghton Mifflin, Boston, 1987.

Baker, R.H. *Michigan Mammals*. Michigan State University Press, Detroit, 1983.

Banfield, A.W.F. *The Mammals of Canada*. University of Toronto Press, Toronto, 1974.

Boschung, H.T. *The Audubon Society Field Guide to North American Fishes, Whales and Dolphins*. Alfred A. Knopf, Inc., New York, 1983.

Hoyt, E. *The Whale Watcher's Handbook*. Penguin/Madison Press, Toronto, 1984.

————. *The Whales of Canada*. Camden House Publishing Ltd., Camden East, Ontario, 1984.

Jefferson, T.A., S. Leatherwood and M.A. Webber. *FAO Species Identification Guide: Marine Mammals of the World*. FAO, Rome, 1993.

Jones, J.K., Jr. et al. *Mammals of the Northern Great Plains*. University of Nebraska Press, Lincoln, Nebraska, 1983.

Katona, S.K.V., V. Rough and D.T. Richardson. *A Field Guide to the Whales, Porpoises and Seals of the Gulf of Maine and Eastern Canada: Cape Cod to Newfoundland*. Charles Scribner's Sons, New York, 1983.

Stokes, D. and L. Stokes. *A Guide to Animal Tracking and Behavior*. Little, Brown and Company, Boston and Toronto, 1986.

Van Zyll de Jong, C.G. *Handbook of Canadian Mammals*. Volume 1: *Marsupials and Insectivores* (1983); Volume 2: *Bats* (1985). National Museums of Canada, Ottawa.

Whitaker, J.O., Jr. *National Audubon Society Field Guide to North American Mammals*. Alfred A. Knopf, Inc., New York, 1996.

———— and W.J. Hamilton, Jr. *Mammals of the Eastern United States*. 3rd edition. Cornell University Press, Ithaca and London, 1998.

CONSERVATION

Busch, B.C. *The War Against the Seals: A History of the North American Seal Fishery*. McGill-Queen's University Press, Kingston, Ontario, 1985.

Lopez, B.H. *Of Wolves and Men*. Charles Scribner's Sons, New York, 1979.

Mowat, F. *Sea of Slaughter*. McClelland & Stewart, Toronto, 1984.

Roe, F.G. *North American Buffalo: A Critical Study of the Species in Its Wild State*. 2nd edition. University of Toronto Press, Toronto, 1970.

Small, G.L. *The Blue Whale*. Columbia University Press, New York, 1971.

SCIENTIFIC JOURNALS

The American Naturalist. American Society of Naturalists. Monthly.

Animal Behaviour. Quarterly.

Behavioral Ecology and Sociobiology. 2 volumes per year, 4 numbers per volume.

The Canadian Field-Naturalist. Ottawa Field-Naturalists' Club. Quarterly.

Canadian Journal of Zoology. National Research Council of Canada. Monthly.

Ecology. Ecological Society of America. Bimonthly.

Evolution. Society for the Study of Evolution. Quarterly.

Journal of Mammalogy. American Society of Mammalogists. Quarterly.

Journal of Wildlife Management. Wildlife Society. Quarterly.

Oecologia. International Association for Ecology. 4 volumes per year, 3 numbers per volume.

INDEX

PHOTO CREDITS

Front cover photograph
© Thomas Kitchin/First Light

Back cover photograph
© Wayne Lynch

Cartography
Robbie Cooke

CONTENTS
4, Wayne Lynch

INTRODUCTION
8, Wayne Lynch

MARSUPIALS
10, 13, 15, Wayne Lynch

INSECTIVORES
16, Rod Planck/Tom Stack & Associates; 19, Dwight R. Kuhn/Bruce Coleman Inc.; 21, Wayne Lynch; 22, Jeff Foott; 23, Gary Meszaros/Bruce Coleman Inc.; 25, E.R. Degginger/Bruce Coleman Inc.; 26-27, Dwight R. Kuhn/Bruce Coleman Inc.; 31, Robert McCaw/Spectrum Stock Inc.; 33, Dwight R. Kuhn/Bruce Coleman Inc.; 37, E.R. Degginger/Bruce Coleman Inc.; 38-39, Rod Planck/Tom Stack & Associates

BATS
40, 42-43, 45, 47, 48, 51, 52, 54, 55, 56, 57, 58, 59, 61, M. Brock Fenton

PIKAS, RABBITS & HARES
62, C. Swift/First Light; 65, Thomas Kitchin/First Light; 67, Wayne Lynch; 68, Jerry Kobalenko/First Light; 70, Robert McCaw/Spectrum Stock Inc.; 71, Wayne Lynch; 72, Thomas Kitchin/First Light; 74, Wayne Lynch; 74-75, Jerry Kobalenko/First Light; 76, 77, Wayne Lynch

RODENTS
78, J.D. Taylor/Hot Shots; 81, Joseph Van Wormer/Bruce Coleman Inc.; 83, Robert Lankinen/First Light; 84, Mike Grandmaison/First Light; 85, Darwin Wiggett/First Light; 86, Wayne Lynch; 88, Robert McCaw/Spectrum Stock Inc.; 89, Wayne Lynch; 90, Wayne Lankinen/Bruce Coleman Inc.; 91, Rod Williams/Bruce Coleman Inc.; 92, 94, Wayne Lynch; 96, Thomas Kitchin/First Light; 97, Kenneth W. Fink/Bruce Coleman Inc.; 98, Darwin Wiggett/First Light; 99, J.B. Dawson/Spectrum Stock Inc.; 100, Darwin Wiggett/First Light; 101, Thomas Kitchin/First Light; 102, 104, 105, Wayne Lynch; 106, Glen and Rebecca Grambo/First Light; 108, Jeff Foott; 110, 112, Wayne Lynch; 114, Robert Lankinen/First Light; 117, Robert Lankinen/First Light; 119, 120, 121, 122, 123, Jeff Foott; 125, M. and P. Fogden/Bruce Coleman Inc.; 126-127, Bob and Clara Calhoun/Bruce Coleman Inc.; 129, Wayne Lynch; 131, Don Standfield/First Light; 132, Thomas Kitchin/First Light; 135, 136, Wayne Lynch; 137, John H. Hoffman/Bruce Coleman Inc.; 138, Robert McCaw/Spectrum Stock Inc.; 139, Wayne Lynch; 141, Dwight R. Kuhn/Bruce Coleman Inc.; 143, Wayne Lynch; 144, Gary R. Jones/Bruce Coleman Inc.; 145, 154, 155, Wayne Lynch; 156, Gary Meszaros/Bruce Coleman Inc.; 157, Wayne Lynch; 159, John Gerlach/Tom Stack & Associates; 161, 163 (left), Thomas Kitchin/First Light; 163 (right), Wayne Lynch

MEAT EATERS
164, Wayne Lynch; 167, Thomas Kitchin/First Light; 168, P. McLeod/First Light; 169, Wayne Lynch; 170, 172-173, Thomas Kitchin/First Light; 174, 176-177, 177, 178, Wayne Lynch; 180, Victoria Hurst/First Light; 181, Wayne Lynch and Aubrey Lang/First Light; 183, 184, Thomas Kitchin/First Light; 186, 187, 188-189, 190, Wayne Lynch; 193, Robert Lankinen/First Light; 195, Jason Puddifoot/First Light; 196-197, Thomas Kitchin; 198, 199, Wayne Lynch; 200, Thomas Kitchin/First Light; 202, Wayne Lynch; 203, Thomas Kitchin/First Light; 204, Wayne Lynch; 205, Roy Tanami/Ursus; 206, Brian and Cherry Alexander/First Light; 207, J.D. Taylor/Hot Shots; 208, 210, 211, Wayne Lynch; 212, Fred Bruemmer/Spectrum Stock Inc.; 213, 214-215, Wayne Lynch; 217, Robert Lankinen/First Light; 218, Glen and Rebecca Grambo/First Light; 219, Wayne Lynch; 221, Victoria Hurst/First Light; 222, Robert Lankinen/First Light; 223, Wayne Lynch; 224, Thomas Kitchin/First Light; 225, Tom Brakefield/Bruce Coleman Inc.; 226-227, Glen and Rebecca Grambo/First Light; 228, Brian Milne/First Light; 229, Jeff Foott; 230-231, Glen and Rebecca Grambo/First Light; 232, 234, 236, 238, Wayne Lynch; 239, Robert Lankinen/First Light; 240, Thomas Kitchin/First Light; 243, Brian Milne/First Light; 244, Glen and Rebecca Grambo/First Light; 245, Erwin and Peggy Bauer/Bruce Coleman Inc.; 247, Wayne Lynch; 248, Thomas Kitchin/First Light; 250, Wayne Lynch; 251, Thomas Kitchin/First Light; 252, Wayne Lynch; 253, Thomas Kitchin/First Light; 254, Victoria Hurst/First Light; 255, Thomas Kitchin/First Light

WHALES, DOLPHINS & PORPOISES
256, Trevor Bonderud/First Light; 258, Glen Williams/Ursus; 261, Kelvin Aitken/First Light; 262-263, Jeff Foott; 265, 266-267, Kelvin Aitken/First Light; 268, G. Williamson/Bruce Coleman Inc.; 269, Frank S. Balthis/Spectrum Stock Inc.; 270, John K.B. Ford/Ursus; 271, Kelvin Aitken/First Light; 273, Steve McCutcheon/Hot Shots; 275, John K.B. Ford/Ursus; 276-277, Flip Nicklin/First Light; 278-279, Paul Nicklen/Ursus; 281, 282-283, Wayne Lynch; 284-285, Flip Nicklin/First Light; 287, J.D. Taylor/Hot Shots; 289, Brian Hay/Spectrum Stock Inc.; 290-291, Jason Puddifoot/First Light; 292, Diana R. McIntyre/Marine Mammal Images; 294, Wayne Lynch; 297, J.D. Taylor/Hot Shots; 298-299, Paul Nicklen/Ursus; 301, Hal Whitehead/Marine Mammal Images; 303, Ron and Val Taylor/Bruce Coleman Inc.; 304-305, Kelvin Aitken/First Light

CLOVEN-HOOFED MAMMALS
306, 309, 310, 312, 314, 316, Thomas Kitchin/First Light; 318, Patrick Morrow/First Light; 320, Brian Milne/First Light; 321, Wayne Lynch; 322-323, Robert Lankinen/First Light; 325, Wayne Lynch; 326, Brian Hay/Spectrum Stock Inc.; 329, Wayne Lynch; 330, Glen and Rebecca Grambo/First Light; 333, 334, 336, 338, 339, 340-341, Wayne Lynch